W9-AEF-296

HUMAN COMMUNICATION THEORY AND RESEARCH
Concepts, Contexts, and Challenges

COMMUNICATION TEXTBOOK SERIES

Jennings Bryant — Editor

General Communication Theory and Methodology

Jennings Bryant — Advisor

STARTT/SLOAN • Historical Methods
in Mass Communication

PILOTTA/MICKUNAS • Science
of Communication: Its
Phenomenological Foundation

SLOAN • Perspectives on
Mass Communication History

HEATH/BRYANT • Human Communication
Theory and Research: Concepts, Contexts,
and Challenges

HUMAN COMMUNICATION THEORY AND RESEARCH
Concepts, Contexts, and Challenges

Robert L. Heath
University of Houston

Jennings Bryant
University of Alabama

LAWRENCE ERLBAUM ASSOCIATES, PUBLISHERS
1992   Hillsdale, New Jersey   Hove and London

Lawrence Erlbaum Associates, Inc., Publishers
365 Broadway
Hillsdale, New Jersey 07642

Library of Congress Cataloging-in-Publication Data
Heath, Robert L. (Robert Lawrence), 1941–
    Human communication theory and research : concepts, contexts, and
challenges / Robert L. Heath, Jennings Bryant.
        p.   cm. — (Communication)
    Includes bibliographical references and index.
    ISBN 0-8058-0164-2 (c)   ISBN 0-8058-1218-0 (p)
    1. Communication.   I. Bryant, Jennings.   II. Title.   III. Series :
Communication (Hillsdale, N.J.)
P90.H39   1992
302.2 – dc20   91-44611
                                                                        CIP

Printed in the United States of America
10 9 8 7 6 5 4 3 2 1

Contents

Preface

This volume introduces students to the growing body of theory and research regarding communication. In the past half century, communication has come to be a particularly important and fruitful topic of research that has drawn attention of hundreds of scholars who have devoted thousands of hours to unlocking its dynamics. Topics selected for discussion in this book reflect the desire that students will acquire an understanding of and appreciation for the difficulties of making discoveries that can help them to increase their insights into communication, one of the most unique qualities of the human species. What is discussed here has implications for how individuals relate to one another as well as for the development of public policy regarding the effects media have on society.

This book acknowledges the contributions of researchers from psychology, political science, and sociology departments. Although their contributions are important, one of the most significant developments in recent decades is the emergence of communication as a research discipline, largely advanced through the development of major departments, schools, and colleges named communication and devoted to that discipline. Most of the work presented here has been drawn from scholars who find their academic affiliation with such programs. The chapters that comprise this book were selected and arranged to give insight into the breadth of studies unique to communication.

Chapter 1 sets an orientation for the social scientific study of communication. It discusses principles of research and outlines the requirements for the development and evaluation of theories. One of the important points made in that chapter is the need for system and rigor in the development of hypotheses, generation of data, and creation of theory. Development of theory entails more than merely thinking abstractly. Only by testing and arguing about theories can they be improved. To know how to do this requires careful examination of the methods and assumptions of social science research as well as re-examination of key assumptions about the communication process, especially those that are sensitive to the similarities and differences involved in how communication occurs in the individual, interpersonal, group, organizational, and mass-mediated contexts.

Chapter 2 examines the dynamic shifts that have occurred in scholars' efforts to define communication and isolate its key variables. Taking the tone of a scholar serving as detective who is intent on determining "who done it," the chapter examines the anatomy of the communication process and discusses the difficulty in knowing which aspects of the process deserve the most attention. By examining key aspects of communication, such as message, source, and channel, the chapter lays a foundation of terminology that is useful to discussing the elements of the process.

Chapter 3 concentrates on language, meaning, and messages. Of particular interest in this chapter is the description and comparison of the three overarching approaches to how words are meaningful. This examination features representationalism or referentialism, linguistic relativity, and the interactional or purposive approach to language. Each theory helps explain how words are meaningful, but none of the theories completely explains this process. Words are a unique part of the human communication process. Their meaning and impact deserve careful attention.

Chapter 4 focuses attention on the importance of uncertainty as a universal motive that leads people to seek and think about information. This chapter examines information as the foundation of communication that leads to a comparison of theories of what information is and how it has meaning for humans who need to learn about and make decisions regarding events that are important to their lives. Once the chapter has established this foundation, it examines how information is important to communication in interpersonal, organizational, and mass-mediated contexts. From this analysis, a case is made that people communicate about something; the essence of that something is information.

Chapter 5 provides an important complement to the discussion on information by addressing the dynamics of social influence, persuasion. Rather than seeing information and persuasion at odds, the chapter demonstrates how leading theories treat them as interdependent parts of social influence and decision making. Starting from the findings of the Yale research project, this chapter progresses to explain how leading researchers have refined the work of each other to establish several leading theories by conducting experiments. As was the case of chapter 4, attention is given to persuasion in the typical communication contexts.

Chapter 6 is the first of two chapters that discuss interpersonal communication. Whereas chapter 6 focuses on factors that improve or harm relationships, chapter 7 studies the processes people use to reduce uncertainty about themselves and their relational partners. Of particular importance to relationship development is the need for disclosure. This examination requires that consideration be given to which variables differentiate between good and bad relationships. As well as looking at the impact of nonverbal communication, this chapter discusses expectations people have of one another and of the conditions that lead to social conflict.

Chapter 7 extends the attention given in previous chapters to how people reduce uncertainty in their interpersonal relationships. Essential to this process is the ways people attribute causes to explain why they and others act as they do. Also important are the communication tactics people use to seek information about relationships, trying to know, for instance, whether other people like them. Research is reported about the processes of second guessing and debiasing. In subtle ways people accommodate to one another and employ communication plans to negotiate relationships.

Chapter 8 captures the dynamics of communication that are typical of organizations. Focal points in organizational communication involve what people think about the companies in which they work, the interpersonal relationships that occur as they work together, and the groups that are used for collective decision making. The chapter compares various approaches to explain how communication allows people to create and act in organizations. This analysis seeks to explain how communication interacts with the climate and culture of each organization. As well as looking at the communication that transpires inside of organizations, insights are provided into the communication that organizations use to affect people outside of them.

Chapter 9 concentrates on the dynamics of mass-mediated communication. This discussion is warranted because of the important roles media play in each person's daily activities. Starting with analysis of early approaches to media studies, the chapter introduces and discusses up-to-date theories that are being used to guide regulatory policies as well as programming and editorial policy. Several key theories enjoy a great deal of scholarly debate and research in the effort to determine how media affect people, as well as to understand how people affect media. A theme central to this analysis is the importance of maintaining attention on the cognitive processes involved in media attentiveness, as well as the interaction between interpersonal communication and media utilization.

Each day leading researchers and theorists shed new insights onto the processes of communication. From relatively primitive starting points, a steady march continues. This trek is beginning to demonstrate how much integration exists between the communication efforts that are typical of interpersonal, organizational, and mass-mediated settings. Welcome to this journey.

Robert L. Heath
Jennings Bryant

1 Why Study Communication Theories and Conduct Research?

Human beings are "symbol-users," as well as "symbol-makers" and "symbol-misusers." With this observation, Burke (1966) underscored how people communicate to manage interpersonal relationships, express feelings, share views of reality, and disseminate informative and persuasive messages through media. Through words, great and magnificent cities are created, problems of health and famine solved, and great drama and comedy written. Words and other symbols allow people to plumb the depths of their souls as well as those of their friends and enemies. People share ideas in order to work together. Other animals, such as humpback whales and elephants, communicate for social purposes by calling to others of their species. Whether other animals use symbols to communicate is a moot issue here; people are more elaborate and complex communicators.

As Burke said, people are symbol-misusers. Through symbols, people categorize one another in ways that lead them to discriminate against some and favor others. If people hold one religious orientation too firmly, they can become intolerant of people who do not hold similar views. Symbols can lead nations to wage war in order to impose their values on enemies. Symbols allow people to scream racial or ethnic slurs at persons they do not like. Words support the development of the science needed to go to the moon and to solve health problems; words provide means to attempt genocide. Words can be used to cast people away as well as welcome them. Advertisers can use misleading advertisements to entice people to buy defective products unworthy of their cost.

People study communication because it is vital to their lives. From infancy, you have watched other people communicate. You have imitated

1

some communication behavior to see if you can successfully use certain strategies to improve relationships, motivate others, or persuade people to go along with your ideas and plans. As a child, you enacted conversations that you observed between your parents and teachers. By this time in your life, you have engaged in thousands of communication interactions and know that friendship and business success require effective communication. You learned early in life that communication can help you satisfy your needs, perhaps by creating friendships. You were quick to realize that communication is strategic; that some words are appropriate in some social contexts but not in others. You noticed that the method in which messages are framed and delivered nonverbally increased their chances of success or failure. Even though you may not have formal theories about how people communicate, you have informal ones; now it is time to study communication instructively, perhaps to make it serve your interests even more.

This chapter lays a foundation for the remainder of the book by setting the study of communication into perspective. It (a) explains the process of inquiry, (b) presents the criteria that guide theory construction, (c) examines several broad research perspectives, (d) discusses assumptions basic to human nature, and (e) shows how communication is best understood by taking a broad perspective based on research into key subdisciplines. These subdisciplines are featured as chapters in this book.

SYSTEMATIC STUDY OF COMMUNICATION

Understanding begins with a theory that can be tested. Explaining the usefulness of theories, McGuire (1981) called them "maps." "Knowledge," he said, "is not a perfect map of the thing known but without it one has to move through the environment with no map at all." Each of us has maps, theories about communication. "The trick," McGuire continued,

> is in making proper use of the theory, which involves recognizing the brilliant partial insight into reality that is provided by any theory's special perspective, seeing its applicability to a specific problem whose puzzling aspects it can illuminate, while at the same time recognizing its limitations and being open to alternative theoretical insights from which guidance can be obtained as one's initial theory begins to prove unsatisfactory. (p. 42)

Theory is needed because no matter how long and hard people examine any object of inquiry, communication in this case, it will not reveal itself. According to O'Keefe (1975), only by developing and testing of theory can its secrets be unlocked.

This book offers many maps. Some increase your understanding of communication. Others give insights into how you can communicate more effectively. Remember that however much you may wonder about the usefulness of the theories you encounter here and elsewhere, without maps, people wander helplessly. When you ask why you should study communication theories and research, realize that *you already are a communication theorist.*

Each day as you interact with others and watch television programs, commercial advertisements, or news, you do so with various communication theories in mind. When you begin to converse with someone, you follow a theory that you have worked out regarding interpersonal interaction. When you participate in a meeting you do so according to some theory you have about group dynamics, leadership, and turn taking. You may not consciously think of these theories all the time, but, if you were pressed to do so, you are able to articulate why you are communicating as you are.

If you want to borrow something from someone, you will have a different theory about what to say and do if the person is reluctant to grant your wish or is willing to do so. Likewise, you might say, "Tonight I deserve to reward myself with a couple of laughs on TV." Or you might decide to tune into the news to find out what is happening or to see how the weather report might affect your weekend plans. You would be less mindful of what you say on the way into an office to work than if you are going to visit a friend who is suffering from cancer.

Exploring this line of analysis, O'Keefe and McCornack (1987) reasoned that during conversations, each participant operates out of a theory of conversation; the success of the participants may depend on the extent to which their goals are similar and whether they use the theory competently to achieve the conversation outcome. Theory can give orderly, not whimsical, explanations of events, interactions, and processes in which you engage each day. When you study theories and research that supports them, you should be able to clarify and improve your theories. Reading the theories and research in this book should increase your insight and help you communicate better, but we make no guarantees.

Theory, research, and practice of communication are interrelated. Broadcasters and editors want to understand how and why viewers use television, listeners use radio, or readers use print journalism. This knowledge can help them develop programming or shape editorial policies. By understanding communication, government regulators and media managers can create policies, such as designating movies by codes (G, PG, R, or X). Research is used by advertisers of products and services, public relations practitioners, public speakers, and other professional communicators. Many large advertising and public relations companies support extensive applied research programs. Insight into communication can improve employee performance in many occupational contexts: business, health and medical service, legal practice, and others. For instance, researchers study doctor–patient communication to improve the accuracy of the information shared and increase empathy between doctor and patient. This research can increase the likelihood that patients will tell their doctors the truth about symptoms and be willing to take the prescribed medication. Understanding interpersonal communication may help people communicate more effectively with family members.

This chapter lays a foundation for studying communication by explaining how systematic inquiry entails observation, analysis, generalization, and prediction. As people engage in daily communication activities, they naively construct and apply theories of communication. In contrast, social scientists go beyond mere intuition and personal observation to understand human communication by constructing theories and then conducting research to test them. Behind systematic inquiry and research is the desire to discover order in our social universe. Systematic study requires researchers to go beyond mere observation of behavior, such as noting that some people watch more television or are more persuasive than others. Researchers are interested in observable behavior patterns, such as noting that people meet and greet one another ritualistically. Research probes the human mind and looks for patterns of communication behavior to discover why people communicate as they do and to learn what effects communication has on opinions and relationships.

Your study of human communication will be easier and more rewarding — even fascinating — if you catch the spirit of observing communication behavior with a sense of wonderment. You may, for instance, wonder why you sometimes get a message across to someone quite clearly and at other times you can't seem to get that person to understand you. Are you causing the problem or is the other person? Or are both of you at fault? Why are some television shows entertaining and others not? Why do some people prefer one kind of television show but not other programs? Why do some television programs make you laugh and others make you cry? Do all people greet one another in the same ways, for instance, saying "Good morning" even when the weather is miserable and they are ill? If not, why are there differences? And what are the different greeting patterns? Why do people ask the questions they do when they meet for the first time? How do they communicate to reduce the uncertainty they feel toward the world around them, their relationships with other people, and their own sense of competence? Why do some companies run smoothly with each employee seeming to understand what is going on, whereas in other companies nothing goes properly? Why do some employees feel miserable about their jobs and believe that no one in the department involves them in the flow of information and decision making? Questions such as these show how inquisitive people can be about the ways they communicate depending on how it affects their needs and interests. Seeking answers for these and other questions indicates the desire to understand communication to make it serve us better.

THEORIES AS COMPETING PERSPECTIVES

Warning! You will encounter many theories and research findings in this book. Some of the theories and findings challenge and contradict one another. Some findings support one theory but not another. This book does not present one theory but demonstrates the robust debate of communication research. The goal is to help you expand your capacity to investigate and understand communication from different perspectives by weighing one theory against another.

Research would be ideal if we had only one theory and if all hypotheses led to helpful and noncontradictory results. But life is imperfect. That is true of communication research as well. Research and theory building are dynamic activities. Any theory may compete against one or several alternative explanations. One way to think of the activities of research and theory construction is as a debate between alternative views.

Posing theories and producing research findings are persuasive activities. Researchers can attract others to their ways of thinking as long as the results adequately explain the variables in the domain under consideration. No theory is without flaws; each has its critics and detractors. In the study of communication, as in other social and physical sciences, you will benefit from thinking of researchers and theorists as advocates who assert a thesis on a topic. They are expected to provide research to support their assertions. Without research findings, a theory is mere speculation.

Nature, Processes, and Limits of Human Inquiry

What makes one theory better than another? How do we know which theory is worth our attention? Questions such as these direct attention to an examination of the processes and criteria of inquiry.

Each theory is tested by the extent to which it is accurate, encompassing, and predictive. A theory must accurately describe and account for the important observable events in communication behavior. Any theory is only as good as its ability to describe, give insight and make prediction. It should be useful. Keep in mind that scholars do not dream up theories just to frustrate students—not usually anyway!

Inquiry Begins With a Sense of Curiosity.   You probably can remember some of the fascinations and wonderments you have had. When you were a child, you might have watched fish in an aquarium and wondered about their behavior; this observation could have led you to understand how dominance, caution, and hierarchy are vital to the ecology of an aquarium. And you probably examined the hardness or softness of some object by seeing whether you could scratch it. You tested the durability of things by throwing rocks at them until they broke — or you learned that they didn't — or that you shouldn't throw rocks at some things in some places.

These valuable lessons taught you something about your world and yourself. That activity also taught you the attitudes and methods of "scientific" inquiry. You had theories, acquired facts about your world, and tested hypotheses to learn more about the nature and relationships of objects. You wondered "what is?" "why?" "if then, what?" and "what if?" If your curiosity continues today, you are now able to learn in a sophisticated way.

Inquiry Must Have System.   Inquiry consists of observation and analysis. To be successful in these activities, you need to know how to discriminate between the important elements of communication activity. Learning the names other people have assigned (or assigning names yourself) to the key elements of communication is vital. Inquiry is systematic when it is used to look for patterns; when communication events are observed to occur in repeatable and predictable ways. A goal of inquiry is to recognize similarities and dissimilarities.

As you look for consistency between communication events, patterns, and relationships, you may discover anomalies — events, patterns, or facts that do not seem to fit your theory. Kuhn (1970) concluded that inquiry is driven by recognition of anomaly, awareness that some fact, event, behavior, or relationship occurs in violation of what a theory says. He believed that inquiry continues until anomalies have been explained. Just when you think you understand an aspect of communication, you may recognize that your conclusions do not completely square with some facts that you see. You may ask yourself whether the "facts" are incorrect or trivial and whether your theory is inadequate.

How you progress from curiosity and systematic observation to draw conclusions about communication is important. You cannot understand communication without a game plan. Systematic inquiry begins by forming theories and testing hypotheses inductively to create, expand, refine, or challenge each theory. Through deductive reasoning, analysis focuses on how well each hypothesis supports the theory and whether competing theories are relevant to the analysis.

To this point, the word "theory" has been used but not defined. Our intention is to have you think about the process of inquiry and to see what it does for people before we define it. The word theory refers to the processes of observing and speculating. It is similar to making an educated guess about some phenomena. You might think, "I guess people communicate in such and such a way because . . ." To make such observations combines a bit of what a theory is and a bit of what a hypothesis is.

A theory is a systematic and plausible set of generalizations that explain some observable phenomena by linking constructs and variables in terms of an organizing principle that is internally consistent. For example,

1. Cultivation theory states that people who view large amounts of television adopt the view of reality, no matter how incorrect it is, that is portrayed in programs they watch.
2. Involvement theory proposes that people who believe their self-interests are involved by a choice, action, or opinion are prone to invest more cognitive effort into forming a point of view on the topic.
3. Uncertainty reduction theory says that people communicate in all contexts—interpersonal, organizational, and mediated—to obtain information because uncertainty is uncomfortable.

These are a few of the theories this book features.

What does a communication theory do? It defines key concepts and explains systematically and rationally the relationships among variables basic to communication behaviors, outcomes, and cognitive processes. A good theory can guide additional speculation, observation, explanation, and prediction. For example, uncertainty reduction theory argues that people strategically communicate to obtain information they need to be comfortable when faced with conditions of social relations and the world around them. Based on this theory, you might predict (hypothesize) that people who are scheduled to meet one another again will ask different or more questions during initial interaction than if they know they are unlikely to meet again. Or social learning theory argues that people learn acceptable and unacceptable opinions and behavior by observing what actions or opinions produce rewards or punishments. Using this theory, you might predict that when persons see behavior rewarded (such as other people becoming more attractive by using an advertised product), they will buy the product.

Inquiry Requires That Key Variables be Isolated and Their Interaction be Understood. Theories help organize hypotheses basic to research and findings that result from it. Some research is conducted merely to observe interaction between two or more variables. This variable analytic approach to the study of communication may lead to interesting conclusions, but each conclusion stands alone because it does not relate to any others or an encompassing theory. For instance, consider this research finding: Television viewing does not hamper academic achievement until it exceeds about 10 hours a week; if young viewers are exposed to programs that are high in information content, television viewing actually enhances achievement (Potter, 1987). This finding is interesting and important. It demonstrates important relationships between variables. But it does not support or deny a theory. Although a widely used, tried and tested approach, researchers must be cautious to not overlook important dimensions of communication by focusing only on variables that are testable (Delia, 1977).

A Theory Differs From a Hypothesis. Often when you think that you have a theory of how communication works, you may only have a hypothesis—or it may be a conclusion based on observed facts—a tested hypothesis. A *hypothesis* is a single conjectural statement regarding relationships between two or more variables that can be tested by empirical observation. For example, someone might hypothesize that, in a business organization, personnel will have higher morale if they are involved in departmental decision making. Researchers might ask, for instance, "*What if* bosses praise their employees' performance frequently, seldom, or never?" And researchers may wonder whether the praise needs to be specific and accurate, such as "You are doing a good job by entering a lot of data and doing your job accurately," or whether general praise, "You are a good worker," will affect employees' performance of tedious jobs. A researcher interested in organizational communication might wonder what kinds and amounts of questions persons ask during employment interviews. Or as researchers discovered, when bargainers are held accountable for the outcome of bargaining, their initial offers are more extreme; they are perceived as being less cooperative. Moreover, according to Roloff and Campion (1987), they take more time to negotiate, are more likely to deadlock, and are less satisfied with the outcome. These kinds of questions are empirically testable as were those when as children we learned what happens to a worn out TV picture tube laying in the junk if we hit it with a rock—or a bigger rock.

Hypotheses are the "work horses" of inquiry. They are single, testable statements, the answer to which may help support or deny a theory. Testing an hypothesis may supply evidence to support a conclusion but does not constitute a theory. Observing events and facts does not constitute a theory. Knowing that most people answer a telephone or greet one another by saying "hello" does not make a theory. But it does say something about communication behavior that should be explained by a theory. A theory constitutes a more encompassing statement of many facts, events, relationships, and conclusions—not just one or two as is the case of a hypothesis. Rather than being a proposition, as is a hypothesis, a theory is often reducible to a summarizing metaphor or overarching concept. For instance, uncertainty reduction theory postulates that much communication behavior is motivated by the desire to predict which actions and judgments produce positive or negative outcomes.

Theories and Hypotheses Interact. Conclusions drawn from tested hypotheses may be grouped in an encompassing statement — a theory. Hypotheses may be tested to examine its viability as well as its leading to a theory. That is, someone might have a theory in mind that seems intuitively valid and may explain some facts and conclusions. By systematically testing relevant hypotheses, the explanatory power of the theory can be examined. Inquiry is guided by asking whether facts and conclusions support a theory. Stressing how theories impose structure and given names to events, Kaplan (1964) reasoned, "A theory must somehow fit God's world, but in an important sense it creates a world of its own" (p. 309). Kaplan made the vital point that theory imposes a view on reality that may not be accurate, but may be believed and used nonetheless. A good example is the belief that persuasive messages always change attitudes and thereby alter behavior. Some communication students reason that if ads do not alter attitudes and influence behavior they would not be used. They draw this conclusion without realizing that they buy and use very few of the products they see advertised. Or as magic bullet theory proposes, media, particularly television, virtually control people's thoughts and lives. These conclusions have been severely criticized, but continue to be believed by persons who have not examined the evidence against them.

Criteria of Theory Construction

How can you know whether one theory is better than another? A good theory explains and predicts, and thereby assists efforts to control communication activities and outcomes. Control can be seen as manipulative, but it also means that communication can be strategically used to achieve good ends. A good theory is useful (heuristic), parsimonious, internally consistent, and capable of being falsified or disproved.

Building a theory begins with explanation. As you observe communication events and patterns, you might speculate on what is going on and hypothesize how these events will work out to some end. The tendency is to ask "what?" "how?" "why?" or "if then, what?" Observation breaks the communication process into discrete events and elements. Kinds of communication events and activities can be observed. An argument is different from a joke. Salutations are different from saying good-bye. Watching television is different from reading a newspaper or sending and receiving memos in a company. Holding a meeting or participating in an interview is not the same as preparing and delivering a speech.

Once different events, relationships, patterns, and processes are observed, they can be named—what scholars call *concepts* or *constructs*. Naming events, processes, and relationships in communication is difficult. For instance, if researchers are going to base research on the assumption that uncertainty reduction is a powerful motive, how can they know for sure what the concept means? Or, what is a *question?* Interviewing studies are interested in strategic questioning activities. A question—a concept vital to interviewing—is an interrogative statement, "What did you study"? Is an imperative, "Tell me what you studied," also a question?

A concept is useful to the extent that other researchers see the same phenomenon in the light that its name distinguishes it from other phenomena. Some phenomena are directly observable. One can observe that the beginning of a conversation is different from its ending. The glare of a person angered during a conversation is observable. But other phenomena are not directly observable. Attitudes, beliefs, or values cannot be observed. Nor can researchers know whether a person is being entertained or enlightened by a television program. All they can go with is what they believe is evidence of these phenomena. When a subject fills out a questionnaire, the researcher hopes the response corresponds to an *attitude, belief,* or *value,*—or *entertainment.* Observation and naming are crucial aspects of theory building because understanding can be advanced only if phenomena are named with sufficient accuracy that people can agree with the terms and find them useful to understand what is going on.

Two terms, *reliability* and *validity,* help determine whether researchers accurately define key concepts and can measure the phenomenon repeatedly. Reliability is a test of whether repeated studies can produce the same results. If not, the results are a function only of the study, not of its ability to examine the phenomena. Validity refers to the accuracy of concepts and measures. For example, what is an attitude? Is it an opinion obtained by having subjects complete a scale, such as Strongly like, _____ , _____ , _____ , _____ , _____ , Strongly dislike? Is it an expression of *agree, disagree,* or *don't know?* A theory that lacks validity or reliability is not useful.

Researchers try to identify key concepts in communication. For instance, *information* may be distinguished from *persuasion,* or *conflict* from *cooperation.* What is *entertainment?* What is *pornography, meaning, channel,* or *attraction?* Is *propaganda* the same as *persuasion?* What is *trust* in interpersonal relationships? What is *attitude* or *belief?* You may notice how difficult these concepts are to define. Often, just as some concept seems to be stabilizing in meaning, someone comes along and frustrates the effort. For instance, in order to study the effects of watching pornography, a researcher must have a viable concept of what pornography is and what distinguishes it from art. Just as researchers think they have achieved a standard definition, culture changes and so does the definition of pornography. Another example: The concept of *channels* and how they differ from *messages* seemed reasonably clear until Marshall McLuhan (1964) called the "medium the message" (p. 23). His observation was designed to show how a channel, such as television, is also a message because each channel gives unique shape to the information it conveys.

Once concepts are identified, the next step is to define or explain the relationships between them. One way to deal with concepts is to put them into a model. Since the 1950s, many articles and communication texts have contained primitive pictorial models. Some of these are shown in chapter 2. Whereas a theory explains key concepts and their relationships, most models are mere pictorial representations that may not be isomorphic analogues of the phenomena being described (Hawes, 1975). To be isomorphic, a model must accurately represent the phenomena under consideration. Few models meet this requirement.

There are at least three kinds of models:

1. *Taxonomy,* the most primitive model, merely lists the key concepts of some phenomena, but does nothing more than suggest that the concepts are related in some way. A good example of a taxonomy is a list of components typically used to describe the communication process: Source, message, channel, receiver, feedback, and context. In this taxonomy, no effort is made to account for how any concept relates to, affects, or is affected by any other.

2. A *pictorial* representation is a more sophisticated model that conceptually describes the phenomena. These are called "spaghetti" models because they have lines going in all directions because they suggest in the most general manner how concepts relate to one another. A typical example of a pictorial representation model results when someone takes the taxonomy of source, message, channel, receiver, feedback, and context and draws elaborate complexes of lines and arrows attempting to describe the relationships between them. Although such models are always incomplete and imprecise, they can be helpful. They postulate relationships so that they can be discussed and so that hypotheses can be posed. They help students understand key concepts and relationships as long as it is understood that they are not replicas of the process being considered.

3. The *mathematical formula*. Those models have achieved a level of definition and precision so that relationships between concepts can be calculated with mathematical precision. Few mathematical

models have been developed to explain communication events and processes.

Each kind of model attempts to express the relationship between concepts and variables. Social scientists typically use the term *variable* to describe what happens when constructs interact or when a construct is measured. As Kerlinger (1973) observed, "a variable is a property that takes on different values." He continued, "A variable is something that varies" (p. 29). A variable is a concept that can be measured numerically.

Variables may be dichotomous, demographic characteristics or male or female for instance, or continuous, such as degree of opinion change or amount of enjoyment produced by watching a particular television program. By assigning numbers to variables and calculating the interaction between them, researchers seek to make accurate observations and predictions.

For instance, a speaker might want to know whether fear appeals of a particular magnitude (high, moderate, or low) increase a listener's willingness to receive and yield to a message. That example contains two other kinds of variables — independent and dependent. An *independent variable* is one that is presumed to produce changes in the *dependent variable*. Here fear appeals is the independent variable, whereas reception and yielding are dependent variables.

A *mediating variable* influences how an independent variable, such as message, will affect the dependent variable, such as attitude; the degree to which a receiver is personally affected by (self-interested) in the topic of a message mediates its impact on recall or attitude change. A *confounding variable* interferes between independent and dependent variables. In doing research, such as the amount of time children watch television, results could be confounded by a variable such as attention; even though television sets may be on and children are in front of them, the children may not be paying attention.

Let's look at communication as a variable. Communication can be treated as a dependent variable by looking for factors that influence it is an outcome. For instance, uncertainty may produce more communication behavior — question asking. Communication can also be treated as an independent variable by examining the variables it influences. Studies of mediated communication treat it as an independent variable that has impact on how people use media (dependent variable) for entertainment or news.

This discussion underscores another criterion of theories, the ability to predict. Although prediction is unnecessary for a theory to be good, it is nevertheless a valuable goal. Theories must describe, but they can also predict how people will behave or respond under certain circumstances. To appreciate the usefulness of predicting outcomes, imagine a communicator who wants to be persuasive (raise a listener's willingness to receive a message and yield to it). The communicator could use fear appeals; in this effort, the person designing the message would have to know what fear appeals are (as a concept) and understand how they interact with cognitive processes of reception and yielding (McGuire, 1968a, 1968b).

Along with its other features, a good theory is heuristic; it can be used to do something valuable. It may guide the design and execution of a communication campaign. A person designing a political campaign, for instance, might be interested in knowing (a) what types of messages will attract attention to candidates, (b) reinforce committed voters, (c) sway the uncommitted voters, (d) convert opponents, and (e) motivate supporters to vote for one candidate or against an opponent.

One heuristic aspect of a theory is the extent to which it can be reduced to a paradigm. What is a *paradigm?* It is the archetypal example or principle that a researcher keeps in mind when thinking about an ideal concept, relationship, or set of relationships. As Kaplan (1964) wrote, a paradigm is "the clearest instance of the general category. In this respect the paradigm functions like an ideal type, but is an actuality rather than an abstract construction, an individual to be generalized rather than a concept already generic in form" (p. 118). A paradigm differs from a theory that requires full explanation of relationships between variables. In contrast, a paradigm reduces a theory to its essence, a single summary model or example.

A theory is heuristic if it leads to successful hypothesis testing. Until hypotheses are tested, they and the theory of which they are a part are nothing but speculation based on intuition or general observation. A good way to think about a hypothesis is that it is the "what if?" "what is?" "why is?" or "if then, what?" statements that are used to focus the research effort so that the answer supports or contradicts the theory that is being explored.

A theory is parsimonious if it can be briefly stated — what some call the "back of the envelope" test. Can the theory be explained in the space available on an envelope? A theory must be internally consistent, meaning that it is logical and reasonable. Finally, a theory should be capable of being falsified. If a theory cannot be disproven, it probably cannot be proven either. In such a circumstance, the "theory" is interesting, but it is not useful for empirical research.

This list of criteria can help you determine which theories do a good job of explaining the phenomena that you are trying to understand. Not all theories are equal. Some are better than others.

Relationships Between Variables

Throughout your study of communication, your inquiry should be guided by the goal of achieving a precise understanding of the relationship between key variables. It is not enough to learn that certain communication variables interact. The higher level of analysis is to know how and why they interact. The following are some major types of interaction that occur.

Linear Versus Nonlinear. Some relationships are linear. This means that the events in the process move from one to another in sequence. The earliest popular communication model portrayed the process as starting from a sender who creates a message that is sent through a channel to have an effect on a receiver. Another example would be the view that a persuasive message is a stimulus that creates a response, such as attitude change, which subsequently leads to a change in behavior. Or, the message in an advertisement may bring up a salient attitude in the mind of the potential buyer and thereby prompt the person to buy (or at least prefer) the product or use the service. A linear model of communication behavior assumes that a logical, causal, sequential relationship exists so that each preceding element affects those that follow.

Many relationships between the elements of the communication process are nonlinear. (The discussion in chapter 2 should help you understand this point more clearly.) Each element in a process interacts dynamically with others. In the aforementioned example of the advertisement, a linear view would assume that the ad content led to an attitude that could lead to a preference to buy. But a person's reaction to advertising is typically nonlinear depending on (a) the time of day when the ad is encountered, (b) the buyer's awareness of competing purchasing choices, (c) peer approval, (d) source credibility, (e) willingness to refute the persuasive message, (f) the buyer's mood, (g) the ease of making the purchase, (h) the buyer's cash flow, and (i) the size of last month's credit card statement—these factors will impinge on (mediate) the likelihood that the message will lead to the desired purchasing behavior. Also, because buyers are dynamic to some extent, they often seek information and ask questions about products and services, thereby selecting information strategically rather than merely yielding to ad content. Each of us has experienced this nonlinear relationship as we weigh factors involved in making a purchasing decision.

A relationship can be colinear. This relationship exists when two variables are not independent. For instance, persuasion research has observed a colinear relationship between attitude toward a behavior and the belief about the norms that should be used in making the decision about the behavior (Ajzen & Fishbein, 1980; Shepherd, 1987). This means that, even though you might have a favorable attitude toward an action, such as going out instead of studying for a final, you consider the norm that says "Study." Or you may not have a positive attitude toward the directive, "Give blood" but you decide to donate because your friends agree to give and think you should as well. In this case, neither variable (attitude toward action or norm) necessarily precedes or follows the other. They may occur simultaneously in the process of persuasive influence.

Curvilinear.   This means that the relationship between two variables is U-shaped. For instance, a curvilinear relationship exists between the impact of source credibility on attitudes and the degree to which receivers are interested in finding out information on the topic. As interest increases, source credibility increases attitude up to a point, after which further interest in the topic lessens attitude change (Stiff, 1986).

Positive Versus Negative.   The relationship between variables can be positive or negative. For instance, high credibility sources have a positive effect on attitude change, whereas low credibility sources may have a negative effect. Another example of a positive relationship exists when, in interpersonal communication, individuals are attracted to those persons who have the same attitudes (a positive relationship). In contrast, a negative relationship exists between persons who have dissimilar attitudes.

Causation Versus Correlation

It is hard to discern whether a relationship is due to causation or correlation. Causation assumes that the relationship between two variables, events, or behaviors is such that one causes another. The antecedent variable under certain conditions produces the consequent change in the other variable. For instance, you know that increased amounts of heat (cause) applied to a tea kettle will increase the speed (effect) with which the water will boil. (You can also vary the condition. Water boils at a lower temperature at high altitudes than at sea level.) One of the perplexing examples of this relationship is that between high amounts of television viewing and low academic achievement. Achievement tends to drop once viewing exceeds 10 hours per week. But studies on this topic are inconclusive as to whether low achievers watch more television or whether watching high amounts of television cause lower achievement. Perhaps high amounts of watching and low achievement are products of some mutual cause (Potter, 1987).

This kind of analysis can be applied to other relationships. For example, persons who have recently made a major purchase read more about the item purchased than do people who have not made the purchase. So, did the purchase cause the result (more reading) or are the two phenomena merely correlated, meaning that they occur at the same time? If all people, rather than some or most, read more about the item purchased, the relationship is more likely to be causation. But if some do not, then more than one factor is likely the cause of the predicted outcome. Conditions such as the magnitude of the purchase or the purchaser's personality may account for the behavior. If so, these factors would be conditions under which the effect would occur.

Correlation states that two events occur or variables change (covary) in either a positive or negative relationship to one another. Even if a causal link cannot be established, the researcher knows that a relationship exists between events. Examples of correlation can be found in the physical sciences. Einstein's contention that $E = MC^2$ argues that a correlation exists between the variables (mass and the speed of light). This is an example of the law of coexistence.

Do we have cause or correlation? This is a vital question. Let's examine an everyday event. Two coworkers frequently go to lunch together. Near lunch time, one or the other shows up at the other's office and says, "Lunch?" A causal model would argue that the invitation produced the response, "I'm ready; let's go." But sometimes the invitation is declined, "I have a different lunch arrangement today." Is the fact that they often go to lunch together due to correlation or causality? The probability is high that one person's arrival will prompt the other person to make a *choice* but the arrival does not cause the choice. Casual observation may lead us to wonder whether height and weight are correlated. Are taller people heavier than short people? As you look around, you find some evidence to confirm this hypothesis, but you also note that some short people are heavy and some are light. More importantly, you should realize that height does not cause weight; neither does shortness cause people to weigh less.

A researcher might wonder whether high amounts of television viewing cause viewers to believe the world is more violent than it is (because TV portrays more violence than is true of the real world). Does watching large amounts of television cause people to perceive high levels of violence? Or do fearful people watch more TV than nonfearful people and thereby find confirmation for the amount of violence they think exists? Some researchers are intent on finding out the causality, if any exists, in this tangle. Others may be willing to settle for some unexplained relationship (in causal terms) between high amounts of televiewing and a sense of apprehension about the amount of violence.

APPROACHES TO THE STUDY OF COMMUNICATION: META-THEORIES

By now you should be aware that communication behavior and individual reactions to it are not merely random. Research could never explain communication behavior if it did not occur according to knowable patterns.

The objective of theory and research is to draw accurate conclusions about relationships between constructs that are essential to understanding some interaction or reaction. To conduct meaningful research, scholars have argued over which approach is best.

Toward this end, some researchers have aspired to discover invariant "scientific" laws about interaction patterns and relationships of communication behavior. Oh, if life were only that easy! An *invariant "scientific" law* perspective assumes that a constant, causal relationship always exists between two variables or events so that the presence or change of one, as antecedent, invariably produces or changes the other. The strict positivistic view of science argues that research findings are invalid unless they are based on invariable relationships. The equation is this: Variable Y varies as a function of variable X under condition Z. Such logic can be used to explain physical events such as objects falling at the same speed under the same conditions or water boiling at the same temperature at the same altitude. But the standard of causal relationships is too demanding to be useful for conducting most communication research.

Carried to its extreme, a general laws approach assumes that human communication behavior is motion, not action. *Motion* is the product of cause and effect relationships. A truck rolling down a hill out of control without a driver is in motion; it is not acting. *Action* assumes willed choices. Much communication behavior is subject to a variety of choices, even though they exhibit patterns whereby people act similarly under similar conditions.

Communication researchers realize that a pure scientific laws approach to communication studies requires an unrealistically mechanistic view of human behavior. Human communication behavior is complex and subject to subtle influences and choices due to (a) situation, (b) personality, (c) personal preferences, and (d) the ability to perform expected communication activity. Communication interaction is a web of multiple causes or correlations so complex that relationships among variables probably are not invariable.

To compensate for this methodological problem, researchers proposed three meta-theories (theories about theories): rules, systems, and covering law. Each of these contains a unique epistemology regarding how to produce reasonable and meaningful research findings.

The *rules* approach argues that behavior and opinion formation are governed by people's efforts to achieve goals by following rules rather than as a response to antecedent conditions, as is assumed by a laws perspective. A rules perspective assumes that people generate, learn, and use rules to make judgments and interact in the same way that they follow rules to play a game. Rules are part of our cognitive or interaction "equipment" and are learned or adopted to guide thought or action.

Those who favor a rules perspective claim that it treats humans more as masters of their fate and less as robots responding to environmental cues. It reasons that strategic interaction choices are guided by learned rules of action, not causal laws of motion. To explain why communicators know which choices to make, theorists search for the cybernetic (feedback) mechanism by which people judge whether their choices bring about the results they desire. The principle is this: If X outcome is desired, then Y behavior or opinion will produce the desired result under Z circumstances.

For example, people take turns during a conversation in order to be thought of as pleasant, amenable persons. They answer questions during an interview to be viewed as competent candidates for a job. They use ingratiation, which follows the rule that if they compliment someone, that person is obliged to be complimentary in return. They know that they must "yield the floor" to allow communication partners to have a turn during a conversation. They believe that they can obtain a favorable outcome by holding a particular attitude—such as believing a specific product is better than other products under the circumstances. The rule "people should buy cars that are economical and durable" contains several attitudes that can guide judgment and behavior. By similar reasoning, persons might watch a funny television program to put themselves in a happy mood. The rules perspective assumes that communication transpires as people follow knowable rules to interact as well as to make judgments (Bandura, 1986; Reardon, 1981).

Reardon (1981) differentiated between rules that are "owned" and those that are "borrowed." *Owned rules* are part of an individual's own repertoire, whereas some rules are borrowed only to "go along." People borrow rules to please the persons from whom they obtained them. Whether someone uses a rule that is personally or socially derived is important. Knowing whether a person is employing a rule because it is personally satisfying or because it has been adopted during interaction can let us determine whether the person is responding to self-oriented or other-oriented rules. People respond differently under those circumstances.

Constitutive rules specify how people should interpret verbal or nonverbal messages or events that occur during interaction. For instance, constitutive rules regarding your relationship with someone (such as spouse, parent, child, or stranger) suggest how you should interpret a statement such as "I love you." "I love you" means something different between a couple whose baby was just born than when it is said by one person to another during an initial encounter in a bar. Or the meaning of "That's an interesting outfit" would be different if spoken by a friend or an enemy. *Regulative rules* govern interaction patterns; for instance, when someone greets you, you are obligated to respond in kind (Pearce & Cronen, 1980). Were you taught to say "thank you" when you receive a gift?

Rules are "what if" statements that link communication behavior to goals that can be satisfied by interacting with other people. One might ask, what strategies do I employ if I want to start a conversation? Or the tactical relationship can be stated as "if—then." *If* person *A* says "Hello," then I should respond appropriately if I want to seem friendly. Each rule links a goal with the communication strategy likely to achieve it. The formula is this: If goal *X,* in situation *Y,* then action *Z*. If hungry, then eat. If an attitude is unrewarding, then change it. If person *A* wants to impress the boss (goal *X*), when the boss needs a favor (situation *Y*), the employee will volunteer (action *Z*).

Because communication behavior exhibits patterns that are knowable and followable, but are not invariant, this meta-theory reasons that they result when people choose to apply specific rules to guide interaction. Researchers seek to discover what rules persons systematically and repeatedly employ to coordinate their efforts and achieve goals in various contexts. Choice presumes that people choose rules that increase their chances of being rewarded through interaction. In this way, for instance, conversations occur because participants know and follow rules of turn taking and topic development logic (McLaughlin, 1984).

Critics of the rules perspective argue that it is impossible to develop a comprehensive list of all of the rules that can apply to all situations. However, the power of the rules perspective is its ability to capture the structure and logic of interaction without being required to explain all communication behavior.

A second meta-theory features *communication systems* (Fisher, 1982; Monge, 1977). This approach helps researchers think holistically about communication interaction and helps express the dynamism of the communication process. Systems theory assumes that reality (including human interaction) is so complex that its variables and relationships can never be known completely. This view treats relationships among people as complex, interdependent, dynamic, self-adjusting, and goal oriented. The advantage of the systems perspective is its ability to give a sense of order to individual communication interactions, as well as those that transpire in a company or entire nation.

According to this view, each person is a communication system as well as a part of many other systems, such as families, businesses, social organizations, universities, news or entertainment media, and countries. As people interact with one another and their environment, they take in information (input), think about it (throughput), and respond to it (output). People form groups, each of which is a system as well as part of a larger system. For instance, a student can be part of an academic club or social group on campus. Each of these is a subsystem, a part of the entire college or university (system). Each college or university is a part of a larger system that contains other campuses, such as a conference or league. That is kind of confusing to comprehend at first, but it is simple when you think of each system as a system—even though it is part of a larger system or composed of subsystems (each of which can be thought of as a system).

Systems meta-theory originated as a means for explaining dynamic interaction and exchange among biological organisms in an ecosystem. The desire was to analyze the efforts and changes organisms make to adapt to one another in their efforts to survive (Bertalanffy, 1968). According to that logic, each person is a system that consists of subsystems—for instance, respiratory system, reproductive system, nervous system, gastrointestinal system, and cardiovascular system.

Systems perspective is used to explain relationships between communicators and their interaction strategies. It rests on many assumptions, particularly the cybernetic principle of regulation and adjustment. Communication systems are self-regulating because of the cybernetic principle that actions should achieve goals; if not, feedback is used to change the goals or tactics.

Applied to communication, systems provides a way to study how people act (or should act) in concert with one another. This approach emphasizes the characteristics of the system, the relationships such as hierarchies among the objects in the system, and the dynamic balance within each system and between it and its environment, which consists of other systems. The parts of a system are interdependent. For example, a university has several kinds of systems: administration, staff, students, and faculty. If a part of a university (system) changes (such as an influx of students), so does the system itself (need for more faculty or increased class size).

Communication events transpire in the context of each system, as its components holistically and dynamically function to achieve the purpose for which it was created. If, for example, researchers want to understand the health of a business, they can use a systems approach to determine how effectively each employee uses communication to survive and excel in the system, and on behalf of it. Each system can be viewed as a means by which people adapt to and interchange with the environment surrounding it. Interchange occurs when one system receives information (input) from another system. This input is processed (throughput) and output for other systems. For instance, news reporters obtain stories by interacting with the world of newsworthy events. These stories are input for the newspaper. Reporters process information into stories and output them to editors. The output of reporters becomes input for editors. And so on!

With a systems perspective, researchers can concentrate on variables and rules and their strategic applications. This study could focus on a receptionist as a person who interfaces with the public (a system) to see if he or she uses appropriate greeting behavior to be friendly with customers and thereby attract business. Analysis might focus on customer relations personnel who interact with unhappy and dissatisfied customers. With its sensitivity to interdependency, a systems approach might encourage researchers to examine whether cordiality by customer relations personnel enhances a business system's ability to succeed — at least to the extent that the business depends on customer satisfaction. Parts of a system are interdependent; what affects one part affects all other parts.

The systems approach demands that communication theory and researchers be aware of a dynamic and far-reaching complex of events and interactions among many communication variables. This approach cautions researchers to view components of the communication process as a system of interdependent parts. A change in one part affects all other parts. This perspective can apply to interaction between two people or capture the dynamics of a corporation with thousands of employees. It explains how people in one system interact with persons in other systems. Thus, a company uses marketing and public relations (bolstered by opinion research) to function constructively with customers and the general public (components of an environment that affects the company's ability to achieve its goals). This observation makes us aware of one last characteristic of a system, *equifinality*. This term refers to the fact that each system can achieve the same goal by different means.

Fisher (1978) reasoned that the systems approach is more compatible with a rule-conforming model rather than law-governed models. When studying complex systems, it is often difficult to make inferences on the basis of antecedent conditions. Thus, he believed, system theory provides an encompassing epistemology for communication theory and research, whereas rules can be used to explain the form of individual episodes of communication interaction.

Social science cannot advance if it is unable to describe relationships among key variables and make general statements, some that can be used to predict communication outcomes. The third perspective, the *covering law* approach, helps fill this void in research and theory development. Berger (1977a) argued that covering laws can be generated by either searching for causal sequences or by discovering covariance (correlation) among events, behaviors, or variables. This meta-theory assumes that, once individuals have learned patterns of communication behavior, they enact these patterns in a fashion that is probable or predictable even if not invariant. This approach acknowledges that the search for absolute and universal mechanistic causality may be too high an ideal for behavioral science.

A covering law must be general enough to account for a broad range of individual behaviors that (a) can be captured within one statement, (b) expresses the essence of the behavior and (c) can be tested empirically. A covering law is nearly as abstract and encompassing as a theory; it embraces many individual behaviors under a general statement.

If this meta-theoretic approach does not assume that people act in a law-like manner, has it fallen short of the requirements of science? You may be quick to notice the difference that exists between people. You might go so far as to say that people are more different than alike. Carried far enough, this logic would argue that communication is essentially random, patternless behavior. To address this position, Berger (1977a) contended that most differences that occur during communication exhibit "irrelevant variety." In this view, the goal of research is to establish covering laws that explain the crucial aspects of communication behavior and ignore that which is irrelevant.

A covering law allows for predictions because it specifies what communication activities go with what conditions and outcomes. For instance, research may reveal that during initial interactions people will ask more questions of their communication partners when they know they will meet again. Or, if a boss notifies an employee that he or she will need to justify the decision to buy certain office furniture, the employee holds him or herself accountable for the decision and uses extensive and appropriate communication behavior to seek to satisfy the expected accountability.

Throughout this book, these three perspectives are used to grasp the essence of communication interaction. The perspectives are complementary, not competing (Cronen & Davis, 1978). Even more important, as is demonstrated in chapter 2, rules and systems perspectives helped convince scholars that the linear, "hypodermic needle paradigm" of communication was static and narrow. The hypodermic needle paradigm assumes that the message sent by the sender is received and accepted unquestioningly, as medicine is injected into a patient. This view has become outdated by the realization that people interpret messages, rather than merely accept them.

Competing Assumptions About Human Nature

Some research views people as passive receivers of information who are influenced by outside persons, media, and environmental conditions. Other researchers take the opposite view that human beings are active participants, dynamically seeking and giving information or persuading and being persuaded. Several questions help illustrate the difference these assumptions make.

• Do readers or viewers actively seek information or do they passively accept what the media provide? Do persons who receive a persuasive message consider its merits and refute some or all of its claims, or do they passively accept all of the claims that are made? Your experiences probably help you make up your mind whether people are passive or active. Perhaps they are passive or active depending on circumstances (Heath, 1976), a position taken by many current communication scholars. One interesting study suggests that young children's viewing behavior (time spent watching TV and types of shows), their understanding of the reality of TV, and the degree to which they are discriminating viewers depends on their parents. Children view less, understand better, and are more discriminating when they are coached by their parents and when their parents show them more affection (Desmond, Singer, Singer, Calam, & Colimore, 1985).

• When people interact, are they mindless, merely voicing scripts that they have learned and used in other conversations, or do they mindfully create each conversational statement anew? Some researchers think that much communication behavior is relatively mindless—requiring little, if any, thought and analysis. This kind of scripted behavior exists as long as it is successful; when it fails, individuals have to improvise. In chapter 5, the point is made that, depending on how important a topic is to us, we may be mindful or mindless. We can be both, but not at the same time.

• Are people complex or simple? Do they prefer (are they satisfied by) detailed, indepth discussions, or do they prefer only the briefest possible amount of information? Some researchers believe that people are complex and insightful, which assumes that they know what they are doing in communication activities. This view argues that people prefer a lot of information and subject it to careful scrutiny. This view might also assume that persons view television or read newspapers to obtain lots of information and insight. The contrasting view approaches the human mind as being relatively uncluttered with detail and disinterested in complex analysis. Sillars (1982), for one, found that people are neither very complex nor accurate in their judgments of the reasons why other people behave as they do. Again, there is substantial room for individual difference between people and the recognition that situations influence the type and amount of information they seek.

• Are persons rational or emotional? Some theories of communication, especially those related to argumentation and persuasion, battle the extent to which judgment is guided by careful, rational analysis versus emotional feelings that lead people to overlook arguments and respond in an emotional manner. Some researchers contend that emotions and reasoning are virtually inseparable, and that the key to understanding their impact is to examine the complementary emotional and rational processes that undergird decision making.

• Is a communication event the product of a single *influence* or multiple *causality* or neither? Researchers try to guard against using too few causes or factors to explain communication activities, but they also know that an infinite list of multiple causes could be used to attribute human communication behavior. In this regard, Berger (1977a) emphasized the goal of discounting irrelevant variety as he concluded that "it is probably the case that relatively few variables ultimately can account for most of the action. We simply do not know what many of these variables are yet" (p. 15).

Research by Domain: Subdisciplines

Communication can be studied by examining core concepts, such as uncertainty or persuasion, and by considering how people communicate in different contexts, such as interpersonal, organizational, or mass mediated. Some concepts, for example information, persuasion, and meaning, are universal to all research domains. For instance, persuasion can be studied in general or as it occurs in context. Persuasion in face-to-face contact typical of interpersonal communication may introduce different concepts and variables than does a corporate public relations effort. Any of these focal points can be considered as subdisciplines; each can be studied by itself or as part of the total communication discipline. However the study is conducted, we must not lose sight of the fact that, eventually, holistic views are more illuminating than particular ones.

Communication behaviors differ, at least to some degree, in each unique context. Context domains include levels of analysis ranging from intraindividual cognitive processes, interpersonal interaction, organizational communication, to mass-mediated communication. Interpersonal communication can be narrowed to the domains of marital communication, doctor–patient communication, or relationship dissolution. In narrow domains such as these, research could focus on persuasion or compliance-gaining strategies.

Shapere (1974) defined a *domain* as "a body of related information about which there is a problem, well defined usually and raised on the basis of specific considerations" (pp. 521–522). A *domain* is a topic of inquiry that focuses on a related group of problems that are worthy and capable of being solved through analysis and research. A domain may be a general concept, such as persuasion; a context, such as mediated communication; or an application, such as advertising. Nonverbal communication and meaning, for instance, are important domains in their own right but also are relevant to other domains, such as interpersonal, organizational, or mediated communication.

Thinking about research by domain should help you understand the continuity and structure of research so that you are not lost in a tangle of competing theories, hypotheses, and contexts. Intuitively, you should notice how research conclusions might differ if source variables, such as credibility, are studied in general, or in one or a combination of the following contexts: public speaking, interpersonal communication, television news, or public relations. You will also note that, increasingly, scholars are viewing communication as being more integrated than segmented. At one point, mass communication scholars and interpersonal communication scholars had little to say to one another. Now, efforts are being made to discover connections between television and the family. Portrayals of families and interpersonal relationships on television may affect the development and dissolution of real-life relationships. Also, power relationships in families determine who watches certain programs, when they watch the programs, and on what specific television set (Bryant, 1990).

The chapters in the remainder of this book present research and theory by concept and context, with some attention to application. Effort has been made to demonstrate how the domains integrate. Each chapter addresses an aspect of communication and features competing interpretations but advocates no single theory of communication.

COMMUNICATION SCIENCE:
THE STUDY OF COMMUNICATION

Some researchers study communication for sheer intellectual curiosity. Their efforts are like those of astronomers, for instance, who want to understand the universe but do not necessarily intend to travel there. Many communication researchers are goaded by curiosity to understand human communication but have no practical applications in mind as they conduct their studies.

Some researchers not only do applied research, but they also adapt findings of pure researchers to solve real problems in practical settings. For instance, researchers have become increasingly sensitive to the effects that media have on culture. They may be interested in understanding how people use media so that they can help networks decide which programs to run at what times. Public policy regarding programming in many countries reflects regulators' views of the effects television or newspapers have on society and culture. Communication researchers are interested in whether news media set the agenda for public policy and political discussions or merely report the debate as it is conducted by politicians and special interest groups. Some researchers study viewing patterns of persons to determine whether television creates "a reality" whereby persons who view lots of television believe that there is more violence in society than do light viewers. Such studies tell us about communication, and how to communicate. This research can lead to improved media policy and programming decisions; practical outcomes, whether self-imposed or promulgated through regulatory agencies.

Research has helped explain why some people suffer from speech fright or speech reticence. It offers insight into why some people are better than others at interpersonal communication. Some people use interpersonal communication research and theory to help people be more successful with their relationships; similar efforts are made to apply organizational communication research to businesses. Results of persuasion studies are applied by advertisers and public relations practitioners. Some persons worry that social science can be applied by corporate communicators to "manipulate" or "brain wash" the public. By the same token research reveals that advertisers are unlikely to do either of these. Each person who studies communication may be more able to guard against the abuse of such research.

During your initial encounter with the many competing theoretical explanations of communication, you may become frustrated. You may find yourself wishing that one explanation could account for the phenomena under consideration. But social science does not operate that way. Scholars advance knowledge by creating arguments, supporting them with data and reasoning, and challenging as well as defending competing explanations of communication behavior. At times research findings tell us what we knew intuitively about communication behaviors or outcomes. So why conduct research and create theories? The answer: To be sure that what we intuit is correct and to understand communication phenomena in a systematic and holistic way.

You can study communication constructively if you keep in mind three basic assumptions:

1. Each person uses communication as a means for reducing uncertainty. People communicate to learn what they need to know to cope with physical and social reality. They tune into the news to get the weather report. They ask questions and share comments to learn how to be social, to know what to say and when, to learn whether they fit in, to know the ropes of the business in which they work. Communication helps people adapt to their social and physical realms. Through communication people create and manage social knowledge, a view of reality that reflects beliefs unique to each group. By sharing meaning with one another, humans live together with a degree of organization and predictability.

2. People communicate to join with others they encounter. They learn strategies of interaction that will help them adapt to one another. Each person is idiosyncratic in his or her need to reduce uncertainty and to adjust and adapt. Some people are extremely competent; others are painfully awkward. But each person is stuck with the problem of needing to be as competent as he or she can be to achieve the desired rewards and avoid the pitfall of incompetence.

3. Because people are symbol-users, they get pleasure from the sheer act of communicating. As you think about why you like to entertain and be entertained through communication, you may realize that entertainment also helps us to reduce uncertainty. Television programs give information about social and physical realities. You can watch people be rewarded and punished for their opinions and efforts. Entertainment viewing or reading reinforces as well as challenges opinions or values. But in addition to this kind of information, you watch, listen, and read simply for pleasure.

This chapter should have armed you with an understanding of key assumptions and methods necessary to appreciate how communication is studied. Along with this foundation, you should be convinced that you have been studying communication throughout your life. By systematically studying communication, you should become more knowledgeable and a better researcher. And you may become a better communicator.

2 Anatomy of the Communication Process

What is communication? What are its components? Is it a process or an act? Is it a series of acts that occur as a process? Is communication a function? Can it break down? Can people "uncommunicate"? Is it the use of symbols to transmit ideas and information from one person to another? Or is it interaction between people—a form of sharing or relationship development? Can personal identity and interpersonal relationships be created without communication? Are some relationships better than others because of how well the persons involved are able to communicate? In this sense communication affects relationships. Is the opposite true—do relationships affect communication? Does mediated communication (radio, television, or newspapers) control receivers' thoughts, or do receivers shape the content of mediated communication by their selections of which shows to watch or listen to or which paper or magazine to buy and read? Questions such as these motivate and guide efforts of researchers who seek to discover how and why humans communicate.

This chapter examines assumptions basic to the view that communication is a process. This analysis should help you appreciate the effort that has been undertaken to decide which concepts are fundamental to the process. This discussion is designed to show how some key concepts have different, even conflicting definitions. It explains how researchers have changed their assumptions regarding what communication is and what concepts help to explain it.

This chapter portrays some dramatic shifts that occurred in regard to how communication is conceptualized and researched. Researchers' definitions of communication affect how they analyze key variables. As you become

28

more aware of key concepts and shifts in perspectives in regard to what communication is, you should appreciate why viewpoints affect how people think about communication.

This century has witnessed dramatic changes in the study of communication. Much of the early communication research of this century was guided by a transmission paradigm dependent on principles of stimulus and response. The belief was that what a sender's message (stimulus) causes a similar response (message reception) in a receiver. According to this view, communication is a means for transmitting ideas from one mind to another to achieve understanding and influence. To some extent that notion persists, but an alternative view—one that features interaction—is beginning to prevail. A major contribution of 20th-century research has been to think of communication, not as a vehicle for transmitting ideas, but as means for interaction.

To examine the anatomy of the communication process, this chapter reviews several definitions, thinks of communication as process, examines early pictorial models of the process, and discusses components of the process.

COMMUNICATION—A HARD TERM TO DEFINE

What is communication? Hundreds of definitions have been proposed, but none is entirely satisfactory. The following examples show the variety of definitions that have been offered. Before studying these examples, jot down your definition of communication and compare it against them.

Featuring the *transmission paradigm,* Devito (1986) said that communication is "the process or act of transmitting a message from a sender to a receiver, through a channel and with the interference of noise; the actual message or messages sent and received; the study of the processes involved in the sending and receiving of messages" (p. 61). This paradigm of communication has been very popular but offers a limited view. Note that Devito said that communication is either a process or an act. Is it both, one at times and the other at other times? Later on in this chapter you will receive information that can help you understand the importance of thinking of communication as process.

Taking the view that communication is interaction, not transmission of ideas or information, Gerbner (1967) defined it as "interaction through messages. Messages are formally coded symbolic or representational events of some shared significance in a culture, produced for the purpose of evoking significance" (p. 430). Note that Gerbner said that messages are "formally" coded. Does his definition exclude informal, unintentional communication behavior, such as nonverbal cues such as head nodding in agreement to what someone is saying? Nonverbal response matching behavior is important to interaction even though it is informal and unintentional.

To what end does interaction lead? Featuring their convergence theory, Rogers and Kincaid (1981) argued that through communication "participants create and share information with one another in order to reach a mutual understanding" (p. 63). The incentive behind communication is to achieve understanding. As one corporate communication firm's letterhead optimistically proclaims, "Communication is the beginning of understanding."

Also featuring interaction, Cronen, Pearce, and Harris (1982) viewed communication as "a process through which persons create, maintain, and alter social order, relationships, and identities" (pp. 85–86). They believed that the study of communication should concentrate on how humans attempt "to achieve coordination by managing the ways messages take on meaning" (p. 68). Pearce and Cronen (1980) contended that through communication "persons collectively create and manage social reality" (p. 7). People interact because they must coordinate meaning sufficiently well to live together with a degree of predictable social order. An interaction view of communication emphasizes the dynamic effort that all parties make while communicating. This paradigm does not feature sender or receiver, but assumes that people's needs and efforts to achieve social coordination are the focal points for studying communication. In this regard, the interaction paradigm is quite different from the transmission paradigm.

Analysis of this kind demonstrates how interaction patterns are crucial to the study of interpersonal communication. According to McLaughlin (1984), conversations do not grow randomly; they follow specific, knowable turn-taking patterns which are rule-like. Because of the principle of systems adaptation, people's evaluations of each situation in which they are communicating influence how they communicate. Based on the definition of the situation and the goals that are present, rules are employed to achieve those goals given the definition of the situation (Cody & McLaughlin, 1985). These patterns have rule-like qualities; one person may not talk too long, people may not randomly change communication topics, and people must take turns sharing the conversational floor with others.

A more extensive commitment to interaction can be obtained by building a definition of communication on a systems perspective. In this way, communication can be said to occur when information output from one system becomes input for another (Ashby, 1963). In a similar way, Hewes and Planalp (1987) argued that communication occurs when one person's behavior affects another. Twenty years earlier, Dance (1967) defined communication "as the eliciting of a response" (p. 289). These definitions make communication synonymous with all stimuli — anything that produces a response or has impact. Do those definitions make communication too basic? Can they account for that range of activities that goes from two people talking, to the sharing of information and influence in a business, to the mass dissemination of information and influence through the media?

Attempting to comprehend the range of definitions, Dance (1970) found 15 different types. Each stressed a different focal point: symbols and verbal speech; understanding; interaction; uncertainty reduction; process; transmission; linking and binding; common experience; channel; memory; modification; stimuli; purpose/intent; time/situation; and power. After this review, he observed, "We are trying to make the concept of 'communication' do too much work for us. The concept, in its present state, is overburdened and thus exhibits strain within itself and within the field which uses it. What may help is the creation of a family of concepts" (p. 210). Indeed, systematic research and theory construction require the identification of key concepts and the explanation of their nature and relationships.

Rather than deciding on one definition, you are wise to look for key concepts and assumptions that make up the anatomy of the communication process. You should learn to understand what concepts mean and know the role each plays in the communication process. As you become skilled in your study of communication, you should be able to spot the unique character of each definition. This analysis will help you note the assumptions the author is making. Such insight is the same as that used by a good detective who can solve a "who-done-it" by using clues to ferret out the culprit. You should understand the crucial differences reflected in each definition and appreciate the assumptions it bears. Through your analysis you may conclude that *communication* is a process by which people create meaning through interaction.

COMMUNICATION AS PROCESS

Imagine yourself going into a strange town or country. You do not know the names of its streets, roads, and places. You do not know where the important places are or where you should be safe, get food, or receive shelter. You do not have a map to help you find your way. This feeling is similar to that experienced by communication theorists of the 1950s and 1960s. They knew that communication had a major impact on thought, relationships, and society. They had an idea of where they wanted their research to lead them, but they did not know which concepts were important. They were unsure which questions were worth answering.

Their inquiry was guided by many questions:

- What impact do media have on society?
- How do persons understand and influence one another?
- How do they know when other people understand them?
- Can communication occur even though there is misunderstanding?
- Do relationships hinge on the extent to which people understand one another, influence each other, or bring about liking or disliking?
- Is communication intentional, fairly random, or virtually mindless, scripted behavior?
- What motivates people to communicate?
- Is one of the major motives the desire to reduce uncertainty?
- Do other motives include seeking to be socially competent or achieving shared meaning?
- How do people use communication to manage relationships?

Questions such as these have been central to communication research and theorizing.

The study of communication produced the belief that it is a process. A process is something that has no apparent beginning or end. It is irreversible. It always goes forward, even when, for example, you and a friend try to resolve a difference that occurred a week ago; the efforts to resolve that difference will carry forward to subsequent communication. Most of us recall instances—whether in conversation, in business, or on television—which linger in our memory. These parts of our memory are recalled and used later. How you communicated with someone before can help or hinder how you deal with that person again. Conversations do not start anew; they have a history. A maxim should help you understand this point: People cannot not communicate nor can they uncommunicate. Efforts to *not* say something communicate any number of "messages": dislike, shyness, rejection, unwillingness to communicate, inability to communicate, and so forth. Telling someone you are sorry for what you said does not erase the statement; it merely adds to it. Recall how a heated argument with someone lingers and colors subsequent conversation with that person.

Some writers say that a process model commits researchers to view communication merely as a product of causality that eliminates the possibility of choice. Without going this far, some events that occur during communication are intentional actions that result from willed behavior, and others are unintentional. The key to understanding communication is not found in trying to determine what is intentional or willed, but in acknowledging that the process continues without end. Each conversation builds on previous ones. Ads people view or read today are filtered through ads previously encountered. Movies or television programs are viewed in the context of previous entertainment fare.

As process, communication has no beginning or end. It was here when you arrived in the world, and it will continue after you are gone.

Communication efforts leave a residue of interaction patterns, experiences, ideas, and feelings that become part of subsequent encounters. To call something a process means that individual events or segments occur over time in ways that are reasonably, but not totally, predictable. The series of events that constitute communication relate to one another by virtue of many reasons—causality, rule compliance, randomness, covariance, or strategic choices by each participant. Carried far enough, process can be viewed as motion instead of action. According to this view, events change, but they do so because of linear causality rather than random chance or choice. Some communication is random or unplanned. You know this because sometimes you say something you did not mean to say or a comment by a friend provokes a nonverbal reaction that you never intended to make. Communication can be viewed as a process of ongoing events, separate acts such as conversations or encounters, all of which continue to prompt subsequent acts, all related to previous acts.

The degree to which communication is mindful and willed or automatic and unplanned is a major issue concerning communication in all contexts: interpersonal, organizational, and mediated. Bargh (1988) saw free will as a challenge to researchers who seek to comprehend how people process information and manage perception, affection, and attribution. Some communication is automatic, but some is purposeful, strategic, and willful.

Researchers have struggled with the dilemma of defining communication as process while using research methods and theories that do not meet the requirements of process. Smith (1972) noted the irony of Berlo's (1960) call to treat communication as process even though he reduced it to a linear Sender–Message–Channel–Receiver model that violates assumptions required for a process view of communication. In large part, this problem was overcome by an enormous amount of research, especially that which examined interpersonal communication as interaction.

If communication is to be viewed as process, then appropriate theories and research methods must be formulated. Cappella (1977) argued that, to understand communication as process, researchers must treat it as ever-changing, unbounded, unsequenced, totally interdependent, and consisting of interaction sequences. It is time dependent because no two communication events are the same. Each event is different, and each moment in each event is different. Thinking about your reactions when watching an entertaining or informational television program can help illustrate time dependency. Each scene builds—as do bricks in a wall—on one another to produce the entire episode—evening's program. Each episode is a part of a series. Some episodes are more entertaining than others. Some parts of each episode are more entertaining. In this way televiewing is time dependent.

Some researchers chide their colleagues to be sure that their research assumptions and procedures match their commitment to view communication as process. For instance, Meyer, Trandt, and Anderson (1980) noted that few mass communication studies adopted a process approach. Most mass communication studies, they argued, are static—looking at discrete variables. They noted how measures used to study television effects "focus on either one minute act or several measured in a single point in time, rather than identifying the interplay of many elements and their changing levels that compose media usage" (p. 264).

Helping to keep process central to theory and research, Reeves, Chaffee, and Tims (1982) claimed that mass communication research has been unduly influenced by Lasswell's (1948) linear model: who says what to whom through what channel with what effect. Because Lasswell's model is sender oriented, it leads researchers to analyze control, content, channel, audience, and effects. Slowly, the influence of Lasswell is giving way to an interest in the receiver. Encouraging this shift, Reeves et al. (1982) advised researchers to concentrate on the "pictures" in peoples' heads that are created and influenced by what they seek and receive from mass media.

Reeves et al. advocated using a social cognition approach, which assumes that each receiver "is mentally active, organizing and processing stimuli from the environment rather than simply responding directly to them" (p. 289). A social cognition orientation to human communication assumes that people construct views of reality. The objective is to understand how people think about one another. As active participants, people are capable of recalling and adding information and thoughts to that which they receive from the media. What they do and how they respond is likely to be influenced by their goals for watching each program.

That communication should be studied as process has become a truism. In the remainder of this chapter, we discuss that notion in detail. We also examine components of the process and explain how researchers have changed their opinions on it.

ORIGINS OF COMMUNICATION THEORY

What is called communication science resulted from the merger of at least four lines of inquiry in this century: (a) the study of rhetoric and public address, (b) propaganda and media effects, (c) transmission and reception of information, as well as (d) group dynamics and interpersonal attribution and interaction. Academic disciplines such as social psychology, sociology, and anthropology have contributed insights to the process. Each of those disciplines offered its unique view of which concepts are basic. A glance at key lines of thought can help you appreciate the effort that has been spent to advance communication science.

Rhetoric and Public Address

Most of what is thought of as communication theory has strong social science foundations. But that does not deny key points of view that have been drawn from scholars who studied the role public speaking plays in society and the tactics by which speakers influence audiences. Studying the history and criticism of public speaking, scholars drew on a tradition of rhetorical theory that has been uninterrupted since at least 500 BC. Most of the public address theory in the early part of this century was based on a speaker-speaking-to-audience paradigm that had its roots in ancient Greece. The capstone of this tradition is Aristotle's *Rhetoric* written in the 4th century BC. He studied the tactics speakers use to affect thoughts and behavior of an audience. He wanted to know the principles of effective public speaking. Aristotle's study focused on message content and structure, use of language and delivery, and the character of the speaker and the listeners.

The heritage of Aristotle is not only found in studies of persuasion, but also in interpersonal conversation. This heritage provides the rationale for unlocking the dynamics of interpersonal communication by disclosing the ways people develop and utilize message design logics (O'Keefe, 1988; O'Keefe & McCornack, 1987) and plan what to say during conversations (Hewes & Planalp, 1987).

Propaganda and Media Effects

Another major impetus in the development of communication theory was concern that mass communication was having enormous influence on people's lives and opinions. Mass communication studies prior to the mid-1950s were conducted primarily in departments of psychology, political science, and sociology or in interdisciplinary institutes. Social psychology studies were heavily oriented to understanding mass persuasion, what is often called *propaganda.* Prevailing interests in rhetoric and persuasion as well as fondness for stimulus–response psychology offered the underpinning scholars used to study mass communication effects or outcomes.

In this vein, Lasswell (1948) offered the formula that asks, "Who says what to whom through what channel with what purpose and effect?" This transmission-effects paradigm was compatible with the rhetoric/persuasion tradition and seemed ideal for comprehending the dynamics of mass communication, particularly under the umbrella of propaganda. That paradigm has been important because many researchers who conduct communication studies are steeped in a traditional search to understand how communication strategies produce effects. Lasswell's interest in propaganda techniques produced *Propaganda Technique in the World War,* published in 1927. This book is often used to mark the beginning of mass communication research. It took the orientation that scholars must know how mass communication affects thought and culture to protect society against unwanted effects.

Motivation for this line of study was the apprehension that a few dominant and exciting media could shape and control thoughts of millions of people. What could result from intrusion of media into the lives of relatively independent and unique people was the possibility that, by watching and reading the same material, they would become similar rather than unique and heterogeneous. Thus began the concept of a mass society created by mass media.

Information Theory: Transmission and Reception

Independent of these lines of analysis—rhetoric and social psychology of mass influence—arose a series of studies in information transmission. They were conducted primarily at research facilities, particularly Bell Labs. Researchers there wanted to understand how information in the form of messages could be electronically transmitted and received with the greatest efficiency and fidelity. This kind of thinking featured a linear model, a sender attempting to get a message across to a receiver.

Group Dynamics and Interpersonal Attribution

In the 1930s, the work of Mead, especially *Mind, Self, and Society* (1934), was extremely popular. His primary contribution to the study of communication was the proposition that people get to know one another and themselves only through communication. The essence of communication, he thought, was symbolic interaction. Lewin's (1951) studies of leadership and the influence people exert on one another in small group situations offered an interactional paradigm from which to study communication. A major breakthrough in the study of interpersonal communication occurred in 1958 when Heider published *The Psychology of Interpersonal Relations*. There he made the point that people can know one another only by what they experience through each other's behavior. This behavior is viewed in patterned ways as people attribute motives and personality traits to one another.

Without full appreciation for the dramatic changes they would bring about, this diverse array of scholars initiated lines of inquiry that altered the study of communication. Slowly, the term *communication* came to be used to label the content of the study, often replacing terms such as *psychology*. Mass communication studies supplanted mass persuasion or mass psychology studies. Communication slowly evolved into a term with its own intellectual territory and research domains, fostered by departments of communication that have burgeoned since 1960. Scholars adopted communication as the central term because they want to study it as a significant and unique aspect of human behavior, not as a manifestation of the psychological, sociological, or political sides of human experience. Communication became the central term modified by many adjectives to characterize domains of study, such as interpersonal communication, organizational communication, speech communication, and mediated (mass) communication. Each of these domains has its own scope and importance.

REEMERGENCE OF COMMUNICATION SCIENCE

One year after Berelson (1959) claimed that communication research lacked promise, an explosion of studies began to prove him wrong. In 1960, Klapper challenged the prevailing fear that the media dominate the thoughts and actions of people. He argued that television plays an important role in the lives of people but does not dominate them. He questioned the prevailing belief that television audiences are passive and reasoned that TV is one of many influences that account for public opinions and mass behavior. He advised a shift from the hypodermic (linear-transmission) model that assumes that media "inject" influence directly into a passive audience. He demonstrated that people resist media influence by relying on community norms, beliefs, and values. When mass communication does produce change in values and norms, one of two conditions is likely to exist: (a) Factors, such as group norms and values, that counter media effects are inoperative, or (b) They actually encourage change.

Klapper's work gave new direction to communication studies by denying the singularity of media influence, by establishing it as one of many mediating influences on opinion, and by showing how audiences are influenced by selective perception, recall, and attention. He was aware that interpersonal influences contribute to, and mediate, media influence; people talk about issues and programs. This talk shapes their reactions to program content and sets norms that may be as or more influential than the media on judgment and behavior. This research was among the first to challenge the linear model of communication. It demonstrated how the influence of communication is more likely to result from many rather than one cause.

Another major innovation in the study of communication was to view it as process, as Berlo advocated in 1960. He favored viewing communication "events and relationships as dynamic, on-going, ever-changing, continuous. When we label something as a process, we also mean that it does not have *a* beginning, *an* end, a fixed sequence of events. It is not static, at rest. It is moving. The ingredients within a process interact; each affects all of the others" (p. 24). But this process is not aimless. For Berlo, all communication was purposeful as he said, *"we communicate to influence—to affect with intent"* (p. 12). This view of process encouraged people to realize that communication transpires over time and is strategic. Even if viewed as a series of episodes, each episode has a history, a present, and a future.

Nearly two decades after alerting communication scholars to the importance of building their studies on a process paradigm, Berlo (1977) observed that four versions had developed:

1. *Process as mystery.* Communication has no starting points, no boundaries, only patterns of development and interaction.
2. *Process as complex organization.* Individual behavior is not the unit of study; relationships are. They change over time.
3. *Process as effect.* This view measures change over time in increments such as attitude shifts or relationship improvement and decline.
4. *Process as activity and change.* People develop, change, and use information to guide behavior and create a shared social reality. The process of communication is central to ongoing changes in social agreement. Information is the fundamental unit of analysis in understanding the presence of communication in society.

The study of communication as process has had many incentives, the most important of which were assumptions permeating the physical sciences and the prominence of general semantics, which advocated that the meaning of words is not static, but process. General semanticists, such as Korzybski (1948), Johnson (1946), and Lee (1952), stressed how meanings of words should not be thought of as static because the world is in a state of flux. They founded their discussion on the word-thing-thought relationship, which assumes that meaning consists of what words mean in relationship to the things they represent. But they cautioned that people should realize that words can be used in ways that treat the world as static. One method they employed to remind people of the process nature of meaning was to "date" key terms. For instance, instead of merely using the word war, they might say war 1863, war 1917, war 1941, war 1952, or war 1967. (Or they would ask that people realize that the war changes each day because on one day one side is winning, whereas on another day that same side is losing.) Each of these is a different war having its own set of enemies, problems, material, logistical tactics, and heroes. Or they might remind us to avoid thinking of our high school chums as though they do not age or change. Words must be used in ways that are sensitive to the passing of time.

The term *process* has enormous implications for how communication is viewed. It flew in the face of traditional studies, which treated each speech as an act separable from what came before it and what followed it. Persons who approached communication as "act" tended to think that an audience takes in a speech, or any other communication message, as a whole. What actually happens is that each person encounters a speech with insights and beliefs created by their own personal, previous communication. What is learned and assimilated from one speech becomes part of the memories that affect how subsequent messages are interpreted.

For some researchers, process means that multiple causal relationships exist between events. Others think of process in terms of an ongoing, uninterrupted flow of events that interact but are not reducible to cause–effect relationships. Communication behavior is viewed by the former group as causal patterns — akin to movement. The latter group views behavior as strategic, willful choices regarding how to act during communication. This action–motion duality forces researchers to consider whether people act willfully or move as a product of causes. This quandary forces researchers to consider how intentional communication behavior is. Do people communicate thoughtfully and intentionally, or do they respond to one another without much insight or strategy? This theme is explored throughout this book. It addresses the balance between mindful communication as calculated action and the flow of communication behavior that lacks thought and premediation.

EFFORTS TO CREATE A COMMUNICATION MODEL

Many studies in the first half of this century operated on a linear model, which assumed that sources design messages that influence passive receivers. This paradigm coupled with a desire to understand how people get a message across to one another clearly and efficiently. Work by Shannon and Weaver (1949) at Bell Labs culminated in an influential explanation of factors involved in clarity and efficiency. Their model was noticeably mechanistic, in part perhaps, because Shannon wanted to help engineers understand the processes of electronic transmission and reception. Despite its limitations, their model prompted other researchers to reduce communication to models featuring a complex of boxes and lines.

As limited as their approach was, Shannon and Weaver contributed a systematic approach to the study of communication. As Ritchie (1986) observed, Shannon was more interested in explaining how to achieve accurate and efficient signal transmission, particularly to improve telephone communication, than he was in proposing a theory of communication. Weaver extended these ideas and intentions to form a rudimentary theory of communication. Shannon wanted to discuss information as it pertained to signal transmission; in this regard, he wanted to be able to deal with information as though it was a fixed entity contained in a message — or a series of messages. Weaver, however, wanted to apply this theory more broadly to issues being addressed by social scientists. Together, they showed how uncertainty reduction motivates people's communication behavior.

Shannon and Weaver (1949) broadly defined communication as "all of the procedures by which one mind may affect another" (p. 3). Weaver showed how their theory could address three broad concerns: (a) The *technical problem* of achieving efficient transmission and reception; (b) the *semantic problem* of increasing the precision with which one person conveys a message to another by selecting the appropriate words; and (c) the *effectiveness problem* of understanding whether the meaning of the message affected the receiver's conduct in the manner the sender intended.

Their classic model (see Fig. 2.1) consisted of an information source, the source's message, transmitter, signal, receiver, the receiver's message, and destination. Eventually, the standard communication model featured the source or encoder, who encodes a message by translating an idea into a code. A *code* is a language or other set of symbols or signs that can be used to transmit a thought through one or more channels to elicit a response in a receiver or *decoder*. In this process, the decoder receives the transmitted message and decodes, or translates, it. Shannon and Weaver also worked to account for how noise could interfere in the transmission/reception process. They tracked down the places where noise might occur. The process started with an information source, such as Person A's mind; A uses a telephone (transmitter) to ask a friend (receiver – Person B) to dinner (message). The signal is the electrical impulse sent over the telephone line to B's telephone. Person B listens to Person A despite some noise and understands the invitation. In this view, noise is any interference in transmission or reception. Later in the refinement of this model, researchers such as Krippendorff (1975) concluded that "noise competes with the information that is transmitted from a source to a receiver" (p. 375). Applying information theory as an explanation, he observed that "noise is the random variable that reduces predictability" (p. 375). This means that noise will affect a sender's ability to predict how a receiver will receive and decode a message. *Noise* is any factor in the process that works against that predictability.

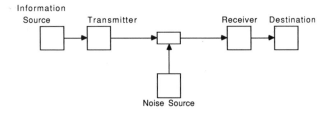

FIG. 2.1.   Model of communication (from Shannon & Weaver, 1949. Reprinted by permission).

Shannon and Weaver helped lay the foundation for an information theory approach to communication that takes two major orientations. One stresses the engineering aspects of transmission and reception. Typical considerations are the engineering design of telephone sending/receiving mechanisms and fidelity of the transmitted signal as it is passed via telephone lines or through the air. This line of study currently has its greatest influence in the development of new communication technologies, such as fiber optics, satellite communication, or computer-assisted communication.

The other orientation considers how people are unable to communicate accurately because people are different and language is not a precise instrument for communication. Differences of opinion, background, and experience provide some of the noise that keeps two people from communicating accurately on a topic. Noise, for example, occurs when people do not share the same meaning of key words or have different attitudes, values, and knowledge.

The study conducted by Shannon and Weaver was motivated by the desire to increase the efficiency and accuracy or fidelity of transmission and reception. *Efficiency* refers to the bits of information per second that can be sent and received. *Accuracy* is the extent to which signals of information can be understood. In this sense, accuracy refers more to clear reception than to the meaning of a message. This engineering model asks quite different questions than do other approaches to human communication research. Engineers want to achieve efficiency and fidelity by understanding technical aspects of transmission and reception. But communication entails more than this. An engineering model does not account for human factors that produce problems such as inattentiveness, difference of experience, or disagreement.

A major step in the evolution of human communication occurred when the focus of study shifted from transmission to an interest in the forces that influence human interaction. Early researchers adhered to the hypodermic, or *direct effects model,* that treated media as a dominant force, virtually controlling thought and judgment, even though they had little if any hard evidence to prove it (Bineham, 1988; Chaffee, 1988).

One of the strongest critics of the direct effects model, Schramm (1954, 1973) advocated a *limited effects model.* To explain communication effects, he needed a model that would define how communication occurs in many settings including, as he said, an author seeking to influence a reader, a person reporting a house on fire, two young lovers talking, and a newspaper trying to stress the virtues of Republicanism.

Schramm contributed substantially to the understanding of the communication process by noting that communicators simultaneously send and receive. In this way, he fostered the trend toward an interaction paradigm for communication. His model (see Fig 2.2) could explain that while one person is speaking, the other is listening. How this listening is done constitutes information for the sender. If a receiver frowns, that provides different information than if he or she smiles supportively. Recognizing the dynamics of interaction countered the tendency to view communication as a linear progression of steps leading to or "causing" each following step. He understood that people respond idiosyncratically to messages as a function of their personality, group influences, and the situation under which the communication occurs.

Westley and MacLean (1957), alert to the implications of the previous models, noted that Shannon and Weaver did not apply their model to mass communication. So Westley and MacLean developed a basic sender–receiver model, with modifications supplied by Newcomb (1953), which they thought could be used to show how communication transpires in many contexts ranging from face-to-face to mass mediated.

Newcomb contributed two dimensions to the basic model of Person A speaking with Person B. He postulated that the relationship between A and B influenced the perceptions B had of A's views on the topic of discussion, X. Thus he examined A speaking to B about X. Newcomb believed that if A likes B, and if A speaks favorably about X on which B has no opinion, then the liking of A will generalize to the liking of X. This scheme has many possibilities. If B likes X and does not like A, what happens if A speaks positively or negatively about X? For instance, you might like your roommate's taste in music. If he or she likes a particular group or album, you will tend to like it as well. If your favorite editorialist takes a particular stand on a tax measure, you may agree. This kind of analysis seemed to add dynamism to the basic process model.

On this foundation, Westley and MacLean offered four versions of the S–R model (see Fig. 2.3). In the first figure (a), they characterize how B receives information directly from X, some aspect of the immediate environment. For instance, B might look at a scenic view. In the second

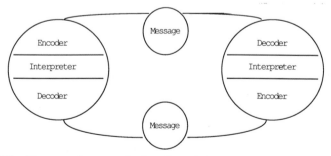

FIG. 2.2.   Elements of communication (from Schramm, 1954. Reprinted by permission).

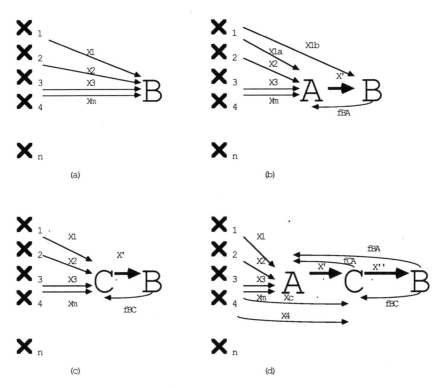

FIG. 2.3. Conceptual model of communication (from Westley & MacLean, 1957. Reprinted by permission).

figure (b), A intervenes to tell B something about an aspect of X. Now A is communicating to B about X, and the FBA (feedback from B to A) loop makes feedback part of the communication system. In (c), the Person C is added who is a gatekeeper and who can withhold or transmit information about X to B. In this case, C is the same as a newspaper — a source of information about X. If B is receiving information about X from A and C, we have an even more complex model as portrayed in (d), which combines interpersonal and mass communication. In this instance C is like a channel — a formal news source that communicates information B wants to know. Westley and MacLean utilized learning theory to reason that B will turn to C as a channel of information only if B is satisfied by (learns from) the information received. Learning theory postulates that a response to a stimuli is learned and will therefore be repeated if it results in what the person believes are rewards. This is one of many views of communication that has employed learning theory.

Westley and MacLean progressed beyond Shannon and Weaver by showing how various communication settings could be modeled, and they underscored how feedback helps a source estimate whether and how a receiver understands a message. But by demonstrating how each setting — given its unique context, relationships, people, channels as such — could be modeled, they also gave evidence of how limited a pictorial representation model can be. Think, for instance, what it would be like to draw a pictorial model to encompass the dynamics of 20 teenagers (10 females and 10 males) at a party chaperoned by one teacher who is well liked and one teacher who is disliked. The dynamics would be impossible to capture. Efforts to model the communication process led to what were called "spaghetti" or "freeway" models. As scholars tried to use pictorial models to capture all of the concepts and their relationships, the lines, boxes, and circles hopelessly tangled.

Early theories featured a stimulus (S)-response(R) paradigm, which dominated social science. As Thomas Kuhn noted (1970) paradigms change when they can no longer explain the phenomena under consideration. The S-R paradigm states that a sender produces a message that causes or stimulates a "meaning" in the receiver. Researchers soon realized that paradigm was limited and imprecise. A major shift occurred when an M was inserted to produce an S-M-R version of the model, which emphasizes that receivers mediate messages. That means a receiver translates into his or her own thoughts what a message "seems" to mean.

In the evolution of models, few if any, had more impact than did Berlo's (1960). By the time his book arrived on the scene, the ideas he expressed were not new, but he popularized the notion that communication is a process and offered an enduring model (S-M-C-R) that contained the now standard concepts: (a) the communication *s*ource (the encoder), (b) the *m*essage, (c) the *c*hannel, and (d) the *r*eceiver (the decoder).

Reflecting major themes typical of the study of communication in the first 60 years of this century, Berlo acknowledged the influence of Aristotle and the general semanticists, as well as Shannon and Weaver. Aristotle's approach to communication stressed how the speech process originates with a speaker who seeks to use a message to influence an audience. This sequence of events transpires in a context, such as a court or public legislative assembly.

Another influence on Berlo was George Herbert Mead (1934) who helped him recognize the impact communication has on the development of individual personality—the self. Borrowing from Mead, Berlo (1960) concluded that *"the concept of self does not precede communication. It is developed through communication"* (p. 125). Mead's primary contribution to communication is the claim that minds, self-concepts, and societies mature and take shape only through the dynamics of "symbolic interaction."

As did Westley and MacLean, Berlo used classical learning theory as the rationale for how and why people communicate. The S in source, he believed, is equivalent to the S in stimulus. And the R's in receiver andresponse are roughly parallel. Thus he concluded that *"a stimulus is anything that a person can receive through one of his senses,"* and *"a response is anything that the individual does as a result of perceiving the stimulus"* (pp. 74–75). A key to his approach is the observation, "The source wants the receiver to change, to learn" (p. 77). This fondness for learning theory made the S–R paradigm central to process of communication.

Learning theory is one of the long-term underpinnings of communication theory. In its most primitive sense, as discovered by Pavlov, people create associations based on two things occurring simultaneously. Pavlov, you may remember, conditioned some dogs to salivate when they heard a bell ring. He did this by ringing a bell as he gave them meat. After a while, the bell alone could cause the dogs to salivate. The stimulus, bell, produced the response, salivation. As you see in this chapter and in chapter 3, many theories of meaning depend on learning theory.

The scholars reviewed in this section played dominant roles in the development of communication models because they identified concepts and relationships basic to the communication process. And they built their models on foundations of theory that led later scholars to adopt their approaches or to have to provide research and theories to repudiate them. By now you should understand how research relies on key assumptions to explain how and why the process functions as it does.

ANATOMY OF THE COMMUNICATION PROCESS

Now that we have reviewed early explanations of the communication process, we examine more thoroughly the anatomy of the process and observe how recent writers created new concepts and stressed relationships overlooked in the early models. As we examine recent discussions of constructs and relationships, you may appreciate how they advance the understanding of communication behavior. Along the way, you can increase and sharpen the vocabulary you use to discuss communication. You may feel frustration that comes from thinking that you have acquired a definition of a concept or understood a principle only to learn that it has shortcomings. Such is the nature of research and theory construction.

Source/Receiver

Early communication models distinguished sources from receivers; as Berlo (1960) said, "some person or group of persons with a purpose, a reason for engaging in communication" (p. 30). Early models emphasized the sender as the dominant figure who used a message to produce a response in a receiver. The model was linear: A source creates a message that is sent, as a stimulus, through a channel to effect a response in a receiver. Sometimes the encoder was portrayed as being the decoder of his or her own message. In this way, elements of the process were thought to be easily segmented. Typical of such thinking, Berlo distinguished the source from the encoder by using an illustration of a sales manager who provides messages that the sales persons subsequently encode into sales presentations. The assumption was that a message is designed to be received and to have an intended effect. When it does not achieve this effect, some writers concluded that a communication "breakdown" occurred.

Today, few if any researchers employ this view of senders and receivers, or if they do, they are cautious to note that only at a moment is one person a sender and the other a receiver. More and more, audiences are viewed as being dynamic—even in mediated settings. Audiences send messages to program directors that some shows are entertaining and others are not. They buy some products and avoid others. *Sender* and *receiver* are terms used now more as a convenience than an accurate description of the elements of the process. Few researchers today view communicators as engaging in behavior that can be reduced to simple stimulus–response patterns. Current researchers prefer to use other terms, such as *actors, interactants, communication partners, communicators, audiences, viewers,* or merely *persons* or *individuals.*

Terms such as these avoid conceptual problems associated with determining who is sending and who is receiving, especially in organizational or interpersonal contexts. This preference comes from a desire to avoid mechanistic S–R assumptions and to stress how each communicator sends and receives. For instance, rather than treating the boss as source and employee as encoder, current research would treat both as sender and receiver. Rather than parroting a sales message prepared by the boss, each employee creates a unique version of the presentation.

A major improvement on early studies is to view audiences as being active rather than passive. One way to decide this issue is by determining whether receivers are willing and able to avoid exclusive influence of a source. McLeod, Becker, and Byrnes (1974) discovered that persons who are self-motivated to participate in a political campaign actively seek information from newspapers and are less likely to form an issue agenda that only corresponds to that of the newspaper they read. They are more likely to seek alternative information than are people who lack self-motivation. These researchers concluded that "cognitive theories require that we take seriously the mechanisms people use to think about mass communications. We must concentrate on the process of thinking rather than the results of thinking" (p. 318).

This shift in focus, Bryant and Street (1988) reasoned, is moving from an emphasis on receptivity to activity and action. The new paradigm features agents who act and are acted on in interpersonal, organizational, and mediated contexts. People select and evaluate information and influence and, in turn, exert influence and provide information that affects other people.

Some recent theories, such as constructivism, stress cognitive activities persons use to receive and process information. As Delia (1977) argued, constructivism assumes that people are able to construct views of their environment and do not merely respond to external forces. According to this view, people perceive reality and engage in communication by imposing an image on what they experience, including the persons with whom they communicate. As persons interact, they see one another as dynamic or weak, active or passive, and in myriad other ways. Such characterizations are used to construct views of other persons that often influence how they will be addressed. As Delia continued, "Since competence at interaction ultimately rests upon individual competencies in social perception and the control of language, variations in communication performance can be understood in terms of differences in the underlying competencies of interactants" (p. 72).

In these ways, the communication process is more complex than a source sending information expressed in a message to elicit a response in a receiver. Moreover, how each person communicates is a function of his or her competencies and idiosyncrasies, a view that goes beyond mere transmission and reception or stimulus–response patterns. The original sending and receiving model of Shannon and Weaver is appropriate for an engineering explanation of the communication process that features electrons being sent and received, but it is too simplistic to account for the dynamics of most communication interaction.

Intent/Purpose

One of the most problematic aspects of communication theory is determining the extent to which communication events are purposeful. Early models stressed purpose too much and did so primarily from the sender's point of view, giving little account of why receivers (seen as passive) acted as they do.

Rhetorical theories that treat the sender as the artistic creator of messages and Lasswell's interest in who says what to whom and with what effect relied heavily on intention or purpose. The linear model relies on the stimulus–response paradigm to determine how the source could achieve its purpose. Applied areas of communication, such as advertising, continue to stress purpose.

In contrast to linear models, uses and gratification theory of how and why people utilize mass media explains that audiences purposefully seek and use television programs and other media to gratify their needs and satisfy their wants. The rules approach to communication assumes that communicators follow a kind of syllogistic logic that is oriented toward purposeful behavior, and purposes are chosen as are the means to achieve them. Thus, communication is said to follow this pattern:

1. A intends to bring about C.
2. A considers that to bring about C he or she must do B.
3. Therefore, A sets out to do B.

Even though *purpose* is a major concept, it is difficult to identify precisely. Some communication behaviors are purposeful, whereas others are not. Some communication is accidental. Each of us communicates messages we never intended. Many purposes can come together at the same time, and sometimes communication occurs for reasons quite different than what is intended. Most newspapers or television stations have multiple purposes for presenting their wares in an appealing manner, especially to attract audiences in order to sell advertising space or time and earn a profit. Some media managers have a larger purpose, such as persuasion to an editorial point of view. But programming and editorial policy are largely a matter of attracting audiences that have favorable dispositions, rather than converting them to a different point of view.

In their review of communication research, Bowers and Bradac (1982) reported that most researchers are vague or ambivalent regarding the matter of intentionality. Persons, when asked why they communicate as they do, may not be able to articulate their intentions. But ironically, when people interact, they usually do so by attributing intentions to one another. One of the most interesting communication questions is the extent to which people accurately attribute intention to those with whom they interact.

To challenge those who believe that all communication is purposeful, Berger and Douglas (1982) proposed "that it is a mistake to assume that most utterances in social interactions are the result of highly conscious thought processes" (p. 43). They continued, "only under rather specific conditions can people be expected to be highly cognizant of concurrent behavior" (p. 46). They contended that much interpersonal communication is a product of scripts (patterns that involve low levels of decision making about what is being said under the circumstances). Thus, "self-consciousness or self-awareness cannot be assumed to be at consistently high levels across persons or situations" (p. 53).

Communication occurs accidentally or incidently. What people do and say is scripted as well as intentional. At times, it is purposeful, the result of carefully defined message design logics and plans. People tune in radio or television programs intent on learning what is happening or to be entertained. They engage in conversations to be perceived as friendly or to borrow class notes or to get a ride home. In these instances, purpose occurs in small or large degrees. The key, however, is to realize that communication occurs, whether intended or not.

Feedback

Perhaps no other term is used more loosely and imprecisely when referring to the communication process. Thousands of times each day, people seek *feedback* from one another. In most cases, they actually want *acknowledgment, comments, reactions,* or *evaluations* — each of which is a more precise term than feedback.

Early studies were fond of the concept of feedback because it fit nicely with the transmission–reception paradigm. Based on the influence of cybernetics, feedback was defined as information a sender receives that allows him or her to determine whether a message had the desired effect on the receiver.

Weiner (1948) fueled enthusiasm for this concept by using a cybernetic model to demonstrate how elements of a system feed back information to one another, so that the efforts of one part could be corrected by assessing the extent to which it was effective. The typical example, although extremely mechanistic, is the thermostat in a house, which turns on a furnace when the house cools. This self-regulating mechanism offered hope for researchers who wanted to understand how responses from the receiver could be used to determine whether the message was getting across as intended. Systems theory relies on the concept of feedback, as do the rules approach and learning theory. Feedback stresses the interactive nature of communication.

Despite the loose way that it is often used, feedback is not a simple concept to define. It often implies a sender-oriented view of communication: The sender uses feedback to determine whether the message was received as intended. How does feedback differ from any other kind of statement made during communication interaction? If an irate reader sends a letter to the editor is that feedback or merely an additional phase in a communication episode? If you say, "Good morning," and a friend replies, "What's good about a rainy day?" is that comment feedback that the receiver did not understand your message or disagreed with it? Or is it a comment that has nothing to do with the accuracy of the statement? Are survey results used to determine the success of a public relations or advertising campaign feedback? Are viewer ratings feedback or an actual part of the communication process?

These questions demonstrate how other concepts, such as *change of opinion* or *conversational behavior,* can be mistaken for feedback. Used precisely, the term is quite useful. If extended beyond its original meaning, it loses precision and blurs our understanding of the process.

Message

Message is one of the most difficult terms of communication science to define, perhaps in part because it is often taken for granted. Writers comment on message, message variables, and message impact. But what is a message? DeVito (1986) said that it is "any signal or combination of signals that serves as a stimulus for a receiver" (p. 201). This view is oriented toward a transmission–reception paradigm and treats message as something that is sent and received.

If we argue that communication is what happens when one person's behavior affects another, what then is the difference between communication—the whole process—and message—a means (part of the process) by which the process transpires? What is the message of a television entertainment program? Are visual images a part of television news, as well as the dialogue? Is the message of news conceptually similar to that of entertainment? If we believe that television news constitutes a message that creates in viewers an impression of reality, what is that message? (Seeing the same news, one person might fear the amount of crime because so much is reported, whereas another person might be reassured that the cops catch the bad guys.) Are interpersonal communication messages the same as those in mediated communication or organizational communication? Is the touch of one romantic partner on the arm of another as much of a message as the words, "You are very special to me"? Is the "touch" the message, or is the message the "meaning" interpreted from the touch? What happens if the message received differs from that intended? In that case, which is "the message"?

If communication is the ball park, then each message must be a play—a part of the game. What if we define message from the sender's viewpoint: It is the vehicle by which information is sent and social influence exerted. Defined from the receiver's point of view: Message is the product of one person's verbal and nonverbal behavior on another. In this way, we distinguish the message sent (message^S) and the message received (message^R). Each may be quite different. This definition reminds us that messages whether interpreted from sender or receiver viewpoints may be quite unintentional and mindless.

This discussion brings in another term, *meaning,* which also refers to the product that results as a person interprets the behavior—verbal and nonverbal — of another. This definition fits comfortably with the cognitive processes associated with attribution, the means by which one person interprets the behavior of others.

Discussions of messages may imply that they are communicated only through words. This is not the case. Nonverbal communication plays a major role in how receivers pay attention to and interpret messages. For instance, the intensity of the words used to state a message can increase its impact on the receiver. When nonverbal communication does not conform to what is expected under the circumstances, a receiver may infer that the sender is lying. Messages — verbal and nonverbal — affect the meaning the communicators create in each situation. Visual messages have a grammar as do verbal messages. For instance, if an advertisement features a product in a pleasant setting, the "visual" statement is this: Product X is pleasant. The news may visually present "good" people in "good settings" and "bad" people in "bad settings." In our more enlightened age, people are sensitive as to whether members of minority groups are visually presented as being inferior or subservient.

Linear models of nonverbal communication are embedded in prescriptions that tell people how to dress correctly or how to dress for success, but they cannot predict the reactions to the complex combinations of gestures, facial movements, body postures, and rate of delivery, for instance, that influence the meaning created by interactants. Nonverbal factors are essential to liking, trust, and estimations of deception. They cannot be ignored by those who feature a behavioral, meaning-centered approach to the study of communication.

Many writers have attempted to explain the interaction of message and meaning. Typical of writers of his time, Schramm (1955) adopted a referential model to explain how messages achieve meaning. A referential approach views words as having meaning insofar as they stand for things (i.e., refer to a person's experience with those things). According to this view, if we want to know what a term means we need to see the thing to which it refers. He wrote, "Messages are made up of signs. A sign is a signal that stands for something in experience. The word 'dog' is a sign that stands for our generalized experience with dogs" (p. 6).

This view of messages, heavily reliant on stimulus-response explanation, is similar to the orientation of Ogden and Richards (1923). They argued that meaning results because people share experiences of things, feelings, and events, and use words to refer to those experiences. A word would cause the mind to think of the thing. Seeing the thing elicits the thought in the mind, which in turn prompts the word to pop into mind. For example, each of us knows what the word "dog" means because of what we have learned; we share a generalized meaning of dog.

Although influenced by the stimulus–response view, Berlo (1960) emphasized the role of the receiver in this process. Thus, he explained, words mean what a receiver thinks they mean. This outcome results because meaning is not in words but in people. Communication occurs, not by transmission of meaning, but because messages elicit meaning stored in the minds of receivers. Considering this line of analysis, Cherry (1978) scoffed that we do not transmit a message; we share it. Even after I talk with someone about something, Cherry wrote, "I still have it" (p. 306). People do not transmit information, they share it.

More than mere tools for eliciting meaning, words affect the views people have—the interpretations they make—of the world around them, including the behavior of others. This point was argued by Sapir and Whorf (Whorf, 1956) who contended that the meanings of the terms and the grammar of the language of each unique group of people contain their peculiar view of the world. According to this view, people express their culture and identity in their language, and their language expresses their culture and identity. This line of analysis challenges the referential model. Indeed, it argues that words "define" reality rather than reality "telling" what words mean. As Burke (1966) argued, people should think of things as signs of words rather than words as signs of things. If, for instance, you hear, "John is a bum," you do not look at John to better understand the meaning of the word bum. Rather, you look at him to see how much of a bum he is.

The concept of *message* can be examined by understanding the nature of information. Here the key question is how does information help people to know what they want and need to know. By taking an information point of view, it could be argued that message is the impact a behavior, idea, or fact has on uncertainty and how that affects the decision-making process. Information is a factor in meaning. If you are to decide between two things, a message is any piece of information that can affect your judgment. In this regard, a message is the content you perceive in what someone else is saying to you. Any piece of information can reduce uncertainty about the content of a message or any decision that must be made in light of the content.

Messages may be the negotiated product of interaction. Some writers (for instance Cronen, Pearce, & Harris, 1982; Delia, O'Keefe, & O'Keefe, 1982) believed that interaction depends on negotiation. Typical of this line of discussion, O'Keefe and Delia (1982) showed how, from the speaker's orientation, "messages are those configurations of elements or features in behavior or human manufactures that are designed to communicate" (p. 47). To communicate, senders "make publicly available some mental state (such as wants, beliefs, or ideas) of the message producer" (p. 47). This is the message "sent" whereas the meaning created by the receiver is the message "received." Message is the effect the sender's behavior has on the receiver.

Viewed from an interaction perspective, message and meaning are created through the dynamic process whereby participants in communication affect each other.

Channels

Channels are typically defined as any means by which a message is sent by a source or obtained by a receiver. People may select channels depending on the kind of message they intend to convey. For instance, people may prefer giving bad news in writing and good news in person. A person breaking a romance or a friendship may do so in writing or through a third party—a mutual friend. If you are going to share good news with someone close, are you likely to want to do so face-to-face, or through writing, or a third party? People rarely propose marriage by placing the proposal on a billboard. In this less-than-orderly world, receivers often obtain messages they were not intended to receive. They get messages via channels other than the ones intended.

To define channels, Berlo (1960) used the human senses: seeing, hearing, tasting, touching, and smelling. He reasoned that every way people experience reality and interact with one another is a communication channel. People communicate by hearing, seeing, smelling, tasting, and touching. Senses are important for studying interpersonal communication. Researchers have made substantial inroads in determining the influence of various channels, verbal and nonverbal. One channel is *what* is said. But other channels include myriad nonverbal means including eye contact, vocal quality, touching, proximity, body position, and appearance. During interpersonal communication, many channels operate simultaneously because parties are in proximity.

In organizational and mediated communication contexts, channels are means by which experts learn how people send and receive information and exert influence, even when they are not in proximity. Communication specialists identify and analyze formal and informal channels to understand communication networks and information flow in organizations. Formal channels typically correspond to chains of command, whereas informal channels are synonymous with "grapevines" and "rumor mills." Gatekeepers are persons who are positioned where they control the flow of information. They determine what information gets into channels. For instance, a boss is a gatekeeper of information that subordinates want to send upward. Likewise, a boss can prevent subordinates from receiving information from above. Reporters and editors are gatekeepers.

In mass communication, each medium is a distinct channel. Key members of a media organization, such as newspaper editors and television program producers, are gatekeepers. Channels also include the hardware used in telecommunications; typical examples would be satellites or computer networks. Researchers who study mediated communication analyze the effects channels have on messages and on the people who use the media to obtain those messages. Advertising media planners spend much of their days deciding which channels are ideal vehicles for their clients.

In many respects, the concept of channel has changed very little since it was coined in the 1940s. But McLuhan (1964) challenged conventional definitions when he claimed that the medium is the message. With this claim, he stressed how channels differ, not only in terms of their content, but also in regard to how they awaken and alter thoughts and senses. Channels allow experiences to be shared directly (television) or indirectly (print). Radio, he wrote, uses spoken writing. Television combines seeing and hearing. He distinguished media by the cognitive processes each required. Reading is an example of linear thought because readers take in one word at a time. In contrast, television is multisensory and nonlinear because viewers see and hear simultaneously — as they do in conversation. Televiewing, he claimed, demands a kind of thought different from reading. A society heavily dependent on reading becomes rigid and linear in thought. Verbal/visual communication, typical of television or face-to-face conversations, can make society less rigid and more multisensory. He reasoned that persons who were reared in a predominantly "print" society exhibit different thought processes than do those reared on heavy doses of television. Following the lead of his mentor, Innis (1951), McLuhan popularized the idea that channels are a dominant force that must be understood to know how the media influence society and culture.

Mediated channels convey information differently. For instance, a book of pictures presents discrete and static images, whereas film and television create an illusion of movement through a continuous display of images. Media convey different material with varying degrees of ease; for instance, body and facial gestures are easy to depict visually, but figurative language is not. Messages conveyed in one medium have more impact than if they are presented in another. Preschoolers recall content better if a story is read to them rather than viewed on television even though the scripts are identical (Meringoff et al., 1983).

Each channel added in the presentation of a message enriches it. Viewing scenery through television enhances the message regarding a vacation spot, and sampling different kinds of chocolate (taste is a channel) enhances a discussion of candy. Perfume ads in magazines often include a sample of the fragrance along with text and pictures. A community with only one medium of information is not as information "rich" as is a community with several media.

Interaction

Slowly, the paradigm of the communication process shifted from a transmission–reception model to a model emphasizing interaction. The transmission–reception model is linear; each component transpires in a linear time sequence at the initiation of the sender. Interaction is dynamic; *all* parties influence the events, the sequence, and the outcomes of the communication. One of several scholars who contributed to this shift, Darnell (1971) argued that "focus on messages or on symbolic transmission is . . . unrealistically narrow" (p. 5). He encouraged researchers to study all of the ways people "affect each other *and* the interactions of those systems of influence" (p. 5).

As early as 1960, Berlo proclaimed that interaction is the "goal of human communication" (p. 129). In making this claim, he subscribed to an influential undercurrent of theory — symbolic interaction — that argues that all communication is interaction. George Herbert Mead (1934) argued that people are dynamic, not passive. They receive their understanding of themselves, their mind and self, as well as their society, through symbolic interaction. By taking this orientation, Berlo tried to make his version of communication dynamic, not static or linear.

Berlo discussed two forms of interaction. One form features feedback, a means the source can use to determine whether the message has been received as intended and if it has the desired effect. This model of communication implies that the quality of interaction depends on whether messages are sent and received accurately. That model is sender oriented. Feedback in this regard is any means a sender uses to determine whether his or her efforts have been successful. This view of communication is supported by cybernetics (Weiner, 1948, 1950).

A better view of interaction is based on empathy, a concept associated with the study of interpersonal communication by examining whether a high quality relationship exists. Stressing this orientation, Berlo (1960) concluded, *"If two individuals make inferences about their own roles and take the roles of the other at the same time, if their communication behavior depends on the reciprocal taking of roles, then they are communicating by interacting with each other"* (p. 130). Communication theory is enriched by the argument that rapport between interactants is a major factor in the process of communication.

What is communication interaction? It consists of a series of interrelated communication events that transpire between communication partners over time and space (Hawes, 1973). Communication transpires over time through a series of comments that go on between people. A conversation can be tracked to see how each statement leads to subsequent ones and eventually to an end. Location or context of the event can affect how interaction occurs. Interaction, in this manner, refers to that moment when people converse (or affect one another in different ways) in keeping with the nature of that relationship. What a friend says to you (a component of the interact) serves as the antecedent to your response, which in turn prompts your friend to reply. And so develops communication interaction.

Hawes (1973) cautioned against believing the process of communication has easily delineated segments and that any segment is free from previous influence and will not shape subsequent segments. If you doubt this notion, think about how you approach someone with whom you have had a heated, angry argument. The new encounter will be shaped in many ways by what happened before. Interaction not only involves progression, by which a conversation develops, but also interdependent behaviors that occur simultaneously.

To examine how interactions transpire, Hawes (1973) suggested that communication research should concentrate on "two dimensions simultaneously—the content and the relationship" (p. 15). He showed how an emphasis on message transmission and reception can distort the view of the communication process. He contrasted his view with that of theorists who think of words and other symbols as something communicators use as though it were a medium of exchange like money which can be traded back and forth. He took a different view that *"communication functions to create and validate symbol systems which define social reality and regulate social action"* (p. 15).

This stance stresses how a symbol system is sustained by interaction. Language is not some static entity that can be codified into dictionaries and used to elicit responses. One person's meaning for a term, at a particular time, cannot actually be imposed on another as *the* meaning. Each symbol system is a product of interaction, between relatively unique yet similar people. To account for the balance of uniqueness and similarity, communication is viewed as a means people use to reduce the uncertainty they have about their world, which happens to contain, among other things, many other human beings. Each has similar and different needs and personalities. *Communication* is a means for decreasing or increasing uncertainty about others.

Ideas such as these added precision and accuracy to the early process models, particularly by amplifying the role of interaction. But Dance (1978), for one, did not agree that interaction is the essence of communication. Although he acknowledged that it is "a vital and essential component of human communication," he doubted that it is the "primary goal." Rather, he argued, the fundamental motivation for "human communication is mentation, or the facilitation of conceptualization" (p. 17). He reasoned that all animals use communication to interact, but only humans use it to think and conceptualize and to share thoughts and concepts (Dance, 1985). People communicate because they want to know something or to reduce uncertainty—about one another, some topic, problem, object, condition, or whatever.

Interaction can be even better understood by appreciating how people conduct conversation. They shift conversational topics based on goals they have for the conversation. They attend to their conversational partner's statements for many reasons, one of which is to show regard through attentiveness. In reciprocation for attentiveness, they can shift topics based on linkages between what is being discussed and what they want to say (Tracy, 1984).

This sense of development highlights the dynamic nature of interaction. Relationships, in this sense, are best thought of as "unfinished business" (Duck, 1990, p. 5). They are ongoing, rather than finished. This perspective is useful for researchers as well as persons who tend to think of their relationships as static rather than dynamic.

Context

Early process models exhibited little awareness of the impact context has on communication. But researchers quickly became aware of the role context plays. The context of each communication event shapes it and influences how it is likely to be studied. So important is context that a few major contexts define the domains of communication science: (a) interpersonal communication, (b) group communication, (c) organizational communication, (d) mass or mediated communication, and (e) public communication.

Context can be thought of as the place or conditions under which communication transpires; it can also be defined as the relationship between communicants. A doctor's office is a place; in this instance, the nonverbal decoration and arrangement of the office are part of context. Doctor-patient communication is a context. In organizational communication, superior-subordinate relationships are a context. If a subordinate is reprimanded in front of fellow employees, that context is different than if the counseling occurs in the privacy of the boss's office.

Contexts often interlock or overlap. While watching television (mediated context), a family is typically also functioning as a small group or interpersonal unit. In this regard, researchers can be quite interested in how one context shapes another. Some researchers think that organizational communication—that which transpires in large and complex organizations—is actually a matter of many interlocking and overlapping instances of interpersonal communication (two people communicating with one another face-to-face, over the phone, via memos or letters, and so on). Others conceive of organizational communication as a special domain of small group communication, and this influences the way the organization is examined.

Cognitive Processes

Many theorists assume that communication grows out of and reflects humans' unique ability to have abstract thoughts and to communicate what they know. Following this line of thought, Dance (1978) argued that mentation is a primary element in human communication—especially because it is unique by comparison to other communication, such as that of chimpanzees or dolphins.

Not all theorists believe that much goes on in people's minds as they communicate. Some researchers argue that much communication is the product of relatively mindless applications of scripts. An example of a script is *phatic communication,* those relatively mindless, but not always meaningless, comments people make when greeting one another. "Good morning" may be the most inaccurate statement that most of us ritualistically make.

An original motivation for studying mass communication was to know its effects on the minds of people who make up large populations. Early studies were motivated by the desire to understand war propaganda and the impact of television. A raging debate continues regarding whether televiewing positively or negatively influences cognitive processes and personality. Does viewing violent programs make people, especially children, more violent? Does viewing fast-paced television programming make children more frenetic and less diligent? Do programming and advertising shape culture and perceptions of reality? Concepts such as *memory* and *recall* are vital to understanding how people respond to mediated communication.

When researchers discuss persuasion, they become keenly interested in the cognitive processes of communication. They want to know how people receive (if they do) and respond to messages. Persuasion researchers have tried to unlock the relationships between attitudes (or other cognitive elements) and behavior. Even intuitively, we know that people may be predisposed to do something, but not do it. People do not act on all of their attitudes. The relationship between attitudes and behavior is quite problematic at times. This persuasive appeal–behavior equation frustrates advertisers who seek to influence buying behavior and program executives who risk fortunes in their attempts to guess audience dispositions toward new programs.

Research and theory have evolved to the point where they can explain the processes involved in creating a message, including motivations behind the message and strategic choices that the sender makes. And increased insight has entered the understanding of receivers' cognitive processes in communication. Early studies conceived of receivers as being relatively passive. Researchers assumed that if a sender made a comment, the receiver understood it *as it was said* and that it had the effect on the receiver that the sender intended. This "magic bullet" approach to communication gave way as insight was gained into how receivers react to messages.

A theory that has done much to fathom the receiving process is *constructivism,* which postulates that receivers are dynamic, interpretative processors of communication who form impressions of people with whom they communicate as well as messages and contexts in which interaction transpires. This theory is operationalized by looking for the number and quality of each individual's interpersonal constructs, which are believed to stabilize discriminations about messages, other communicators, and contexts. This means that, as people listen to one another, they apply constructs that help them assess the kind of person the other is and, on that basis, evaluate the message. This assessment is not random; it is systematic and thereby allows people to adapt to one another in relatively predictable ways because each has some knowledge about who each other is, how information is processed, and how interactions transpire (O'Keefe & Delia, 1982). This theory assumes that the number and kinds of thoughts people have about one another is significant. In response, critics of the theory have claimed that it confuses cognitive complexity with loquacity (Beatty & Payne, 1985).

This inquiry seeks to understand how persons involved in communication perceive one another. And it considers whether how people perceive one another influences how they communicate. Studies such as these have expanded the understanding of the relationship between interactants in the communication process.

CONCLUSION

The early view of the anatomy of the communication process created a transmission/reception paradigm, often called the hypodermic needle or magic bullet model. Many researchers who studied communication in the 1960s adopted that model and used the term *breakdown* to describe what happens when the outcome of a communication effort differs from what the source had intended. Challenging this orientation, Smith (1970) observed that "*breakdown* implies a disruption or a malfunctioning of an element or part of a mechanical system. To correct a communication breakdown one either repairs the system or replaces one of its parts" (pp. 343–344). "Parts" cannot be replaced or repaired; we can only continue to communicate in the hope that we may be understood more clearly, achieve the influence we desire, improve a relationship, or be newsworthy or entertaining.

Recent theories challenged that original paradigm in favor of an interactional approach. Subsequent chapters discuss and evaluate those theories. As you come to understand them, you should be able to draw on the terms and concepts introduced in this chapter. Having analyzed why certain concepts and models are preferred, you ought to appreciate the roles theory and research play in the effort to understand communication phenomena.

Earlier in this chapter, you were encouraged to define communication. If you did so, did it change as you became more familiar with the issues that were addressed in this chapter? If so, don't feel alone. It is a difficult concept to define, but as we continue, you should have a better idea of the concepts and issues that are vital to it.

3 Language, Meaning, and Messages

Language is vital to human communication. Through words, people create, manage, and share interpretations of reality and interact socially. For society to function, people must share knowledge of, and give meaning to, their physical and social realms and understand one another well enough to be able to coordinate their activities. Through words, people name and evaluate the objects, sensations, feelings, and situations they experience. With words, people externalize and internalize thoughts (Burke, 1961). This sharing provides the basis for cooperative behavior through *social reality,* the understanding each person has of what other people know (Berger & Luckman, 1966). Language is not only a means by which people contact one another through interaction, but it is also vital to the cognitive processes they use to define and evaluate one another (Berger & Bradac, 1982).

Demonstrating the importance of studying cognitive processes people use to create and share interpretations of reality, Hewes and Planalp (1987) argued that, without such knowledge, communication theorists would have no means for explaining misunderstanding and its effects on other relational variables such as deception, conflict, and failure to coordinate efforts. As Seibold and Spitzberg (1982) reasoned:

> communication can hardly be treated without reference to the *interpretations* actors bring to their attempts to symbolically interact. Without attention to the ways in which actors represent and make sense of the phenomenal world, construe event associations, assess and process the actions of others, and interpret personal choices in order to initiate appropriate symbolic activity, the study of human communication is limited to mechanistic analysis. (p. 87)

Extending this idea, Hewes and Planalp (1987) concluded, "Effective communication requires not only that people share knowledge (intersubjectivity) but also that they know they share knowledge" (pp. 165–166). Language is the means by which people function on two levels; that of their individual thoughts and the realization that others have similar meanings and interpretations.

From these opening comments, you may have inferred that this chapter does not cover language and meaning by focusing on grammar and vocabulary, as might be discussed in English classes or the basic structure of language typical of research by linguists or psycholinguists. The chapter examines theories about how people use symbols as a social reality to reduce uncertainty, coordinate activities, shape relationships, express feelings, and be entertained. An understanding of language and meaning can explain how people develop an idea (the form of a sentence or extended comment) or interact by knowing how symbols are put together in structured sequences, whether of sentence length or an entire communication episode. And the discussion of language considers how words name and evaluate reality.

Patterns are vital to language. Each sentence requires a *grammar*—a set of rules and conventions—that guides its development and expression of thought. (This grammar can be successful even though ungrammatical.) Knowing the rules of their language lets people recognize that a pattern of words, such as "John went along the quickly sidewalk on his knowing that others would" is jibberish. This pattern violates the expected grammar so much that a recognizable message cannot be inferred.

As is the case for individual sentences, conversations can transpire over time only because patterns or rules are followed (McLaughlin, 1984). Interactions must be executed by applying rules that eliminate the randomness that would make communication impossible. If you ask someone, "Are you going to class" and the person answers "The duck flies only in the dark," you might think the person is stupid, joking, or not listening. Persons are expected to follow rule-based patterns during discourse.

Scholars attempt to define which language variables are most important. Some studies center on message impact, such as the effect intense language has on the persuasiveness of a message, or a receiver's perception of a speaker, based on the kind of language he or she uses (Bradac, Bowers, & Courtright, 1979). To advance the understanding of the effect words have on communication, these researchers proposed three candidates: intensity, diversity, and immediacy. *Intensity* is "the quality of language which indicates the degree to which the speaker's attitude toward a concept deviates from neutrality" (Bowers, 1963, p. 345). *Lexical diversity* is the extensiveness of a person's vocabulary. *Immediacy* is a measure of the degree to which a source is emotionally involved with the topic of conversation. To better understand immediacy, compare the degree of involvement exhibited in the following statements: "I like your suit." "That suit is stylish." "You probably get lots of compliments on that suit." The first statement exhibits the most involvement, and the last one the least (Bradac et al., 1979).

In this way, language is an independent variable that influences communication outcomes. Because of the inseparability of language and thought, words ought not to be viewed merely as means for dressing up the presentation of ideas. According to Blankenship (1974), more than a "cosmetic" placed on an idea, the language used to express it is inseparable from its meaning.

Studies of language delve into the nature of *meaning* by concentrating on relationships between words and things and by examining how interaction transpires. In this vein, scholars come to different conclusions:

1. Meaning is the response the source's words produce in the receiver's mind.
2. Meaning is the product of the relationship between thoughts and the objects of thought — what people think about.
3. Meaning is the impact conventionalized symbol systems (idioms) have on perceptions and actions of the people who use and live the perspectives embedded in each idiom.
4. Meaning is what emerges when persons involved in communication interpret the intentions behind what each other says.

Each of these conclusions adds insight into the way words have meaning and serve efforts to communicate. Each statement reflects different views of the communication process.

Examination of the four statements requires an understanding of three theories: (a) the representational or referential view of meaning, (b) linguistic relativity, and (c) a view of language that treats meaning as arising largely because of interaction rules and the need to coordinate social actions. This chapter explains and compares those points of view. But before you examine those theories, you should appreciate how language makes human communication unique.

WORDS AND THE UNIQUENESS OF HUMAN COMMUNICATION

Ability to use complex and powerful symbol systems makes human communication unique. Other animals communicate. Bees use ritualistic movements to tell one another where pollen is located and how far they must travel to get it. Elephants and whales use sounds as social cues to other members of their species. Researchers have trained bottle-nosed dolphins and apes to use signs to engage in rudimentary conversations. Researchers are astounded if an animal learns a few hundred signs and uses them strategically.

No matter how novel such studies are, the uniquely human use of language is demonstrated by the ease with which most human infants obtain a large vocabulary in a few years with a minimum of the rote training and imitation other kinds of animals (such as apes) require to learn far fewer words. And humans are the only animals that use words to store knowledge in libraries.

Computers use language to communicate with one another and with people. But computers know only the language they were taught and, as of yet, develop none by themselves. And computers, unlike humans, do not change their language over time. Human language changes constantly as is demonstrated by comparing modern contemporary English with that used by Chaucer or Shakespeare.

Words are vital to perception—to the ways people see reality and attribute meaning to it. A sensitivity to words can help you understand the processes of social cognition and human behavior. People interact with one another based on characterizations they impose on one another and motives they attribute to each other's behavior. If you "see" someone as a crook or a bum, you are likely to act differently toward the person than if you think he or she is honest and decent.

People characterize one another by how they use language; for this reason, a person who uses the vocabulary of a stockbroker is likely to be a more credible financial advisor than one who does not use that jargon. The way people use language can affect how they judge each other's competence and estimate the degree to which they identify with one another. The words used to make a statement is a factor determining whether the language reinforces or changes an attitude (Bradac et al., 1979). In this way, words have perceptual and interpersonal outcomes.

If you think words are only used to convey factual or evaluative messages, you can miss the fact that they are also used ritualistically—as scripts—where the meaning is more in the interpersonal process than the content. A "good day" may be rainy. "How are you?" usually does not invite details. Words are used to govern the flow of conversation. Comments, such as "Please tell me about the courses you took in college that most prepared you for this job," are employed to shift topics during a job interview and invite a response from the interviewee.

In business organizations, words are used to define and evaluate, as well as coordinate, inform, and influence. Images you have of a company and its products or services are flavored by the words used to describe them. Words are used to coordinate work, exchange information, and give employees a feeling of being involved in the company as well as reward or punish them.

From the previous comments, you may have inferred that two broad themes guide the discussion of language—*cognitive* and *constitutive*. The first focuses on the cognitive function of language to explain the role meaning, thoughts, and judgments that play in the relationship between words and "things." The term *things* is a convenient concept to direct attention to the phenomena to which words refer. Things can include any experience—situations, actions, feelings, or sensations. Everyday facts like eating, automobiles, clothing, traffic, people, and weather take on unique meanings through the words employed to characterize them. Through words, you can imagine things that do not exist, such as unicorns or poltergeists, and talk about them as though they do exist.

The study of the relationship between words and things is akin to *epistemology*—the philosophical explanation of how people come to know the phenomena in their world. The key question is that of the chicken and the egg. Which comes first in the shaping of cognitions—the word or the thing? Do words shape views of reality, or does contact with things and experiences in reality influence the meaning these things have?

The relationship probably goes both ways. Two examples can help you appreciate this quandary. Recall the first time you ate liver, if you have. When you did so, you may have had some forewarning about how it might taste. But what you thought of the taste and texture was affected by your direct experience when you took your first bite. The impact of this experience "flavors" your meaning of the word "liver." Here is the other side of the coin: Liver is a traditional, although not universally enjoyed, food in our society. But toasted grubs are not. To people in other countries, toasted grubs are a delicacy, as are the eyes and entrails of goats and sheep. You probably do not eat horse or dog meat, but people in other countries do. To some extent, tastes (the liking of certain foods) are derived from direct contact with reality, and in other cases tastes are "filtered" through cultural biases regarding what is acceptable to eat.

Meaning is not only based on conventional interpretations of words but also their context and function in a conversation. The second broad theme in the study of language involves *constitutive* rules that function during interaction. People learn to interpret meaning based on rules that operate during each communication episode. Meaning is shaded by interpretations idiosyncratic to persons involved in each communication encounter and the nature of the encounter. Meaning depends on the situation, the time the encounter occurs, the relationship between communicators, and the intent that is perceived to guide the comments each person makes. In this regard, "Drink!" or "Give me a drink!" can have many meanings. The meaning changes if the words are spoken by a thirsty child or by an alcoholic. In this sense, meaning is not in the words or in what they refer to but in the perceived intentions and interaction that occur during each episode.

Insights can be increased into the relationship between meaning, words, and messages by examining and comparing three theories: *representationalism, relativism,* and *purposive.* Each theory offers a unique explanation of how words acquire meaning, influence judgment, shape perception, and serve interaction. These theories are not mutually exclusive; each makes unique contributions as well as falls short of providing a complete explanation of what language is and how it creates understanding and enables interaction. By comparing these theories, a clearer view can be obtained of how language and meaning interact.

WORDS, COGNITION, AND PERCEPTION

The first two theories, representationalism and relativism, offer contrasting views of cognition and perception. *Representationalism (referentialism)* postulates that words take their meaning in large part because they stand for (represent or refer to) things, feelings, or situations people have experienced. This theory builds on the principle that people learn that phenomena have names; the meaning of words that refer to those phenomena results from experiences with the phenomena (e.g., the taste of liver). In contrast, *linguistic relativity* contends that people's views of physical and social reality are filtered through the structure and idiom unique to each language culture. Thoughts and perceptions are shaped by language. As people learn a language, they take on its unique views of reality.

Both theories have implications for epistemology because they seek to explain how words help and hinder efforts to know and understand the physical and social realms and to communicate about them. Language is basic to the human motive to know — to reduce uncertainty. In this way, it can be questioned whether people know reality accurately or merely live a view of reality that is contained in the language they share with others in their culture.

Representationalism: A Referential View

What view of language dominates communication theory? Reflecting on this question in the early 1970s, Stewart (1972) concluded, "Speech scholars view language as fundamentally a system of symbols, and meaning as a matter of symbols representing or naming objects, ideas, or behavioral responses" (p. 124). Although no recent survey of texts and articles has updated these findings, representationalism probably enjoys less popularity today because of its limited ability to explain the nature of meaning. But representationalism persists because it is so intuitive.

To explain how words come to have meaning, referential theory relies on a view of learning theory that was popular early in the 20th century. The basic premise of the theory is that people learn the meaning of words by associating them with things and experiences. As children, we learned names of animals, for instance, by thumbing through a book or seeing the actual object and learning the name of each animal. And a child who touches a hot stove learns the meaning of the word "hot" as a parent says, "Don't touch that stove; it's hot!" The sensation of pain becomes a thought that is associated with the word "hot." Later, the word "hot" stimulates some residue of the experience. The word represents or refers to the thing or experience. The process goes in this sequence: Experience results in thought, which becomes associated with words or other symbols, which subsequently are used to make statements about the experience. Words have meaning to the extent that persons have similar experiences, but meaning is not in words but in the thoughts that result from the experience.

Ogden and Richards (1923), leading advocates of this theory, concluded that meaning cannot be understood without recognizing the relationship between words and things. To explain this relationship, they created their famous triangle (see Fig. 3.1), which consists of three components: experience, which acts as a referent, reference or thought (the residue created by the experience), and symbol or words. The relationship between referent and reference is causal, according to Ogden and Richards; contact with the referent (dog) causes the reference (warm, cuddly animals). Likewise, these theorists believe the symbol is causally related to the reference. If you hear or read the word "dog," you think of the animal. In contrast to these two causally connected relationships, the relationship between words and things is indirect. This indirect relationship they stress by using a broken line to

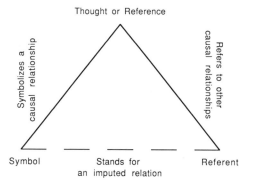

FIG. 3.1.   Triangle of meaning (from Ogden & Richards, 1923. Reprinted by permission).

demonstrate that words and things are related only by an intervening thought or reference. Based on this analysis, Ogden and Richards concluded, "When we hear what is said, the symbols both cause us to perform an act of reference and to assume an attitude which will, according to circumstances, be more or less similar to the act and the attitude of the speaker" (p. 11).

This statement—the foundation of the referential approach to language—makes two important points. First, things in reality and encounters with them govern the meaning that people hold. Second, because other people have similar experiences, words can be used to elicit thoughts. In this way, language enables people to communicate. Meanings of words depend on the things and experiences to which they refer. This theory can account for why people have different meanings for terms. For example, the word "dog" means something different to a person who was attacked by one as a child than it does for a person with no similar experience.

For these reasons, Richards (1925) argued that people can communicate only to the extent that they share experience. With Ogden, Richards concluded (1923), "communication may be defined as a use of symbols in such a way that acts of reference occur in a hearer which are similar in all relevant respects to those which are symbolized by them in the speaker" (pp. 205–206). By applying this reasoning, Ogden and Richards offered a criterion by which to assess the accuracy of communication: A word is correct if it produces the same reference in the receiver as in the sender. This theory assumes that, at least within each group of people using the same language or idiom, the accuracy of a statement is a measure of the degree to which it corresponds to reality. Recall how this line of reasoning supported the transmission–reception model of communication discussed in chapter 2.

Extending this theory, Richards (1936) argued that meaning grows as words are associated with, or modify, one another. Perception is a sorting done in context. Context "is a name for a whole cluster of events that recur together—including the required conditions as well as whatever we may pick out as cause or effect" (p. 34). As Richards concluded, "language, well used, is a *completion* and does what the intuitions of sensation by themselves cannot do. Words are the meeting points at which regions of experience which can never combine in sensation or intuition, come together" (pp. 130–131). By this analysis, he argued that language can encompass many experiences and offers means by which thoughts in varying degrees of complexity can be created and exchanged.

A more complex explanation of the referential theory of meaning was presented by Osgood and his associates (Osgood, 1953; Osgood, Suci, & Tannenbaum, 1957). They also used learning theory to contend that meaning is the behavioral response a term creates in the receiver. Hearing a word (or seeing the thing) stimulates a thought that mediates between a stimulus and a message that is finally created in the mind of the receiver. Mediation occurs because the receiver compares this immediate response to previous ones. How does mediation work? Osgood (1963) explained, "The greater the frequency with which stimulus events (S–S) or response events (R–R) have been paired in input or output experience of the organism, the greater will be the tendency for their central correlates to activate each other" (p. 741). The meaning that arises in response to a word or the object is a composite of a complex of previous encounters with both the stimulus and our responses to it.

The components of Osgood's model parallel those commonly used in the 1960s to explain the communication process: *encoding* (receiving stimuli), *associating,* and *decoding* (responding to the association between thought and stimuli; Osgood, 1963). The reasoning is this: When stimuli are received, they become associated with one or more responses such as pleasure or fear. This response to the stimuli—actually seeing the thing or having the experience—constitutes the reaction that becomes the meaning associated with the thing or experience. Once people learn that this thing or experience (stimulus) has a name, the word is associated with the response that represents the stimuli. Subsequently, the word can produce the response even in the absence of direct contact with the experience. If the experience has several components or attributes to it, which is often the case, all of them together form the composite meaning of that experience. The meaning of the word that stands for the stimuli contains all of the component attributes. In this way, many component attributes associate together to form the substance of a term, such as *grandmother.* For example, you may associate many attributes with the word "grandmother," such as kind, warm, good food, big hugs, gray hair, wrinkles, twinkling smiles, and frailty. The word grandmother prompts you to bring into your consciousness the component attributes of the meaning of the term.

This reasoning brought Osgood to an important contribution to under- standing meaning—the concept of *semantic space.* He coined this concept to describe two dimensions of meaning. One is the many attributes that can be associated with a single term, such as grandmother. The second dimension is the degree to which any term applies to the central concept. He reasoned that

each judgment represents a selection among a set of given alternatives and serves to localize the concept as a point in the semantic space. The larger the number of scales and the more representative the selection of these scales, the more validly does this point in the space represent the operational meaning of the concept. (Osgood et al., 1957, p. 26)

This analysis led Osgood and his associates to create the semantic differential as an instrument for measuring meaning by having respondents indicate what concepts they associate with a central concept (Snider & Osgood, 1969). This differential allows researchers to allocate a concept to a point in a multidimensional semantic space. As Osgood et al. (1957) reasoned, "Difference in the meaning between two concepts is then merely a function of the differences in their respective allocations within the same space" (p. 26). In this way, researchers can measure the degree to which any concept is a part of the total meaning of the central concept, such as grandmother. Many versions of the semantic differential have been developed as researchers attempt to understand and measure meaning. Thus, for instance, product researchers might measure audience reactions (semantic space) to a product, such as a breakfast cereal, by having the audience mark the appropriate point in each of the following differentials. (These researchers want to know which concepts are associated with the cereal and how strongly each is associated.)

tasty :	:	:	:	:	:	tasteless
pleasant :	:	:	:	:	:	unpleasant
nutritious :	:	:	:	:	:	unnutritious
attractive :	:	:	:	:	:	unattractive
fun :	:	:	:	:	:	not fun

The strength of each concept in semantic space is measured by its location on the scale. If a survey respondent marks the space next to *fun,* that indicates that the attribute is strongly associated with the cereal. Or if the respondent marks the middle space, that means the attribute is neutral—or essentially irrelevant. And if the space next to not fun is marked, that expresses that this respondent did not think the cereal is fun. Similar marks for other semantic items can give researchers a composite view of each subject's impressions of the cereal. The data can be analyzed to derive a total view of all subjects' impressions. Thus, this sample population might believe the cereal is sort of tasty and pleasant, very attractive and fun, but not very nutritious.

Drawing on the work of Osgood and his associates, Berlo (1960) applied this theory of meaning to explain the communication process. The key to meaning, he agreed with Osgood, depends on how people learn to connect stimuli. Proximal stimuli are produced by direct contact with the physical world through the senses. For instance, touching a hot stove or tasting food elicits a response. Distal stimuli do not result from direct contact, but as reaction to a snake that is in a room but not in direct contact with a person. The two kinds of response are paired. Thus, Berlo continued, "People begin to respond (internally) to the distal stimulus, by detaching and internalizing some of their original responses to the proximal stimulus" (p. 183). These internal responses become fixed—learned. They prompt the individual to make some sort of overt response. "The internal response—and the internal stimulus that comes from it — can be defined as the 'meaning' of the external stimulus, for the person who is responding" (Berlo, 1960, p. 184). The first phase in learning is a response to proximal stimuli — direct contact. Distal stimuli, the second stage, provide indirect contact that calls on what was learned from proximal stimuli. The third stage, that which is essential to communication, occurs when individuals learn that words are connected to distal and proximal stimuli. The word "snake" is a linguistic stimulus associated with the proximal contact with a snake and the awareness of what it is (distal stimuli). Affective memories cause emotional responses to the object and to the word; words can elicit these memories.

This line of reasoning became the focal point for work by the general semanticists who believed that by studying language they could increase clarity of communication. General semanticists worry that people are uncritical of the associations they make between words and things. The meanings people possess may not accurately reflect the nature of the things being referred to. Working to prevent false conclusions and misunderstanding, they stress the need to perceive reality accurately. They want people to avoid the filtering effects of biases that are embedded in thoughts and words.

A leader in this movement, Lee (1941, 1952) observed how words name that for which they stand. Thus, *table* is the name of an object, *red* is the name of a quality, *run* is the name of an activity, and *over* is the name of a relation. According to this view, people use words to name the stimuli they receive. This naming process can lead to errors if people come to believe that words are more than mere references to things, or conclusions about things. To avoid this mistake, Semanticists rely on the axiom: Words are *not* things as maps are *not* territories. By this statement, semanticists hope to prevent people from thinking reality is what their words say it is. Thus, Lee pressed for a standard of clarity: "To be most useful, statements must fit, must be similar in structure to the life facts being represented. Words can be manipulated independently of what they represent, and so made false to fact both consciously and unconsciously" (Lee, 1941, p. 22).

To help people avoid making false references, semanticists have offered a variety of remedies, including warning that terms are most accurate when they express one-word/one-thing relationships, such as the name of a person. Semanticists observe that dictionaries are history books, merely reporting what terms meant at the time they were published. They cautioned that the meaning of words should not be considered as static. If meaning is thought to be static and unchanging, two kinds of problems can occur. One flaw is forgetting that the meaning of words changes over time. Another flaw — "time binding" — is the tendency people have to stop time rather than realizing that the world is in constant flux. This fault can be easily recognized by recalling how surprised you were to see how a friend whom you have not seen for years has changed; your recollection of the person is as you last saw him or her. "Baby" John is now a 6'3" tall teenager. Janet is no longer a flower child of the 1960s; she is a senior partner in a law firm.

The theories so far discussed in this section rely extensively on the referential nature of words and things. If we carry our discussion into the realm of how people make more extended statements about reality, we can examine the assumptions of representationalism as they apply to more complex cognitions.

Many theorists stress how important language is to mentation. Such theorists do not merely acknowledge the association between words and things as is posited by Ogden, Richards, Osgood, and Berlo. Instead, these theorists emphasize the impact language has on thought and communication about physical and social phenomena. Accurate and insightful description and analysis of physical and social realities are the criteria that underpin this school of thought.

Although part of the referential school, Langer (1951) and Cassirer (1946) went beyond the rudiments of the referential relationship among words, thoughts, and things to argue that words are vehicles for conceiving and expressing complex ideas about reality. Langer reasoned that humans, "unlike all other animals," employ signs or symbols "not only to *indicate* things but to *represent* them" (p. 37). Symbols can be used to think about things in their absence. Words remind us of things and can excite feelings and emotions from past experience.

For Langer (1951), meaning is not merely the reference a term makes to that for which it stands. For instance, the meaning of a dog is not merely a furry, four-legged animal that barks and chases cars. The meaning of the term *dog*, for instance, changes based on its context in each sentence and in the minds of the persons interpreting the sentence. Thus, meaning is the product of abstraction, of thought.

Regardless of the degree of abstraction, words are tested by their ability to make accurate statements about reality:

> This means that as many propositions as possible shall be applicable to *observable fact*. The systems of thought that seem to us to represent "knowledge" are those which were *designed as hypotheses*, i.e. designed with reference to experience and intended to meet certain tests: At definite points their implications must yield propositions which express discoverable facts. (Langer, 1951, p. 231)

In this way, Langer demonstrated how the representational theory of language is the foundation of thought, analysis, and debates about the nature of our physical and social realities. No matter how abstract terms become, they are to be held accountable for their ability to accurately define and evaluate the objects of thought and analysis. She concluded that *"language is the only means of articulating thought"* (p. 81). Reality serves as the standard or measure against which the accuracy and insightfulness of ideas is tested. As Cassirer (1946) reasoned,

> Before the intellectual work of conceiving and understanding of phenomena can set in, the work of *naming* must have preceded it, and have reached a certain point of elaboration. For it is this process which transforms the world of sense impression . . . into a mental world, a world of ideas and meanings. (p. 28)

Naming consists of focusing on key attributes. But naming reality involves more than making a mere copy of it. He believed that the copy theory of knowledge has been discredited. In addition to naming the objects, situations, feelings, and events of our physical and social reality, the intellect is capable of evaluation (Cassirer, 1953). His epistemology assumes that pure cognition can translate particulars that exist in nature into universal laws. Individual objects and sensations of reality become joined into categories through the processes of naming and evaluation. Language, Cassirer contended, allows humans to "progress from the world of mere sensation to the world of intuition and ideas" (p. 88). As did Langer, Cassirer believed that language helps us move our thoughts from the concrete representation of things to abstractions about them.

Langer (1951) believed that people have an innate desire to abstract. It is the essence of rationality. Abstraction is the process of leaving out details about an object, event, or situation. Whether merely a name for a thing or the expression of a more complex and abstract thought, a word is not in a one-to-one relationship to things. Words make statements about things and suggest or highlight their properties. Words show the place of things in the culture of those people who use the language being used for the thought. Human brains carry on the process of ideation. They take in external stimuli and translate them into ideas through language.

Representational theory of meaning is provocative and helps explain how words allow people to communicate. Based on the word–thing relationship, this theory struggles to explain the difficulty and value of achieving accurate references. Many of these theorists rely on an accuracy paradigm to explain how words relate to reality; they want to know how well people use words for naming, abstracting, and sharing meaning.

The representational theory of meaning seems intuitively valid for many reasons. But, as critics of this theory contend, it is too simplistic to completely explain how words come to have meaning. Making this point, Cherry (1978) observed that most words do not have a direct relationship to things. To prove his point, he offered terms such as *democracy, freedom, tyranny,* and *happiness.* Even the terms that refer to things, he argued, denote categories of things—as well as specific things. And Stewart (1972) observed, "Neither 'abstract' terms like 'democracy' or 'semantics' nor exclamatory utterances appear to stand for or name something else" (p. 126). Articles, such as "a," "an," or "the," and prepositions are problematic. What is the referent for terms such as "of," "in," or "about?"

Cherry doubted the referential theory can help people use words more precisely. He was aware of the suggestion by the semanticists that one-word/one-thing relationships eliminate ambiguity. Without doubt, if every thing, every feeling, and every experience had its own name, precision could be increased. But as Cherry added,

> Language cannot give precise representation of things or ideas because there are simply not enough different words to express the subtlety of every shade of thought. If we had words for everything, their numbers would be astronomically large and beyond our powers of memory or our skill to use them. (p. 71)

Burke (1969a) added to this criticism by charging that the advice by the semanticists to focus on specific cases "leaves us with a world of individuals" (p. 251). Once we resort to abstraction to compensate for the impossibility of naming every thing, we move away from the optimal one-word/one-thing standard.

The referential theory explains that meaning results when a word becomes associated with the concept of some phenomenon, a spider for example. Note, however, that an expert on spiders might have a different view of them than would a lay person. Even a moment of thought can suggest that meaning depends on what words impose on reality. For instance, in a delivery room, once the doctor announces "It's a girl!" or "It's a boy!," a lot can be imagined about the different social experiences and customs the baby will enjoy or suffer as he or she grows in a culture that has different meanings for what it is to be a boy or a girl. The terms *boy* and *girl* are not merely descriptive. Men and women are treated according to the mores of each culture; these mores are embedded in the language of that culture, a theme explored extensively by linguistic relativists.

LINGUISTIC RELATIVITY

Instead of assuming that words take their meaning from the things to which they refer, what if we argue the opposite—that the meaning of things reflects the content of the words assigned to them? This line of reasoning concludes that, as people encounter reality, they use that experience to define a term such as *hot,* but they also use words to define reality, whether specific things such as "girl" or "boy" or abstractions, such as *democracy.* Each word, each idiom imposes a unique view on reality, both physical and social. This conclusion is the heart of linguistic relativism. This section discusses that theory and contrasts it to the referential, representational theory.

The central theme of linguistic relativism is that people impose meaning on social and physical reality because each language—each idiom—expresses a different world view. Therefore, reality cannot serve as an infallible test of the validity of propositions because it is perceived through shadings unique to each idiom. For instance, in this culture, a cow is a domesticated bovine of the genus *bovinus,* a kind of livestock that is raised for food. The lot of most cattle is to end up on the butcher block. That view of cattle is embedded in perspectives carried in the American language. But Hindus have a different view of cow. They see cattle as a temporary home for the spirit of another human being. To kill a cow, accordingly, is to disturb that spirit. Thus, a cow is whatever any linguistic culture says it is.

Languages are not neutral. They cannot be free from ideology. Ideologies influence perceptions by giving one preferred version of physical and social reality. Each ideology prescribes a view of what people see, as well as how they define and evaluate it. Thus, for instance, socialism views labor and workers differently than does the kind of capitalism championed by ruthless robber barons of the past century, who had little regard for the health and well-being of employees. Words often contain stereotypes that are imposed on reality and through which perceptions are filtered.

One of the best expressions of this view was made by Sapir who observed:

> Human beings do not live in the objective world alone, not alone in the world of social activity as ordinarily understood, but are very much at the mercy of the particular language which has become the medium of expression for their society. We see and hear and otherwise experience very largely as we do because the language habits of our community predispose certain choices of interpretation. (quoted by Whorf, 1956, p. 134)

The principle contained in that statement forms a cornerstone for linguistic relativity.

In a similar vein, Whorf (1956) argued that how people name a situation will affect their behavior in that situation. He made this discovery while working for an insurance company. He noted that employees' perceptions of what causes fires had a hypnotic effect on their views of fire prevention in their working environment. He observed how the term *gasoline drums* caused people to act with more care than they did in the presence of what they considered to be empty gasoline drums. They disregarded (or were unaware) of the fact that empty drums often give off combustible vapors. The formula contained in this view of language is this: "The situation is named in one pattern and the name is then 'acted out' or 'lived up to' in another, this being a general formula for the linguistic conditioning of behavior" (Whorf, 1956, p. 135). He pointed to an instance where a substance that seemed nonflammable, limestone, had its chemical properties altered so that it was combustible. (When limestone is exposed to acetic acid, it becomes calcium acetate, which becomes acetone when heated. Acetone is extremely flammable.) But the employees took no caution around the limestone until a fire occurred. A similar instance occurred when water in a pool became flammable because its properties changed.

Alert to how perception is tied to vocabulary, Whorf and Sapir found that the structure of each language gives its users a unique view of reality. To illustrate his point, Whorf compared how Standard Average European (SAE) language and the Hopi (native American tribe in Southwestern United States) language each expressed quantities. Whereas SAE might say "a glass of water" the Hopi would say "water." Standard Average European language might request a "piece of meat" but the Hopi would merely ask for "meat." The notion of modifying collective nouns, such as "water" or "meat," is not vital to the Hopi way of thinking and therefore not part of their language. Rather than thinking of "a hot summer day," the Hopi would make no such distinction because summer is the hot time, so the day should be hot. Another example of cultural differences is observed by noting that West Africans who speak Ewe use the same word for "yesterday" and "tomorrow." That words mean "not now."

At this point, the referential theorists might claim that just because people do not carefully use thought and words to accurately describe physical or social reality does not cast doubt on the referential theory of meaning. Indeed, such imprecision could fuel the efforts of referential theorists to help people use language more clearly. But relativists make the point that people think and act toward the world around them and toward one another because of perspectives and biases built into the vocabulary they use. Such biases are unavoidable. Reality is sufficiently ambiguous that no one can truly be sure that he or she accurately understands it. Relativists are willing to acknowledge that because of the power words have over perception, thoughts and observations can never eliminate the biases built into each idiom, which is never free from underlying ideologies and other frames of reference.

For this reason, relativists view language as a conventionalized symbol system. Each vocabulary is a collective property created by a group of people to enable communication. The meaning of each word is nothing more or less than what the people who use it believe it to mean. As Deetz (1973) concluded, people participate in human interaction by taking on "an already meaningful language through immersion in the stream of heritage" (p. 48). Your language was here when you entered the world. You took on the idiom of your parents and friends as a conventional and functional means for communicating. As you adopted that language, you accepted certain perspectives — values, beliefs, attitudes, ideologies and such. Thus, for instance, if you were raised in a Democratic family your view of politics is different than if you took on a Republican vocabulary. As Cherry (1978) said, "Words are signs which have significance by *convention,* and those people who do not adopt the conventions simply fail to communicate" (p. 69).

Each language expresses a culture. As Cherry (1978) reasoned,

> A text, when translated from one language into another, may lose or change a great deal of its emotive force. When I read French I need to become a different person, with different thoughts; the language change bears with it a change of national character and temperament, a different history and literature. (p. 72)

For Cherry, "The language of a people largely constrains their thoughts. Its words, concepts, and syntax, out of all the signs people use, are the most important determinant of what they are *free* and *able* to think" (p. 73). According to this view, a translator's dictionary and grammar book may aid your efforts to understand a document written in a foreign language, but you may not comprehend the ideas of the document if you were not reared in that culture.

Symbolic interactionism offers some of the rationale for linguistic relativism. To explain the process by which words become conventionalized, Mead (1934) expanded on the principles of stimulus and response. The result is one of the richest, most important communication paradigms. The foundation of Mead's model is a gesture made by a "sender," an interpretation of the gesture by the "receiver," and the subsequent development of a shared meaning or interpretation of what that gesture meant. In this way, people come to know the meaning of terms through interaction; meaning is a shared response to each term, which has achieved the status of a significant symbol, the meaning of which is shared by many people.

This theory offers a different rationale for how people come to share meaning than does the referential theory. Recall the story used above to describe how a child might learn the word "hot" because it is associated with a stove. The important point is not that the word and the thing become associated, but that the child realizes that in this society that a sensation of pain is associated with the word "hot." The word is not only important because it can describe a sensation, but also because it can be used to interact (conduct conversations with others).

To illustrate the basic point of symbolic interaction, Mead noted that communication begins with one entity making a verbal or nonverbal gesture to another. One dog growls at another. The second dog (receiver or interactant) interprets this growl and, henceforth, both dogs have a shared meaning of what that growl means. Similarly, one person may shake a fist in the face of another. Likewise, a vocalization becomes conventionalized as soon as both parties share a meaning for a symbol. As Mead (1934) reasoned, once a "gesture means the idea behind it and it arouses that idea in the other individual, then we have a significant symbol" (p. 43). Once a symbol becomes meaningful for both partners in a conversation, it is language. In this manner, meaning is conventionalized through symbolic interaction. *Meaning* is the impact the words have on the communication partners. This line of analysis has been refined by writers who feature a *convergence theory* of meaning. Such discussions argue that shared meaning is produced when people comment about their experiences or the objects that they have encountered (Bormann, 1983; Rogers & Kincaid, 1981).

Simply stated, words are meaningful for humans because they know what the words mean for them. This dynamic and organic view argues that words are not static, nor are meanings easily prescribed. Meaning is the product of interaction—action and reaction. In contrast to those who stress the referential relationship between words and things, Mead (1934) reasoned that the meaning of any object depends

> upon the relation of an organism or group of organisms to it. It is not essentially or primarily a psychical content (a content of mind or conscious-ness), for it need not be conscious at all, and is not in fact until significant symbols are evolved in the process of human social experience. Only when it becomes identified with such symbols does meaning become conscious. (pp. 80–81)

Meaning is dynamic because what a gesture means to one person is the interpretation and response another person makes to it. The response of the second person is directed toward or related to the completion of that act.

Many of these themes of linguistic relativism were either reinforced or amplified by Burke, who produced one of the most complete theories of language created in this century (Heath, 1986). His theory features the concept of dramatism, a model of interaction that views people as actors in a drama; all people act with one another through words. This theme is similar to Mead's contention that meaning is created through symbolic interaction. Burke (1966) reversed the basic equation of the referential theorists by concluding, that at least to some extent, "things are the signs of words" (p. 363).

Burke (1966) argued that vocabularies express perspectives. For this reason, he observed, "there will be as many different worldviews in history as there are people" (p. 52). Words, perceptions, and actions are intertwined. Consequently, each person shares perceptions and incentives typical of all other people who use a particular language, with its unique perspectives. Not only do we get a sense of physical and social realities through language, but we also acquire an understanding of the expectations of what constitutes social competence—how to act. "The human animal, as we know it, *emerges into personality* by first mastering whatever tribal speech happens to be its particular symbolic environment" (Burke, 1966, p. 53).

Burke (1966) demonstrated the difference between words and things by reminding us "how easy it is to turn the *word* 'tree' into 'five thousand trees,' and how different would be the processes required for the similar multiplication of an actual tree" (p. 480). By making this point, however, he does not contend that the universe is nothing more than a figment of our interpretations. People's characterizations of reality cannot vary too far from "fact" without experiencing a sense of recalcitrance (Burke, 1965). For instance, a stone cannot be made edible by calling it a potato. Thus, "the *thing* tree is not a *word*" (1966, p. 481). Likewise, "*words are mere words. Nothing could be farther from 'food,' for instance, than a mere word for it*" (Burke, 1952, p. 61).

Words shape people's perceptions of reality, Burke (1964) said, because people "see" through "terministic screens." Words constitute "a kind of photographic 'screen' which will 'let through' some perceptions and 'filter out' others" (p. 105). He was alerted to this phenomenon when he observed how photographs of the same subject matter appeared different when they were taken with different colored lens. Each color of lens produced a different view of the subject matter (Burke, 1966). A quick illustration shows how terms constitute screens. Think how your view of an adult human female changes if she is called *girl, woman,* or *lady.* In this way, our method for examining the physical and social objects and situations in the world around us *"reveals only such reality as is capable of being revealed by this particular kind of terminology"* (Burke, 1969a, p. 313). This is the case because our instruments for knowing are nothing but structures of terms and therefore manifest the nature of terms (Burke, 1969a). For this reason, people are separated from their natural condition by language, an instrument of their own making (Burke, 1966). This analysis suggests that words join us with wordless nature while at the same time mediating between us and it (Burke, 1961).

Burke (1966) realized how difficult it is to use our observations of reality to verify the truthfulness of our statements. Problems of verifying truth arise because our conclusions imply *"the particular terminology in terms of which the observations are made"* (p. 46). Because ideologies are imposed through words, our universe appears to be "something like a cheese." People slice it in an infinite number of ways. After each person choses his or her own pattern of slicing, other people's "cuts fall at the wrong places" (Burke, 1965, pp. 102–103). He cast doubt on the veracity of the referential approach to language when he illustrated how similar events, objects, acts, or feelings appear different when named differently. Thus, he noted how "we call *obstinacy* in an enemy what we call *perseverance* in ourselves — or we call another man's frankness 'incaution' and label as 'caution' our own *lack* of frankness" (1965, p. 109). Burke cautioned, "the last way on earth to transcend the deceptions of *words* is by a mere 'tough-minded' beginning with 'things' " (1952, pp. 62–63). Sheer nonsense can arise if we lose sight of the need to make words correspond to reality as much as possible, but views of reality can never be free from the shadings imposed by idioms.

For this reason, Burke (1958) concluded that people *are* vocabulary. To manipulate their vocabulary is to manipulate them. Language is "the basic instrument by which social relationships are managed." For this reason, "if there is an 'organic flaw' in the nature of language, we may well expect to find this organic flaw revealing itself through the texture of society" (1934, p. 330). Aware that perspectives, and therefore ideologies, are based on language and that flaws in thinking can result, he felt the need to discuss language to help correct the social evils he witnessed. He knew that false *and* worthwhile ideas can be passed from one generation to the next because language is useful for "inventing, perfecting, and handing-on instruments and methods" (Burke, 1965, p. 276).

Based on his theory of language, Burke (1969b) developed a theory of rhetoric that proposes that, if people identify with one another, they will think and act in similar ways. This theory offers support for believing that language is vital to persons' efforts to share social reality and to be competent in interpersonal activities. Identification is possible because people attempt to minimize their differences by sharing views that allow them to act in concert. Because they share identities by viewing themselves in similar ways, people are able to persuade one another by ingratiation, by talking each other's language, and by sharing the same speech, gesture, tonality, order, image, attitude, and idea. Identification assists interpersonal interaction because people can enact the perspectives embedded in the idioms they share with others.

Burke's theory is particularly instructive for understanding interpersonal role behavior. Many actions and opinions are implied in terms such as farmer, *laborer, banker, father, mother, teacher,* or *terrorist.* Each term suggests behavioral patterns that prescribe what interaction patterns and beliefs are expected of those who hold those titles. These terms play a powerful part in interpersonal attribution. Individuals attempt to understand one another — to reduce uncertainty — by attributing motives to one another. Attribution is predicated on the implications and expectations that are embedded in the terms they use to describe one another. Burke's theory of language, as does the work by other linguistic relativists, helps explain how attributions are made—and why they can be false.

Linguistic relativity argues that, because people tend to live a world based on intersubjective knowledge, they are wise to wonder what other people use words to mean. However, the choice is not between representationalism or linguistic relativism. Both theories contribute to our understanding of language and meaning. Both have a degree of validity. Words for tangible objects or experiences, such as "bumble bee" or "bee sting," take on some degree of meaning because of experiences people have with the object or experience. In this way, reality helps people to define terms. But even more importantly, words are conventionalized through social interaction. Meaning is an expression of the ideology and unique world views of the people who create and live that particular language through social interaction.

Linguistic relativism is particularly helpful in explaining the meaning and power of language in many contexts. Interpersonally, individuals characterize one another and attribute motives and personality characteristics, in part through applications of prototypes and stereotypes. These are "terministic screens" people carry that allow them to "know" one another. Internally and externally, organizations create images of themselves and the products and services they provide. Preferring the relativistic over the referential theory of language, Eisenberg (1984) argued that strategic ambiguity is a reasonable, useful, and normative approach to language used by members of organizations. He believed that it is too much to expect people to have the same meaning for terms by having the same experiences. Many people throughout an organization have quite different experiences. Strategic ambiguity promotes unified diversity, enough consensus for the organization, through its members, to operate successfully, but not so much as to be stifling.

This is not only true for companies, but also for organizations such as churches and educational systems. Each offers different terministic screens based on the words used and their conventionalized meanings. News broadcasts contain perspectives; one year's *enemies* are next year's *allies*. The presidential election campaign of Richard Nixon succeeded because he pledged to get tough on "law and order." Years later, George Bush won by wanting a "kinder and gentler" society.

LANGUAGE AND INTERPERSONAL INTERACTION

Given what you now know about language, do you know how people read or interpret others' comments and thereby know how to participate in communication interactions? If someone enters your room and says, "What are you doing?," how do you know what that statement means? Referential theorists cannot answer this question, nor can the relativists. What does "I love you" mean? Or "The boss is really angry"? Or "You play the game my way or you'll be looking for a new game to play"? The point that you should realize is that many comments do not refer to any *thing* at all. They may use conventionalized statements that we understand because we have learned the code of our society, but how do we know what each statement means at a particular moment? The remainder of this chapter will address these issues.

Partial explanation of this problem can by found in the work of constructivists, such as Delia, O'Keefe, and O'Keefe (1982), who argue that people interact with one another based on their ability to segment experience into meaningful units so that thought and action can be structured and controlled. People are born into a world that is defined by ongoing cultural processes of social organization and interpretation. Interpretive processes develop through interaction with other people who share this social world. For this reason, constructivists reason, culture is (a) an evolving social organization, (b) a conception of reality, and (c) a complex of symbols employed by persons who encounter one another.

In this way, people create interpretive systems primarily through communication in order to adapt to their social world. Once people acquire these interpretative frameworks, their "action is guided by context-relevant interactions and beliefs produced by schemes of interpretation" (Delia et al., 1982, p. 155). *Interaction,* therefore, is

> a process in which persons coordinate their behavior through the application of shared interpretive schemes; it is a process of implicit negotiation in which strategic choices reflect the emerging consensus about the reality that participants share. (Delia et al., 1982, p. 159)

To know the meaning of statements such as "I love you" or "What are you up to?," people must employ a set of interaction–interpretation rules that may be complex or simple, depending on the case. One response to this quandary could be merely to ask the other person, "What do you mean by that?" Indeed, that response is possible; however, people rarely are this direct. Can they trust the answer they receive? How do they reduce uncertainty while showing their own communication competence? One answer to those questions is provided as the coordinated management of meaning.

COORDINATED MANAGEMENT OF MEANING

This theory begins with the proposition, similar to symbolic interaction, that communication enables people to "cocreate, maintain, and alter social order, personal relationships, and individual identities" (Cronen et al., 1982, p. 64). Treating communication as more than a vehicle for conveying thought, this theory views it as "the process of creating the perspectives that give rise to ideas and facts. Communication is not simply one of many things that persons do in relationships; it is the process of maintaining and creating relationships" (p. 65).

To illustrate the importance of understanding this process, Pearce and Cronen (1980) noted that people interact with one another in a manner similar to the actions of characters in a play, but unlike a theater production, life is "an undirected play" (p. 120). People learn some scripts from parents and peers. They learn to say "Hello" when answering the phone and "thank you" when receiving a gift. But often, the play of life has no script and we, the actors, must improvise. This theory believes people coordinate activities by managing the ways their messages have meaning for one another.

Burke and other linguistic relativists might explain this process by featuring the terms by which people characterize themselves and thereby give motive to their actions. In contrast, the coordinated management of meaning depends on the rules and content or message structure of the interaction. In this view, communication is "a process in which each person interprets and responds to the acts of another, monitors the sequence, and compares it to his or her desires and expectations" (Pearce & Cronen, 1980, p. 68). Coordination of what goes on during any communication episode does not require that the participants share mutual understanding. They can coordinate communication episodes even though they assign different meanings to key messages, but without coordinated management of meaning, communication cannot transpire.

To be able to join in meaningful conversation, the actions of each person must be meaningful to the communication partner. All that people can ever know of one another during interaction is what they see and hear; they know one another only by experiencing each other's behavior. In this context, messages produce meaning at two levels: content and relationship (Watzlawick, Beavin, & Jackson, 1967). Meaning occurs because of what each person thinks the other's statements mean in the context of the relationship. "I love you" is interpreted differently if the relationship is romantic rather than platonic. Through these kinds of meanings, people not only interpret one another but also regulate their relationship. One person might want a friendship relationship while the other seeks to be more romantic. The meanings of what they send and receive will be shaped by these factors.

People interpret messages and know what actions constitute appropriate responses because they have rules to follow that correspond to these two levels of meaning. This theory postulates that communication acts are coordinated because people can employ two kinds of rules, *constitutive* and *regulative,* to negotiate each interaction no matter how routine or unique it might be. These types of rules help individuals to know what behavior is appropriate and likely to be productive (regulative), and what the behavior of others means (constitutive).

Pearce and Cronen (1980) thought of people as being able to employ complex, multileveled systems of rules for meaning and action. These rules help people to understand (constitutive) what others' actions mean and how to respond (regulative). To accomplish their communication outcomes, people must be able to interpret what their senses perceive as information and translate this information into actions. To achieve this interpretation, people create theories to explain when their actions are correct.

How do people know how to create these theories? They learn behaviors that are appropriate to many situations. Then when they find themselves in a similar situation, they rely on an interpretative process that consists of six levels: content, speech acts, contracts, episodes, life-scripts, and archetypes.

Content consists of "referential cognitive processes by which individuals organize and interpret the world as it is ultimately perceived" (Pearce & Cronen, 1980, p. 130). According to Kelley (1955), human behavior is influenced by the perceptual process of each individual (in a collectivity) that intervenes between that person and his or her physical and social realities. These perceptions are filtered through the interpretative process that explains the experience. Content consists of the meaning the parties of a conversation assign to what they and their partners say and do.

The second level is *speech acts.* These are what one person does or says (Pearce & Cronen, 1980). This notion is drawn from Austin (1962) and Searle (1969, 1976) who argued that the meaning of each speech act is the impact its perceived intent has on communication partners. The question "When are you going to wash the car?" can be interpreted in many ways. Its meaning in a particular conversation consists of the impact it has on the person who receives it. It can be meant merely as a question used to seek information or it can be intended to motivate the receiver to get busy with soap and water. Speech acts include threats, promises, efforts to inform, suggestions, advice, insults, compliments, and such. Each of these speech acts has a set of rules that governs what it means and how it should be executed (Searle, 1969). Rules implied by each kind of speech act regulate social interaction (Pearce & Cronen, 1980). The meaning of any speech act is a combination of what the interactants thought its content is and what it implies for the relationship.

The third level is *contracts,* which range from formal agreements (such as legal contracts) to informal social arrangements. People engaged in conversation have a repertoire of contracts (regulative rules) that can be applied. For instance, the repertoire of rules available in an argument can be used to make the argument worse or to lessen the friction. A relevant part of each interaction is each participant's recognition of the relevant contracts as well as a willingness and ability to abide by them.

Episodes, the next level, are definable, recurring communication events, such as "having coffee," "interviewing for a job," "making a date," or "planning a family outing." Each episode implies one or more sets of contracts that can be used to guide participants through the event. Episodes, because they define a communication event, give participants the opportunity to know the meaning of specific events within an episode. A greeting at the beginning of a job interview can give participants an idea of what kind of person each other is (as well as perspectives of the self—"I think the person will believe I am a strong person because I shake hands firmly and comment on what a forward thinking company this is"). Comments at the beginning of an interview serve quite different purposes than do those at the end. The definition the parties hold of the interview, as an episode, will help them interpret what their behavior and the other participant's behavior means. Is willingness to emphasize achievements a display of confidence or bragging? Is hesitance to answer questions a sign of deception, falsification, insecurity, or a strong desire to be precise and accurate—even if hesitant—when making an important comment? Continuing their metaphor of the dramatic event, Pearce and Cronen (1980) observed, "The repertoire of episodes known by a particular communicator is analogous to the snatches of scripts known by actors in the undirected play" (p. 136). Episodes help participants predict events and know what of their communication repertoire to select to coordinate efforts with each other.

Life-scripts, the fifth level, refer to communication options each communicator believes fits his or her self-perception at a particular moment. Typical of this kind of statement are these: "This is who I am" or "This is something I would do." Pearce and Cronen avoided the term *self-concept,* which they believe is a static concept. They "prefer to think of the self simply as that cluster of episodes defined by the person as those in which s/he does or might participate" (p. 137). Life-scripts are patterned, repeated series of comments that are used routinely and repeatedly as people engage in the same kinds of episodes. A life-script is, for example, that set of comments typical of one married couple's routine conversations. Parents and children play out life-scripts throughout each day. "Don't go out . . ." "Be sure to . . ." "Can I . . . just this once?" "You don't really understand me." Most of these comments probably sound familiar to you. Note also that we often are not actually interested in the extent to which comments such as these refer to reality. Such statements are not designed to define physical or social reality. They are employed to achieve purposes within communication episodes. Their meaning is the impact they have on the participants in the episode given the nature of the relationship.

The final level in this hierarchy is *archetypes,* which offer a fundamental logic that interactants can use to frame or define experience. Archetypes are the large organizing patterns of behavior that are so universal to human experience that each culture, no matter how different in other ways, will address these experiences. Every culture has some way of defining and acting meaningfully toward birth, death, pain, agony, leave taking, reunions, returns, and so on.

These six levels of interaction and meaning give researchers a way to focus on what kinds of cues and rules interactants are using at a particular moment as they negotiate the protocols of interpersonal interaction. This analysis combines the rules of interaction to the ways in which the logics of discourse allow people to act and interact. People negotiate and conventionalize communication interactions. As Eisenberg (1986) concluded, "through communication, individuals over time create, maintain, and transform the social realities they inhabit" (p. 89).

Even though interaction rules may account for some of the dynamics of conversation, they do not explain how conversations grow topically or whether they grow coherently. Investigating conversational coherence, Planalp, Graham, and Paulson (1987) found that connections between turn taking in conversations are based on cues that one segment of a conversation provides for the next. Using these cues, participants connect their comments to the comment that preceded. *Syntactic cues* result from the use of pronouns, substitutions, ellipses, and conjunctions. For instance, one person might say *"He* saw your car there" and the interactant might say, using the pronoun as a cue, "He who?" *Pragmatic cues* are conversational pairs, such as questions and answers. (In the previous example, the question "He who?" cues a reply, "John.") *Lexical cues* are based on meaning relations; for instance, the flow of conversation might center on the development of an idea, such as sports or flowers, until one person says something about a related topic prompted by what someone else said. The discussion of sports (including comments on aggressiveness) might lead into comments on aggression in international relations; aggression is the conversational cue. Or a discussion of flowers might shift into a discussion of colors cued by a comment about a flower of a particular color. The researchers compared the use of syntactic, pragmatic, and lexical devices as cues in conversations. Only lexical cues were found significantly more often in coherent conversations. This work is significant because it emphasizes that meaning is vital to conversational coherence, not just syntactics or pragmatics.

Studying this issue, Villaume and Cegala (1988) concluded that people mesh comments during conversation to achieve coherence as a form of collaboration. Cohesive devices explicitly connect comments. Three grammatical cohesive devices are prevalent in conversation: *reference devices* such as pronouns, indefinite articles, demonstratives, and comparative forms; *substitution devices* based on the employment of counters or marker words (e.g., "Who wants gum?" "I'll have some." "Some" is a *marker* standing for "gum."); and *ellipsis,* a kind of substitution, where a respondent replies without being explicit (e.g., "Is that your book?" "Yeah," implying that is.) This study was based on interaction involvement—the extent to which each person facilitates a conversation by being sensitive to its evolving flow and by integrating his or her thoughts, feelings and behaviors into the flow. The results were that each pair of communicators differed in the patterned use of interactive ellipsis and noninteractive references. The discourse strategies reflect the relative certainty, or uncertainty, each person feels during interaction and whether appropriate means are being used to develop conversational topics. This occurs, Villaume and Cegala reasoned, because interaction involvement is related to communicators' degree of certainty/uncertainty about the interaction. These factors influence interactants' confidence to execute communication moves and connections. Reference devices are more difficult to execute than are ellipsis and substitution; the former requires that respondents interpret the meanings of their communication partners. Partners may use interactional direction to tie their talk to their partner's. The degree of involvement in the conversation is a powerful indicator of the kinds of communication tactics persons use. A speech accommodation explanation of this situation is that a low-involved person interacts with a high-involved person by attempting to adjust to the socially approved and powerful style of the high-involved in an effort to manage impressions and seek social approval; the second explanation for the reaction is uncertainty/certainty differences. Perhaps low-involved persons are uncertain about how to track conversations and take appropriate turns. In this way, interactions are a product of the chemistry between the interactants taking into consideration their communication competencies; their ability to accommodate themselves to others to be seen as socially competent.

ACTION-ORIENTED LANGUAGE THEORY

As does coordinated management of meaning, other action-oriented approaches to interpersonal communication draw their rationale from *ordinary language philosophy.* Whereas other language theories focus on cultural meanings or the relationship between word and reference, speech act theory concentrates on performance (Austin, 1962, 1964; Searle, 1969). According to this theory, meaning is inseparable from intention. The key to successful communication is each speaker's ability to communicate his or her intentions as a part of the communication event. To be successful, the speaker must get the receiver to understand the intent behind the statement. Just as important is the ability of the receiver to interpret the message by determining its purpose.

Categorizing statements by what they do, ordinary language philosophy features four kinds of statements.

1. The simplest statement, an *utterance,* is the articulation of sounds, perhaps the vocalization of a single word, such as the greeting, "Hi!"
2. A *proposition* or *locution* states a reference, such as "Houston is approximately 250 miles south of Dallas."
3. An *illocution* is intended to elicit a cognitive or behavioral response because of the way it is framed; for instance one person might say to another, "That sunset is too beautiful for us to pass up" inviting the response "Let's go for a walk."
4. A *perlocution* is designed to have some consequential effect on the feelings, thoughts, or behavior of the receiver. The sender may state "Please pass the salt" or "No Trespassing." The message leaves no doubt regarding the appropriate response.

Discerning between each of these latter three types of statements probably requires more cues than those embedded in the sentences themselves. For this reason, interactants often turn to the nature of the episode, along with its typical life-scripts and relevant contracts and archetypes as well as nonverbal cues to determine the content of the exchange.

Messages exchanged between individuals often have the same referential power but differ in terms of what the words mean for each relationship. For instance, directives, a type of illocutionary act, can have at least four effects during negotiation. They can convey levels of politeness, provide relational messages, define participant rights and obligations in dealing with the directive, and indicate the significance of the information requested (Donohue & Diez, 1985).

Some language forms convey powerfulness and others express powerlessness. Kinds of expression associated with powerlessness include hedges ("I sorta finished my homework"), unnecessary intensifiers ("I'm a good kid"), or tags ("My painting is good, isn't it"). Whether these are interpreted as powerful or powerless depends on the perceived purpose and the *paralanguage* (the vocal inflection that accompanied the statement). Research suggests that during conversations, people are able to distinguish between powerful and powerless statements. The criteria by which these distinctions are made are quite stable. Moreover, what could appear at times as powerless statement forms may be said in ways to be powerful (Bradac & Mulac, 1984).

Action-oriented theory of meaning argues that meaning is more than a reference to a referent. This theory contends that meaning is at least partially unique to each communication interaction, but not so idiosyncratic that two people cannot know what meaning to assign to the interaction. Meaning is created each moment throughout each interaction. It is not necessarily testable by checking statements against reality, but by seeing their impact on participants. Marriage vows, "I do," or "I pronounce you man and wife," are not referential. But they are important in everyday life. They give meaning to our lives, and help us to know what constitutes the requirements of social competence (Stewart, 1972).

This theory is full of promise. Intuitive and scientific evidence abounds to justify its conclusions. For instance, Bell, Buerkel-Rothfuss, and Core (1987) studied the correspondence between the use of private idiom, interpersonal context, and quality of relationship. They examined idioms that could be used during confrontation, to express affection, and for labeling outsiders. Results revealed that for both sexes, loving, commitment, and closeness are associated with an increased use of idioms to express affection, initiate sexual encounters, and refer to sexual matters. Context is a factor. In such relationships, references to outsiders are made in public, whereas sexual invitations are usually made in private.

As Brenders (1987) cautioned, any action-oriented theory of meaning (especially the coordinated management of meaning) can overemphasize the idiosyncratic, intrapersonal rules people use to develop meaning during interaction. This error can lead someone who is analyzing others' communication to mistake conventional or routine functions of language with those that are unique and idiosyncratic. For this reason, researchers and people engaging in conversation can confuse semantic (dictionary or conventional) meaning and pragmatic meaning, which depends on interpreting intentions behind statements to understand their meaning. Pragmatic meanings may differ from semantic meanings. As people interact, they strive to balance semantic and pragmatic meanings by attempting to determine when conventional meaning is used and when the perceived intention of the speaker should be applied to determine the meaning of statements. For this reason, purposive and affective dimensions of meanings often can only be interpreted in the context of each unique interaction. Fathoming this kind of problem presents challenges to researchers, and to each of us as we interact each day.

CONCLUSION

This chapter demonstrates how language, with its impact on cognitive processes and peoples' relationships with one another, is a useful vehicle for interacting, reducing uncertainty, entertaining, and exchanging thoughts. A unique human capability, language plays many roles in all communication contexts and domains.

People select words that present themselves in various degrees of powerfulness, an aspect of social competence. To explain the dynamics that guide the selection of words during interactions and their use to exert influence, Giles and Wiemann (1987) reasoned that refinements in the understanding of language should achieve three goals:

> 1. integrate the symbolic and referential functions of language for our individual, relational, and multiple group identities. 2. focus upon the creative role of majority and minority collectivities in society while recognizing the dynamic nature of language change and evolution. 3. feature the interface between the ways that language reflects, builds upon, and determines social reality, as well as highlight the dynamic, skeptical, crafty communicative qualities we all share. (pp. 367–368)

This endeavor is necessary because language represents and defines reality as well as serves as a vital means for interaction. The search to understand language depends on comprehending the principles people use to generate meanings for statements that are predominantly open ended (Jacobs, 1985).

Studies suggest that people follow patterns of behavior and employ words that are contextually meaningful. Meaning results from interaction and is not merely based on references between words and things or the expression of idioms. As further insight is gained regarding how words are used to create meaning and coordinate interaction, we will better understand why communication can reduce uncertainty, regulate social interaction, and entertain.

4 Information and Uncertainty: Concepts and Contexts

Communication studies have been significantly affected by the concept of *information*. Few concepts have been as important, or as troublesome. A moment's reflection can help you realize how central information is to your communication activities. When you pick up a newspaper, tune in radio or TV news, or join a conversation, you are probably seeking and providing information on some topic (perhaps a ball game score, a fashion change, or a new album by a popular group). You may ask a friend whether someone in whom you are romantically interested likes you. These illustrations point out that people seek to reduce uncertainty. People do not like to feel uncertain; it produces emotional and cognitive discomfort.

Information is important because it lets people know who and where they are and how well they are doing. People acquire information about others, their environment, and themselves. Information is a basic ingredient in change and adaptation. A systems perspective should remind you that information obtained through interpersonal contact in an organization or through mediated communication can help you adapt to your environment and monitor your success. Without information, people cannot make good decisions; they cannot know who their friends (or enemies) are, how they need to operate in an organization, who won an election, or what the weather report is.

Some information is sought, but it can come to you without your having to exert much effort. The front page of the newspaper or radio or TV news announces that someone was murdered or three persons died in a car accident. These persons are strangers to you, so how does that information affect your certainty? As is typical of most persons, you carry many propositions or conclusions that you continually test: "Crime is a problem in our town." "People die in car accidents if they drive recklessly." "Pollution is killing wildlife." Information acquired through conversations or news stories confirms or disconfirms propositions that people test to understand events and other people as well as themselves. By testing these conclusions, they estimate how secure they are or what the nature of the world is. People acquire information—sometimes aggressively and other times passively—with the goal of increasing the certainty that they know what is going on.

Information exchange can be viewed as the basic communication paradigm—people seeking, giving, or exchanging information to reduce uncertainty. However, more than describing how information is sent from one person to another during communication, information theory supplies a rationale to explain how people make meaningful contact with others and their environment. Information has been described as the means by which people come to know one another as well as physical and social realities (Watzlawick et al., 1967).

Information, as a concept, was popularized in the 1950s and 1960s by researchers who relied on the work of Shannon and Weaver (1949) and Weiner (1948). In that period, *cybernetics* developed as the science or study of regulation and control. It seeks to explain the processes by which people or other systems receive information in regard to their attempts to achieve their goals; information can be used to decide to continue or abandon those attempts or to change the goals. For example, a person might shoot a free throw so hard that the basketball bounces back from the backboard without touching the rim; the second shot would be guided by the information (feedback) gained from the first. The second attempt might be shot too easily and fall short. Using information gained from the first two attempts, the third shot might be made in such a way that it goes through the hoop. If attempts achieve goals, these attempts are likely to be repeated; if they are unsuccessful, they will probably be abandoned. That simple premise demonstrates why an understanding of information is valuable to efforts to explain and improve the communication process.

This chapter emphasizes the need humans have to seek and exchange information to reduce uncertainty about physical and social reality and to achieve social competence. This discussion demonstrates how information is vital to messages and meanings. *Meaning* is the interpretation of the information a message contains, and *messages* are means by which information is obtained. The chapter compares two views of information, defines key concepts, and discusses research findings regarding the presence of information in interpersonal, organizational, and mass-mediated contexts. In this analysis, information is defined as the aspect of messages that increases or reduces uncertainty.

INFORMATION: FOUNDATION FOR COMMUNICATION THEORY AND RESEARCH

Despite its popularity in the 1960s and 1970s, information has also had an uncertain status with communication theorists. Part of the trouble information has encountered comes from unsound assumptions. For instance, information and persuasion have been treated as mutually exclusive, when, for instance, people reason that a source can inform or persuade. At other times, information and persuasion have been viewed as enemies. This division led to unfortunate assumptions and battles. Some writers have argued that some components of the communication industries and of our discipline—journalism, for instance—provide information, but do not persuade. Those who adhere to this belief often suggest that in contrast to providing information—which somehow seems to them to be "pure"— others, such as advertising or public relations personnel, persuade—dealing in the "impure." In this sense, persuasion is equated with manipulation, deceit, and lies.

Such distinctions are unproductive. Indeed, information is a major part of persuasive influence. For instance, Danes (1978) showed that if receivers accumulate information that differs from their beliefs, they are likely to change those beliefs. Reviewing 50 years of persuasion research, Reinard (1988) concluded that evidence influences opinions, especially when it is relevant to topics with which audiences are involved. Public communication campaign messages can affect opinions when they provide information publics think is relevant to their interests (Douglas, Westley, & Chaffee, 1970; Mendelsohn, 1973; Winett, 1986).

Several variables probably interact to increase consistency between the amount of knowledge persons have on a topic, their attitudes on the topic, and the likelihood that their behavior will be consistent with their knowledge and attitudes. One of the most important of these variables is involvement, which can be operationalized in at least four ways: (a) the number of messages a person can report on a topic, (b) the extent to which personal risk is thought to exist, (c) the extremity of the attitudes on the topic, and (d) the amount of reading that each person does on the topic. The best predictors of consistency between knowledge, attitudes, and behavior are cognitive involvement—number of messages held on a topic—and extremity of attitude position on the topic (Chaffee & Roser, 1986).

A problem researchers have had is the tendency to treat information as being tangible. As Fisher (1978) observed, it is a mistake to treat information as a thing—an entity that can be transported from one place to another or as having a referent (something for which it stands). A better view, he believed, is to think of it as the means by which people know about one another and their environment. By obtaining information, people can adjust their behavior and adapt to one another. Adjustment and adaptation are vital to the self-organizing and self-regulating activities of systems.

This relationship among the parts of a system and between the system and its environment can be understood by recalling that energy, for instance, is one of the basic ingredients of a biological or physical system. Animals take in (input) energy in the form of food from the outside and metabolize (process or throughput) it so that it enables them to perform activities (output) such as work or play. This analogy should help you understand the roles information plays in a system. Social systems, such as individuals, families, businesses, or schools, cannot survive without information. People need information to know one another, to be able to adapt to each other, and to know whether they are achieving their goals. According to systems theory, information is to communication what energy is to biological or physical systems; information flows between systems, giving the systems the means to adapt to one another. In addition to being received and transformed by a system, information can also be created by a system (Krippendorff, 1977).

During the 1960s, information theory refined the definition of "message." As discussed in chapter 3, *messages* are means by which communicators obtain information. *Meaning* is an interpretation that one communicator assigns to verbal and nonverbal behavior of another. Meaning depends on communicators' experience and language, as well as the context in which it is formed. By contributing the word "bits" to our vocabulary, information theory added to the understanding of what a message is. A *bit* is any unit of thought that allows a person to reduce an alternative or choice by half.

For instance, you might ask a friend whether you left your coat in his or her closet. The friend can answer this question with one bit of information, "yes" (or "no," depending on the facts). If the answer is "yes," it is there and nowhere else. The decision at the moment is "closet" or "somewhere else." See how "yes" (or "no") reduces the choice by half. In this vein, messages contain bits of information (Fisher, 1978). What any bit means depends on the interpretation of the persons involved. What is information to one person may not be to another. *Information* is the impact each bit has on a choice or decision being made.

Researchers have argued that "*information* must not be confused with meaning" (Shannon & Weaver, 1949, p. 8). In this sense, information refers to aspects of messages that are free of values (Broadhurst & Darnell, 1965). For instance, a telephone system is designed with consideration of the quality of the signal to be received, not the quality of the information conveyed. Telephones can be used for gossip, financial transactions, medical discussions, or illegal drug deals. The technical problem is to transmit information accurately, efficiently, and correctly. The concern is for *capacity*—the amount of information that can be transmitted given the quality of the sender, message, channel, or receiver. Information theory can address the capacity of channels, messages, systems, networks, and the human mind.

Disagreeing with the contention that information is unrelated to meaning, Deetz and Mumby (1985) reasoned that all contact with reality provides information. Knowledge and understanding depend on verification via perception. Terms used to define objects, situations, and experiences filter the meaning (the interpretation and importance of bits of information). Bits of information cannot stand as messages separate from the experience, language, or context that gives them definition. For instance, if an expert on snakes heard two children describing the one they had seen in the backyard, the "message" would have different information for the expert than for a worried parent who could not recognize poisonous snakes.

Discussions of information were generated from technical inquiry regarding the engineering of telephone transmission systems. In its infancy, this topic interested electrical engineers, but not the majority of communication scholars. Once communication researchers saw how the concept could be applied to everyday communication, its importance increased. Now this engineering concept is important for the entire range of communication situations. For this reason, advances in telecommunications, including those called information technologies, have led to a dynamic renewal of interest in communication–transmission efficiency and systems analysis. It has led to discussions of how information affects societies. For the most part, this line of analysis began once Porat (1977) and Dizard (1982) proclaimed that many economies, particularly Japan, the United States, and Europe, are becoming "information societies."

The industrial worker, according to this point of view, is being replaced by the "information worker." Instead of manufacturing automobiles, this new type of worker generates, stores, transmits, and sells information. Telecommunications offers solutions for communication problems experienced by complex organizations that need to communicate with thousands of people who are in many locations — some a hemisphere away. More and more researchers have begun to study and develop computer-assisted and global, satellite communication. Satellite telecommunications links allow millions of people to witness, virtually simultaneously, the same events — whether news, entertainment, or sports. People have become fascinated by the potential of storing and retrieving information from huge databases. Dozens of newspapers can be read online each day by accessing databases through personal computers hooked to telephone lines. Dow-Jones databases offer instant retrieval of information on approximately 750,000 U.S. companies.

The years since Porat's (1977) famous proclamation have generated many studies that have only scratched the surface of what the future holds

(Dizard, 1982). Information is a medium of exchange that has enormous social, cultural, and political impact. New information technologies, policies, and practices are dramatically changing society (Schiller, 1983). Included among these changes is the trend toward privatization of information. Information that once was publically available, such as data from governmental agencies, now has to be obtained through private database companies. Information is power; the people, companies, and countries that control information wield power. Information is changing the nature of society; for instance, with the ability to obtain and process information quickly, physicians can perform complex diagnoses in their offices. Personal credit histories are contained in massive databases. People who have home computers and modems can link into database services to gain instant access to libraries full of information on virtually any topic imaginable.

In these ways and many more, information is a vital aspect of communication theory and research. By understanding this theory, you can appreciate the principles of message design, transmission, and reception; it explains how communication is affected by several capacities—such as the ability of a channel to transmit information in large quantities and at rapid rates or the mental capacity of people to process information. Information is the "energy" in the communication process.

Information: Toward A Definition

How do you define information? You may think of it as what one person says to another—objectively. This view might contrast information and persuasion or manipulation, believing the latter activities are long on emotion and devoid of information. You might define it as facts and figures stated without elaboration. Or in keeping with the new information age, you may consider information as a commodity that is bought and sold. You might think of it as tangible, a "thing" conveyed from one person to another.

Stressing the problems involved in defining the term, Ruben (1985) summarized several definitions to show how broadly (and loosely) it is used. He found it used to refer to data, decision making and problem solving, commodities, and constraints on choices; it is used in conjunction with stimuli, learning, thinking, cognition, memory, knowledge, media, and linkages between a living system and its environment. To remedy the problem of the definition of *information,* he suggested that the concept be narrowed into four broad categories: (a) *data,* what it expresses; (b) *process,* how it is acquired, transmitted, transformed, stored, or retrieved; (c) *channel,* how it is transmitted, stored, transformed, or retrieved; and (d) *uses* and *outcomes,* its impact.

To define information, Devito (1986) wrote that it is "that which reduces uncertainty," as "something that the receiver does not already know" (pp. 155–156). If a person already has the data, according to this definition, it is not information. It is information only as long as it is affects uncertainty. In this vein, Cherry (1978) concluded that information is valuable (has meaning) only when doubt is present. The amount of information conveyed in a message is always relative; it depends on the amount of doubt a receiver has before and after receiving a message.

To illustrate the concept of information, Krippendorff (1975) noted that the amount of information conveyed by a message is the difference between the amount of uncertainty before a message is received and the amount of uncertainty that exists after it is received. This definition is consonant with Krippendorf's (1977) contention that "*information* is equated with making choices" (p. 157). He explained that "a message conveys *information* to the extent that it is, in fact, and is perceived as the *product of choices*" (p. 157). Senders make choices in regard to what they say, and receivers use information to reduce uncertainty – about what is said or about some choice – or both. This view assumes that people seek and share information to reduce uncertainty produced by choices they must make.

For this reason, human cognition is fed by information. *Cognition* is a computational process that handles quantities of information that stem from past experiences as well as fictional accounts, projections, and values. This line of reasoning follows the metaphor of the human individual as information processor; each processor is a system and all are parts of larger information systems. Information is the medium of exchange between systems, within a system, and between a system and its environment.

Placing information into a systems context, Krippendorff (1977) concluded that

> organizations develop procedures for handling information internally: sorting, coding, selective transmission, storing, deciding on and executing instruction to its executive organs, consulting social memories – explicitly, in the form of libraries and files, and implicitly in the form of net attitudes, etc. (pp. 159–161)

In this regard, a family is a system. Each day, its members provide information (or fail to do so) in ways that affect one another. One member forgets to tell another that the boss called. A note, "I'll be home this afternoon," does not contain sufficient information to reduce the uncertainty about what time the person will arrive.

A systems orientation views information as a basic ingredient in each person's efforts to achieve social understanding, which is needed to produce the self-correction required to increase self-efficacy. This paradigm explains communication behavior that transpires in social groups, complex organizations, and the media. *Information* is data an individual (or a social unit such as a family or company) uses in its attempts to adapt to its environment, to reduce uncertainty and achieve gratification (Weiner, 1948).

Entropy

Before turning attention to theories about information and viewing its role in various communication contexts, we need to examine the concept of *entropy*, the degree of disorganization that exists in any system—whether physical or social. Entropy is the degree of uncertainty that results from randomness, lack of predictability, in a situation or message. The relationship between information and entropy is this: When certainty or predictability is present in a situation, no additional information is needed, and no entropy exists. In this way, information is based on the assumptions of probabilities.

Maximum entropy, according to Shannon and Weaver (1949), results from maximum information. This means that entropy is highest when all bits of information are present and equally possible. For instance, you would be uncertain which card would be dealt first from a deck of 52 cards (maximum information equals maximum entropy, unpredictability, and high uncertainty). If you kept track of the first 51 cards dealt from the deck, the last card would be easy to predict. Randomness would be eliminated because only one bit of information remains regarding that last card. Another example of this point can be made by referring to a maternity room where only one question, "is it a girl or boy?" need be answered to announce the sex of a newborn child. Information theory postulates that certainty is high when entropy is low and vice versa.

Entropy is concerned with the range of messages possible in a given situation. Ambiguity or vagueness is an example of high entropy. It results when a receiver cannot accurately decode a word or statement and know what the sender means. Ambiguity means that more information exists regarding which interpretation of the message is correct than is the case when a message is clear. It is difficult to predict what the first comment in a conversation will be, and if the receiver of this comment does not know the sender, that prediction is even more difficult to make. Unpredictability is maximum when we have unlimited choices regarding what we are going to talk about and what we are going to say about it, and regarding what others are going to talk about and what they will say about it. In this way, entropy refers to the amount of freedom people have in the design and interpretation of messages.

Discussions of information often use the term *randomness*. In the strictest sense, randomness is a dichotomous variable; something is random or not. Used in this way, we could not talk in terms of degrees of randomness. Because uncertainty is a continuous variable, it is advisable to use terms such as *likelihood, probability,* or *predictability.* These terms allow us to imagine, for instance, that persons are unlikely (or highly likely) to obtain the information they need to reduce uncertainty. Any piece of information might increase (or decrease) uncertainty. In this regard, pieces of information can have large or small effects on uncertainty.

Predictability is a key concept for discussing how information is supplied by media and sought by readers, viewers, or listeners. For instance, when people place news (information) on TV or in a newspaper, they position the information so that a person wanting it is likely to find it. Sports, weather, food, or financial sections help receivers find each kind of information with greater likelihood. Think how difficult a newspaper would be to read if the information was scattered throughout rather than grouped by topic. Likewise, one ad does not stand much chance of being seen or read, even by a target population. Consequently, advertisers increase the likelihood that intended audiences will get the information by placing it in many places on the same day or by repeating it over several days. Many advertisers do both. Advertisers also try to place the information where targeted audiences are predicted to find it.

In an information environment, repetition or redundancy increases the likelihood that people will encounter the message, which, in its own turn, is designed to reduce the audience's uncertainty about the qualities of a product or service. This concept can also apply to interpersonal relationships. For instance, if you want to find information about a friend whom you believe you can no longer trust, you may seek data from the person most likely to have it or ask many people on the assumption that lots of contacts increase your chances of getting the information you want.

Likelihood is the test of information richness. An information environment is rich if many topics are discussed by many people and media. *Richness* is a measure of the likelihood that senders will have their messages received and senders will obtain the information they desire. This is a way of thinking about the difficulty an advertiser faces when attempting to send information to a buyer or when a buyer seeks information needed to make a purchase. The greater the number of messages available on a topic, the more likely the receiver will get the intended message and reduce uncertainty. An increase in sources also enriches the information environment. People in a large organization may have trouble getting information they need due to a lack of information richness, (insufficient number of communication sources people need to obtain the information they want).

Theorists postulate that entropy by its nature tends to increase. Physical systems, such as an iron bar exposed to the weather, tend toward entropy; the bar is likely to rust and disintegrate—iron particles tend to become random. Living organisms are likely to deteriorate if they cannot get needed information and apply it to corrective behavior in order to find food needed to survive. In such a situation, entropy is present—and the organism is likely to perish—without appropriate food—if all things are equally likely to be ingested but cannot be equally digested.

This principle applies to social situations. In a social setting, such as a communication context (whether interpersonal, organizational, or mediated), entropy is present if an individual is likely to generate or receive any message; this means that entropy occurs when no message is more likely to be sent or received than any other. In this way, we might imagine that a child's communication is more unpredictable than is a supervisor's when giving instructions. (Some supervisors may give instructions as unpredictably as a baby babbles.) The concept of predictability increases the understanding of complex systems. Systems theory assumes that entropy will increase unless some force intervenes; physical and social systems tend to become less organized and more random.

In keeping with this view of information, the objective of effective message design is to limit the range of possibilities the receiver has for interpreting the message received, thereby reducing unpredictability and increasing certainty. This view of information explains why communication rules limit, but do not totally constrain, the allowable possibilities of what can be said and what is likely to be meant by what is said.

One argument for a rules perspective to explain communication interaction is that, if appropriate rules are not followed, communication behavior can become increasingly unpredictable and therefore less likely to reduce uncertainty. Patterns, both of interaction and structure of message content, are necessary to mitigate entropy and thereby reduce uncertainty. Similarly, a systems approach to human communication aims to explain the needs and corrective mechanisms individuals require to make systems thrive rather than perish.

During interpersonal communication, the flow of conversation would be very unpredictable and hard to coordinate if persons were equally likely to say one thing as opposed to another, or to imply many meanings rather than one. But conversations are not unpredictable. Each comment, in one way or another, suggests the allowable possibilities that can be used to continue a conversation. People could not conduct conversations if they were totally unpredictable. In similar fashion, organizations could not operate if the people who operate them obtain and provide information in highly random ways.

When we consider the systems typical of complex organizations, such as a business or university, unpredictability can mean that people do not have or cannot understand the information they need to make decisions or conduct business. If an employee's search for needed information is random, he or she is equally likely to get needed *and* unneeded information. Or looked at from the sender's orientation in mass media, this unpredictability can mean that the targeted public is as likely to encounter (or miss) one message as any other.

Such unpredictability is a problem, for instance, for persons who are involved in product advertising or publicity. They work hard to increase the likelihood that their messages will be received from among advertising clutter. For that reason, people advertise in places where they believe they are more likely to encounter people who are interested in the messages. Toys are advertised on Saturday morning television. House cleaning products are advertised during weekdays, but not during sports events. Cosmetics, cars, food, and beer are advertised at night. Women's magazines carry women's products, whereas men's magazines carry products of interest to men. All of this conventional (and social scientific) wisdom follows the proposition that entropy is a measure of the amount of disorganization or unpredictability in a system.

INFORMATION: A FIXED DECISION MODEL

As is typical of all complex topics, the discussion of information has taken several paths, some of which are not directly related to communication. But each in its own way has helped solve the puzzle of how best to comprehend what information is and how it can be conceptualized as a means by which people adapt to one another and to their environments. The most important early studies on information were the work on transmission and reception by Shannon and Weaver, Wiener's study of cybernetics, and probability theory (Krippendorff, 1977).

Few concepts have been more central to information theory or made it more important to communication theory than has probability. This model centers on the likelihood that any bit of data will be received or obtained and whether it will reduce the uncertainty present in a situation. As Weiner (1950) wrote,

> it is possible to treat sets of messages as having an entropy like sets of states of the external world. Just as entropy is a measure of disorganization, the information carried by a set of messages is a measure of disorganization. The more probable the message, the less information it gives. Cliches, for example, are less illuminating than great poems. (p. 21)

In a similar vein, Weiner believed that feedback is important to communication; by using it, people, individually or in organizations, as well as communicating machines such as computers, can lessen entropy—uncertainty. The reasoning is this: Information is sought to reduce uncertainty, and *feedback* is a means by which communicators can assess the extent (probability) to which their behavior is producing the response they desire. Feedback, in this sense, is a corrective device—in keeping with cybernetics—that allows people to determine whether they are undertaking the actions needed to achieve their goals. They want to increase the probability that they have the information necessary to achieve their goals. One way to answer this question is to see whether the information is satisfactory to achieve those goals. Feedback is the means for answering this question: Test whether information is sufficient by using it to reach the desired goals. A grade is feedback in regard to whether you had enough information to pass an exam or score high on it. Obtaining a teacher's reaction to your answers on review questions is feedback that can be used to increase the likelihood that you are prepared for a test. Getting lost (or arriving successfully) is feedback on a friend's ability to give (and your ability to obtain) directions.

Feedback can be used to determine how well you are doing. You might ask a friend, "Do you like my car," seeking a binary (either/or) reaction, "Yes" or "Not really." Much of the information you receive under these conditions may not seem binary. In answer to a question about the car you could get comments that appear to fall in a semantic range, "terrific," "great," "good," "OK," "pretty old," "a junker," and "heap." But this problem is more a matter of precision of thought or response rather than a flaw in the conception of information. The binary nature of information exists even in a range. "Really like your" car excludes all other possibilities. What do you think of my car? "I like it because it is a convertible," as opposed to its not being a convertible. "The tires are in bad shape and the body needs work." "The sound system is good, but one speaker rattles." "Is that a drip of oil from the engine?"

Responses such as these help the questioner get information. The information accumulates or sums to a total, interpreted by the perceptions of the receiver. It helps the questioner gain information to estimate his or her standing in regard to this question. The value of information can only be estimated in terms of the goal to which it is being put. Such is the nature of information in everyday conversation when cast in a cybernetic model.

Using probability as the basis of their model, Shannon and Weaver (1949) contended that information relates not so much to what is said as to what could *be* said. That is, information is a measure of freedom of choice in selecting a message. The source's freedom of choice in constructing a message is equal to the receiver's uncertainty about which message will be transmitted and what it means. When a source has maximum freedom of choice between independent and equally probable symbols, uncertainty about the next symbol to be selected and used during communication is maximum; such situations reach maximum entropy. *Relative entropy* is the ratio of the actual entropy in a given situation to maximum entropy. Content that does not reduce uncertainty present in a situation contains no information. When source and receiver possess the same information, communication can cease.

In this way, Shannon and Weaver equated information and communication. They provided a rationale for message design, which argues that, in any situation, the amount of information present is based on the probability that a sender will say what needs to be said and do so in a manner that increases the likelihood that the receiver will get the information and need no further communication. Berlo (1977) advocated a model with which individuals can estimate the probability of something happening, what he calls *expectation of occurrence,* a comparison of the expected versus what actually occurs.

> An expectation set is maximally uncertain when no prediction can be derived from it that is better than any other prediction (i.e., a random distribution of expectations). Given a random distribution, an amount of uncertainty is determined solely by the number of alternatives that are expected. As alternatives rise, uncertainty rises and control and predictability are reduced. (p. 25)

In this view, information is measured by the logarithm of the number of available choices. The *unit of measure* is the bit that represents a decision between two alternatives. The number of bits of information in a set of equally probable alternatives is equal to the number of times the set must be divided in half to leave only one alternative. In other words, a *bit* is an arbitrary unit that serves to quantify the information needed to predict the next symbol to be drawn from a set of symbols.

For instance, approximately six bits of information are required to identify which card was selected from a deck of 52 standard playing cards. This means that a person will need to have six questions answered to determine (reduce uncertainty) what card was selected from a deck. The first question could be, "Is the card black?" The answer "Yes" eliminates half of the cards. The next question, "Is the card a club?" could be answered "Yes" or "No" to eliminate thirteen more cards. By using these two questions, a person can eliminate 39 cards. Four more questions should be all that are needed to identify the card that was drawn from the deck: (a) odd or even, (b) face, (c) higher than X, and (d) X or Y. This example illustrates the probability approach to information theory, which postulates that for any set of information, there is an optimal method of communicating, based on the probability that the desired information can be conveyed by providing the fewest bits of information needed to reduce uncertainty. The game "Twenty Questions" assumes that skilled question askers who have a good knowledge base ought to be able to solve the problem in 20 or fewer questions.

Shannon and Weaver postulated that, in a message, each word may or may not help the receiver understand what the source of the message means. In this way, information can lead us to be able to predict, to varying degrees of accuracy, what a sentence will lead to in the way of a complete message. The sentence, "I want a . . .," leaves a lot of uncertainty regarding how it will be completed. But we know the kinds (however infinite they might be) of terms (reflecting wishes) that the person might use. Context can be helpful, either the context of this term in a conversation, for example, teenagers talking about cars, or the physical context, such as a child standing in front of a sink pointing to a drinking glass. If a young child who is a stranger to you says, "I want blaa," you probably would experience high entropy. You would have the "freedom" to assign many meanings to that sound because you would not know which one is probably correct. If the child approaches you in a kitchen and points to a glass on the sink, entropy would likely be lower as you infer that the child wants a drink of something. If the child makes the same attempt at getting a drink over several days, a pattern (redundancy) is established that reduces the uncertainty regarding the child's request.

Just as you figure out that the child wants a drink, entropy rises again as you consider, *of what?* Sometimes we offer the child opportunities to give bits of information by holding up the milk, or water, or juice container to see if any of these is what he or she wants. Information, according to this model, is

> a measure of one's freedom of choice in selecting a message. The greater the freedom of choice, and hence the greater the information, the greater is the uncertainty that the message actually selected is the best one. Thus greater freedom of choice, greater uncertainty, greater information go hand in hand. (Shannon & Weaver, 1949, pp. 18–19)

Shannon and Weaver used this principle to define noise and describe its impact on communication. Any bit of information that increases uncertainty is *noise.* Any addition or omission of a symbol or signal during communication results in a difference between the sender's message and the one received. Noise makes redundancy necessary. Shannon and Weaver (1949) wrote:

> If noise is introduced, then the received message contains certain distortions, certain errors, certain extraneous material, that would certainly lead one to say that the received message exhibits, because of the effects of the noise, an increased uncertainty. But if the uncertainty is increased, the information is increased, and this sounds as though the noise were beneficial! (p. 19)

When noise is present, the received signal exhibits greater information. Stated differently, a signal that is received must be selected out of a more varied (lowered probability of accuracy) set of messages than was originally intended by the sender. Thus, Shannon and Weaver (1949) made a key distinction: "Uncertainty which arises by virtue of freedom of choice on the part of the sender is desirable uncertainty. Uncertainty which arises because of errors or because of the influence of noise is undesirable uncertainty" (p. 19).

Shannon and Weaver's approach stresses that information is the number of messages (defined as bits) needed to totally reduce uncertainty. The objective is to understand the problem producing uncertainty, estimate the availability of information, and calculate how much effect each piece of information has on the uncertainty in the situation. Shannon and Weaver concluded that a well designed message is low in entropy.

Shannon and Weaver viewed communication as a process, a series or chain of events. During these events, several factors can increase or decrease entropy. One factor is redundancy, where combinations of bits of information work together to decrease entropy; thus in the English language it is nearly 100% certain that "u" will follow "q" in a word. Another factor is context; the example of the child requesting a "drink" in a kitchen is an instance of context. Realizing that someone knows a piece of information can help increase the likelihood that another piece will be understood. The phrase, "Rm w riv vu," becomes less entropic when it is known to be a real estate advertisement. With this kind of analysis, Shannon and Weaver defined what they thought are the key factors of the communication process.

Finn and Roberts (1984) claimed that the influence of Shannon and Weaver reaches far beyond the sender-message-channel-receiver model often associated with them. Their major contribution is their rationale for using an *entropic* model to measure the array of observations among variables in a well-defined problem—such as determining what card has been selected from a deck. This model was extended to communication research by Schramm (1955), who advocated that researchers should investigate the relationship between channel capacity and audience capacity. Thus, Schramm postulated that entropy can be a measure of the amount of news in a story, the proportion of news in it versus other stories, and the amount received by readers or viewers. Chaffee and Wilson (1977) used this entropic model to suggest that communities can be media rich or media poor depending on the number of issues people hold to be important. Richness is a measure of the number of media in relation to the range and variety of issues discussed.

In a similar way, Kennamer and Chaffee (1982) called for media effects studies based on "collective" and "individual" levels of uncertainty. A society can have too little or too much information for its needs. Examining this hypothesis, they concluded that the level of uncertainty in each political campaign is positively related to the number of candidates and the extent to which they are equally likely to be elected. They concluded that the audience that is exposed to the most political information will (a) hold more information than the low exposure audience, (b) add to its information more quickly, and (c) have the lower level of uncertainty as the media indicate how well each candidate is faring in the campaign.

To this point we have hinted at an important issue basic to understanding information. The issue is this: Is information something that can best be measured by estimating the likelihood that a bit of information will be available and helpful to reduce the uncertainty at hand? Or, is information something that is best measured by the degree to which the persons feel that any piece of information reduces their uncertainty? The first view of information is basic to the studies of Shannon and Weaver (1949). The latter view assumes that information is best treated in terms of its impact on judgment rather than as a measure implied in some decision system, such as determining how much uncertainty is decreased when we know something (e.g., what cards have been played out of the 52 that constitute a deck). Keep in mind that Shannon and Weaver said that, as information increases, uncertainty decreases, and vice versa. The next section discusses a contrasting view.

INFORMATION: A RECEIVER IMPACT MODEL

If you go to make a major purchase such as a washing machine, car, or stereo, for instance, you probably do not have a fixed equation that can be used to calculate how much each bit of information contributes to a final decision. You get some information from one salesperson, which can reduce uncertainty. Other bits of information can increase uncertainty. If you get conflicting information from several salespeople, uncertainty may increase drastically or you may find some means to resolve it by focusing on certain decision rules. This case, which is typical in our lives, shows that a "theory of information" must be able to explain everyday events.

This example of making a purchase illustrates how information can be defined in terms of its impact on the person seeking it. Thus, in contrast to the entropic model, the *evocative* or *impact* approach to information features the effect any bit of information has on people's need to know, their desire to reduce uncertainty in ill-defined decision circumstances. Taking a different orientation than the one provided by Shannon and Weaver, Conant (1979) defined information "as that which changes what we know" (p. 177). He made the point that we are constantly bombarded by signals—stimuli, some of which are sent intentionally and some which are not. He defined message as "any input to a system that has, or *might* have an effect upon it" (p. 177). He continued, "Every message is potentially a carrier of information in the everyday sense of that word. That is, the receipt and interpretation of a message always entitles the receiver to adjust its knowledge about its environment in some fashion" (p. 177). After this reasoning, he came to this thesis: "Information is that which changes knowledge, and a message can be said to convey information to a receiver if and only if the receiver's knowledge is changed as a result" (p. 177).

To justify his view, Conant (1979) pointed to several weaknesses of the view advocated by Shannon and Weaver. "For one, viewing the information of a message as dependent only on its probability (in an ensemble of possible messages) makes it extremely artificial, and usually quite impossible as well, to calculate the information carried by real messages transferred in the real world of human conversation" (p. 178). If someone shouts "Fire!" listeners do not calculate the probability of what it means. In this way, he reasoned, the importance of a message is its effect on those who hear it. If a person in the room shouts "Aklee!" instead of "Fire!" the information content of "Aklee!" in the view of Shannon and Weaver would be higher than that of "Fire!" This is true, Conant reasoned, because of Shannon and Weaver's formula, which assumes that each bit reduces uncertainty by half and that information is greatest when uncertainty is highest. But we know intuitively that a nonsense message carries virtually no "information." Conant argued that Shannon and Weaver's theory provides little help in understanding communication because it assumes that probabilities involved in decisions are stable and do not change over time. Consequently, this model of information, and its implication for communication, is limited.

Communication and information are not stable or fixed. The need to communicate and the value of any piece of information fluctuate over time. A theory of information should take into consideration the impact of the information on receivers. Conant preferred not to define information as "a property of the message stream" and argued that "information is associated with the *relation* between message and receiver. The perspective here is that the *effect* of the message on the receiver is more basic and fundamental than the message itself" (p. 179).

In light of this reasoning, Conant proposed a model that treats the impact of information as belief strength measured on a scale between 0 and 1. He reasoned, "When a message induces a receiver to modify its knowledge, the result is a change in the vector (but not, we presume, in the *interpretation*). The *meaning* of the message consists in the change in the vector, along with the associated interpretation" (p. 180). The likelihood of rain would move from 0.4 to 1.0 when rain drops began to fall on one's head. "A message is meaningful if the receiver's knowledge is a result of it." He continued, "a message conveys information if and only if it causes movement of the receiver's knowledge in knowledge-space" (p. 181). People want information to be able to reduce uncertainty and increase control of their lives.

The major feature of information is, according to Conant, the effect a message has on the belief strength of the person receiving and using it. It is not a measure of how any bit "should" resolve a decision, such as figuring out which card was drawn from the deck. The impact theory of information has the advantage of treating people as being different. People need more or less information under different circumstances and have different levels of self-confidence. This theory assumes that the information contained in a message is not the same for all people. It acknowledges the cognitive complexity, prior knowledge, and self-confidence of the receiver. This definition of information explains how information has market value. *Value of information* is a function of the effect it can have for a receiver who wants to reduce uncertainty and is willing to pay for the information.

The value of information is measured by the difference it makes on a receiver's degree of uncertainty. This approach to information adds insight into how information relates to communication and motivation typical of interpersonal, organizational, and mediated communication contexts. The next three sections show how information applies to these contexts.

INFORMATION IN INTERPERSONAL CONTEXTS

One theory of interpersonal communication posits that people are motivated in their communication behavior by their desire to reduce the uncertainty regarding what they know about each other, about physical and social reality, and about their own social competency. Through contact with others, people create social reality (Berger & Luckman, 1966; Watzlawick et al., 1967) and seek to know one another (Berger, 1987; Berger & Bradac, 1982; Berger & Calabrese, 1975; Roloff & Berger, 1982). This view of interpersonal communication, called *social cognition,* concentrates on the processes and motives behind individual efforts to receive and interpret information obtained by scrutinizing others, one's self, and reality. Efforts to obtain and process information become more pronounced when habitual or scripted thoughts, cognitions, and patterns of interaction do not suffice the persons involved.

Interpersonal communication patterns change as a consequence of information-seeking behavior that occurs as people attempt to reduce uncertainty. For instance, as they get closer to voting age, to become competent voters, people tend to seek political information, often by asking others about candidates (Woelfel, 1977). According to Kellerman (1987), information is the only means by which people involved in a interaction can determine whether they want to continue a relationship and get to know one another. Without information, a relationship cannot progress.

Crediting Shannon and Weaver (1949) with starting the uncertainty reduction paradigm, Pavitt and Cappella (1979) reasoned that uncertainty is present when people do not know other communicators or cannot predict their actions. Uncertainty results when one set of events or reactions is as likely to occur as another and when communicators want a correct description of each other or when they want to predict some event. Information is sought to lower uncertainty and improve the ability to predict events.

Feelings of uncertainty produce a state of emotional or cognitive arousal—a desire to achieve certainty—in many but not all cases. People may not want to know really bad news that has personal, negative consequences, and at least, for a while, may even deny such information. But in most cases, uncertainty leads to information-seeking communication (Berger & Calabrese, 1975; Pavitt & Cappella, 1979). In an attempt to build consensus, people may talk only with people with whom they agree and avoid those with whom they disagree.

According to Shannon and Weaver (1949), the value of information is measured by how much each bit reduces uncertainty. This view of information is insensitive to information-seeking behavior, which is relative to the needs of the persons involved. To partially satisfy this problem, McLeod and Chaffee (1973) postulated that the success of persons engaged in communication can be measured by the degree of coorientation—the extent to which their perceptions of each other are accurate and satisfying, based on mutual understanding.

Despite their desire to obtain and use information to get to know one another, conclusions people draw based on their perceptions of one another are rarely accurate beyond chance (Sillars, 1982). This means that their perceptions of each other, their perceptions of the facts involved in the situation, and the other person's perceptions of them probably do not agree. A great deal of communication theory and research explores how people try to understand one another, and, using the coorientation model, it measures the extent to which they do. Pavitt and Cappella (1979) stressed the importance of examining the factors that affect the accuracy of judgments people hold of one another and of including context variables in such discussions.

To advance research into factors and motivation affecting accuracy and uncertainty, Pavitt and Cappella advised researchers to examine "within-dyad accuracy," "outside-dyad accuracy," and "consensus task accuracy" (pp. 124–125). A dyad is two people communicating. *Within dyad accuracy* refers to the ability of each participant to be accurate about the other's views on relevant topics through communication. *Outside dyad accuracy* refers to each participant's ability to be accurate about the other's views regarding a person or group of persons. *Consensus task accuracy* refers to participants' ability to use communication to reach agreement on some issue.

Pavitt and Cappella postulated that liking and amount of communication will influence within-dyad accuracy. People who like one another are likely to seek information from one another. But liking distorts perception of agreement; people tend to believe that they agree with persons they like and disagree with those they dislike. Perceived disagreement increases the likelihood of disliking. People tend to like the ideas of persons whom they like. This analysis assumes that people strive to keep their perceptions and feelings in harmony.

Thus, Pavitt and Cappella reasoned that accuracy of judgment is likely to exhibit a U-shaped (curvilinear) relationship with liking, because when people like one another they tend to have unrealistically high perceptions of the amount of agreement, whereas those with extreme degrees of disliking tend toward exaggerated perceptions of disagreement. If people like others, they may tend to agree with their judgments rather than seek information that could disrupt that liking; and they may ignore information that could diminish disagreement with persons they dislike.

Because liking is such a strong motive, people tend to be open to increased amounts of information sharing with those they like. This communication may lead them to be similar in their opinions of the object, but not necessarily accurate. Agreement or similarity has little to do with whether opinions about some object or situation are accurate, but agreement or similarity is a measure of the accuracy of perception regarding the other communicator's opinion on the object. Thus, Pavitt and Cappella (1979) postulated, "Actual agreement between two communicators about a relevant object is a monotonically increasing function of amount/time spent in communication with each other concerning the relevant object" (p. 129). This contention predicts that interactants will change toward each other's expressed attitude as interaction continues. Closely related is another hypothesis: "Accuracy in judgments concerning another person's view toward a relevant object is a monotonically increasing function of amount of communication with the other person" (p. 129). And Pavitt and Cappella added a third postulate in this vein: "Under conditions of actual agreement, accuracy in judgments of another's view concerning a relevant object is directly related to perception of agreement with the other concerning the relevant object. The greater the actual agreement, the more an increase in accuracy will lead to an increase in perceived agreement" (pp. 129–130).

This line of analysis has many implications for interpersonal communication, liking, information seeking, and agreement. When persons are engaged in "within-dyad tasks," accuracy is a function of A's knowledge about B's views about the details related to a task. If A is uncertain about B's information, the task cannot be completed until more information is obtained in order to increase confidence. In regard to "outside-dyad tasks", A's success does not rely only on knowledge of B's views, but also on information and assumptions acquired independent of B. Other sources of information and direct contact with the object can supplement information acquired from B. Some of the factors influencing judgments in this case will be confidence in one's own opinion and the opinions of others. For these reasons, information is a key factor in the development of interpersonal relationships.

Information is important to processes that occur during negotiation. Investigating the factors that affect exchange of information during negotiation, Donohue and Diez (1985) found that negotiators need information to coordinate their expectations and identify expected outcomes. In their study, Donohue and Diez defined *information* "as any statement or set of materials that may provide knowledge of the opponent's expected outcomes" (p. 309). Negotiators strategically increase or decrease the amount of information they supply to one another. They use directives to get one another to reveal information, for instance "Tell me about . . ." Face-threatening directives are used to challenge or force the partner to comply. Negotiators use more face-threatening directives when their goals are different, when they are unwilling to cooperate, when procedures for conducting the negotiation are not rigid, when participants have a substantial relational history, and when participants feel personally involved with the negotiation content. During combative negotiation, information is strategically used on a win–loss basis. In integrative negotiation, participants are more willing to share information. During combative negotiation, participants attempt to impose rigid obligations on one another to respond to directives.

This analysis suggests that several factors are basic to information seeking, its impact on judgment, and degrees of interpersonal liking. The value of most information is not determined by its ability to solve some problem with fixed probabilities, such as a card game. Information is best defined in terms of the impact data has on persons, given a variety of factors such as interpersonal attraction, willingness to seek information; and then allowing the information to affect judgment and self-confidence.

These factors are likely to impinge on your estimates of when you have sufficient information to reduce uncertainty and make your decision, whether about interpersonal partners or purchases. This kind of reasoning explains why you estimate whether you like the salespeople you meet and calculate whether their statements match your perceptions. You should be able to understand even better why you behave differently if you are confident in your judgment about the purchase regardless of your relationship with the salesperson. In friendship situations, people seek information from those they like, but mostly to ascertain agreement rather than find disagreement. If they find information that can affect their liking of a friend, they tend not to want or believe the information; they require additional information to decide about the friendship. Many other applications of this theory are likely to come to mind, but this brief summary suffices to show some relevant variables involved in information-seeking and interpersonal communication. This theme is expanded in chapters 6 and 7.

UNCERTAINTY REDUCTION – SEEKING INFORMATION IN ORGANIZATIONAL CONTEXTS

A great deal has been written about the role of information in organizations. As was discussed earlier in this chapter, information theory and systems theory became close allies in the 1960s and 1970s. Together, they can account for how systems – large or small – need and obtain information to adjust dynamically to their environment. Every day, new communication technologies are designed and produced to help people in companies communicate more successfully within and outside of their corporate confines. Such innovation may be implemented with disregard for the humans who are expected to create, store, and transmit the information. For that reason, assumptions regarding which information systems to implement and their consequences on the people in organizations pose major challenges to people who manage these organizations (Walton, 1982).

Underpinning this research is the theme that the desire to reduce uncertainty motivates people in organizations to obtain and share information. This model applies to all aspects of systems: interpersonal interaction, networks, and contact with external audiences through public relations, marketing, and advertising. Some interpersonal communication research addresses the ways individuals seek, share, and use information during interactions with other members of organizations. Given this range of topics, Fisher (1978) believed that network research "expanded the 'connectedness' dimension from that of merely a message-exchange channel to a broader concept of relationship or kinship" (p. 95). Communication can be used to transmit and receive information; humans use feedback to determine whether their communication is achieving the goal of adapting to the environment and other systems (Fisher, 1978, 1982; Krippendorff, 1977; Schramm, 1955; Weiner, 1948).

Information theory, once it became augmented by cybernetics, gave the rationale needed to understand organizations as dynamic information processing organisms. The best metaphor for understanding a system is the *dynamic organism* — a living creature that takes energy from its environment by eating. Through dynamic interaction with its environment, an organism takes in the energy needed to survive. Social systems use information as "energy."

Information, coupled with other cybernetic, adaptative behaviors, gives organisms the means to steer a course by which to achieve their objectives. Open systems let in information that helps them adapt; closed systems do not. Rather than thinking of systems as either closed or open, it is best to think in terms of degrees of openness. Open systems take in information to assess whether their actions are moving them toward their goals. For instance, marketing studies are conducted to determine whether companies are selling the right goods or radio stations are playing the music the public wants to hear. Through the influence of cybernetics, terms such as *intelligence, adaptation,* and *growth* have become key variables for explaining how communication networks operate and how organizations achieve self-modification.

Placing cybernetics in context, Krippendorff (1977) reasoned that "systems theory emphasizes properties of *wholes* and *parts, relationships* and *hierarchies,* while cybernetics focuses on *behavior, processes,* and *circular communication*" (p. 152). Systems theory describes the components of an organization whereas cybernetics offers a rationale for how it adapts to its environment. Krippendorff believed that information theory expands the basic stimulus–response paradigm, which only links incoming stimuli and triggered responses to explain how organizations adapt. Beyond this foundation, he explained, "the information processing approach considers cognition as a computational process that involves possibly large quantities of information stemming from past experiences, including fictional accounts, future projections, values, and purposes" (1977, p. 159). People are information processors, and social systems are means for handling information. Information theory linked to cybernetics enriches the explanation of how people in complex organizations, through their abilities, adapt to their environments to think and use information for strategic decision making.

Explanations of how communication supports organizations feature the characteristics of a system. One characteristic is *homeostasis,* the tendency for the system to adapt dynamically to survive and prosper. Another characteristic is *equifinality,* the ability of systems to reach the same goal with different means. *Wholeness* means that a system is a collection of parts but it is nonsummative; it is more than the sum of its parts. *Openness* refers to a system's ability to interchange information dynamically with its environment to adapt and survive. *Complexity* means that systems are not simple and tend to become more complex and differentiated over time. Systems have the characteristic of *self-regulation,* the ability to set goals and guide their actions using feedback to evaluate their efforts to achieve those goals. Systems are characterized by *hierarchy,* which means that an organization is a suprasystem that consists of layers of subsystems, which are in turn divided into sub-subsystems and so forth. By understanding hierarchy, we should be able to better understand systems' tendency to become increasingly complex (Fisher, 1978; Krippendorff, 1977).

Each of these characteristics has implications for how communication and information exchange occur in an organization. A company publishing a newspaper is a good illustration of these principles. A newspaper strives to maintain homeostasis by keeping a balance in many ways, one of which is to get information which is interesting to and desired by readers; the size of the newspaper will be influenced by the number of readers, the amount each is willing to pay for each day's copy, and the willingness and ability of advertisers to spend money that defrays printing costs and increases profit. A newspaper must balance itself with other news sources in a community, such as radio and television. Two reporters exhibit equifinality by getting their stories in different ways; one reporter may be subtle and the other very aggressive. All of the systems of the newspaper constitute its wholeness; a newspaper must have reporters, printers, accountants, editors, procurement, maintenance, sales, and distribution. Reporters help the paper to be open to the environment, and readership surveys are another kind of openness by which the newspaper management attempts to understand and adapt to its environment. A small town newspaper may have few people who do many tasks (low complexity) whereas a major city newspaper may have many people, each of whom does few tasks (high complexity). A newspaper must self-regulate; if circumstances change, so must the paper. For instance, legal interpretations of libel may make reporters and editors more cautious in regard to what they print about persons. Hierarchy refers to the organizational structure of a system. You might immediately assume that hierarchy follows the patterns of the organizational chart with management at the top because it is most important. *Hierarchy* in systems terminology refers not to importance but to arrangement, because each part of the system is important; take one part away and the entire system changes. If reporters do not report well or maintenance does not keep the presses operating, the paper will not be produced despite the "power" of management. Hierarchy refers to levels of specificity; a system is divided into subsystems, and sub-subsystems. One system is reporters, which is divided into subsystems such as local news, sports, business, and fashion.

This illustration portrays the routine efforts an organization makes to adapt to its environment. Dynamic changes occur when information becomes more complex, the information environment becomes turbulent, or people experience information overload. Under these conditions, companies use scanning and probing to acquire information (input) from the external environment. This information is throughput (processed and used to reduce uncertainty) and output (the product of the throughput is sent to the appropriate personnel). Once information has been acquired, several factors affect what is done with it. For instance, information can be routed from people in one part of the organization to people in another part. During this process, the information may be altered, summarized, or delayed at each point where one person has access to it before passing it on to others.

Huber and Daft (1987) explained this process by featuring several concepts. *Complexity* is a measure of the number of variables that must be considered when processing information about an organization's environment. A situation is complex if it requires attention to many variables. A crash of a major airline might be complex if variables such as terrorism, pilot error, or structural flaws are equally probable as causes. *Turbulence* refers to the degree of stability or instability in the environment; maximum turbulence results in maximum entropy, randomness, or uncertainty. While the stock market was wildly fluctuating in October of 1987, so many factors were occurring that most people had a hard time keeping up with the turbulence. Turbulence results from two factors: instability (frequency of change) and randomness (unpredictability of frequency and direction of change). *Information load* is the amount of information and the difficulty of obtaining and processing it in meaningful ways within the organization to adapt maximally to the environment. A student who has too many difficult classes in a semester may experience information overload. Add to this load the problems of a family member who is suffering from cancer and the load increases. In times of turbulence, Huber and Daft reasoned, organizations seek to protect the basis of their business and increase their means for adapting to their environment. Huber and Daft predicted that information load, complexity, and turbulence will increase. These changes will have dramatic implications for organizational communication and organizations' abilities to reduce uncertainty. How quickly and effectively any person handles information in an organization depends on many factors, especially workload and competence. Thus, Huber and Daft (1987) concluded, if the sender is either cognitively or logistically overloaded, it is likely that messages will be modified (distorted or abbreviated).

Applying the uncertainty reduction paradigm, Huber and Daft (1987) studied how companies monitor their environments to discover problems or opportunities and how they extract, process, and act on information from those environments. One problem, information load, occurs when information processing becomes difficult due to its quantity, ambiguity, and variety. *Quantity* is the number of messages received per unit of time. If a person gets several conflicting reports on the same topic, he or she is experiencing quantity. *Ambiguity* means that symbols or messages can have multiple interpretations. A person with whom you are romantically interested may signal that he or she likes you but also indicates what you could interpret as disinterest as well. *Variety* refers to the complexity and turbulence of the information stream. While studying for an exam, you may have lots of information (complexity), and members of your study group may have different opinions in regard to what the information means and how it can be used to answer questions (turbulence). Perhaps members of your study group have different notes from the same lecture.

Complexity can be subdivided into three components: numerosity, diversity, and interdependence. *Numerosity* is the number of components in the environment; for instance, if you try to keep up with all teams who participate in a sport (and all of the players of that sport) you are required to deal with more information than if you only follow one team and its players. *Diversity* refers to the differences among markets served; for example if a company provides one line of clothing for men only, getting and making sense of customers' reactions to the quality and style of the clothing is different than if the company produces ten lines of clothing for different age groups of both sexes. *Interdependence* refers to the relationship that exists when many companies share the same environment and develop complex relationships and dependencies on one another. As an example of this last variable, you might think how buyers and sellers of used homes are both interested in the current market values of homes, but for quite different reasons. Buyers want to be able to see how little they can pay for a piece of property, whereas sellers want to use those data to maximize their profits. Using these constructs, Huber and Daft (1987) postulated that the more complex the environment, the more resources the organization will have to commit to scanning for information that can be used to take advantage of opportunities and avoid problems. In this way, Huber and Daft defined "perceived environmental uncertainty," which consists of several factors: amount of information, specificity of messages about the environment, and the quality of messages about the environment.

Organizations need the ability to change; to do so requires effective acquisition and processing of information. How well organizations obtain and transmit information internally and externally is vital to their ability to innovate. Innovation within an organization is influenced by the degree to which management encourages it, the number of channels used to transmit information about it, and the degree to which supervisors personally seek information about the innovation. Impetus to adopt any innovation correlates with the emphasis an organization places on innovation in general (Hoffman & Roman, 1984).

In this way, companies vary in their abilities to obtain and utilize information. The same can be said about the departments or subsystems of those organizations. Depending on how cybernetics is used, an organization's adaptation can be mechanistic or dynamic (Morgan, 1982). The mechanistic view of cybernetics features the selection of those activities that are most likely to achieve an organization's goals. A classic example of this mechanistic approach is a thermostat, which regulates the comfort of a room by reading its temperature and making the appropriate signals to the heating or cooling system. Adaptation occurs within a limited range of goals and activities. In this view, systems are designed and set into operation to satisfy a narrow range of goals that may ignore many others that are not noticed because they are perceived to be outside of the immediate system.

In contrast to this mechanistic view, Morgan (1982) argued that cybernetics should be approached as an epistemology—a way of thinking about an organization as the means for looking for new and better goals by which to guide its actions. This, he believed, is a constructive way to seek information—in a sense by looking for uncertainty that needs to be reduced. To illustrate the point, recall the story of the fellow who felt successful that he had cornered the buggywhip market only to discover that there no longer was a market. The point is this: Cybernetics can be applied narrowly to argue that a company is in harmony with its society because the organization is at peace. Cybernetics can be viewed too narrowly in this regard. The search for information must include surveillance of the environment to see how it is changing and why. A cybernetic device such as a thermostat does not draw information from the environment to determine how and why changes are occurring, but knows only that they are—the temperature is warmer or colder. Reading this information, a thermostat instructs the heating or cooling system appropriately. Cybernetic adjustment to the environment must include the possibility of establishing new goals, developing new criteria for evaluating success, and being sensitive to change and turbulence. A cybernetic system that does not include these features can become static and close itself to its environment.

In these ways, systems theory and information theory have made important contributions to efforts to explain how and why people communicate in their capacity as members of organizations.

UNCERTAINTY REDUCTION-SEEKING INFORMATION IN MEDIATED CONTEXTS

To apply information theory to mediated communication seems almost too obvious to require explanation. After all, don't the media exist to provide information and entertainment? But the issue is more complex than that.

Developed in its "bare bones" fashion, the role of information in media might be described in terms of who is saying what to whom under what circumstances and with what effect (Lasswell, 1948). This linear model is typical of the views expressed by Shannon and Weaver (1949), Westley and MacLean (1957), and to a lesser extent, Schramm (1954, 1955). What can be said of information in mediated contexts?

How this question is answered depends largely on whether a receiver of information is viewed as a passive receptacle into which a sender injects information or as an active participant who seeks information. Reinforcement (selective exposure) theory and uses and gratifications theory, as well as other theories of mediated communication, challenge the sender-to-receiver paradigm.

Reinforcement theory rests on research findings that the media have limited effects because viewers, readers, and listeners select programming and information to which they want to be exposed. The notion that people seek information that serves their needs is fundamental to selective exposure theory. For instance, subjects who experienced high threat by hearing about a violent crime that occurred near them (on campus) or low threat (hearing about a crime across town) expressed preference for film clips containing retribution, but did not want to view film clips regarding information on attacks, or comedy, or romantic sequences (Boyanowsky, 1977).

Uses and gratifications theory contends that receivers are dynamic because they can and will seek sources of information and entertainment to satisfy their needs. This theory can be modeled this way: Needs that have psychological and social origins lead individuals to have expectations of the mass media and other sources, which lead to differential patterns of media exposure to gratify those needs.

Researchers have debated which list of needs is most accurate. One list of needs features diversion or escape, personal relations and affiliation, personal identity and self-esteem, and surveillance (Katz, Blumler, & Gurevitch, 1974). In a study of students (middle school, high school, and college), three categories of gratification behavior were found to influence selection of communication channels: surveillance/entertainment, affective guidance, and behavioral guidance (Lometi, Reeves, & Bybee, 1977). The first category is oriented to information seeking whereas the latter two reflect the desire to learn the norms that indicate which feelings and behavior are appropriate.

Preferences regarding kinds of information and gratification sought are used to predict media use. Media selection and use behavior are not merely influenced by the gratification to be received by watching a specific program (a favorite newscast) or that type of program in general (news). An estimation of the amount of gratification that will be derived by watching one program is meaningful only by comparing it to other programs that could be watched or other activities in which the person could engage. Viewers may monitor their behavior to infer that they must like a certain kind of program because they watch it often (Palmgreen, Wenner, & Rayburn, 1981).

People seek information in product purchase situations (e.g., buying cosmetics) for social comparison as well as personal reasons. Interpersonal–social influence variables are as important for predicting the types and amounts of information sought as are personal variables, such as education or desire to reduce uncertainty. Social comparison influences operate when individuals are uncertain whether their judgments about a product are correct and when they need social approval (Moschis, 1980).

Entropy is a valuable concept for discussing information in mediated contexts. If an audience experiences needs and desires gratification, and if the number of media is large or the amount of information is rich, then individuals are more likely to satisfy their needs. Applying the concept of entropy, Chaffee and Wilson (1977) found a significant relationship between the number of local mass media institutions and the ability to diffuse diverse ideas in a community. When many media outlets discuss a wide array of topics, the information environment is "rich." The amount of information being provided by the media can be described as constituting a news hole. The amount of news space and time is fixed: Each day approximately the same amount of time is given to all news on TV and radio, and newspapers are approximately the same length each day—except Sunday. The importance of each topic discussed by the media depends on how much time and space it receives in proportion to all other news topics.

Entropy is used to refer to the likelihood that people will find information they want and that the media will get the information to them. A long-standing assumption of media effects is that if a public's knowledge is to be increased on a topic, then media have to provide more information to increase the public's chances of being exposed to it. In this regard, the number of media outlets in a community can remain constant and amount of information can increase if the proportion of media space or time devoted to an issue increases. If more time or space is devoted, the probability of people encountering the information increases. During an information campaign, the proportion of time or space given to one bit of information increases at the expense of another. Thus, Salmon (1986) concluded, the impact of an information campaign probably depends on the extent the information being disseminated relates to people's self-interest, the amount of information available in the environment prior to the campaign, and the magnitude and duration of the campaign.

In addition to using entropy to discuss information diffusion throughout a large population, the concept is used to analyze the content of individual programs, for instance the degree of abstractness present in a television program. Age and education level of viewers correlate with tolerance for entropy (amount of complexity). Older and better educated viewers can understand more abstract television programs than can their younger or less educated counterparts (Krull, Watt, & Lichty, 1977).

Diffusion of innovation is one of many typical contexts in which media as well as interpersonal contacts provide information and influence opinion and judgment. Studying how innovation occurs, Rogers (1962) argued that it consists of three stages: invention, diffusion (or communication), and consequences. Diffusion means that an idea spreads from a point of origin to others and eventually achieves general or limited acceptance. The information flows through networks. The nature of networks and the roles key people play in them determine the likelihood that the innovation will be adopted. Networks are more than simple information linkages among people. The key is the extent to which convergence occurs where people who could adopt the innovation begin to get the same information from credible sources. The process by which innovation spreads throughout society is not linear (Rogers & Kincaid, 1981). Although promoters of an innovation try to channel information to adopters, to a large extent the information is randomly diffused. Information is sought primarily by persons who adopt more quickly than others.

Innovation diffusion research has attempted to explain the variables that influence how and why users adopt a new information medium, such as *videotex,* the process of receiving printed messages through a computer or video screen instead of reading them in a newspaper. Adoption of a new medium depends on adopters' information need, which medium adopters prefer, availability of the medium, and familiarity with it. Adoption of a new medium depends on the extent to which it is perceived to be more effective, convenient, or gratifying than old ones. A new medium has its greatest impact on media or leisure activities that are its closest equivalents. For this reason, movie going declined after the adoption of television (Heikkinen & Reese, 1986). Media use preferences depend on availability and accessibility more than content. The most useful and gratifying media are television, newspapers, and books, in contrast to radio, magazines, and films (Kippax & Murray, 1980). Findings such as these vary according to the kind of audience that is studied.

Another variable that influences how people accept and use information is capacity. The term *capacity* is used to address the extent that the parts of the communication process can handle information. *Sender capacity* refers to the amount of information that a source (person or object such as a computer or a library) can supply at a given time vis-à-vis the receiver's needs. *Message capacity* is the amount of information that can be contained in a single message, such as a specific combination of words (the space of a memo, or duration of a conversation). Some messages efficiently deliver the content; others, for instance, are "too wordy." *Channel capacity* is "equal to the maximum rate (in bits per second) at which useful information (i.e., total uncertainty minus noise uncertainty) can be transmitted over the channel" (Shannon & Weaver, 1949, p. 21). Such measures could apply to the kind of conductor involved; for instance fibre optics has more capacity than does standard transmission cable. *Time capacity* is a measure of how long communicators have or take to transmit a message as well as process it. If time is shorter, the message must be more brief or efficient or information must be omitted – or other types of capacity must be increased. *Receiver capacity* refers to the ability to receive and process information. This capacity can be a function of each individual's cognitive ability or experience with the information. It could refer to the person's need for information. The human mind files and retrieves information based on associations (which ideas, thoughts, objects, feelings, or concepts go with one another) as well as the level of interest the person has for the information (Anderson, 1985). To illustrate sender and receiver capacity, imagine a small computer drawing information from (or sending it to) a large one. A small computer has less capacity and therefore sends or receives at a slower rate, measured in bits per second.

This brief discussion of information in mediated contexts demonstrates that an interactive, reciprocal relationship exists between the audience that wants information and the media that provide it. Key factors in this process are the probability that people will encounter and be satisfied by the information. People seek and use media and message content to reduce uncertainty and achieve social competence.

CONCLUSION

Information is basic to communication in all contexts. Craig (1979) urged communication researchers to study cognitive processes to understand the content of what people say and the effect it has on interaction. Cognitive science stresses that people communicate about something, a view that requires understanding the effects that perception, forgetting, memory, and recall have on communication.

During interpersonal communication, people lower or raise certainty by asking questions, eliciting responses, and attributing personal characteristics to one another. People communicate by using conventional patterns or interaction rituals to lower entropy. In organizations, information is a medium of exchange that can be used to correct activities of individuals, groups, or companies. Individuals use media to reduce uncertainty even though they seek information selectively. Prior to finalizing decisions, people seek information that reinforces the decision they want to make, and after they make a decision, they seek information to reduce the dissonance associated with the decision (Wheeless & Cook, 1985). An understanding of information supplies additional rationale to explain how and why people communicate to come into meaningful contact with one another and their environment.

5 Persuasion: Concepts and Contexts

Persuasion theory and research deal with social influence — people communicating to affect one another and themselves. Society could not exist if people did not influence one another's opinions and behavior through discourse.

Having said that, we could claim that all communication is social influence. Berlo (1960) made communication and persuasion synonymous by concluding that "we communicate to influence — to affect with intent" (p. 12). In interpersonal communication, people want to know how to influence each other's judgments and behaviors and to understand how they themselves are influenced so that they can control the degree to which they are persuaded. Corporations influence employees' opinions and behaviors, shape images the external public has of them, and create customers' preferences for their products or services. The opinion climate inside companies results, at least in part, from management's influence on employees. Persuasion, media effects, advertising, marketing, political communication, and propaganda are terms that have become so entwined they are often used synonymously.

The previous chapter showed how information and persuasion are interrelated — especially because both concepts are used to study influence. So what is unique about persuasion, a concept that has been widely studied for centuries? More than 2,000 years ago, Aristotle (1954) called *rhetoric* the art of creating persuasive arguments. Since at least that time, *persuasion* has been viewed as strategic behavior whereby one person influences the opinions, judgments, and behavior of others. However, as Petty and Cacioppo (1986b) noted, "after accumulating a vast quantity of data and an impressive number of theories—perhaps more data and theory than on any other single topic in the social sciences," researchers do not agree "if, when and how traditional source, message, recipient and channel variables affect attitude change" (pp. 124–125).

Persuasion research is so complex and problematic that generalizing about the influence process can be misleading, if not downright incorrect. Efforts to study persuasion are frustrated by the vast complexity of the human mind, which is capable of receiving and handling many influences simultaneously. Moreover, persuasive impact can result from interaction of many factors such as message variables—especially content, structure, and style. This list of variables includes those related to sources—especially credibility, interpersonal relationships (such as liking or conflict), channels, and idiosyncratic characteristics of receivers (including the extent to which people are self-interested in outcomes and expect to obtain rewards or avoid punishments by taking one action instead of another).

Research and theory are hard pressed to explain the interactions between these variables and thereby predict how to achieve persuasive influence. For these reasons, this chapter cannot encompass all of what is needed to understand and achieve persuasive influence, but it will review major concepts, theories, and research related to social influence and show how they are relevant to interpersonal, organizational, and mediated contexts.

TOWARD A DEFINITION

Persuasion, Miller (1980) reasoned, is the use of messages to modify behavior by using some combination of coercive force and appeals that affect reason and emotion. Emphasizing the role threat and coercion can play in persuasion, he recognized the influence that can result when, for instance, a child threatens to run away from home rather than eat vegetables or when terrorists hijack a plane demanding release of their compatriots. Quite accurately, he does not view reason and emotions as qualitatively different concepts that can be easily separated. Some researchers believe *reason* is the logical, analytic part of judgment whereas *emotion* involves feelings that influence judgment and behavior. But each plays an important role in social influence, and both can account for shifts in opinion and behavior. Receivers (persuadees) can be active participants in social influence, although they do so in response to persuaders (Miller, 1987). Rather than being passive, persuadees often seek persuasive influence. Is that not what people do when they look through a catalog, enter a car dealership, or go to a political rally to have their voting preference influenced? Persuadees ignore, resist, and refute messages with which they disagree. They can be dynamic and may distort messages through selective perception.

Instead of using reason and emotion as key terms, most researchers prefer concepts such as attitude to define the cognitive processes involved in the reception and consideration of messages. By 1935, at least in the judgment of the esteemed psychologist Allport, attitude had become the most important term in social psychology and persuasion research. In the tradition of persuasion studies that feature attitude and attitude change, Devito (1986) defined it as "the process of influencing attitudes and behavior" (p. 225).

Although extremely difficult to define, attitudes, often in conjunction with companion terms such as beliefs and values, are featured in persuasion research. The dominant paradigm behind such studies is this: Attitudes and attitude changes precede behavior and behavior change. One reason that attitudes continue to be used to account for motivation is that they readily lend themselves to research techniques. Rare is the student who escapes a four-year college education without being asked to participate in a study that measures attitudes, whether for clinical, career diagnostic, or research purposes. Such research can lead to the conclusion that thoughts are neat and orderly and people receive and process persuasive messages mindfully. Many people involved in advertising believe, naively, that a message containing an appeal will necessarily stimulate a favorable attitude response and guide behavior.

Two landmark studies challenged the attitude–behavior relationship. One was the work by LaPiere (1934) who toured the country with a Chinese couple who ate at cafés and stayed at hotels. Afterward, LaPiere sent a post card to the establishments asking whether they would serve Chinese customers. The vast majority said they would not even though they had. Even though his research suffered methodological flaws, LaPiere led many to question seriously whether behavior necessarily follows attitudes.

A second conceptual breakthrough in the attitude–action relationship was produced by Bem (1965, 1968, 1972), who noted that people often infer their attitudes from their behavior rather than inferring their behavior from their attitudes. An illustration of his classic principle is this: "I must like (attitude) brown bread because I often eat it" (behavior). The paradigm behind this statement differs from the attitude-to-behavior paradigm reflected in the following statement: "I should buy brown bread because I like it." You may intuit that both models work in your life. But the first one is a powerful counterbalance to the traditional one, which assumes that attitude and attitude change must precede behavior. It allows researchers to discuss the relationship this way: At times people change their behavior, and then their attitudes.

Such is the case because people change their attitudes to conform to their behavior, as well as change behavior to conform to attitudes. Many employees experience this phenomenon when, after working at a company for several years, they express liking for their jobs to rationalize why they have worked there so long. Each of us feels cognitive discomfort when our behavior and attitudes do not coincide; if behavior cannot change, then attitudes may. This approach to the attitude–behavior relationship argues that people monitor their behavior to know what their attitudes are and act in ways (manage impressions of themselves to others and themselves) so that their attitudes and behavior are consonant.

One explanation of how behavior change can lead to attitude change was supplied by forced compliance research (Festinger & Carlsmith, 1959). Parents "force" children to brush their teeth, take baths, and eat proper meals. Eventually, these behaviors become the norm, and attitudes are formed to correspond to them. Likewise, social change can be created by requiring people not to discriminate on the basis of race, sex, age, handicap, or religion. Eventually, such behavior may become ingrained and result in new, adjusted attitudes.

These observations are made early in this chapter to have you consider why persuasion should *not* be thought of as a linear process, nor one in which sources are always active and receivers are always passive. Your definition of persuasion must acknowledge that people sometimes persuade themselves. It should account for the impact of many kinds of communication stimuli, including words, other symbols such as numbers and pictures, nonverbal cues, veiled and overt threats, and coercion. It must deal with opinions that result from careful consideration, based on reasoning and evidence as well as nearly mindless responses to clever ads — nearly void of information — that claim products to be "new and improved."

Your definition of persuasion must be sensitive to persuasive methods that occur in different contexts, such as interpersonal, group, organizational, and mediated — including what some call propaganda. Persuasion theory must account for a great deal of resistance on the part of the target persuadee, as well as easy compliance. The definition must account for idiosyncrasies of personality, such as high or low self-esteem and need for peer approval. Given these conditions, *persuasion* can be defined as the facet of communication that focuses on processes of social influence.

AN OVERVIEW

Many misconceptions about persuasion result from incorrect assumptions about the ways receivers are influenced. Communication students, particularly those interested in advertising, public relations, and mass media effects, often overestimate the impact that messages have on receivers.

Some of these students defend their bias by saying, "Advertisers would not spend all of that money if their ads did not work." This view can be corrected partially by recalling how many ads you watch, listen to, or read that do not create a favorable attitude or lead to action. Think of the wreck on your home and budget if you purchased everything you see advertised. Many ad campaigns with enormous budgets have failed; some have backfired. Many messages designed to influence opinion or behavior do not.

Before analyzing the major theories of persuasion, we should examine some factors that are basic to persuasion theory. This foundation will increase your insight into how people receive and process persuasive messages.

1. Receiver exposure, attention, perception, and retention are selective. This selectivity is based on a vast array of idiosyncrasies that depend on the persons involved—messages, type of decision, circumstances, and values people believe to be relevant (Heath, 1976). Receivers of the same persuasive message often perceive and interpret it differently; what one receiver sees as an attractive item, for instance, may be viewed as wasteful by someone else. Some research finds that people prefer messages that are consistent with their existing opinions; other research finds just the opposite. People often pay more attention to ads and statements about a product after, rather than before, it is purchased. This information is used to confirm the purchase, exemplifying a postdecision rather than predecision attention model. People tend to ignore or forget information that conflicts with their purchase decision. They attend to messages provided by people who are similar to them more than by persons who are dissimilar—unless dissimilarity is overridden by other circumstances, such as status or competence. You might seek advice on making investments from someone who is different from you, someone who is rich and therefore of different status. When you ask strangers for street or road directions when you are lost in an unfamiliar town, you probably check to see if they are competent more than if they are similar to you. (Some people you ask for directions may seem similarly lost because they are unsure how to get from here to there!) A message may gain attention because the audience is self-interested in its usefulness, or attention can have nothing to do with self-interest but result from other stimuli, such as novelty (Wheeless & Cook, 1985).

2. Reactions to persuasive messages depend on the extent to which receivers are self-interested and whether holding opinions or taking actions can help to achieve rewards or avoid undesirable outcomes. These two powerful variables affect how people receive, process, and act on messages (Ajzen & Fishbein, 1980; Petty & Cacioppo, 1986a; Sherif, Sherif, & Nebergall, 1965).

3. The message-impact model must account for simple and complex relationships. Some messages have a lot of impact even though the persuadee expends minimal effort in the process of receiving and thinking about them. Advertisements for soft drinks are good examples of how people make some decisions based more on glitz than fact. In other instances, the message alone cannot influence judgment or behavior. In such multiple-factor situations, many variables interact to produce acceptance or resistance to the message. For instance, peer approval may increase or decrease message impact, and receivers may have conflicting pieces of evidence that need to be incorporated into the final decision.

4. People are capable of resisting persuasion. Such resistance can result from reactions to message content, but it can also result from a negative reaction to the source. Resistance is likely to occur when people need to comply with group norms that are contradictory to message content or advocated behavior. People who do not see the benefits of action, or think it fraught with liabilities, are likely to resist messages.

5. To some extent (probably varying with circumstances and individual differences), people are capable of self-persuasion. They solicit and accept information and influence, sometimes from many sources, and weigh it to reach conclusions, form attitudes, or decide on behaviors.

6. Some social influence occurs so subtly that people do not think of it as persuasion. This is the case when people acquire norms, values, judgments, preferences, and behavioral intentions merely by adopting the idiom used by those with whom they associate. The language you use is loaded with attitudes, many of which are so much a part of your thoughts that you have difficulty recognizing them. Idioms contain social reality; along with the words we learn, each of us takes on attitudes toward people of other nationalities, ethnic groups, or religions. For instance, people raised in one religion will think that attending a particular movie is a sin, whereas people raised in other religions will not.

7. Attempts to separate persuasion from information create an inaccurate division. Studies demonstrate that information is invaluable to persuasive impact. For instance, beliefs can be held with a high degree of certainty despite the lack of information to support them. However, beliefs that are based on accumulated information are more resistant to change than are those merely held with a high degree of certainty (Danes, 1978). When attitudes are stable (held for a long time), they reflect increasingly the information (number of messages) that the individual knows supports them (Saltiel & Woelfel, 1975). Studying media impact, Alper and Leidy (1969) concluded, "Information need not lead to attitude change, but attitude change is improbable without any input of information" (p. 556). When people receive messages that contain conflicting information, they are less likely to recall that information or to have a favorable attitude toward the

message than are people who do not receive conflicting information (Burgoon, 1975). Examining the impact of information on persuasion, Morley and Walker (1987) found that it produces belief change only when it is very important, novel, and plausible. This study did not confirm previous results, which found that information could change beliefs even if all three factors are not present. Studies such as these argue against separating information from persuasion.

8. People want useful and "accurate" attitudes because a major function of an attitude is to help them adapt their behavior to circumstances. Information helps people understand reality and reduce uncertainty.

CONCEPTUAL AND RESEARCH FOUNDATIONS: LEARNING THEORY

Rhetoric, propaganda, attitude change, motivation, and media effects studies—all of these helped establish the underpinnings for contemporary persuasion studies. Before the 1960s, most approaches to persuasion were linear, predicated on the model of an active sender influencing a relatively passive receiver. Attitude change was featured as a consequence of a message provided by a source, whereby the receiver learned information that affected opinions or behavior—or both.

Until the mid-1950s, persuasion research was driven by a model of human thought and behavior that placed attitudes central in the cognitive system. Communication—often in the form of messages—was used as the independent variable, and attitudes and behavior were dependent variables. One limitation of persuasion research has been an over reliance on an attitude, attitude change, and attitude–behavior model. Defining attitudes is difficult, as is linking them to behavior. Much of this kind of research is driven by the convenience of doing pencil–paper response item tests of attitude. The logic often goes this way: Give an audience several response items and use the results to shape a persuasive message. By this method, a politician might discover that people prefer candidates who are moderate, honest, strong on law and order, and fiscally responsible. By this analysis, a candidate should assert to be all of these. But what happens if the opponent makes the same claims? A campaign could come down to which person can prove with information that he or she is more moderate, honest, committed to law and order, and fiscally responsible.

The drive-motive model that was popular in early persuasion studies assumed that people had many drives that could be tapped by persuasive messages. The reasoning was this: Attach an action to a motive and people will respond accordingly. By this logic, many people thought that anything could be sold if attached to a drive-motive. But what happens if all perfume or cologne is marketed by appeals to sex, or food is marketed by appeals to taste? What distinguishes one product from another? Such a model was too unrefined to be helpful. Drive-motive approaches to persuasion remain popular among some students of advertising and marketing, who continue believe that behavior is largely an outcome of inherent and learned drives and motives that can be tapped by persuasive messages. This model is limited for at least two reasons: (a) People do not always respond in singular, causal ways to satisfy motives. Motives often conflict; all cannot be satisfied. Much of our behavior is not merely a response to inherent or learned motives. (b) Even if people respond to motives, it would be impossible to list all motives and connect them to all behaviors in ways that would allow persuaders to move receivers to act like a puppeteer makes marionettes move.

To address inadequacies of these models, a major series of persuasion studies was conducted at Yale in the 1940s and 1950s. This work also grew out of efforts to understand the impact of "propaganda" on society and individual beliefs and behavior. This research project was especially important given a desire to build public commitment during wartime and divert public opinion away from "foreign" propaganda that many believed could subvert the United States war efforts. This research relied heavily on learning theory, which was very popular and subscribed to Lasswell's (1948) linear model: Who says what to whom with what effect.

The research led to the proposition:

> A major basis for acceptance of a given opinion is provided by arguments or reasons [obtained from a message] which, according to the individual's own thinking habits, constitute "rational" or "logical" support for the conclusion. In addition to supporting reasons, there are likely to be other special incentives involving anticipated rewards and punishments which motivate the individual to accept or reject a given opinion. (Hovland, Janis, & Kelley, 1953, p. 11)

These researchers argued that stimuli–data (messages) lead to learning through repeated actions (including statements made to oneself) and rewards. The task, the Yale group thought, was to understand how people accept and comprehend messages that subsequently guide behavior.

The original Yale model consisted of five parts thought to occur in this order: Once a message is received because it gains *attention,* and if it is *comprehended,* it will lead to *acceptance,* yielding to the message by deciding that it is reasonable. To have impact, a message must be *retained,* the ability and motivation to remember the information. If all of these factors are present, the message leads to *action.*

As is typical of research projects, the number of variables used in the model changed over time. For instance, the model was reduced to four components: attention, comprehension, anticipation, and evaluation. Attention, comprehension, and anticipation are learning factors; whereas evaluation is an acceptance factor. If individuals are motivated, they are likely to pay attention to messages, devote energy to comprehending them, and anticipate the implications of each, such as its rewards. Persuasibility was thought to be a product of ability factors, such as intellectual capacity and training in thinking about persuasive messages, and motive factors, such as temperament and habits of processing messages.

These researchers concluded that the variables which influence learning are facilitating factors whereas evaluation is an inhibiting factor. If motivating factors increase evaluation, a person is unlikely to be persuaded because flaws will be discovered in the message. Persuasibility was thought to result from the interaction of facilitating and inhibiting factors. For instance, when persons are low in motivation to use facilitating factors, persuasibility will decrease. However, low motivation to use an inhibiting factor increases persuasibility. Low motivation is likely to lessen the effect of all four factors, which has the same effect on persuasibility as does deficiency in those factors (Janis et al., 1959).

To refine the Yale model, McGuire (1968a, 1968b) reduced it to two variables: The probability (Pr) of opinion change *(O)* equals the product of reception *(R)* and yielding *(Y)*, which he expressed in the formula, Pr *(O)* = Pr *(R)* × Pr *(Y)*. He corrected the original model because he realized that reception does not always lead to yielding. His study produced the *compensatory assumption* that receiver characteristics, which increase reception, will decrease yielding. For instance, the ability to comprehend — as a part of reception — will decrease yielding. McGuire argued that anxiety usually lessens reception but increases yielding. Self-confident people will let in information (reception) but are willing to disagree with the source (not yield). The second major principle that McGuire contributed was the *situational weighting assumption*. If a message is easy to comprehend, reception is unlikely to be as important as yielding. When messages are complex, reception and comprehension are at least as important as yielding.

Without abandoning his commitment to reception and yielding as the central concepts, McGuire (1981) saw them as encompassing several specific stages of persuasive influence. Presented in the sequence in which they are likely to occur, the variables are:

1. being exposed to the message,
2. attending to it,
3. liking it and becoming interested in it,
4. comprehending it,
5. learning how to process and use it,

6. yielding to it,
7. memorizing it,
8. retrieving it as required,
9. using it to make decisions,
10. behaving in accord with the decision,
11. reinforcing the actions,and
12. consolidating the decision based on the success of the action.

Persuasive influence is possible at each stage.

In addition to striving to make encompassing statements about the persuasion process, Yale researchers examined how each component of the communication process figures in persuasion. Thus, for instance, by focusing on source variables, the researchers spawned decades of research into the effects source credibility has on attitude and behavior. The argument is that who the speaker is perceived to be affects the impact of the message. The Yale group argued that credibility depends on the extent to which the source is perceived to be expert, trustworthy, or affiliated with groups the receivers view positively. High credibility sources are more likely to create opinion change than are low credibility sources. This research team found that, over time, receivers dissociate the source from the message so that opinions received from a low credibility source can increase and those from a high credibility source decrease (Hovland et al., 1953). Fast talking sources are more credible than slower talkers. Although experts have high credibility on topics related to their expertise, the ideal source is one that is similar to but slightly higher in status than the receiver (Wright, 1981).

In recent years, the debate regarding source credibility has centered on which characteristics (such as dynamism, expertness, intelligence, trustworthiness, safety, or qualification) constitute credibility (Berlo, Lemert, & Mertz, 1969). Studies such as these are problematic for several methdological reasons; for instance, the categories used to define credibility are generated by researchers and may not the subjects' (Cronkhite & Liska, 1980). Although researchers differ about which factors are most important, they agree that receivers hold standards of credibility against which the sender and his or her presentation are compared favorably or unfavorably. Moreover, in the past several years, it has become apparent that what constitutes credibility changes according to situations and specific receiver expectations.

Pursuing this line of thought, Cronkhite and Liska (1980) reasoned that factors leading to credibility are dynamic and interactive, not static or singular. They are not static, for instance, because a source can perceive what standards of credibility a receiver expects under a set of circumstances and adapt to them. The receiver can observe characteristics of the source and use them to decide whether the source is credible; such decisions are sensitive to the goals that are salient in a particular situation. The credibility of a physician, for instance, regarding a medical problem might not be the same regarding playing golf or buying an automobile. Cronkhite and Liska concluded that people use the situation and the goals they have in that situation to construct their list of attributes of credibility relevant to those goals in that situation.

As additional evidence that credibility is not static, research indicates that if the qualifications of a source are identified late in the message, credibility has less effect than if that identification occurs prior to presentation of the message (O'Keefe, 1987). Although people claim that advertising in general lacks credibility, they recognize differences in credibility on an ad-by-ad basis. Attitudes toward advertising do not significantly influence attitudes toward content of specific ads (Muehling, 1987).

Nonverbal cues are vital to receivers' assessments of speaker credibility. Speakers are perceived to possess competence and composure when they exhibit greater vocal and facial pleasantness. Facial expressiveness increases perceptions of competence. Speakers who exhibit naturalness, dominance, and relaxed posture are viewed as sociable, especially when they have a pleasant voice. Speakers are thought to be more persuasive when they exhibit naturalness, facial expressiveness, and relaxed posture (Burgoon, Birk, & Pfau, 1990).

Miller (1987) argued that credibility is different for interpersonal situations than for other situations because, as conversations progress, the need for credibility may change. On one topic, one conversational partner may be more credible than the other; this relationship can reverse as conversational topics change. At one point in a conversation, one partner may be viewed as sufficiently credible, but the seriousness of the topic or the statements (verbal or nonverbal) by the individual may increase the need for credibility or alter the extent to which that partner is viewed as credible by the other. Interpersonal credibility depends on communication style and other tactics people use to induce others to like them.

This logic can apply to corporate communication as well because companies interact with various publics and respond to different circumstances. Companies must be aware of the consequences of the credibility of their claims regarding products, services, or their images. Their credibility changes over time. Regardless of the context, credibility is multifaceted, dynamic, and constantly changing.

In addition to source variables, the Yale research group studied how message variables affect opinion change. Their findings on fear appeals are particularly instructive. Studying how messages foster attention, they found that fear appeals increase attention to the extent that people see the threat applying to themselves or to persons for whom they are responsible. Intense fear appeals can inhibit attention and increase distraction, which impairs comprehension and leads to avoidance (Hovland et al., 1953).

Since the Yale studies, fear appeal research has produced conflicting results. Some studies concluded that high amounts of fear produce attitude change, but other studies found low amounts to be more effective. Evaluating the relationship between fear appeals and attitude change, Boster and Mongeau (1984) suggested that the amount of perceived fear results from a colinear relationship (direct interaction) between age and anxiety, which in turn affects attitude and behavior. Demographic and personality variables mediate the ways and extent to which fear affects attitudes and behavior. These findings suggest that caution be used when generalizing about the relationship between fear appeals, attitudes, and behavior.

Three factors appear to be important in regard to the impact of fear appeals: (a) the extent to which the object of fear is presented in extreme or noxious language, (b) the likelihood that the fear event will occur, and (c) the persuadee's ability to make a protective response. An assumption is that fear appeals are powerful because they are associated with negative outcomes, a prediction based on expectancy value theory (Rogers, 1975).

Studies of message effects compared two-sided versus one-sided presentations. Two-sided messages—those that present pros and cons—are more likely to be effective for receivers who are initially opposed to the arguments, who will hear the opposing side later, or who are better educated. One-sided presentation is best for people who initially support the message. Messages that are used to refute other messages are more effective when they present two sides rather than only one side. However, one-sided refutational messages are more persuasive than two-sided nonrefutational messages (Allen et al., 1990).

Since the Yale studies, other researchers have determined that sidedness may not operate alone. Persons who believe that an issue relates to their self-interest are more persuaded by two-sided arguments than by one-sided arguments. This is particularly true for persons who are more able to cope with uncertainty. The opposite is true for people who are less comfortable with uncertainty (Sorrentino, Bobocel, Gitta, Olson, & Hewitt, 1988).

Continuing the work of the Yale researchers, recent attention has been given to sidedness in advertising research. After years of avoiding comments about other products and assuming that only good news should be presented, researchers have discovered that two-sided presentations achieve higher commitments to purchase products (Golden & Alpert, 1987). Sidedness in advertising can include making negative comments about competitors' products as well as acknowledging limitations of the sponsor's products or services.

The study of persuasive messages also discussed the order in which message components are presented. Such research compared the impact of arguments heard early in a message or campaign (primacy) versus those heard at the end of a message or campaign (recency). Primacy is superior when it creates an incentive to learn—to take in the message. Strong arguments presented at the beginning of the message have more impact on those who are initially disinterested. Anxiety arousing arguments can disrupt the comprehension process and be counterproductive (Hovland et al., 1959).

Many subsequent studies have examined the impact of message variables on persuasiveness. A recurring theme is the persuasive impact of intense or figurative language. To further demonstrate how the factors of persuasiveness complement or mediate one another, language and source credibility have been found to interact; sources that use extensive figurative language are seen as being more authoritative (Reinsch, 1974).

Another instance where message and credibility interact is the effect evidence has on credibility. Factual evidence (information) increases the impact of persuasive messages. Although statistics increase persuasive impact, they have no greater effect than do other kinds of evidence. Use of evidence can increase speaker credibility. The quality of evidence is less a factor with disinterested audiences; for this reason, more arguments, regardless of their quality, will have more impact with less interested or uninvolved audiences. This is not the case for involved receivers; they are more discriminating in their reception and use of evidence (Reinard, 1988; Stiff, 1986). In fact, when people are involved with an issue, relevant information can change their opinions (Petty, Cacioppo, & Goldman, 1981).

Interested in how all elements of the communication process affect persuasion, Yale researchers also examined the receiver by looking for factors that influence persuasibility—the extent to which receivers can be readily persuaded. Believing that demographic factors (such as age or education) are unrelated to persuasibility, they concluded that it is a function of several factors that are situational. Females are not always more persuasible than males; nor are older people always less persuasible than younger people. People are more persuasible when they need information and when the information they receive does not conflict with what they know about the topic. When evaluating incoming messages, people rely on information with which they are familiar (Janis et al., 1959).

The Yale group also studied the effects of group affiliation on opinion change. They discovered that people who desire to belong to a group are most likely to accept the opinions of that group. Self-confident individuals who are less needful of a group are likely to be more independent in forming opinions (Hovland et al., 1953).

Even though the Yale studies relied on a sender-to-receiver paradigm and learning theory, they made a major contribution to persuasion research. This section has also presented research that extends and corrects the findings of the Yale researchers. This foundation undergirds the remainder of the chapter, which discusses other approaches to persuasion research. Among the most important corrections that have been made to the original Yale studies is the argument that people are active, as well as passive, in the formation of their opinions. Also, whereas much persuasion research is oriented toward antecedent–outcome relationships, some researchers use a rules perspective to explain how cognitions and behavior are influenced (Reardon, 1981).

SOCIAL LEARNING – SOCIAL COGNITIVE THEORY

To modify the orientation taken by Yale researchers, social learning – social cognitive theory developed to show how people actively participate in their own persuasion. Its major proponent, Bandura (1986) concluded, "Social cognitive theory embraces an interactional model of causation in which environmental events, personal factors, and behavior all operate as interacting determinants of each other. Reciprocal causation provides people with opportunities to exercise some control over their destinies as well as set limits of self-direction" (p. xi).

This theory is based on a learning theory paradigm, which argues that people seek to learn how to achieve rewards and avoid punishments. Although acknowledging humans' biological nature, the theory proposes that most motivation is not the result of internal drives but of preferences created to maximize rewards and avoid punishments. Preferences for action grow, at least in part, out of internal standards and evaluative reactions to one's own ability to perform to achieve rewards or avoid punishments.

This theory views behavior as being directed toward goals and outcomes projected into the future. Persons have some say over which of these goals they prefer, and based on that decision, they explore their options to achieve reward and avoid punishment. Projections into the future and self-motivation are possible because people are able to acquire knowledge through communication, forethought, vicarious experience of others' successes and failures, self-regulation, and self-reflection. The theory features three processes of change: acquisition, generality, and stability. The theory is interested in how people acquire beliefs and rules for obtaining rewards and avoiding punishment. It studies the extent to which beliefs about reward behavior generalize to various circumstances and attempts to determine which factors cause beliefs and behaviors to be stable.

This theory relies on the learning process. "Learning," Bandura observed

(1986), "is largely an information-processing activity in which information about the structure of behavior and about environmental events is transformed into symbolic representations that serve as guides for action" (p. 5). Social learning theory argues that people are neither driven by inner forces nor helplessly shaped by external ones. People can set goals and reward themselves; they are insightful as well as foresightful and do not rely exclusively on external forces for rewards. Social learning theory views people as capable of self-regulation, through self-reward and self-punishment. Individuals receive information from their environment that is used to create motivation. From this information, they learn the consequences of certain opinions and behaviors and select those that seem most likely to produce reward and avoid punishment.

At least four means are employed by each person to learn which opinions and behaviors are likely to produce desired results: direct experience, role playing, modeling, and information acquisition. By *direct experience,* people learn the consequences of opinions they hold and the behaviors they employ. *Role playing* allows them to try out opinions and behaviors without direct experience. For instance, children can play a role of "adult" to see how the attitudes and behaviors of adults are rewarded. *Modeling* is observational learning; other people (including actors who appear in ads) are used as models. If an individual believes that he or she can perform as the model does, then action is likely, given the assumption that action will produce the same rewards (or avoid punishments) as it did for the model. People learn from experiences of models to the extent that the model is similar and to the extent each person believes himself or herself able to perform as the model does. (For this reason, extremely attractive models in advertisements may not be as persuasive to average receivers as are models more similar to receivers in attractiveness.) Modeling can teach cognitive skills and processes as well as supply opinions, behaviors, preferences, and rules. Models' behavior not only sets examples to be followed, but it also directs the observer's attention to objects and circumstances to be sought or avoided. This behavior establishes examples of thought processes observers can use to guide their choices. Not all thought or behavior that is observed leads to immediate imitation, but it can establish patterns or rules that are cognitively stored for retrieval under appropriate circumstances. Individuals learn rules that have led themselves or others to obtain rewards and avoid punishments. A cybernetic principle underpins this theory; it reasons that people use feedback to assess their success in obtaining rewards and estimating the extent to which certain actions and opinions are satisfying. By *acquiring information,* individuals learn what attitudes and actions to adopt to achieve rewards and prevent negative consequences.

Whereas other theories assume that messages lead to attitude formation, ⁺his one is less reliant on that relationship. People receive information (as well as experience direct and indirect action) from others, which is used to create beliefs. Beliefs take the form of assessments of which opinions and behaviors produce rewards and avoid punishments. In making assessments, self-esteem is vital, Bandura (1977) argued, because it is an estimate of how highly individuals value their own opinions. Learning creates "if–then" rules that guide behavior: "If this behavior is taken, then the desired consequences will result." If people perceive themselves to be inefficacious, they are less likely to use modeling as means for guiding behavior; they feel that even though others can obtain rewards, they will be unable to do so.

Social learning theory contributes a foundation for explaining media effects because it argues that characters in television programs, motion pictures, or advertisements serve as models that are imitated on the assumption that viewers can also achieve the rewards and avoid the punishments. For example, numerous studies have found that children who observe violence on television are more likely to resort to violence than are those who do not witness the violence, at least in the short run.

Bandura (1986) concluded that the closer the reward is to the action taken, the more impact it has on the learning curve. He pointed out that what people expect to get out of behavior is more likely to serve as motivation than is what they actually obtain. Since monitoring of behavior–reward relationships is quite complex, individuals do not always accurately estimate what factors cause rewards or punishments. Typically, they rely on factors most immediately associated with the rewards in attributing the reasons for success or failure. Cues that can be used to predict outcomes sometimes are complex. In the formation of beliefs about which actions are preferred, people often have to weigh some factors more heavily than others. Estimating what the factors of success are and how much each contributes to success can be bewildering. The model assumes that people estimate the likelihood of achieving desired outcomes in terms of a probability model. The beliefs they hold about outcomes are largely a function of how well they think they can function in a situation.

Social learning theory is powerful because it captures the interaction between people and their environment, and it features foresightfulness, self-direction, and self-esteem. Building on learning theory, it can explain how and why people adopt beliefs and behavior rules. Its weakness is its inability to indicate which variables go together in what circumstances. It tells us more about beliefs in the context of rewards and punishments than it does about them as factors of knowledge or judgment.

SOCIAL JUDGMENT-INVOLVEMENT THEORY

Social judgment-involvement theory improved on earlier studies by emphasizing the roles that self-concept and prior attitude play in persuasion. This theory takes the tack that "attitudes are not discrete elements in human psychology, but are, on the contrary, constituents of persons' self-esteem" (Sherif & Sherif, 1967, p. 4). Consequently, the theory postulates that any attitude change results in a new "self-picture." This change also can result in uncertainty, disturbance, instability, and puzzlement. Attitudes are part of the "ego constellation" and remain stable until disrupted by communication that challenges them. They are "the stands the individual upholds and cherishes about objects, issues, person, groups, or institutions" (Sherif & Sherif, 1967, p. 4). These attitudes are present in the mind whenever a person receives a new message.

Each new message is compared to this existing attitude and is evaluated by considering the extent to which the two are similar or dissimilar. This theory reasons that individuals' willingness to change their opinions depends on the proximity between the opinions they hold and the opinion in the message, and to the extent they are ego-involved in their judgment. Ego-involvement increases as self-interest increases. The greater the difference between the opinion a person holds and the one expressed by the persuader, the less likely that the new opinion will be accepted, especially if the change would require alterations of the self-concept. If ego-involvement is high, a person is even more likely to reject the new message.

According to this theory, an attitude is "a range or latitude of acceptance" (Sherif et al., 1965, p. vi). People use anchoring attitudes to assess what is said and done by others. How closely an espoused attitude agrees with an anchor attitude can affect one of three latitudes: *acceptance,* where the attitude being espoused is close enough to the anchor to be accepted; *rejection,* where the espoused attitude is objectionable and is therefore rejected; and *noncommittal,* where the new attitude is seen as neutral or produces "no opinion."

To change an attitude, a source can express an attitude that is slightly different from the existing one, but not so different as to be rejected. If it is close enough, it is accepted and shapes the anchor attitude; this is the product of *assimilation effects,* the tendency to subjectively minimize the difference between an anchor attitude and attitudes that are similar to it. Attitudes that differ from an anchor attitude and are not close enough to be acceptable suffer rejection because of contrast effects. *Contrast effects* result when persons maximize the difference between their attitude and those that are objectionable (Sherif & Hovland, 1961).

To change an attitude requires alteration of self, a change in the person — thereby producing ego-involvement and resistance (Sherif & Cantril, 1947; Sherif et al., 1965). Persons who are highly ego-involved have narrower lattitudes of acceptance than uninvolved persons do. Ego-involvement increases the tendency to evaluate messages, even when subjects are instructed not to do so. When people are ego-involved, they use their attitude position to evaluate other positions (Sherif & Sherif, 1967). The amount of change depends on the degree to which attitudes are structured and familiar. When they are neither structured nor familiar, they are more likely to be changed, especially if the message is stated by a high credibility source. In cases where involvement is high, information is sufficient, the source is credible, and discrepancy is great, the anchoring attitude may change, but if it does not, a boomerang effect is likely to occur and increase resistance to change (Sherif et al., 1965).

Social judgment-involvement theory was popular for several years, but was criticized for relying too heavily on single, anchoring attitudes as the factor for predicting message influence. It does not take into account the likelihood that, in most important decision situations, many attitudes are involved, not just the one provided by a source and the anchor against which it is weighed. Decisions often require weighing several conflicting attitudes. Social judgment-involvement theory does a better job of accounting for the impact messages have on judgment than it does of explaining how attitudes relate to behavior. Despite its limitations, it contributed the concept of *ego-involvement*.

COGNITIVE-INVOLVEMENT THEORY

Social judgment-involvement theory fostered research into the cognitive processes that operate once a person receives a message advocating an attitude. One of its predictions was that high amounts of involvement lead to lowered attitude change. To refine this research, new investigations have examined the cognitive processes people use, whether complex or simple, when they desire information about objects and issues related to their personal interest. Petty and Cacioppo (1979) discovered, in contrast to social judgment-involvement theory, that high levels of involvement do not invariably decrease persuasion; rather, high involvement can enhance persuasion if the message contains cogent arguments and if people have enough knowledge regarding an issue to enable them to process issue-relevant statements.

Cognitive involvement theory defines cognitive response as "a unit of information pertaining to an object or issue that is the result of cognitive processing" (Cacioppo, Harkins, & Petty, 1981, p. 37). An argument is any bit of information that is "relevant to a person's subjective determination of the true merits of an advocated position" (Petty & Cacioppo, 1986a, p. 16). Cognitive processes reduce each persuasive argument to its component parts—the information contained—and compare them to opinions held.

Petty and Cacioppo (1986b) offered a model of cognitive processing that sees individuals as progressing from mere positive or negative associations in regard to a topic or object to the point where "the formation and change of some attitudes become very thoughtful processes in which issue-relevant information is carefully scrutinized and evaluated in terms of existing knowledge" (p. 131). When people encounter a topic that relates to their self-interest, they elaborate on it by receiving and storing messages relevant to it. In this process, elaboration is a continuous, not dichotomous variable. Thus, in contrast to social judgment-involvement theory, this theory predicts that high involvement increases the likelihood of receiving a message and changing attitudes or behavior.

Cognitive involvement theory assumes that people want correct and useful attitudes and will expend the effort needed to obtain and process information to do so. Persons who experience high levels of involvement are willing to read, talk, and teleview to obtain information on those topics. They also have more messages on a topic than do their low involved counterparts (Heath & Douglas, 1990).

Once they believe their self-interest is affected,

> people are likely to attend to the appeal; attempt to access relevant information from both external and internal sources; scrutinize and make inferences about the message arguments in light of any other pertinent information available; draw conclusions about the merits of the arguments based on their analyses; and consequently derive an overall evaluation of, or attitude toward, the recommendation. (Petty & Cacioppo, 1986a, p. 7)

Persuasive messages change opinions, according to this theory, because thought about arguments results in new arguments, which are then integrated into the beliefs about the object or issue. The more people are prompted to think about the arguments, the more likely opinions will change.

This research differentiates between opinions that require a high level of cognitive processing and those that do not. The difference is the degree of involvement. Cognitive involvement is a product of how important message content is for a receiver's self-interest and how aroused that person becomes.

Level of involvement depends on the extent to which people believe their self-interest is affected by a message, purchase, issue, situation, or such. If they feel their self-interest is affected, they experience a high level of arousal and become involved. Involvement is a mediating variable that influences how a message will affect attitudes or behavior. Thus, for instance, advertising messages that associate soft drinks or beers with enjoyable activities require a different kind and degree of cognitive processing than do those that address solutions to the problem of illegal drugs or nuclear arms reduction.

Acknowledging that high and low levels of involvement are typical, the Elaboration Likelihood Model (ELM), the heart of cognitive involvement theory, features two "routes" of persuasive influence: central and peripheral. When people experience high levels of involvement, they pay attention to messages and scrutinize them by comparing them against existing information and arguments. This central route requires mindful cognitive processing that includes evaluation of message content. This route is likely to lead to lasting cognitions and predict behavior — until these cognitions are challenged by other cogent arguments.

The peripheral route is based on pleasant or unpleasant associations, requiring only a relatively mindless consideration of affective responses to extra-message cues such as source credibility, context in which a message is received, or attributes of the object. For instance, soft drink or beer ads typically associate the beverage with refreshing scenes, happy fun-loving people, rich and vivid colors, warm puppies, and the like. Ads for these products feature ice sliding down the sides of the bottles. Pleasant embellishments — such as accompanying up-beat music — help reinforce a positive impression that remains in affective memory. This kind of influence is not cognitively involving and therefore not particularly powerful, enduring, or predictive of behavior (Cacioppo, Harkins, & Petty, 1981; Cialdini, Petty, & Cacioppo, 1981; Petty & Cacioppo, 1981, 1986b; Petty, Cacioppo, & Schumann, 1983; Petty, Kasmer, Haugtvedt, & Cacioppo, 1987). These two cognitive processes are diagrammed in Fig. 5.1.

The ELM accounts for the differences in persuasive impact produced by arguments that contain ample information and cogent reasons as compared to messages that rely on simplistic associations of negative and positive attributes to some object, action, or situation. The key variable in this process is involvement, the extent to which an individual is willing and able to "think" about the position advocated and its supporting materials. When people are motivated and able to think about the content of the message, elaboration is high. Elaboration involves cognitive processes such as evaluation, recall, critical judgment, and inferential judgment. When elaboration is high, the central persuasive route is likely to occur; conversely, the peripheral route is the likely result of low elaboration.

Studying receivers' ability to process information in an advertisement for disposable razors, Petty et al. (1983) discovered that strong arguments had more persuasive impact than did weak ones. High involvement increased recall of brand names but had no effect on recall of ad content. Subjects who were more involved were more critical of arguments than were low-involved subjects; high-involved subjects were more persuaded by strong arguments than were low-involved subjects and were more critical of and less persuaded by weak arguments. Low-involved subjects were more likely to use peripheral cues, such as source credibility, rather than issue-specific argumentation, whereas the opposite was true of high in-

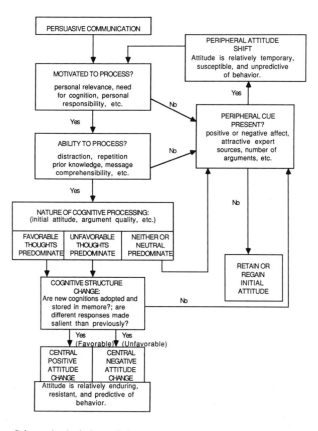

FIG. 5.1.   Schematic depiction of the two routes to persuasion (from Petty et al., 1987. Reprinted by permission of the Speech Communication Association).

volved people. When individuals are prepared to deal with more information, they will be more likely to act on those arguments and resist later change than will individuals who receive many arguments but are not involved (motivated or skilled) to assess the accuracy and worth of the messages (Petty et al., 1987).

The ELM holds that variables, such as messages, source attributes, or situation attributes, can play any of three roles in cognitive involvement: they can be an argument, a cue, or a factor, each of which can influence the extent to which people will process the information. For instance, a source can serve any of the three roles. A person who is ill from excessive smoking is an *argument* or a message about smoking. For instance, the famous tough guy actor Yul Bryner made an antismoking commercial that was aired only after he died from cancer, which he believed was related to smoking. His apparent physical ill health was a *cue* to listeners that, if they wanted to avoid a similar condition, they should be involved or self-interested in what he had to say. The fact that Bryner had been a "tough guy" actor was a factor that could have influenced people to be *more involved* in the ad because it said that even tough people can be killed by cancer. All three variables—argument, cue, and factor—can operate at the same time (Petty et al., 1987).

One factor relevant to persuasive impact, according to ELM, is message repetition. An evening spent watching TV or listening to the radio will convince you that advertising sponsors believe that repeated messages increase the likelihood that persuadees will recall messages and use them when formulating opinions about a product. Parents also seem to believe that repeated messages "drive their point home" because they give their children the same instructions over and over. Studying the power of repetition, Cacioppo and Petty (1979) found that a sender can use repetition to increase the likelihood a message will be recalled. When people receive repeated messages, their agreement first increases and then decreases. This occurs because counterargument at first decreases, then increases, as messages are repeated.

A high level of cognitive involvement and the need-to-know predicts the impact information received from a public information campaign has on receivers' on knowledge, attitudes, and behavior. The need-to-know motivates information seeking on topics such as those related to health. When situations produce little involvement, behavior is likely to be a product of situational factors rather than attitudes or knowledge. When involvement increases, behavior should be a product of attitude and knowledge. Under low involvement, people are likely to respond to cues such as the likability or credibility of sources; high involvement is likely to produce careful analysis, thought, and consideration. Perceived risk produces erratic relationships among knowledge, attitude, and belief and does not always lead to a desire for more knowledge (Chaffee & Roser, 1986). A curvilinear relationship exists between the degree to which a persuadee is involved in a persuasive topic and the effects of source credibility on that person's attitudes. As involvement increases, so does the impact of source credibility to a point after which further involvement can actually reduce attitude change (Stiff, 1986). One explanation for these findings is that, when people are worried about some matter, such as their health, even though they have high levels of involvement, they ignore information on the topic because they want to avoid increases in their level of fear.

You can provide intuitive support for these findings. When you first discover information on some topic, it is likely to influence your opinion even if it is incorrect. This is the case because you have no information against which to evaluate the new information. As you become more involved in a topic, you can evaluate information more thoroughly and accurately. Thus, the central route leads to attitude positions that resist change, and behavior is based on information because it is reasonable to do so (Reinard, 1988). Lacking knowledge, people rely on peripheral cues, which result in less lasting persuasive impact (Wood, Kallgren, & Priesler, 1985). This theory is promising because it integrates an array of variables into a single explanation of persuasion. One problem involved in researching and applying this theory results from the difficulty—or impossibility—of knowing when a sufficient level of involvement or self-interest has been generated to produce the related effects.

INFORMATION INTEGRATION-EXPECTANCY VALUE THEORY

Each previously discussed theory contributes to the understanding of persuasion. The Yale research program attempted to explain how each part of the communication process affects the learning that leads to attitudes and behavior. Social judgment-involvement demonstrates the ego-involving interaction between anchoring attitudes and self-concept, as they affect reception and response to persuasive messages. Social learning–social cognition features people as dynamic participants who help to form their own opinions regarding which opinions and actions achieve rewards or avoid punishments. Elaboration-cognitive involvement distinguishes between complex and simple persuasive efforts.

Although each of these theories makes contributions, none describes how attitudes interact and people assess the expected value of holding opinions or decide to act. To remedy that deficiency, information integration-expectancy value theory explains how attitudes are composed of complex and often conflicting components and how behavior is a product of two factors: (a) attitude toward the action, and (b) belief about the subjective norms that approve or disapprove of the action. Going beyond the notion that behavior is predicated on "motives," this theory argues that behavior results from a colinear interaction between the attitude that a specific action is good or bad and awareness of social pressures or norms favoring or disfavoring it (Ajzen & Fishbein, 1980).

This theory makes two major arguments. The first is that attitudes are not singular or undifferentiated cognitions as is suggested by other theories such as social judgment-involvement. Second, affective and cognitive components of attitudes are interrelated, not separate. The evaluative dimension of attitudes consists of affective qualities that can be expressed as likes or dislikes. Thus, a child might like (positive attitude) ice cream and dislike (negative attitude) liver or spinach.

Emphasizing the notion of likes and dislikes, Fishbein and Ajzen (1975) defined *attitude* as *"a learned predisposition to respond in a consistently favorable or unfavorable manner with respect to a given object"* (p. 6). Once they are acquired, attitudes provide consistency for judgment and behavior because they reflect patterns of preferences that each individual establishes. But attitudes are not only affective; they also have cognitive dimensions that can be measured as *degrees of certainty*—the extent to which people hold some idea or opinion to likely be "true."

A *belief* is the cognitive dimension of an attitude that expresses the extent (subjective probability) to which an evaluation (positive or negative attribute) is associated with an object, concept, situation, or action being evaluated. Thus, an attitude such as "harmful to health" contains a negative evaluation, but it also depends on how strongly (belief) each person associates that attribute, "harmful to health," with an object such as cigarettes. A person who does not believe they are harmful would have a different attitude than one who believes cigarettes are harmful. But both persons would agree that "harmful to health" is a negative evaluation.

This notion of belief is the same as the one discussed in chapter 4 regarding the impact data have on degrees of certainty measured in percentages. A belief—measured as a percentage of certainty—can be increased or decreased with information. For example, a person who plans a picnic might look at low, menacing clouds the morning of the picnic and have a relatively strong belief (based on apparent information) that rain is likely. That belief (percentage) would lessen if the clouds begin to lift and sun pops through periodically. The belief, "We'll have good weather," replaces its opposite as the clouds clear and the sun shines continuously. In this way, beliefs are conclusions that are affected by information.

For this reason, Fishbein and Ajzen (1975) concluded that beliefs are the building blocks of the cognitive structure, the information base that supports evaluative systems as well as intentions and behaviors. One strength of this theory is its ability to show how beliefs and attitudes are integrated, whereas other theories either feature only one attitude at a time or do not see that judgment involves many positive and negative evaluations along with beliefs of various degrees of strength. To express this integration, Fishbein and Ajzen use the following formula:

$$A_o = \sum_{i=1}^{n} b_i e_i$$

This formula consists of Ao, the attitude toward some object O; *bi*, belief *i* about O, (the extent to which any attribute *i* is related to the object); ei, the evaluation (positive or negative) associated with the object; and n, the total number of beliefs involved in the attitude, expressed as a summation Σ.

This theory captures many opinions about an object or action and expresses them as the product of interactions between belief strength and evaluation strength. To understand this evaluation, imagine the following analysis a person (in this case the mother and father of a family) might perform when considering the purchase of an automobile. As you go through this illustration, remember that belief is calculated by obtaining a degree of certainty, a percentage expressed in a range from 0 to 1, and that evaluation is a response on a continuum from -3 to $+3$. The interaction of the belief and evaluation is the product, be. Keep in mind that Brand X is evaluated by comparing it to all other brands. A similar matrix must be created for each competing brand, and the final preference should be based on the comparison of all Ao's. Imagine that this decision is being made by a family that has a limited budget and consists of six members. The attitude they hold is one that is expected to achieve the most rewards and avoid negative outcomes. The components of the mother and father's attitude toward Brand X are provided in Table 5.1. Note how this decision reflects the unique circumstances of this family. Comfort and size are important as is serviceability, economy, and reliability; style is unimportant. Another family might use a completely different matrix. Before you can predict the behavioral outcome of the buyers' attitudes, you need to know that their attitudes regarding other automobiles are as follows: Brand A, -1.35; Brand B, 1.87; and Brand C, 2.12. Based on the integration of beliefs and evaluations, you should predict that the family would buy Brand C.

This theory is useful because it helps the persuader to know what decision ingredients might be changed through a persuasive message. For instance, a sales person could convince the potential buyers that Brand X is larger than they originally thought. If "small and uncomfortable" could be changed to "large and comfortable," by informing the buyers of the internal passenger space, the decision should change. The relevance of the criteria "small and uneconomical" could be lowered by reminding the buyers that the two oldest children of the family (twins) will soon be away at college so the

TABLE 5.1
Illustration of Components of Attitude Toward Brand X

	b	e	be
Brand X is reliable	.75	$+3$	2.25
Brand X is economical	.70	$+3$	2.10
Brand X is small	.99	-3	-2.97
Brand X is uncomfortable	.99	-3	-2.97
Brand X is hard to service	.65	-1	-0.65
Brand X is stylish	.80	0	0.00
The total Ao regarding Brand X is			-2.24

family car needs to be only large enough to carry four passengers instead of six. This illustration should help you understand how this theory manages judgments about objects and predicts behavior.

Information integration-expectancy value theory can help you to appreciate the relationship between judgments and behavior (Ajzen & Fishbein, 1980; Fishbein & Ajzen, 1975). The theory suggests that behavior is a product of attitude toward the behavior (especially its expected reward value) and the subjective norms involved. Subjective norms consist of actual and assumed opinions that valued others (persons whose opinions are important) would have regarding a decision. The model takes into account two kinds of information: (a) desire to behave so as to obtain the most rewards, and (b) desire to conform to the norms of individuals who are important to the person making the decision. The formulation of this norm is based on a decision maker's beliefs that specific individuals or groups think he or she should or should not perform the intended action. (Note how beliefs about the subjective norm can explain why people sometimes do what they don't want to do, and why they don't do what they want to do.)

Let's return to the car buying illustration. Recall that the key subjective norm supporting the decision is this: This family should buy an economical and roomy automobile that is reliable and easy to maintain. Where did that decision criterion come from? It came from the decision maker's experience as well as the opinions of others. The person making the decision may have a belief intention toward the action of $+2$. (The figure could be $+3$, but we believe that in the back of each reasonable car buyer's mind there is "lust" for a small and racy car.) How this number ($+2$) is translated into motivation to act depends on perception of the opinions of other people regarding this decision. The opinions of others, a normative belief, could be modeled by calculating each person's agreement/disagreement with the norm ($+3$ support the norm/-3 oppose it) and the extent to which the person making the decision wants to comply with the advice of the person ($+3$ to 0). This phase of the decision process, development of subjective norms of behavior, consists of the norms others favor (NB) and motivation to comply (MC) with those persons' expressions of what should be done. Expressed algebraically, this relationship is $SN = \Sigma (NB_i)(MC_i)$, as is illustrated in Table 5.2. The normative belief is favored by the individual ($+2$) and by the others ($+9$). The $+9$ should give the person making the decision confidence that it is proper. This decision matrix is sensitive to the valued opinions of the spouse, a neighbor, and a co-worker. The opinion of the salesperson, who wants to sell a car that is small, uncomfortable, and expensive is discounted. The two oldest children in the family prefer a small and sporty automobile to a "tank." Although given positive regard ($+1$), their opinions on the normative belief do not overweigh others' opinions.

TABLE 5.2
Illustration of Components of Behavioral Intention

Valued others	Normative belief		Motivation to comply		Product
Spouse	+3	×	+3	=	+9
Respected friend	+2	×	+2	=	+4
Respected coworker	+2	×	+1	=	+2
Salesperson	−3	×	+0	=	−0
Oldest boy in family	−3	×	+1	=	−3
Oldest girl in family	−3	×	+1	=	−3
Total estimation of prevailing normative belief					+9

These kids argue for style and against the criteria preferred by their parents. Note that this argument lessens the parents' commitment by a total of (−6). If not for the kids' arguments, the parents' overall commitment to the criteria of comfort and economy would be +15 instead of +9. See how others' opinions and arguments have a measurable effect.

In this way, we can model the attitude toward the object and estimate the normative belief regarding the correctness or wisdom of an intended behavior. Both factors influence behavior. This theory combines insight into the complex nature of attitudes, which often must balance conflicting information that consists of positives and negatives. It indicates that behavior is predicated on an estimation of the goodness or badness of the decision, which can be modified by an individual's estimations of what others think. This theory can explain why people do not buy every product or service they see advertised. Even if they have a positive attitude toward the product, they do not intend to buy it now or at all because of personal intentions or because they yield to the prevailing subjective norms perceived to be held by others whose opinions they respect.

Refining this theory, Shepherd (1987) discovered that the degree of colinearity between attitudinal and normative beliefs differs, depending on how clearly the persons differentiate the issues or choices involved and how much information they bring to the situation. For instance, people with undifferentiated opinions on political candidates evidence substantial colinearity, whereas people with differentiated opinions do not. Insight into the decision leads the individual to prefer either the attitude toward the action or the prevailing normative belief. The key to the decision is which of the two seems likely to result in the most favorable decision—expectancy value.

This theory is instructive for those who wish to be persuasive. It allows them to see that they can change one or several components of an attitude by changing the evaluation or the belief (degree of certainty). They can also change a person's intention by focusing on the goodness or badness of the decision or by influencing a person's perception of the prevailing subjective norm. All of this is founded on research that supports Fishbein and Ajzen's (1981) belief that "Information is the essence of the persuasion process" (p. 339).

SELF-PERSUASION

One issue that is central to persuasion research is the role the persuadee plays in the process. Most of the research reported in this chapter sees the persuadee as relatively dynamic in the process. For at least thirty years, researchers have been aware that when people create messages, they are likely to influence themselves by the content of those messages. An individual's attitudes may change as the result of being induced to make a statement or take an action that is contrary to his or her attitudes prior to the statement. Making a statement or taking an action (such as eating grasshoppers at survival school) is likely to change attitudes to conform with those expressed in the statement or consonant with the action. The outcome is more likely to occur if the action is taken or the statement made with minimal reward or to comply with the request of an unattractive person. Miller (1987) said that this result occurs because individuals persuade themselves. Miller and Burgoon (1978) characterized this as an *active participation* paradigm rather than *passive reception*.

Two broad explanations can be given for this outcome. One reasons that people attempt to avoid or reduce dissonance — an uncomfortable feeling — when confronted with conflicting attitudes, information, beliefs, or choices (Festinger, 1957). To reduce dissonance experienced by stating something contrary to existing beliefs, an individual may adopt the new attitude. The second explanation is predicated on individuals' tendency to manage their impressions. Impression management, particularly when it is associated with self-monitoring can lead an individual to believe, as Bem (1970) reasoned. An illustration of Bem's point is the typical self-reflection: "I must believe what I am saying otherwise I wouldn't be saying it." Bem observed that people often monitor their behavior to determine what their attitudes are. For example, people reflect on their behavior to infer their attitudes: "I must believe this statement (or approve this behavior) because I just said (or did) it."

If people can be prompted to make a minimal proattitudinal commitment, they are likely to agree subsequently to an even larger request on the same subject. This is called the *foot-in-the-door* phenomenon. People can also be persuaded if a large request is made of them, followed by a smaller request. This is called *door-in-the-face*. These are strategies often associated with a sales scenario. A salesperson gets a potential buyer to make a small commitment. This kind of strategy may be employed when the car salesperson gets you to take a test drive. Even if you don't buy that car, you at least are in position to persuade yourself that you must want a new car otherwise you would not be test driving them. Sales people like to get a public commitment to a minor request, "Do you like the color?"

Door-in-the-face tactics occur, for instance, when a solicitor for an environmental or humane society group asks for a $100 donation for a worthy cause. The solicitor will gladly accept this amount, but is willing to settle for less. Likewise, most sales people "sell down," starting with expensive merchandise and going to less expensive. As typical as these examples are, research suggests that neither strategy has a very strong relationship to eliciting a final response. The final request in the door-in-the-face situations must be made soon after the first one, whereas time does not seem have an effect in the foot-in-the-door situation. Researchers explain these phenomena by using self-perception and reciprocal concessions theories (Dillard, Hunter, & Burgoon, 1984).

RESISTANCE TO PERSUASIVE MESSAGES

When people hear or read messages, they process and respond to them with varying degrees of willingness to believe. Each of us can attest to the accuracy of this statement as we encounter millions of ads during our life. We pay little attention to most ads, but some we find agreeable and others we argue against. According to social judgment-involvement theory, people reject messages that conflict too greatly with attitudes central to their self-concept. Sometimes people accept almost any information uncritically; at other times they are quite critical. The difference, at least according to ELM, is due to the degree of involvement—ability and willingness to process useful information and strong reasons.

Examining what makes people resist persuasive messages, McGuire (1964) studied the efficacy of forewarnings—telling persons that a counter message is coming—to prepare them to resist the message. He based his analysis on an analogy to medical *inoculation;* a small dose of a disease is injected into a patient to stimulate the body to develop immunity to it. He reasoned that if people feel a mild threat from learning that someone is going to challenge their opinions, they will increase their resistance. He examined the efficacy of preparing people to resist by giving them *proattitudinal* statements to reinforce their existing attitudes or *refutational* statements to challenge the espoused statements. Two kinds of refutational arguments are viable, those that are similar to the espoused argument and those that directly challenge it.

Evidencing the complexity of the persuasion process, Burgoon and King

(1974) found that messages presented in intense language can overcome forewarnings if receivers are actively involved in the composition of the message. This research reinforces findings that language is a factor in the impact of persuasive messages (Miller & Burgoon, 1979).

Following McGuire's lead, Wright (1973, 1974, 1981) argued that individuals respond to message content by comparing it to their existing opinions. This comparison may manifest itself in three forms: Counterargument, source derogation, and support argument. Counterargument consists of spotting discrepancies between existing opinions and those contained in the espoused message. Source derogation attacks the credibility of the message source. Support arguments are generated in behalf of existing opinions. Wright observed that counterargument is the most powerful mediator of content expressed in advertisements. When people heard an audio version of the ad, they were more attentive and therefore more likely to generate support arguments and resort to derogation than were those who read the ad. When individuals are involved in the decision outcome they are likely to participate in these three mediating processes.

Expectations of how a persuader will communicate affects how a persuadee responds to the message. When a persuadee expects an intense attack on an attitude and this attack is more moderate than expected, the persuadee is prone to favor the position espoused in moderate terms, but will eventually return to the previous level of counterargument. In contrast, people who receive intense messages after expecting low intensity messages are initially negative toward the espoused message but become less likely to counterargue. Derogation of the source seems to reduce the need to counterargue.

Research such as this demonstrates that many factors influence how individuals receive and process persuasive messages. Although some messages prepare people to resist new messages, others do not. Involvement and personal disposition toward the topic affect willingness to accept or reject new messages.

INTERPERSONAL CONTEXT

Because persuasion depends on the cognitive impact of messages coupled with the persuadee's desire to cope, principles of persuasion would seem to be universal to all contexts. Some research findings, however, are particularly relevant to contexts.

Examining how men and women think of themselves as persuaders in interpersonal settings, Andrews (1987) found that women are less confident of their ability to be persuasive in interpersonal settings than are men. This self-consciousness is unwarranted because trained coders who observed interactions during the research did not detect that women were less competent. Some gender-based differences do appear. The kinds of arguments men use differ from those of women. Men use more criterion-based arguments (arguments that are based on criteria unique to the message under consideration), whereas women are prone to invent their own arguments, particularly sensitive to social responsibility. Men attribute their persuasive success to their abilities whereas failures are blamed on the situation. Women believe that their success as persuaders results from hard work in preparing strong arguments.

Each day in dozens of interpersonal settings, you make requests of persons whom you encounter. Some requests are scripted and casual, whereas others may be carefully planned and require some skill in their execution. So typical is this kind of behavior, that researchers have devoted many studies to the processes of compliance gaining.

The concept of *compliance gaining* has been used to explain how people in interpersonal contexts attempt to influence each other with requests. The basis of compliance gaining research is this: Messages can induce compliance because of expectations, relationships, or consequences of actions by or in behalf of the person who receives the request.

One means for studying compliance utilizes a list of typical kinds of statements people use when making requests of one another. This research assumes that people are more or less familiar with the kinds of statements available to be used for making requests and seeking compliance. Researchers are interested in the kinds of statements people select to use.

A list created by Marwell and Schmitt (1967) contains 16 types of messages. The list includes *promises* and *threats,* recommendations based on *positive expertise* (do as I say and you will gain rewards) or *negative expertise* (if you follow my recommendation you can avoid negative consequences). Compliance gaining messages can include *liking, debt, moral appeal, pregiving* (whereby the source gives the reward in advance of the requested action), and *aversive stimulation* (a request which promises to discontinue punishment if the request is granted). The list of compliance gaining strategies also includes requests based on *positive self-feeling* (compliance will make you feel good) and *negative self-feeling* (noncompliance will make you feel bad). *Positive altercasting* bases a request on claims that a person of good character will comply, whereas *negative altercasting* claims that persons who do not comply are of bad character. *Altruism* is an appeal to comply because the person is altruistic. Compliance messages can claim that people will like the person if he or she complies *(esteem-positive)* or will dislike the person if he or she does not comply *(esteem-negative).* These statements probably sound familiar to you. You probably use some or all, and perhaps you have acquaintances who use some of these all of the time.

A typical kind of compliance gaining research has subjects read the list of 16 strategies and check which kinds of strategies are used or useful in gaining compliance in different situations and in the face of different kinds of counter moves. Such research methodologies seem to lack validity because people do not actually communicate that way. It is rare, if ever, that people consider all of the available strategies relevant to a situation or desired outcome. Such methodologies truly put "words" into the "mouths" of subjects that they otherwise might not have. For this reason, this approach to study compliance should be used with extreme caution or avoided completely (Burleson et al., 1988).

Can the list be shortened to fewer than 16 items? Miller (1987) believed that it need only include these compliance strategies: rewarding activities, punishing activities, expertise, impersonal commitment, and personal commitment. The version of the list Miller offered included:

1. reward oriented statements (one or both parties can receive rewards from compliance),
2. punishment oriented statements (compliance helps avoid punishment),
3. communicator onus (threat, negative expertise, aversion, or negative esteem), and
4. recipient onus (negative moral appeal, negative self-feeling, or claims of indebtedness).

This model employs expectancy-value theory, which predicts that people prefer to comply with requests that produce positive outcomes (or avoid negative ones) and which conform to their norms of behavior.

Featuring relational variables as the basis of compliance requests, Cody and McLaughlin (1980) claimed that six factors influence the selection of messages by persons trying to gain compliance:

1. amount of *intimacy* between the persons,
2. extent to which compliance will *personally benefit* the person making the request,
3. *consequences* of the compliance-gaining effort on the relationship,
4. *rights* of the persons,
5. extent to which the person making the request typically *dominates* the other, and
6. degree of *resistance* the person initiating the request expects from the other during the compliance-gaining effort.

Even though relational variables are important and obvious, Hunter and Boster (1987) argued that the person seeking compliance is unlikely to use a request type that would make him or her uncomfortable.

Compliance strategies are sensitive to situations. For instance, self-oriented credibility statements are used when seeking compliance, at least by proponents of environmentalism. In such cases, persuaders seek to demonstrate the negative expertise of opponents and the positive expertise of proponents. Altruism is an effective appeal for addressing persons who are socially oriented, whereas aversive comments are effective when targets of the request are self-oriented (Baglan, Lalumia, & Bayless, 1986).

Compliance strategies are sensitive to self-justification and relationships. Dillard and Burgoon (1985) observed that if people believe they are justified in making a request, they are more likely to use verbal aggression as a message tactic. If people think they have lots to gain from the request, they are likely to use many strategies. If the person making the request senses a high degree intimacy in the relationship, he or she is less likely to use verbal aggression or harsh messages.

Compliance-gaining strategies differ depending on the kind of request. A person who is seeking to borrow something is likely to make contractual statements designed to reduce the cost of granting the request. When people request favors, they inquire about the cost of the target's compliance, ask about the ability of the target to comply, and offer compensation. When borrowing requests are denied, the person seeking compliance is unwilling to express forgiveness and seeks to persuade the person to comply. In contrast, when favors are denied, the person seeking compliance is prone to be forgiving (Roloff & Janiszewski, 1989).

When communication tactics fail, people may turn to physical threat and force to gain compliance. Males are more likely than females to use force against noncompliant males in situations when a relationship is not at stake. Males are more likely than females to use force in interpersonal situations, especially those with short-term consequences. The quality of interpersonal relationships influences which compliance-gaining strategies are used (de-Turck, 1987).

Married couples differ in their use of power to achieve compliance. For instance, "traditional" couples state their expectations of one another to gain compliance; this tactic is used because of the couple's commitment to interdependency as the basis of their marriage. This kind of couple is able to discuss the positive and negative outcomes of the requested behavior and use relationship as a basis of power. "Separates" (people who are less committed to interdependence and who avoid conflict in relationships) do not use messages that express relationships or lead to conflict to gain compliance. They are more likely to use open appeals to influence their partners. "Independents" hold less traditional relationship values and are mildly committed to interdependency. They appeal to obligations and the values of their partner (Witteman & Fitzpatrick, 1986).

People seek compliance by disclosing their vulnerabilities (indicating that they need someone's help) or by expressing hostilities toward persons other than the other participant (seeking to gang up against someone else). When people recognize that these tactics are being used, they respond with positive messages and report a positive attitude toward the request and the relationship with the person making the request. However, such strategies do not increase willingness to comply (Shimanoff, 1987).

Compliance gaining seems to be guided by the assumption that willingness to comply (or not) is governed by contingency rules that are selected to achieve anticipated consequences. These rules are refined by self-identities of the participants, personal values, and image-maintenance rules—all of which are aimed at supporting self-presentation. How these rules are used depends on the circumstances of the moment, rules governing the particular relationship, and salient social norms (Smith, 1984).

One major compliance-gaining rule is equity. People are concerned that others are treated fairly (as they themselves wish to be treated). Thus, people will work harder to persuade another if they believe that person can benefit from the outcome (Boster & Stiff, 1984).

Studies such as these demonstrate the progress that is being made to understand how people seek to gain compliance in interpersonal contexts. But more work remains because, as is the case of all communication studies, many factors interact to influence the outcomes of compliance tactics. Research is needed to consider the weighted interaction of several factors:

1. motivation and cognitive factors relevant to requests;
2. relational and identity goals and the ways participants use messages to manage them;
3. characteristics of influencers and targets;
4. message tactics; and
5. factors related to relationships and reciprocation (Miller, Boster, Roloff, & Seibold, 1987).

ORGANIZATIONAL CONTEXT

Throughout the chapter, references have been made to organizations' use of persuasion to influence opinion and behavior, especially through advertising. Rather than go into additional detail, it will suffice to say that as a source of persuasive messages, an organization is similar to a person, being assessed according to criteria of source credibility and being met with varying degrees of receptivity and resistance. Organizations attempt to create social realities that influence how their members and outsiders perceive them. Organizations use compliance gaining messages. As receivers, organizations are subject to influence whether through information, other types of appeals, or coercion and forced compliance such as that exerted by governmental regulatory agencies.

MEDIATED CONTEXT

Many persuasion tactics are employed through the media. Television, radio, and print advertising brings claims about many wonderous goods and services to homes around the nation. Many of the studies cited in this chapter help explain the impact of persuasion in mediated contexts. According to social learning theory, people use the media as means for formulating attitudes and adopting behavior. Media form opinions primarily by portraying successes or failures of models. People attend to media content to learn which opinions and behaviors produce rewards and punishments — lessons they want to learn. Advertising can have central or peripheral influence on the cognitive system. Marketing research can operate on the assumption that satisfaction occurs when the attributes of products coincide with those desired by buyers (Oliver, 1981).

One line of analysis joins persuasion theory — especially expectancy-value — to uses and gratifications research (Palmgreen & Rayburn, 1982, 1985a, 1985b). The argument is that people select and watch television programs because of the interaction between gratifications sought and obtained. People select television programs that produce the gratification they desire and based on their perception that others would approve or disapprove of the selection. Viewing behavior is guided by desire for information and entertainment, and as well as creation of a social bond or dependency with a prominent media personality or entertainment program character. Each of these factors constitutes an expectancy value for watching television (Babrow & Swanson, 1988).

CONCLUSION

This chapter has concentrated on research and theory related to social influence. It supports the proposition that persuasive influence occurs because people construct and live a social reality in coordination with others. Social influence assumes the ability to reduce uncertainty, to hold opinions and behave in ways that are rewarding or avoid negative outcomes. People often expose themselves to others' persuasive influence.

Influence requires information, albeit of varying amounts. People seek and receive information and compare it against what they already know in their effort to achieve accurate views. To maximize rewards and minimize losses or punishments, people acquire information by watching the behavior of others, obtaining messages, and monitoring their own behavior. They draw conclusions about what behavior produces which rewards under what circumstances. These efforts are related to individuals' estimations of their ability to acquire rewards and avoid punishments by regarding which opinions or behavior is preferred. In the process of participating in social influence, people are sometimes active and sometimes passive. In these ways, people communicate to exert social influence.

6

Interpersonal Communication: Relationships, Expectations, and Conflict

A desire to understand what factors improve relationships fuels the study of interpersonal communication. People assume that analysis of interpersonal communication can explain how relationships grow, remain static, or deteriorate—*From Greeting to Goodbye* (Knapp, 1978). Ever since Mead (1934) demonstrated that people grow in personality and relationships through communication, scholars have been sensitive to the importance of interpersonal interaction.

Few if any aspects of communication receive more attention than does the quality of relationships—the subject of countless poems, songs, stories, dramas, and conversations. In the past two decades, thousands of popular books, articles, and advice columns have advised people on ways to get along better, be assertive, think well of themselves, and enrich their lives through communication. By the time you reached adolescence, you acquired a long list of rules by which to guide relationships. You were told how to be polite, to defend yourself verbally, to get along with others, to ingratiate, to resolve conflict, and to enhance relationships.

Interpersonal communication research and theory continue to address a wide array of topics, but concentrate on four major themes: quality of relationships, social conflict, accuracy of people's understanding of one another, and communication planning and competence. Throughout this discussion, uncertainty reduction is a central motive because interpersonal communication entails efforts to gain and share information to understand other people as well as ourselves and our competencies. To do so requires interpersonal competence and involves estimates of the communication competence of relational partners.

People assess the quality of relationships by attempting to understand themselves and their communication partners. Analysis of interpersonal communication has an "economic" dimension; as people negotiate relationships, they calculate the costs and rewards of compliance, conflict, disclosure, and relational commitment. A lot of research assumes that people seek to maintain and negotiate relationships so that rewards outweigh costs.

How people communicate not only affects the quality of relationships but also reflects their quality. For instance, although all couples seem to voice the same amount of complaints to one another, the kind of relationship influences the types of complaints that are voiced. Couples who enjoy a good relationship complain about each other's behavior, make complaints that carry positive affect, and deal agreeably with partner's complaints. In contrast, maladjusted couples complain about one another's personal characteristics, voice negative feelings, and make counter complaints in response to complaints made by partners (Alberts, 1988).

Relationships depend on how individuals form and manage meaning. As discussed in chapter 3, some meanings are referential, leading participants to recall experiences they have had with objects, situations, and feelings, but many other meanings exist in the content of the terms used to characterize people, things, situations, and relationships. This relativistic view of meaning constitutes the basis of stereotypes that people use to identify with one another, such as "members of this company," "my best friend," "university students," or "our family." Words are used to attribute causation such as saying, "Nobody but a 'scumbag' would do that." The meaning of words used in conversations is also influenced by perceptions of the intentions behind statements people make. For instance, the statement, "You're a good kid," takes on meaning more from context and the intentions of those involved than from any reference to "good kids."

Prior to the 1970s, little research was done to understand interpersonal communication, despite its prevalence in people's lives. The hypodermic needle model dominated communication research, which assumed that senders "injected" information and influence into receivers. Soon researchers realized that this model was inappropriate for studying interaction and relationships. In the 1960s, several events heightened interest and offered a new paradigm for studying interpersonal communication. Humanistic psychology, popular in the 1970s, argued that people should enable rather than manipulate one another. A goal of humanistic psychology was to help people achieve personal growth individually and through relationships. Topics such as negotiation and cooperation gave increased insight into how interpersonal communication could be studied without focusing narrowly on concerns such as how one person affects the attitudes of another (Berger, 1977b).

The study of interpersonal communication was prompted by many lines of discussion focused on relationships. Seminal work in psychiatry considered how personality shapes and is shaped by relationships; people's psychiatric problems are not only the result of personal problems, but also the product of interpersonal problems. Humanistic psychology, European philosophy (particularly existentialism), and the peace/love movement of the 1960s popularized the notion that lives and relationships could be improved through effective communication. Rules theory, speech act philosophy, linguistic relativity, and systems theory supported by the concept of cybernation gave perspectives that fostered research on interpersonal communication.

In that tradition, this chapter examines how people use communication to shape interpersonal relationships. Unique insight can be gained regarding relationships by understanding that how people communicate affects relationships — and vice versa. Research has demonstrated that people reward or punish one another through verbal and nonverbal communication, and by those means they negotiate and shape relationships. During relationships, people seek and share, as well as hide, information from one another. They are concerned about their competence and constantly weigh the costs and rewards of creating, maintaining, and dissolving relationships.

One challenge in studying interpersonal communication is to gain insight without coming to believe that people are mindful of each comment they make. Some people are more mindful of what and how they communicate than are others. People are more mindful at some times than others. But none of us are aware of what we are doing and saying all of the time.

Part of the challenge of studying interpersonal communication is deciding what variables account for the differences in relationships. Most people intuit that several variables seem characteristic of successful and rewarding relationships as well as make others unrewarding. Terms such as *trust, openness, conflict, harmful,* and *supportive* typically come to mind when people think about the qualities that characterize relationships. As you are, researchers are faced with trying to determine which variables account for the quality of relationships and how those variables interact. Before examining that kind of research, we should stop to define interpersonal communication.

WHAT IS INTERPERSONAL COMMUNICATION?

Interpersonal communication is dyadic interaction in which people negotiate relationships by using communication styles and strategies that become personally meaningful as the persons involved attempt to reduce uncertainty (about themselves, their partners, and their relationships), to be self-efficacious, and to maximize rewards through interaction.

In the most basic sense, interpersonal communication occurs when what one person does or says affects another person. In this sense, what one person does has impact on what the other person does. In relationships, people estimate the likely reaction the other person will make in response to what is said and done. To understand interpersonal communication requires insight into how interactions provide partners with information about each other, themselves, and their relationship (Cappella, 1987).

Miller and Steinberg (1975) argued that the primary content of interpersonal communication is psychological, rather than sociological or cultural information. People can only know one another by experiencing each other's behavior—what they do and say. The key to understanding psychological information is not to focus only on the content of conversations—what people say to one another—but also to examine the effects of what they say and do during interaction.

By learning about interaction and relationship variables, people may increase the predictability of how relationships can be influenced and made rewarding. This view assumes that communication is motivated by uncertainty reduction and the desire to maximize rewards and minimize losses during interactions. This paradigm, Berger (1977b) believed, differs substantially from a rules-based approach, which assumes that persons prefer rule consensus—participants playing by the same interaction rules—to achieve agreeable communication outcomes. Stressing the differences between the two positions, Berger agreed with Miller and Steinberg (1975) that people may break rules to gain rewards, even for the short term. Based on this view of interpersonal communication, Berger advised that the key concepts needed to study interpersonal communication are communicator style, communicative competence, and communication process.

Interpersonal communication involves a high degree of direct contact. It need not be face to face; many relationships rely on letters or telephones as communication media. It is that form of communication where people are immediately interdependent and interlocked; what each does affects the other and the outcome of the interaction. Persons involved in interpersonal communication co-define the dynamics of relationships. For instance, it is impossible to fight if a relational partner does not want to fight.

Interpersonal communication research begins from the premise that people perceive and respond to one another based on what they experience each other doing and saying. This entails all behavior, verbal and nonverbal, that participants perform during interactions. Not only is behavior essential to a relationship, but so is the way participants cognitively process what that behavior means to them and the relationship. People come to know one another only through exchanges that have content and relational characteristics.

Interaction transpires over time through a process involving turn taking, interruptions, topic shifts, disclosures, and confirmations. How interaction occurs is fostered or hindered by variables such as complementarity (how what one person does complements the other), divergence (moving apart) or convergence (coming together), and compensatory reactions (making up for what the other person fails to do).

Concepts such as these are central to this chapter and the next one. This chapter concentrates primarily on variables that advance or harm relationships; the next chapter examines social cognition (how people "know" one another) and communication competence (how well people interact).

INTERPERSONAL COMMUNICATION: THE DYNAMICS OF ACTION AND REACTION

Who are your friends? Your enemies? How do you know? Who can you trust? What do you do to get people to trust and like you? Do you know when other people are trying to control you? Do you let some people control you more than others? How do you exert control — or counter the control moves others employ? What nonverbal cues are most important to you in getting to know someone? Questions such as these should help you to focus on some of the issues basic to interpersonal communication. The objective is to address the variables that account for the qualitative differences between relationships and affect their growth, stability, or decline.

If they fail to capture the dynamics of the interactive process, interpersonal communication studies fail to be revealing. Persons engaged in interpersonal communication interact in ways that define their relationship. How they interact is a result of this definition. "At the core of this definitional process are the relational messages exchanged between participants" (Burgoon & Hale, 1984, p. 193). The meaning a relationship has for each of its participants exists in their minds rather than in the relationship per se. Each participant will have unique definitions of each relationship, but a few characteristics seem universal to all relationships.

Morton, Alexander, and Altman (1976) offered several propositions to stress the relationship between action and definition while noting how interactions progress naturally.

1. They postulated that viable relationships demand that the parties engaged in communication have mutual control over one another. This assumes that the parties need a consensual definition of that relationship. For instance, Person A has control of Person B only if B allows that to occur.

2. Relationships are defined by multiple modes of communication (verbal, nonverbal, time, context, and occasion) that occur at multiple levels (superior–subordinate, formal to informal).
3. As a relationship develops, modes of exchange increase and diversify. For instance enemies find more ways to fight, as lovers find more ways to express affection.
4. If a relationship lacks a sense of mutuality, it is likely to suffer crisis. Most lopsided relationships do not last, or if they do, they rarely produce happiness.
5. Individuals are involved in a relationship consensus regarding the means by which they can negotiate the relationship. They like to know the groundrules of their relationships. For instance, they want to know when and how to be open — or whether they can be open or are expected to be open. They share an understanding of the rewards (or their withdrawal), punishments, and coercions that are appropriate for influencing how each other performs in that relationship. For example, they know that if they talk too much the other persons are likely to tell them to be quiet; if they do not listen, they may find their relational partners unwilling to listen. The parties also seek consensus regarding the degree to which any communication tactics can be used and the way their use is distributed between the parties. Is it okay for you to lose your temper, but you don't want your friends to lose their tempers at you? Can both partners use the same means of reward and coercion — and to the same extent and for the same purpose? The answer to that question may become clearer when you recall that parents sometimes "scream" at their kids or "whine" to show them they too can use those control tactics.

Throughout the study of interpersonal communication, verbal exchange plays a prominent role, but this study involves more than tracking verbal aspects of interactants' communication styles. Words are also important because they influence perceptions interactants have of one another and of their relationships. If the terms people use to characterize each other contain stereotypes, the interaction may fulfill those stereotypes. For instance, a person will think differently of a communication partner who is dominating rather than strong, even though either trait is only a matter of perception. At some point in a relationship, the "strength" one person admired in another may become "smothering." Even if the degree of strength does not change, the perception of it does.

Although discussion of interpersonal communication focuses on means by which people interact, we cannot ignore the impact of the perceptions the participants have of one another. Communication styles, strategies, and competencies are important, but what transpires in a relationship depends on what the participants think occurs and the impact those thoughts have on the relationship.

This brief summary emphasizes how interaction follows a cybernetic model whereby people use positive and negative responses to influence each other and guide interaction. Through interaction, participants define, refine, and negotiate the meanings they assign to one another, to themselves, and to their relationship. Participants calculate the rewards and costs of the relationship and reflect on their competencies to improve it. Featuring a rules perspective to explain this process, Millar and Rogers (1976) concluded, "A transactional perspective of communication behavior tries to look directly at the combinatorial rules characterizing the system's message exchange process and not at the individual characteristics brought to the situation by the individual participants" (p. 90).

SOCIAL PENETRATION

To understand the process of interpersonal communication, researchers attempt to determine what cybernetic responses guide the development of relationships. This inquiry addresses several broad questions. (a) Is the process strategic? (b) If so, how does it operate? (c) What is the nature of the message exchange process? (d) What motives underpin the process? Some answers to these questions have been provided by social penetration theory (Altman & Taylor, 1973; Taylor & Altman 1987).

Social penetration refers to the process whereby people come to know one another in varying degrees of detail and intimacy. This theory views the quality of communication—what is exchanged between relational partners—as vital to the development and maintenance of relationships.

According to this theory, positive communication produces positive relationships, whereas negative communication results in negative ones. People prefer positive to negative relationships. In positive relationships, persons are willing to disclose. Disclosure, communicating openly, is gratifying, whereas being closed to others produces negative outcomes. For the most part, each relational partner is flattered by the other person's willingness to disclose; this willingness asserts that the person is worthy of receiving this disclosure. However, too much disclosure can become negative, a burden on a relationship. According to this theory, relationships grow through overt interpersonal behaviors and internal cognitive processes whereby participants create messages, prepare message strategies, and think about the quality of the relationship.

Social penetration theory argues that relationships grow or dissolve by passing through developmental stages. The metaphor of penetration is used to emphasize how people "get into" each other, come to know and willingly disclose to each other. According to the theory, the growth of a relationship is gradual and relatively orderly, moving from superficial awareness, to recognition, understanding, and appreciation of one another. Deterioration of relationships follows the opposite path. In a deteriorating relationship, people become increasingly closed.

Each moment of communication, regardless of the quality of the relationship, transpires in a context that has a past—a history—and can be projected into the future. Projection into the future allows participants to forecast and estimate the rewards and costs of becoming more intimate, getting to know each other, and maintaining a relationship. The history of the relationship lets the partners know what rewards were received or losses incurred from previous disclosure. Relationships grow, this theory postulates, because people hope to achieve more satisfying interactions.

This theory suggests that relationships progress through four stages: Orientation, exploration, affective exchange, and stable exchange (Taylor & Altman, 1987). *Orientation* occurs in public areas. At this stage, the level of intimacy is that typical of initial interactions when people first meet and start to become acquainted. The tone of conversations at this stage is likely to be cautious and exploratory. Initial, superficial efforts are made to reduce uncertainty and forecast the reward/cost ratio of getting to know the other person.

A relationship progresses to the second phase if participants become willing to have *exploratory affective exchange*. This stage involves preliminary attempts to reveal aspects of personality and more private thoughts. The tone of this stage is more friendly and relaxed. An exchange of feelings and emotions is vital at this phase. This reveals information about the person who volunteers them that the partner would not otherwise have. A level of trust is developing because each person is willing to share intimate details and to be more expressive and less guarded. This stage may be characterized by "what do you think (or feel) questions." It may involve open expression of feelings, "You're nice" or "I enjoy your company."

The third stage, *affective exchange,* is a continuation of the previous stage. It is typical of close friendships and romantic relationships, in which intimacy increases because participants disclose to each other in more casual and free-wheeling ways. The final stage, *stable exchange,* is characterized by continuous openness. Because of disclosure at previous stages, participants have come to know one another sufficiently well to reliably interpret and predict feelings and behavior of each other.

Participants cannot progress through these stages without using verbal and nonverbal communication as well as situationally oriented behaviors, including nonverbal cues of space, distance, and physical objects. As relationships become more intimate, participants can make transitions through space—even into intimate space—easier and with a prediction that the outcome will be positive. This phenomenon is easy to appreciate as you recall how you become "closer" to others physically as well as psychologically. It is uncomfortable for most people to put an arm around a stranger. Most people have encountered the awkwardness of initiating, accepting, or repelling a kiss—a good example of the penetration of intimate space. People test distance in space when they are physically separated, sometimes by hundreds of miles.

Taylor and Altman (1987) acknowledged that relationships cannot grow without conflict. Crises and relationship stress occur. How participants negotiate such crises depends in part on their calculations of the reward/cost ratio of the relationship. If crisis and conflict lead to forecasts that costs will outweigh rewards, the relationship is likely to dissolve or at least become less intimate. This outcome could result from failure to manage conflict effectively.

According to this theory, all relationships entail costs. To understand interpersonal relationships requires insight into this formula: Relationship outcomes = rewards − costs. Taylor and Altman (1987) presented five propositions in this regard.

1. When rewards outweigh costs, a relationship is satisfying.
2. In assessing the reward/cost ratio, people can estimate an absolute reward/cost ratio and use it as a yardstick against which to measure each specific relationship.
3. As interaction transpires, critical moments are assessed in terms of the absolute reward and cost ratio of the relationship. In this way, participants calculate immediate obtained rewards and costs.
4. As the relationship continues, participants *forecast* rewards and costs based on apparent progress, given its history and immediate rewards.
5. Participants calculate the cumulative rewards and costs over the duration of the relationship.

Because efforts to increase intimacy produce costs, exchange at superficial levels usually occurs before progressing to more intimate levels. This progression can be conceptualized in terms of *quantity* (number of topics which can be shared) and *quality* (depth of intimacy on each topic). Most social relationships exhibit stability and change. This process is a tug-of-war involving polarities such as closedness–openness, acceptance–rejection, or disclosure–secretiveness. Change is necessary if relationships are to develop, but they must have a sufficiently stable relationship history to support subsequent levels of intimacy.

Change can be *quantitative,* more topics become open for discussion, and *qualitative,* more disclosure is possible on each topic. Dissolution of relationships assumes that the opposite processes occur, less depth and fewer topics. You probably recall how you spent time talking about topics with a relational partner when the relationship was good, but found that you really did not have much to say as the relationship became less satisfying.

In this process, sources of opposition can be either internal or external. Internal forces range from visceral biological responses, such as negative or positive emotional arousal, as well as cognitive idiosyncratic preferences and tolerances ("I just didn't like his/her looks"). External forces include social pressures, norms, and approval. Interactions vary in the amount of openness or closedness that occurs; they tend to vary over time, even with the same person, and according to circumstances.

Stability is important because participants need to feel that they can act and be acted toward in ways that are predictable. But a relationship cannot grow if it remains stable. Whether the quantity or quality of openness or closedness remains stable or changes probably depends on four factors: *frequency* (how often a person is open or closed), *amplitude* (the degree of openness or closedness), *regularity* (the patterns of openness or closedness), or *relative duration* of either state (how long a person is in either state).

These processes operate on the assumption that people seek to maintain balance, a concept consistent with the cybernetic, systems approach to communication. Rather than striving for any ideal state, persons interact to achieve balance among closedness, openness, stability, and change as they achieve a level of comfort in each relationship. Tensions involved in efforts to achieve balance provide the dynamism of a relationship. Rather than striving for an ideal relationship, people are likely to enjoy relationships in which they are able to balance these four factors so that there is enough but not too much openness, closedness, stability, or change. How these dimensions operate in an interaction is related to timing and synchrony. *Timing* refers to the moments when each party is open or closed on a topic. *Synchrony* focuses on whether they are in complementary states at the same times so that their efforts match one another (Altman, Vinsel, & Brown, 1981).

This analysis suggests that rather than using some ideal to measure the quality of relationships, you should look at what persons want from their relationships to determine how satisfied they are and how likely they are to make dynamic adjustments to increase the level of satisfaction. Taylor and Altman (1987) predicted that when the ratio of rewards to costs is high, the penetration process is likely to increase.

One reason for this increase is the presence of norms of *reciprocity.* Disclosure by one person invites disclosure by another. This exchange process is regulated by norms of *equitable exchange,* implying that each person is obligated to achieve the same degree of disclosure. These processes are influenced by the ability of people to perceive the degree to which others are disclosing and their willingness to match that disclosure. Although the metaphor of mental bookkeeping of rewards/costs, closedness/openness is a bit crass, some method of account keeping seems to be vital to the increase or deterioration of social penetration. This view fits the notion that, although intimacy ought to increase or decrease in developmental fashion, it may be cyclical, whereby people are periodically more open or more closed.

Disclosure is strategic behavior that is sensitive to at least four factors: Setting, receiver, sender, and relationship. To decide whether to disclose, women rely more on sender and receiver characteristics than do men, and they place more importance on prerequisite conditions for all topics than do men. Although women are more willing to express empathy than men, have greater need for affiliation, and be more responsive, they also seem more sensitive to the circumstances required for self-disclosure (Petronio, Martin, & Littlefield, 1984). Comforting is also strategic. Highly apprehensive individuals do not engage in as much comforting behavior as do their less apprehensive counterparts. Comforting behavior is unrelated to empathy or locus of control (Samter & Burleson, 1984).

Understanding how and whether a sequence of disclosure occurs can provide needed insight into how relationships become more intimate (or fail). Social penetration theory predicts that breadth and depth of self-disclosure should increase. Early stages in a relationship should be characterized by periods of public disclosure. This kind of disclosure involves relatively nonthreatening details known to others with whom the discloser has contact. This level of disclosure should lay the foundation for semiprivate disclosures, and eventually private-personal disclosures. Uncertainty reduction theory postulates that disclosure should tend to diminish over time as each partner feels that enough uncertainty has been reduced for the relationship to be maintained (Berger & Calabrese, 1975).

To better understand whether and how mutual exchange of disclosure occurs, VanLear (1987) investigated whether relationships show incremental increases in depth and breadth of disclosure topics (public, semiprivate, or private-personal) and, if so, by what pattern. This research found that levels of disclosure tend to follow norms of reciprocity; intimate disclosure is matched by intimate disclosure. This reciprocity was strongest for semiprivate disclosures. Development of relationships seems to follow a cyclical model of self-disclosure reciprocity. One person's disclosure may prompt the partner to reciprocate at least for a short time, but intimate disclosure is difficult to maintain for very long. Although this progression is cyclical in some dyads, it does not occur in all. This research offers partial support for social penetration theory and demonstrates the important role relational history plays in interpersonal communication.

Any moment of interpersonal communication has some past that affects what partners do and say. A relationship has a present (what is happening), and to some degree, what is said and done is predicated on where the relationship seems to be going—whether it is likely to be rewarding. One way of patterning this history of relationships is to think of them as cycles, whereby participants recall the relational history to check, for instance, the amount of trust. Whether a person is willing to trust another depends in large part on whether that trust was violated or accepted in the past. If all is well with the relationship, it can progress to a new level—a mix of cyclical and linear patterns (Duck & Miell, 1986). Linear patterns mean that the amount of openness by one partner is reciprocated by the other and that the amount of openness achieved does not lessen or increase in a cyclical fashion.

In this development, each relationship may change at different paces or rhythms; some relationships achieve intimacy more quickly than others do. Each relationship and, within it, each segment, lasts for a period, and thereby has *scale*. Sometimes during a relationship a person might mention some intimate detail briefly to see how the partner reacts. Although mentioned briefly at one point, this intimate detail could be the subject of a longer discussion at a later time. Relationships exhibit *sequences* of changing and recurring patterns. Sometimes during a relationship, people "go over the same ground" time after time. To an extent, the history of the relationship depends on the *salience* of any event—the extent to which it is at the forefront of one or both persons' thoughts. These patterns suggest that interpersonal relationship histories—their progression—may be subject to many variables (Werner & Haggard, 1985). During interpersonal communication, people go back over topics previously discussed and advance into unexplored grounds, if rewards outweigh costs.

One of the keys to relationship development is what the participants remember about previous encounters with one another. Contrary to what most people think, they are able to recall relatively little (about 10%) of what was said in a previous conversation. And they remember selectively (Stafford & Daly, 1984). What people remember is likely to be behavior-specific (what other people did) rather than the qualities of the relationship (such as control) or the situation in which it occurred (Planalp, 1985).

What people remember about their interpersonal encounters may be based on what they think are prototypical interactions. What this means is that people seem to remember relational history by categorizing events according to what they think a typical relationship should be. They create their interaction plans according to a similar set of expectations (Honeycutt, Cantrill, & Greene, 1989). This research explains why two people in an encounter remember differently what happened. They focus on different features of their encounters because of their unique expectations of what should happen in interpersonal communication.

In this way, social penetration theory offers many interesting ways to think about interpersonal communication. One of its most important dimensions, estimations of cost/rewards, will be featured in the next section to explain how people decide what makes a good relationship and negotiate its boundaries and define its obligations.

SOCIAL EXCHANGE THEORY

How do you know what is required to achieve and maintain a friendship or some other relationship? That question can be answered in terms of dynamics unique to each relationship. Each friendship is different. You may have one relative who demands a lot of you whereas another gives more than he or she receives. You might have a good relationship with someone based on the mutual willingness to disclose—at least that is what social penetration theory suggests. Positive communication, especially in the form of disclosure, is a major part of the development of such relationships. Perhaps so. But what do you do or expect of others with whom you have ongoing relationships?

Part of the answer to that question rests with the willingness and ability of relational partners to negotiate and comply with obligations and rewards of relationships. You probably have several friends with whom you have different relationships, but you might say that each friend is a good friend, even if each is a different kind of friend. You might be willing to disclose some of your personality to one of your parents but not to the other parent. What is the difference? In pondering that question, you might also intuit some of the shortcomings of social penetration theory, such as its reliance on disclosure and the difficulty of knowing when any amount of disclosure is enough or too much.

To close some of these gaps in the understanding of relationships, social exchange theory postulates that people negotiate the "rules" and "requirements" of each relationship. As does social penetration theory, social exchange theory assumes that people prefer positive to negative relationships and that positive communication leads to positive relationships. According to social exchange theory, individuals, who are involved in interactions that they want to be positive, define and negotiate what *they* consider to be required for positive and negative communication, and "agree" on the rules and behaviors required to foster the relationship. Rules and actions that make up a relationship are defined by each person's expectations and needs as well as by what each person is able and willing to perform in behalf of the relationship. Capturing the essence of this approach to interpersonal communication, Roloff (1981) concluded, "Interpersonal communication is a symbolic process by which two people bound together in a relationship, provide each other with resources or negotiate the exchange of resources" (p. 30).

Roloff (1987) shed insight into the relational exchange that occurs when people negotiate the means for improving or harming efforts to establish relationships. Everyday rewards that people give to or withhold from one another constitute "payments" that affect how they negotiate the responsibilities and limits of achieving intimacy with one another. These payments occur in the form of communication. If one person discloses too much (or too little) or interrupts too often or does not listen attentively, the partner is likely to act in ways that demonstrate that these behaviors are inappropriate. By this means, the partner attempts to set limits on the activities needed to foster the relationship. Through negotiation of the amount of each kind of action—for instance, how much disclosure is enough—partners define relationships. At a given moment, one partner might believe that an amount of disclosure is sufficient, but if the other person says, "Tell me more about yourself," the amount was insufficient.

By defining and meeting obligations, people demonstrate to one another that they desire to know each other's innermost thoughts and share mutual regard. For instance, marital happiness is positively correlated with the number of positive communication exchanges received each day. These communication exchanges cover a wide range of activities too long to list here, but some examples are helpful. For instance, the list includes kind looks (eye contact), a pat on the back, listening or disclosing at appropriate times, including the other in a conversation, or introducing that person to one's friends. People seem to be happiest when others whom they like perform positively and avoid negative jabs. These kinds of communication acts are the basis of social exchange that people use to reduce uncertainty and define rewards (and costs) to enhance relationships.

In many respects, this theory features a process that is analogous to monetary exchange. In situations regarding monetary reciprocity, people are interested in giving and receiving fair value for their efforts. If one person gives something of value to another, according to social exchange theory, reciprocation of equal or sufficient value is expected. But what is fair value? What is "fair" exchange to one relational partner may be too much (or too little) in the estimation of another.

The goal of the theory is to explain how people negotiate what is expected to satisfy the amount of relational rewards and how long one can take before repayment. Resources in this context can be many: kindness, regard, love, complements, and requests to be involved (inclusion). They can be verbal or nonverbal. A smile, for example, is a valuable resource, as is a kind touch. Rewards can be as tangible as a dinner invitation or as intangible as willingness to listen attentively.

Roloff (1987) set out some norms that are basic to social exchange.

• The first of these, *norms of reciprocity,* depend on several factors that can affect relationships. *Homeomorphic* exchanges require returns of the same benefits. That is, if one person compliments another a similar compliment is expected to balance the exchange. A return of an equivalent but different resource is *heteromorphic.* A sincere compliment by one person may be exchanged for a heartfelt "thank you" by another. Norms of reciprocity govern whether resources must be the same or merely equivalent.

• The second norm refers to amount of time allowed or required for the exchange to be satisfying; the length of time allowed is a factor of each relationship and may be carefully negotiated. Sometimes people feel obligated to perform an exchange immediately (or expect an immediate exchange). Others who are more "laid back" may be in no hurry to exchange. (Do you send greeting cards to persons who do not send them to you? If you receive a card, do you feel compelled to reciprocate?) People who expect an immediate exchange may get the response but interpret it as being "late"—payment took too long. In this case, failure to respond as expected constitutes negative communication that can be used to decide that the partner does not desire to achieve or maintain a friendship. No such slight might have been intended, but in interpersonal communication, people interpret each relationship through the behavior of the other parties—and judge them based on criteria that may not be voiced.

• A third norm refers to whether the exchange must be of equal value. A rich friend could invite a poor friend to an expensive lunch and be satisfied by a sandwich in exchange; this is an equivalent rather than an equal exchange but could serve nicely as a fair exchange of friendship.

• A fourth norm relates to whether a clear link must be made between the resources exchanged; if a link is not expressed, but required, the person may have received the exchanged resource but did not know it. This means that one person thought the exchange had been made but the other person did not. One person is satisfied and expects further reciprocation whereas the other is dissatisfied and may withhold reciprocation.

Not all resources can be exchanged for fair value. Thus, norms of reciprocity may specify which resources may be exchanged to meet specific obligations and foster relationships. Some resources may be inappropriate, at least in a given context.

Norms may specify whether and in what ways resources are transferable. The exchange may require that resources not only be returned to the original giver, but also to persons close to that person. Or, other people associated with the person who receive the resource may be obligated to return the resources to the original giver. For this reason, one strain on marriage partners is taking on members of their spouse's family. A wife may like her uncle, but her husband does not. She may believe that her marriage is not strong if her husband cannot be nice to her uncle.

Norms of reciprocity refer to how the initiation of giving resources starts. People may initiate a relationship and give resources (a) without any expectation of return, or (b) because a specific response is needed by the original giver.

Norms imply the potential for one person to invoke sanctions against their communication partners who do not give fair exchange in return. Thus, for instance, if you did not listen to a good friend the last time he or she had something to say, that person may not listen to you the next time you are together. The person may actually tell you that he or she is not listening because you did not listen. That is an explicit sanction. Those that are not explicit are much more difficult to identify and, therefore, are more difficult to resolve. Sometimes people use questions to reduce uncertainty as whether a sanction has been placed on them. We have all asked, "Are you mad at me?" Persons who do not return resources (of equal or equivalent value or in a timely fashion) may experience various sanctions. Norms may prescribe how many resources can be given without reciprocity before sanctions are permissible. They may also prescribe the kind and degree of the sanction and the amount of time that must elapse before sanctions are appropriate.

These norms of reciprocity not only help clarify the exchange basis of this theory, but they also suggest a variety of lines of research to determine how the exchange mechanism operates between persons seeking intimate relationships. Intimate relationships are characterized by indepth understanding of one another as well as high levels of mutual regard. Partners in intimate relationships may be better at knowing and following norms; they may be superior in their ability to perceive when certain exchanges are needed and have the communication competencies to perform appropriate exchanges. Persons who are not so competent, either in perception or exchange, may find creating intimate relationships more difficult. To achieve intimacy, both partners need to be able to know what resources are regarded as such, what norms apply, and how effectively each party is in meeting them.

Drawing on the assumptions of social exchange theory, Roloff (1987) offered several hypotheses. He speculated that as the degree of intimacy increases, several factors will be at play:

1. As a relationship matures, it will exhibit more heteropathic responses because intimacy allows, perhaps even warrants, greater latitude of exchange. As intimacy increases, people come to have more knowledge of one another and can better appreciate the value of each resource in the perception of their communication partner.

2. As intimacy increases, the time expected for exchange becomes more variable. Partners trust each other to repay resources and, therefore, need not exchange on such a short time frame.
3. As a relationship matures, partners are less likely to use a resource merely to get a resource and are less likely to expect or state explicitly that a resource is given in specific payment. People need to do less to be sure the other person knows that a resource has been repaid. Trust and understanding as well as ability to reduce uncertainty increase as a relationship becomes more intimate. Indeed, one of the tests of increased intimacy may be that the level of regard remains high even though explicit exchanges are not made. (But partners must guard against "taking the other for granted.")
4. Increased intimacy makes more resources available for exchange,
5. requires more transferability of exchange,
6. obligates partners to initiate exchanges, and
7. allows partners to be more tolerant of asymmetrical relationships, whereby one person gives more than the other without harming the relationship.
8. Intimates are less likely to be upset and willing to impose sanctions if exact reciprocation does not occur.

Focusing on factors that can affect relational growth, Roloff (1987) suggested that, as individuals sense or desire that a relationship is becoming more intimate, they are more likely to engage in reciprocation. To foster the growth of relationships, participants may engage in need assessment interactions whereby they inquire about the other to see what resources are needed and to know whether "the ledger" is balanced.

Increased intimacy prompts interactants to be more disclosive because they know that their partner is capable of reading the need for reciprocity and will know what to do. Increased intimacy is associated with willingness of participants to accept an offered resource and to be less likely to express gratitude for receipt of a resource. In an intimate relationship, if the need for resources is imbalanced, participants are likely to tolerate unilateral giving and receiving without harm to the relationship.

How people negotiate the relational quality of an interaction becomes important. Thus, as intimacy increases, people become more willing to seek needed resources from the other, and less explanation is needed for why requests are made and fewer inducements are given for these requests. Prior to development of intimacy, partners desiring intimacy may have to work hard to achieve appropriate exchanges. Dating behavior, for instance, may in the beginning be characterized by lots of effort on the part of one or both partners. As a relationship continues, it is likely that at various times one or both partners will fail to give the desired exchange and may suffer some sanctions. Statements indicating the presence of imbalance might include, "You did not call me," "You do not call me enough," "Tim gave Susan flowers," or "Joanne doesn't flirt with other guys the way you do." These comments probably sound familiar. If so, you probably have pretty good insight into the presence and operation of social exchange.

This is a powerful explanation of why each relationship is different and how those differences are negotiated. In keeping with our central themes, this theory emphasizes the importance of social competence, rests on an uncertainty reduction model, suggests that people persuade others to be friends, and features rewards and costs of building relationships.

WHAT VARIABLES SHAPE RELATIONSHIPS?

To this point, we have discussed two theories that reason that people seek positive relationships and use disclosure as well as negotiation to create or dissolve them. As research progresses, one objective is to determine which variables influence how relationships grow, remain static, or deteriorate. Researchers seek to discover which variables best indicate the quality of relationships.

Two researchers, Millar and Rogers (1976, 1987), were instrumental in this effort by arguing that the quality of relationships depends on control, trust, and intimacy. They built their work on the assumption that self-identity is a social product, the result of interaction. For this reason, people seek and prefer other persons who can predictably satisfy their desire for role identity. In this vein, interactants either complement or contradict one another. If complementarity exceeds contradiction, the relationship is likely to be satisfying.

For this reason, interpersonal relationships are redundant, interlocked, and co-defined rather than unilaterally defined. Patterns of communication behavior are played over and over *(redundant)*. What one person does affects the other which in turn produces a counter effect *(interlocked)*. Partners involved in relationships *co-define* those relationships; for example, if you ask one person to describe a relationship, he or she is likely to do so in terms of what he or she thinks of its quality and what he or she thinks the partner thinks of the relationship.

If the same question were put to a relational partner, he or she would have the same two perspectives (what he or she thinks and what he or she thinks the partner thinks). Another good way to realize that relationships are interlocked is to recall that one person cannot carry on an argument if the other person is unwilling. (Most of us know how to bait someone into an argument, but it takes two to argue.) Trust is co-defined by what each does for and to the other. With these principles in mind, we can examine what Millar and Rogers believe to be the variables that have the most effect on relationships.

Control refers to the right and ability each participant has to define, direct, and delimit the actions that transpire during interaction. Control often varies, at least by topic and context, between participants. For instance, in a marriage, one partner might exert more control over budget matters whereas the other might exercise more control over recreation. In some relationships, control is distributed relatively equally between partners, and in other relationships it is disproportionate—one partner exerts more control over a broad range of topics, matters, and conversations. Although researchers assume that control is best when it is equally distributed, they recognize that a good relationship can exist with one person exerting disproportionate amounts of control (as long the partner willingly yields to this control). A key in a relationship is the extent to which partners support each other's role identity. A dependent person can be supported by another's strength. That person is rewarded for having strength by the other person's need for guidance.

Control is the most basic of the three concepts. It is exerted through commitments, norms, rules, promises, threats and contracts. During interactions, people estimate the probability of how their partners will behave under control constraints. If they exert control in a particular situation, will their partners yield or resist? What will happen if one person seeks to change the dynamics of a relationship by attempting to exert control whereas before that person yielded to the partner's control? If one person withholds control, will the partner exert control?

To answer questions such as these, Millar and Rogers (1987) offered three measures of control. *Redundancy* refers to the amount and kind of control tactics each person exerts. Redundancy refers to the kinds of constraints used to wield control or the tactics used to negotiate the rights to define the relationship. If one or both parties repeatedly use the same patterns of control, redundancy is high. High redundancy equals high rigidity, the unwillingness or inability to change tactics. *Dominance* is the amount of influence or control exhibited by A relative to B. To measure how control is distributed in a relationship, all of the control can be divided by the amount of control A exerts. The result of this calculation is the extent to which dominance is distributed. If one person has all of the control, he or she is dominant. Keep in mind that relationships are codependent; one person can dominate only if allowed to do so by the other person. The last measure of control, *power,* is the degree to which one person can influence or constrain another's behavior.

The second major variable affecting a relationship, Millar and Rogers (1987) contended, is *trust*—the extent to which participants experience uncertainty in regard to amount and kind of control exerted in a relationship. Trust is a counterpart of control; it refers to the control persons exert over themselves and their partners. They consider whether they can trust one another to handle control responsibly—in ways that produce rewards rather than costs. Because people are interdependent, their actions influence one another, and outcomes depend on what each one does regarding the other. Trust is contingent on the extent and ways one person can depend on the other; in this regard, trust involves predictability and obligation. Based on the assumption that people seek rewards during relationships, trust involves attempts to increase predictability and reduce uncertainty.

Trust has three indices: vulnerability, reward dependability, and confidence. *Vulnerability* is an estimate of the frequency that A is willing to be vulnerable to B. Vulnerability depends on the difference between subjective cost of risking and the reward to be derived from risking. Person A is vulnerable to Person B if B can deliver or withhold rewards to A. Vulnerability is a function of the cost of getting the reward and occurs when cost may not equal reward. The parties in a relationship must be vulnerable for it to grow. A second factor of vulnerability is *reward dependability,* a score based on the frequency that A has been (or will be) rewarded for being vulnerable to B. Reward dependability is high if one partner can depend on the other for rewards. Trust results when reward dependability is high, or the extent to which the relationship of A's need for reward is met by B; A's need for reward divided by B's giving reward equals 1 when trust is high. *Confidence* is the extent to which persons believe others will not betray them. This estimate is set against the vulnerability score which is a estimate of the ratio between costs and rewards.

Intimacy, the third major construct in this model, depends on one person using the other for self-confirmation. It refers to the extent relational partners have depth of attachment. Intimacy is high if partners are exclusive with one another—meaning that only the partner can provide some need or satisfy some part of the relationship. Statements such as "I can't live without you" or "I really miss you when you are away" characterize intimacy.

What are the factors of intimacy? One is *transferability* which refers to the number of persons who can confirm Person A. If transferability is high (many people can satisfy Person A), the amount of intimacy and confirmation any person has for Person A is low. *Attachment* refers to subjective feelings partners have for one another. If one person likes the confirmation the other can give, attachment is high. *Knowledge* is vital because it refers to what one partner knows about the other's transferability and attachment. Person A's attachment for Person B depends on the extent to which A believes B views A as a relational partner.

Based on this model, Millar and Rogers (1987) defined dominance in marital relationships as occurring when reward dependability and knowledge ratios are small. If the control system is flexible, dominance is low; rigidity means that dominance is high. If B's needs are not transferable beyond A and if B is attached to A, A is dominant.

Defined in this way, Millar and Rogers distinguish between domineeringness and dominance. *Dominance* assumes that one partner must reciprocate or yield control to the other. If neither wants to yield and both want to control, *domineeringness* occurs and results in neither partner being pleased by the relationship. In keeping with this line of research, Warfel (1984) discovered that people use communication style (how they communicate) to determine which person is powerful. People who use "powerless" language are viewed as less dominant but more competent as communicators because they employ a wide range of relationship-building strategies and do not force relationships.

Research such as that reported by Millar and Rogers is intuitively interesting but it has been criticized from a research methodology standpoint (Folger & Poole, 1982). The difficulty is that the research is often conducted by having coders listen to conversations between subjects. The coders are asked to code the kinds of statements they perceive and estimate the depth of feeling expressed in the statements. Knowing, as an outsider, whether a statement exerts (rather than exhibits) dominance, control, trust, or intimacy can be difficult and inaccurate.

Each of us has experienced this research methodology flaw during everyday conversations; many times we misjudge intensity of feelings or relational meaning of comments we hear exchanged among our acquaintances. A statement such as, "I thought you were really mad at her" exhibits how we can be wrong; such a statement might be found to be in error when our friend says, "Oh, I always talk to her like that. She knows I don't mean that. We've been friends for years." Such misperceptions not only plague researchers, but they also have implications for how each person interacts with others. Some people seem to be more competent than others in telegraphing the relational meaning of comments and in interpreting the relational meaning that others' comments contain.

In addition to the problem of coding relational responses, another difficulty in studying interpersonal relations is determining which variables actually should be studied because they account most for differences between rewarding and unrewarding relationships. In contrast to the three-part taxonomy proposed by Millar and Rogers, Knapp (1978) suggested an alternative list: Depth, breadth, evaluation, smoothness, difficulty, spontaneity, flexibility, and uniqueness. The first two of these concepts are featured in Altman and Taylor's (1973) social penetration theory that argues that relationships depend on the breadth of topics and depth of detail participants share with each other.

Smoothness refers to degree to which a conversation synchronizes and interactants' conversational styles are similar and free of strain. *Difficulty* is an estimate of the extent to which interactants are able to accurately understand one another. *Spontaneity* relates to amount of strain or tension present in interactants' efforts to get to know one another. *Flexibility* and *uniqueness* refer to the variety of channels participants use to communicate and their ability to adapt messages to each other as unique personalities.

These eight factors, Knapp, Ellis, and Williams (1980) argued, can be reduced to three.

1. *Personalized communication* refers to the degrees of intimacy in a relationship; it results from private conversations, expressions of feelings, sharing of secrets, and such.
2. *Synchronized communication* relates to conversational styles, the ease with which people interact.
3. *Difficult communication* is the opposite of synchronized communication.

Burgoon and Hale (1984) criticized Knapp's taxonomy for featuring communication styles or quality of relationships rather than the content of messages that foster or harm them. Based on a review of several other taxonomies, Burgoon and Hale reasoned that the best taxonomy is one that stresses message content. In this vein, *dominance–submission* is one of the major pairs of concepts because it includes comments participants use to exert and share control. *Intimacy* can be subdivided to include statements that convey affection-hostility, intensity of involvement, inclusion–exclusion, trust, and depth-superficiality. Factors such as these define the degree of immediacy in a relationship. *Immediacy* refers to the extent to which a relationship is based on liking; it depends on the closeness participants convey to one another by verbal and nonverbal behavior that signifies intimacy, such as touching, eye contact, rapport, physical closeness, and vocalizations of closeness such as the use of the pronoun "we."

Immediacy is an important variable because people approach and get involved with appealing or pleasing people and avoid those who are not (Mehrabian, 1981; Weiner & Mehrabian, 1968). If messages contain immediacy, they are likely to attract people to each other. *Emotional arousal* and *composure* are closely related, but are independent of one another. Even though people may be aroused (angered, for instance) during conversations they can remain composed. *Formality* refers to norms unique to each interaction; message content can convey a tone of formality or informality. The *task-social* dimension focuses on message content because some statements are designed to achieve tasks, whereas others foster (or hamper) a socioemotional climate conducive to performance of the task.

Burgoon and Hale used their taxonomy to argue that other researchers' sets of terms are too narrow and focus on communication style or outcome rather than message content.

Having refined their taxonomy, Burgoon and Hale (1987) expanded the list of variables from five to eight: dominance, similarity/depth, immediacy/affection, formality, task-orientation, equality, receptivity-trust, and composure. The effort to determine what list of variables is not trivial, even though it is often confusing to remember which researchers prefer which list. Without an accurate list of key elements of a relationship, it is impossible to determine what communication styles and message variables affect what relationship variables leading to better or worse relationships. This kind of effort strives to realize what Berger (1977a) believed to be the essence of social scientific research, the search for the few variables that are essential to understanding a relationship as opposed to those that are not, those that constitute irrelevant variety.

The usefulness of Burgoon and Hale's taxonomy is demonstrated by studies such as one that investigated what kinds of messages used by physicians are likely to gain compliance and be satisfying to patients. Patients are more satisfied when physicians express receptivity, immediacy, composure, similarity, formality, and low levels of dominance (Burgoon et al., 1987). Patients seem more satisfied when their doctors exhibit nonverbal communication styles that are similar to those of their patients. Doctors tend to match or reciprocate patients' nonverbal patterns, such as response latency (time between statements), pauses during speaking turns (hesitance), body orientation (such as turning toward someone instead of turning away), and interruptions (breaking into statements by one another) as well as duration of turns (how long one person speaks) and gestural patterns. Doctors are less domineering and more responsive to patients over 30 years old. They are responsive to patients who experience anxiety (Street & Buller, 1988). Many of these relationship cues are nonverbal.

Studying romantic relationships, Baxter (1990) featured three relationship pairs: Autonomy–connection, openness–closedness, and predictability–novelty. As subjects reflected back on a romantic relationship, they recalled all three variables and were able to indicate the communication strategies they used in response to each. Openness-closedness is the dominant pair at early stages of romantic relationships, and the other two dominate later stages. How satisfied partners are with a relationship correlates with their use of strategies: Selection, separation, neutralization, and reframing. *Selection* entails deciding to use strategies that feature one end of the continuum, such as becoming more open or more closed. *Separation* involves assigning one of the polar concepts to topics or events, such as saying that the two partners should spend Friday evenings together, a loss of autonomy for the good of the relationship. *Neutralization* occurs when the parties lessen the emotional intensity associated with one of the polar terms, perhaps by agreeing to be less upset by one person's closedness. *Reframing* is a relatively complex strategy that results when one of the terms is redefined, such as autonomy not being viewed as the opposite of connection, but its enhancement. In this last sense, a person may argue that the romance is strong because he or she feels even more connected during absence and that absence proves the strength of the romance (Baxter, 1990).

This section has discussed efforts being made to determine which variables foster the understanding of why some relationships are superior to others. Throughout this chapter, one theme is central: People favor rewarding relationships and avoid those that cost more than they offer in exchange. Such observations are almost too facile to be helpful. By digging into the nature of relational communication, researchers are slowly discovering which factors of communication content and style influence how people understand and relate to one another in interpersonal communication. We must discover exactly what variables stand the test of describing satisfying relationships.

EXPECTATIONS IN RELATIONSHIPS

As you communicate with others, you probably think about whether those persons meet or violate your expectations of how they should interact. Even if you do not consciously have those thoughts, you probably react to others based on how well they meet your expectations. You might conclude, "Well, I never expected her (him) to react that way." Or you might think, "Do you need to stand so close to me"?

People expect one another to communicate in certain ways. Without such expectations and the ability to meet them, communication would be chaotic. People have expectations in regard to which communication styles, strategies, and messages should be used at various points in a relationship. These expectations guide what people do and what they expect others to do during interactions. People may misinterpret one another because they have difficulty knowing what each other means or why the other acts as he or she does. Moreover, some people are more competent at sensing which communication behaviors are expected and in performing the appropriate behaviors. Usually, when expectations are met positively, the relationship is rewarding.

What happens when expectations are not met? This section explores that question, giving attention to the roles nonverbal communication plays when individuals satisfy or violate expectations. Most people believe that they and others should conform to communication norms to be successful; this assumption is basic to the rules perspective, as well as theories that postulate that violations produce arousal that leads to negative consequences (Andersen, 1985; Cappella & Greene, 1982; Patterson, 1982, 1983). Some violations of expectations harm communication, but some violations, whether verbal or nonverbal, enhance communicator effectiveness (Burgoon & Hale, 1988).

A basic assumption is that nonverbal patterns of relational partners should match or complement one another if a relationship is positive and likely to progress. Nonverbal cues and patterns that do not match may prompt interactants to abandon a relationship. For instance, one might assume that the more supportive someone is, the more he or she will be liked. Berger, Weber, Munley, and Dixon (1977) examined five types of relationships: formal, acquaintance, friend, close friend, and lover. Three factors—sociability, character, and supportiveness—affected interpersonal attractiveness. Across the five relationships, supportiveness showed the greatest difference.

Although relationships do not develop in an orderly, linear progression, what individuals do in regard to one another at each moment in an interaction can affect whether the relationship improves, remains static, or declines. People who adapt or accommodate to one another are likely to be acceptable and attractive conversational partners (Giles & Powesland, 1975). Liking tends to increase when people see their communication partners as being supportive and similar (Berger et al., 1977).

Interpersonal expectations are intimately related to nonverbal aspects of communication. Nonverbal communication is a vital part of interaction because participants use it to give and gain information about each other. People interpret nonverbal communication to reduce uncertainty about the people with whom they communicate and the likelihood that a relationship is rewarding. The most important nonverbal cues are ones that are used intentionally and regularly within each social community (Burgoon, 1985).

Nonverbal cues can complement or contradict what is said. How nonverbal cues accompany what is said can have a lot to do with the interpretation the receiver makes of what he or she thinks is said. You might say something to a friend that you do not intend to be interpreted as unpleasant, but if you say it the "wrong" way, your friend can be hurt or angry. A statement, for instance "You know what I mean, *don't you,*" can be said so that it is interpreted as an expression of uncertainty or as a threat. Vocal qualities modify the statements they accompany. The context in which a statement is made can modify the meaning of nonverbal cues. Nonverbal cues are so subtle and situational that people often use one set of nonverbal displays in private and a different set in public (Burgoon, 1985).

People rely on the extent to which nonverbal cues correspond to expectations. This is especially the case for spotting deception. Despite the tendency to believe that they are expert at spotting deception, people are not very skillful (Bauchner, Brandt, & Miller, 1977; Ekman & Friesen, 1974; Hocking, Bauchner, Kaminski, & Miller, 1979). Changes in arousal, emotion, cognitive difficulty, and control may indicate deception. People who are deceiving are likely to respond more quickly, have shorter periods of eye contact, and be more restrained or inhibited in the display of nonverbal cues (Greene, O'Hair, Cody, & Yen, 1985).

If conversational partners know one another well enough and have a sufficiently long conversational history, they are more likely to spot deception because of perceived discrepancies between what is said, how it is said, and what is expected (verbally and nonverbally). Deception is often associated with

1. less contact,
2. more control of what is said and how,
3. less smiling,
4. more postural shifts,
5. longer response latencies (longer pauses between what one person says and the other's response),
6. slower speech rate,
7. more speech errors (such as wrong word selection),
8. more hesitancies,
9. less immediacy,
10. higher pitch,
11. more nonverbal adaptors,
12. less time spent answering questions, and
13. decreased use of illustrators — gestures used to illustrate comments such as the length of "the fish that got away."

(Burgoon, 1985; deTurck & Miller, 1985; Zuckerman, DePaulo, & Rosenthal, 1981).

In intimate situations, familiarity may not necessarily lead to ability to recognize deception, but produce a level of trust sufficiently high that partners do not expect and therefore do not look for cues of deception. In such situations, ability to spot deception is enhanced by a general suspicion of others and situational suspicion (McCornack & Levine, 1990).

When a person who is deceiving believes a relational partner is "wise to the game," the communication behavior is managed more closely. Clues that deception may have been spotted include nonverbal cues of suspicion and the use of probes. Once deceivers spot these strategies, they mask their arousal cues and encode with a positive demeanor (Buller, Strzyzewski, & Comstock, 1991).

Before continuing to discuss nonverbal communication and expectation, a review of key terms used to describe nonverbal cues can be helpful. The study of body movement, posture, and gestures is called *kinesics*. Kinesics can involve studying whether leaning toward a person during a conversation shows signs of liking for and interest in that person, or whether leaning is a threat.

Paralanguage includes vocal elements that accompany, complement, contradict, or substitute for vocalized words. These elements include vocal qualities, characterizers, qualifiers, and segregates or hesitancies. *Qualities* refer to factors such as pitch, rate, articulation, and rhythm. *Characterizers* are sounds that signify, for instance, whether a person is happy or sad. *Qualifiers* are vocal cues that vary from the norm, for instance, by being too soft or too loud. *Hesitancies* include sounds such as "uhs" or "uhms" and pauses. *Paralinguistic cues* are important to the ability to interpret feeling; they more accurately indicate feelings than does verbal disclosure; people use their own feelings as reference points against which to interpret feelings others express through paralinguistic cues (Sillars, Pike, Jones, & Murphy, 1984).

How vocalics accompany compliance-gaining requests influences whether those requests will be granted. Positive violations increase the likelihood that requests will be granted, whereas negative violations lessen the likelihood of compliance (Buller & Burgoon, 1986). For example, a child's request to be taken to the zoo should be accompanied by vocal cues showing a desire to go. If the child is very excited (positive violation), the request is more likely to be granted because of the person's desire to please the child. If the request is made in vocal tones that suggest the child is not actually interested (negative violation), the request is unlikely to be granted because of the belief that the effort will not be rewarding because the child does not truly want to go.

Proxemics is concerned with the ways people communicate with space ranging from architecture (design and lay out of a building or selection and arrangement of furniture) to the positioning of one person's body in relation to another's during interaction. Proxemic distance includes touch, closeness, eye contact (gaze), and thermal factors (warmth of the body) resulting from proximity. Through proxemic adjustments, for instance, people welcome others and move close to show signs of greeting through eye contact. In contrast, people can turn away and ignore others, avoiding eye contact or glaring. Elevator "politics" give you many opportunities to see how people act with space; the dynamics between two friends alone in an elevator change, for instance, once their space is invaded when others enter the elevator.

Touch can be studied by itself, under the taxonomic heading, *haptics*. *Chronemics* refers to the use of time in communication; for instance, some party guests show up late to give the impression that they are busy and therefore socially important and attractive. This kind of expectation depends on culture and context. *Physical appearance* can include how people dress or groom themselves to manage impressions. Appearance can include cues derived from size, body shape, age, sex, race, or ethnicity; each of these factors can affect communication interaction.

When people interpret one another's nonverbal cues, they tend to do so by using them in combinations (multidimensional). For instance, high amounts of eye contact, close body proximity, forward body lean, and smiling combine to indicate intimacy, attraction, and trust. In contrast, the combination of little eye contact, turning away, leaning backward, and absence of smiling and touch combine to indicate detachment. People who display high amounts of eye contact, close proximity, and smiles are seen to be calm, not aroused, and composed. High amounts of eye contact and close proximity are interpreted together as signs of dominance (Burgoon, Buller, Hale, & deTurck, 1984).

In a similar fashion, estimates of how involved a communication partner is with a topic of discussion are calculated by looking for combinations of kinesic/proxemic attentiveness (leaning forward), smiles, laughter, synchronized speech, few silences and latencies, and less toying with objects. Other indicators of involvement include facial animation, vocal interest, deeper vocal pitch, less fidgeting, and vocal tones indicating attentiveness (Coker & Burgoon, 1987).

Nonverbal cues serve many functions. They illustrate, point, highlight, and regulate. People signal to others to speed up or slow down during conversation, an instance of regulation. Nonverbal cues are used for greetings and to end conversations. For instance, a teacher may stand up to signal the end of a conference once a student has taken long enough to discuss a problem or complain about a grade. People may use nonverbal communication to show relational harmony or disharmony. They may match one another's nods in synchrony to signal approval or avoid synchrony to indicate displeasure.

Turn taking is an important nonverbal part of conversation. One aspect of turn taking is allowing the other person to finish a statement rather than interrupting. This nonverbal pattern can affect rapport during a conversation. Researchers are interested in patterns of who interrupts and who allows interruptions. It might be assumed that men interrupt more during conversations than women do. However, Dindia (1987) discovered that some people, regardless of sex, interrupt more than others do. Interruption patterns cannot be predicted by sex; men do not interrupt more than women, and women are not interrupted more than men. People who interrupt more than others do so in same and other sex interactions. Women are less likely to interrupt supportive comments, whereas they tend to interrupt informative statements more than men do.

Amount and kind of eye gaze can affect rapport between persons joined in conversation. People watch conversational partners to regulate and adjust to them; gaze is used to determine when a partner's conversational turn is ending. While communicating with one another, women use more mutual gaze/mutual talk and mutual gaze/mutual silence than occurs in male-to-male or male-to-female interactions. In mixed-sex dyads, women tend to adopt patterns of eye gaze used by their male partners, whereas in those dyads men do not adapt to women but use patterns typical of male-to-male interaction. Women tend to accommodate to one another and to men in interpersonal communication, but men do not accommodate as much to women. Interaction patterns exist, but they are not always guided by response matching or accommodation. Women, more than men, seem sensitive to the importance of accommodation in interpersonal communication and have more skills to accomplish it (Andersen, 1985).

When people violate eye gaze expectations, the results will be evaluated differently if the violator is thought to be able to reward the partner, or if the relationship is nonrewarding. Eye gaze patterns can affect impressions of attraction, credibility, and how partners communicate. Eye gaze aversion — not making eye contact — harms the relationship (Burgoon, Coker, & Coker, 1986).

People use nonverbal cues to define relationships. Although partners periodically discuss their relationships, for instance, "We are good friends," they continually make nonverbal "comments" about the relationships. Relationships are defined by several key nonverbal patterns, such as composure, dominance–submission, immediacy–nonimmediacy, and intimacy–similarity. Nonverbal cues can indicate trust, liking, attraction, and friendliness. They can suggest how much one partner is involved with the other. Distance and use of space are particularly important in this regard. Communication reticence or uncommunicativeness gives an impression that a person is disinterested or uninvolved in a relationship. When communicators are reticent with friends, quality of relationship is perceived to be mixed, (but more positive than negative). Such is not the case when reticence occurs between strangers, where uncommunicativeness is a sign of disinterest. Strangers often match reticence with less facial pleasantness while displaying tension, disinterest, or anxiety (Burgoon & Koper, 1984).

Nonverbal communication is guided by norms that foster compliance. People who comply with norms are thought to be more competent communicators than are those who violate them. However, *nonverbal expectancy violations theory* posits that under certain circumstances violations of social norms and expectations can enhance communication rather than harm it (Burgoon & Hale, 1988).

People use their expectations about nonverbal communication of others to evaluate their communication competence. Violations, whether positive or negative, can influence communication outcome. Expectations follow social norms unless communication partners know one another well enough to ignore their idiosyncrasies. How norms are used may be a function of

gender, age, personality or sex; they can be triggered by relational characteristics such as degree of acquaintance, status, or liking. These variables
interact in a matrix that makes predictions about communication strategies
and outcomes difficult, but norms, expectations, and known idiosyncrasies
help to make communication systematic and predictable. In terms of
nonverbal distance, for instance, communicating at moderate distance is
preferred to being far apart or too close. Whereas you might find a friendly
person invading your space on first meeting (norm violation), you might
become comfortable with the person's use of distance as a friendship
develops. Some of your friends are likely to get physically close to you and
even touch you, whereas others will not. You might be offended if a
stranger touched you the way a friend might touch you.

Some violations are positively evaluated. You know this because you
think that some persons you meet are "phony" or "syrupy" in their efforts
to be warm; whereas others who are quite competent in this regard leave
you thinking of them as "warm" and "cordial," a person you want to know
better. Both persons may have violated the same norms of nonverbal
communication by being "extremely" friendly during greeting phases of
acquaintantships. But the consequences are different—liking versus disliking.

People assume relational partners will comply with expected communication behaviors, including nonverbal cues, such as amount of distance
between people. Violations may produce negative reactions, but that is not
always the case, especially when the violator can reward the partner.
Deviation from the norm by moving closer can communicate attraction,
interest, and affiliation, whereas deviation from the norm by being further
away can communicate the opposite. Violators are likely to be seen as
insensitive if they lack the potential to reward their partners. When
violation produces signs of arousal, persons should prompt partners to
comply with norms (Burgoon & Aho, 1982).

To explain these different outcomes, Burgoon and Hale (1988) advanced
the nonverbal expectancy violations theory that, as does social exchange
theory, reasons that people continue to communicate as long as benefits
outweigh costs. A key factor in this theory is the reward relationship
between participants. If a person who can reward another violates a norm
or expectation, that violation is disregarded or in some instances increases
the positive regard of the other person. If a violation carries with it the
possibility of high reward, it may increase attraction and credibility. Once
a person spots a violation on the part of another communicator, an
evaluative process starts with the question, "Do I like/dislike this violation?"

Because immediacy is a vital part of communication, friends and
strangers are evaluated positively as being credible when they show the

expected amount of immediacy. When communicators show less immediacy than expected, they may be negatively evaluated and viewed as less competent. Failure to achieve the minimum amount of immediacy communicates detachment, nonintimacy, dissimilarity, and more dominance than normal immediacy. Whether the violation results in negative or positive evaluation is mediated by the ability of the violator to reward the communication partner (Burgoon & Hale, 1988).

These findings have refined the *discrepancy arousal theory* proposed by Cappella and Greene (1982). This theory views the communication process as consisting of moment-by-moment occurrences by which each communicator affects and is affected by the other. Arousal-positive or arousal-negative feelings result from any discrepancy between one person's expectations of what the other's actions should be and what those actions are. Levels of arousal correspond to amounts of discrepancy; the greater the discrepancy, the higher the arousal. Expectations can be both affiliative and activity related. Persons can expect one another to exhibit certain feelings or to perform certain activities; when they do not, discrepancy and arousal occur.

Responses to violations can take the form of reciprocity (matching) or compensation. Reciprocity is characterized by approach-approach sequences whereas compensation is characterized by approach–avoidance or avoidance–avoidance sequences. Patterns of reciprocity and compensation are accompanied by physiological, cognitive, and affective reactions. Whether an interaction is going well or poorly, individuals tend to reciprocate or compensate in response to one another.

Reciprocation and compensation exhibit levels of intensity, duration, or frequency. How each person responds depends on the involvement or affiliation he or she feels toward the other person in the situation. Expectations and reactions to arousal are personal and produce responses that are signaled through actions such as vocalizations, pauses, response latencies, loudness, eye gaze, distance, body orientation, smiling and laughter, touch, body lean, and verbal intimacy. When expectations are met, participants enjoy a sense of pleasantness.

What one person does, in large part, depends on what the other does. Cappella and Greene (1982) reasoned that arousal occurs because individuals depend on one another. When interactants' dependency is mutual and contingent, one person's action is likely to be a response to the other person's action. Responses can be immediate or delayed as well as positive or negative and abstract or concrete. Reactions to violation are affected by the amount of compatibility between partners, their social competence, and their attractiveness and empathy.

As you think about adjustments by persons with whom you communicate, imagine that the kind of response each makes fluctuates during each interaction—and throughout many interactions. At times each person compensates or reciprocates. By tracing these patterns on graph paper, we can chart the interaction patterns of each relationship. Whether participants in a dyad are likely to compensate or reciprocate in response to each other can be predicted by juxtaposing their response curves and estimating the degree of overlap.

Similar expectation levels and widths of acceptance regions indicate that overlap is high and reciprocity (approach–approach sequences) is likely. If expectation levels and widths of acceptance regions differ, compensation (approach–avoidance or avoidance–avoidance sequences) is likely. The determining factor of acceptance is the amount of arousal that will be tolerated before it leads to aversion. Cappella and Greene (1982) postulated that compensatory behavior is likely to occur when people involved in interaction have different expectation levels and acceptance region widths.

If those factors become similar, reciprocity is likely to occur. Relational history of the participants leads them to make compensatory or reciprocity responses to each other. For instance, the degree of toleration for discrepancy is likely to be greater when one or both persons like each other, than if they do not. Similarly, if one person can reward the other, the violation is likely to be discounted (Burgoon & Hale, 1988). In these ways, persons engaged in interpersonal communication use expectations to evaluate the competence and attractiveness of one another.

INTERPERSONAL CONFLICT, AFFINITY, AND RELATION DISSOLUTION

The three topics discussed in this section are not inherently linked, but they give us a useful contrast. They imply potentially "good, bad, and ugly" dimensions of interpersonal relationships.

Conflict can be defined as a contest for scarce resources or positions in which participants are ego-involved. This means that, when persons can grant or deny each other some position or resource, conflict can result—if both participants truly want the position or resource. For instance, no conflict exists in a game if everyone who plays can win or if no one cares whether he or she wins. As long as lots of cookies are in the jar, no conflict exists, but once the cookies are nearly gone, a contest for scarce resources can produce conflict.

This view of conflict can be expanded to include perceived interference with communication partners' efforts to achieve relational goals. Conflict may result from loss of potential pay-offs, rewards, or benefits. It may occur when communication partners have incongruent or incompatible behaviors.

Viewed this way, conflict is not misunderstanding. Misunderstanding can be remedied by communicating more clearly. However, conflict is not necessarily resolved by clarity. Even though conflict produces distortions, persons engaged in it often know what is going on and what each other means.

Conflict is not inherently harmful to relationships. If conflict occurs because of honest differences that can be resolved, it can enhance a relationship. The quality of each relationship (trust, control, and intimacy) relates to the likelihood that participants will resolve conflict constructively. Conflict resolution tactics reflect the rules and compliance behaviors people use to create and manage it, as well as contexts in which it occurs (Smith, 1984).

To resolve conflict, people may employ compromise, competition, accommodation, and avoidance. To *compromise,* participants exchange resources, to the extent they can, in an attempt to maximize their own and each others' outcomes. *Competition* is predicated on a win–loss paradigm, but even under that condition, it may not be harmful if the relationship is solid and if the prospect of the conflict leading to other relationship outcomes is high. For instance, friendships can be based on healthy athletic competition. *Accommodation* means that one person tries to resolve conflict by smoothing the feelings of the other. Such a tactic can be helpful, especially when ego-involvement leds to competition rather than other resolution strategies. *Avoidance* is the tactic of leaving the area of combat. Sometimes a conflict resolves itself merely when combatants have time to cool. You probably have been engaged in many conflicts that a day or two later seemed so trivial that you and your partner had a hard time recalling why the conflict became emotional. Each conflict resolution tactic can be used constructively or be inappropriate.

Examining how college roommates resolve conflict, Sillars (1980) found that they often employ passive (indirect) strategies, including withdrawal. Distributive strategies promote individual over mutual outcomes, whereas integrative strategies feature information exchange and mutually beneficial outcomes. The strategies roommates employ affect the outcomes of the conflict. When roommates think their partners will select positive strategies, they reciprocate with integrative strategies. This kind of strategy is also likely to be used when a party believes that he or she is responsible for the conflict. Once a roommate relationship becomes stable, integrative relationships are more likely, and passive ones are less likely.

How persons in conflict perceive one another can affect resolution. Likewise, beliefs relational partners have about one another and relationships in general influence how they solve problems — or whether they try to solve them — rather than merely ending a relationship (Metts & Cupach, 1990).

One factor central to conflict is power, the ability one person has to affect the behavior or feelings of another. In a relationship, power may be symmetrical or asymmetrical; it requires moves and countermoves. These moves involve choices: approach–avoidance, positive–negative, and direct–indirect. These moves affect the development and resolution of conflict. In a symetrical relationship, for instance, approach will be met with approach. During conflict, one person might begin by using positive tactics; if they are responded to positively, that mode will continue. If a response is negative, the countermove is likely to be negative. Moves are employed to the extent that each participant is able, and to the degree that the tactic produces desired results (Berger, 1985).

Several communication strategies are typical of conflict situations: apologies, explanations, inducements, contingencies (limitations placed on a request or offer), counterpersuasion, and coercion. How requests are made and conflict is resolved depends on the degree of intimacy between participants. When people make requests of others with whom they are relationally close, they assume that the requests will be granted, as much out of obligation as for any other reason. This kind of generalization can be explained by a rules approach, which prescribes that requests are to be granted—if the partner is able. Or it can be explained by a systems perspective, whereby each participant knows that what is done to or granted for the other will affect how the conflict matures. Requests in intimate situations require less elaboration to justify why they were made or should be granted. If their requests are denied, people seem less inclined to be polite in their reaction if they are involved in an intimate relationship; impoliteness is not as likely in nonintimate relationships. Relational intimacy is characterized by contrasting communication styles: cooperative/friendly versus competitive/hostile, equal versus unequal, intense versus superficial, and socioemotional/informational versus task/formal (Roloff, Janiszewski, McGrath, Burns, & Lalita, 1988).

Believing that unstructured conflict resolution leads to negative outcomes that can defeat efforts to bring harmony, researchers advocate the use of decision rules as a remedy. These rules can help persons engaged in conflict to focus on issues and the decision process rather than on personalities. If conflict becomes personalized, it may be more difficult to resolve because people defend their feelings and egos rather than attempt to resolve the conflict. However, people who are instructed to use conflict resolution methods are less immediate and more formal in their communication styles. Attempting to follow decision rules may lead participants to use less friendly, "liking" language and to resist resolution. Decision rules appear to have less inhibiting effect on men than women involved in conflict (Donohue, Weider-Hatfield, Hamilton, & Diez, 1985).

According to O'Keefe and Shepherd (1987), communicators' ability to resolve conflict depends on their skill in devising goal management strategies. These strategies include selecting one goal outcome in preference to others, separating the issues basic to the conflict, and integrating or reconciling competing aims. Integration as a message strategy enhances the persuadee's impression of the persuader; it is the best tactic for being persuasive and liked. Persons who are able to see many issues and strategy options and who rely on integration and face-saving tactics are likely to resolve conflict. Effective conflict resolution depends on the ability to recognize the relevance of, and simultaneously pursue, multiple and competing objectives.

Burggraf and Sillars (1987) observed that communication styles that married couples use during conflict are negotiated and do not differ by sex. This conclusion suggests that the tactics married couples use during conflict are determined by how they have taught each other to communicate (negotiated and reciprocated). In this vein, conflict is a relational process, which may be ambiguous and improvised or culturally defined and regulated (Sillars & Weisberg, 1987).

Married couples, Fitzpatrick (1977) reported, base their conflict resolution tactics on the kind of marriage they have: independents, separates, and traditionals. *Independents* consider themselves to be less restrained in the use of verbal tactics than do other types. They use contracts as the basis of creating obligations and resolving conflict. *Separates* show very little willingness to share and avoid conflict. *Traditionals* rely on stereotypes of a traditional marriage. They are not autonomous in their tactic selection, relying on their view of the rules and values of a traditional marriage during conflict.

Conversational topics and themes are part of the communication styles of married couples. Traditional couples tend to use communal (togetherness) themes. Individualistic themes are typical of conversations by separates. Communal themes are more satisfying than are individual themes (Sillars, Weisberg, Burggraf, & Wilson, 1987).

One principle that runs throughout interpersonal communication research is that people select strategies to obtain communication goals, and they do so with varying degrees of insight or mindfulness and employ them with different degrees of skill (O'Keefe & Shepherd, 1987). An example of the difference in message/strategy selection is found in how females and males seek to establish relations with one another (Richmond, Gorham, & Furio, 1987).

Getting others to like us is a vital communication goal. People employ affinity-seeking behavior to lead others to like them. One model that explains this behavior features four interrelated units:

1. Antecedent factors (interaction goals, motives for seeking liking, and level of mindfulness).
2. Constraints (dispositions and social skills) and characteristics of the communication partner.
3. Strategic activity (strategy selection, integration, and quality of enactment).
4. Responses by the person whose liking is being sought. Affinity-seeking strategies involve control, trust, politeness, involvement with the other, self-involvement, and commonality. Many affinity-seeking strategies can be employed such as altruism, control, equality, openness, nonverbal immediacy, similarity, supportiveness, and trustworthiness (Bell & Daly, 1984).

When people begin to realize that a relationship costs more than it produces in rewards, they consider dissolving it. This is the first stage, called *intra-psychic* phase, in the process of ending relationships. At this point, partners think about one another's behavior, assess the partner's performance, and weigh the costs and rewards of maintaining the relationship as opposed to ending it. If the discomfort is sufficiently high and the person believes that communicating with the partner might correct the cost/reward imbalance, that people is likely to enter the *dyadic* phase of talking with the partner. This stage can entail confrontation, negotiation, attempts to repair damage, and joint assessments of the future of the relationship.

Depending on the success of the dyadic phase, a person considering ending a relationship is likely to enter the *social* phase, which involves conversations with others about the relationship, efforts to repair it, calls for intervention, and face-saving and blame-placing statements. Once the relationship ends, the partners move to the *grave dressing* phase in which they communicate to get over the relationship, engage in retrospection, and present the "break up" story to acquaintances (Duck, 1982).

Baxter (1982) discovered that persons who suffer relationship break ups like to think of themselves as the person who made the decision to end the relationship. Such situations are likely to incur four kinds of strategies: withdrawal/avoidance, manipulation, positive comments, and open confrontation. Efforts to end relationships often begin with (a) direct statements that the relationship is over, (b) indirect statements that avoid asking about and involving the partner in conversation or activities, and (c) nonverbal withdrawal — for instance, avoiding touching, standing less close, or seeing the other less often (Wilmot, Carbaugh, & Baxter, 1985).

In these ways, people use communication to fight, to demonstrate liking, and to dissolve relationships. Communication styles and strategies are important to relationships. Part of the success of each relationship depends on skills partners have and are willing to employ. This is especially true as they find themselves in conflict and seek to resolve it.

CONCLUSION

Relationships seem to endure because participants find them satisfying—at least to the extent that rewards appear to outweigh costs of maintaining them. In a similar way, the quality of relationships appears to be characterized by certain types of communication strategies. People in good relationships communicate differently than do people in bad ones. With these basic observations in mind, you might ask, "But how do I know when I am in a good relationship and what can I do to make it better?" The need to reduce uncertainty about the people with whom you communicate and about relationships you create is the theme of the next chapter.

7

Interpersonal
Communication:
Social Cognition and
Communication Competence

Interpersonal relationships begin, grow, remain static, or deteriorate. How do persons involved in them know whether these relationships are sound or deteriorating? Chapter 6 discussed variables that affect interpersonal relationships by noting that, as people communicate, they have expectations—of themselves and others—in regard to what interpersonal action is appropriate and what is not. When communication partners do not satisfy expectations, people may experience arousal that can affect, negatively or positively, attractiveness as relational partners. People negotiate and co-define the limits, conditions, and obligations needed for a relationship—including how much disclosure is sufficient or excessive. Limits and obligations in a relationship are negotiated through social exchange. Given these conditions, each participant is continually confronted with the need to obtain information that will help him or her assess the quality of each relationship and better understand the relational partner.

Because people cannot know others directly and as they actually are, they do the best they can to know them through communication. The need to understand how interpersonal partners acquire and use information, for this reason, is a most important communication topic. Throughout this chapter runs the theme that the need for information and to be competent influences the communication plans people employ. Conversely, the information people have leads them to conclude that some communication plans are more appropriate than others.

To understand how people strive to reduce uncertainty during interpersonal communication requires insights into processes of *interpersonal attribution* and *uncertainty reduction*. These concepts have to do with the ways people come to know each other and how people perform competently. This discussion shows why and how individuals attempt to reduce uncertainty (about others, themselves, and relationships) during interpersonal communication. This analysis pursues the theme that people select, with varying degrees of mindfulness, those communication strategies most likely to achieve goals. One major goal is to be a competent, a desirable communication partner.

As discussed in chapter 6, the quality of each relationship appears to depend on disclosure, costs, and rewards of social exchange, compliance with communication rules or norms, and management of conflict. Chapter 7 describes the processes by which individuals attempt to figure out who each other is and whether particular relationships are worth their cost. This chapter stresses the role information plays in building relationships and considers how people plan to use communication to get to know one another.

GUESSING AND SECOND GUESSING

This chapter assumes that we cannot let others into our minds to know us nor can we get inside their minds to know them. Because of these limitations, some amount of uncertainty exists in relationships. Uncertainty is unpleasant and, therefore, motivational. People want to reduce uncertainty they feel toward others (getting to know who they are), and they want to know what others think about them and why other people act as they do. "Does he/she really like me?" "Do people see me as a nice person?" "Does my boss think I am a competent worker?" "Will I be able to say the right things to get a date (or make a sale)?" "Am I a competent communicator?" During interpersonal interaction, people seek to answer these questions and many more. As you were cautioned in the last chapter, you need to guard against coming to think that people are always mindful of what is happening during communication. But by gaining insights, they increase their chances that when they are mindful of what is going on they will be more competent.

The process of getting to know others may be short circuited. When people are involved in interpersonal communication, they often assume they know who the other person is and why he or she is acting in a particular manner. This process of characterizing others (and oneself) is called *attribution,* the basic process of social cognition.

Even though participants in communication do not actually know why their partners act as they do, they speculate about or attribute causes to that behavior in an attempt to feel comfortable that they know what is going on. For instance, as you communicate with others, you probably find yourself thinking, "He/she likes me because she/he smiles and looks at me when we talk," or "No one really listens to me; I guess I'm not the sort people like to be friends with." You make many self-attributions based on your involvement with others. "I would have been better in that interview if the interviewer had not tricked me" "I did well on that test because I studied hard." "I would have done better on that test if my roommate had not persuaded me to go to a movie instead of studying."

Giving perspective to this discussion, Berger (1987) observed that relational communication is affected by people seeking rewards through communication. When rewards for being in a relationship exceed costs, the relationship is likely to improve. Conversely, when costs of an interaction exceed rewards, the relationship is likely to deteriorate. This line of analysis directs researchers' attention to outcomes, such as increased intimacy or trust, rather than concentrating on means by which interpersonal communication transpires.

Via processes of social cognition, Berger (1987) argued, "interactants determine which stimuli are rewarding and which are costly to their partners" (p. 57). Much of what goes on during interpersonal communication is aimed at reducing uncertainty in regard to the persons involved in communication, quality of relationships, and communicator competence. "Hence," he continued, "uncertainty reduction is a necessary condition for the definition of the currency of social exchange, and it is through communicative activity that uncertainty is reduced" (p. 57). Because a rewards/cost matrix is present in relationships, as proposed by social exchange theory, the fundamental question in interpersonal communication is how do people know when rewards justify costs. Thus, Berger reasoned, "What gives individuals the ability to exert control in relationships is the *knowledge* of what is rewarding and costly to their interaction partners and to themselves" (p. 57).

Attribution and disclosure are interrelated. When people disclose positive aspects of themselves and the relationship, their partners are likely to self-disclose. If negative attributions result from what a communication partner discloses, that disclosure is unlikely to be reciprocated and the relationship may even terminate. Disclosure has a positive affect on attribution because it suggests that the person who makes the disclosure likes the person to whom it is made. This analysis adds credence to social penetration theory, but also suggests that disclosure alone is not the key. Attributions made about disclosure influence whether the relationship seems rewarding (Derlega, Winstead, Wong, & Greenspan, 1987). Attribution affects how people make sense of what others disclose to them.

Social cognition assumes that persons involved in interpersonal communication do so with varying degrees of thought or mindfulness. This thought focuses on the interaction and participants (self as well as others). A great deal of communication consists of scripts — routine comments that are made without much thought. What and how people think require schemata — patterns and assumptions by which they construct their view of social reality. These constructions are, to varying degrees, designed to achieve veridical representations of self, others, and relationships (Roloff & Berger, 1982).

When people interact, they exchange information that may or may not be accurate. Perhaps it is fabricated through deception or it may be biased. To reduce uncertainty, people want to solve riddles of this kind: "How competent are people under these conditions?"

They have strategies that enhance their competence. One research project (Hewes, Graham, Doelger, & Pavitt, 1985) investigated how people "debias" information, a process called *second-guessing*. Once people suspect they cannot wholly trust the information they have received, they resort to alternative interpretations. Contrary to the notion that people are gullible and easily misled, research finds that they are skilled at debiasing when they sense the need. People frequently employ this strategy. When people are trying to determine whether others' comments are biased, they look for inadequate sampling (generalizations made from too few instances), inaccurate reports (ones that differ from known facts), inconsistencies, self-serving bias, opportunity to adequately know the truth, lack of information the partner should know if the story is not biased, errors in attribution, or diagnostic errors (inaccurate analysis of circumstances). In the process of debiasing, people look for *explanatory cues,* those that suggest that the source is biased due to motivational or cognitive processing patterns, or *warning cues,* the way the message is constructed or delivered, especially nonverbally (Doelger, Hewes, & Graham, 1986).

Messages are reinterpreted during debiasing in hopes of achieving a more accurate picture of what is going on. Persons who have a high need for information are likely to seek information to assist their debiasing, particularly if it is not difficult to obtain. If people have a high need to assure themselves that information is accurate, they are likely to think of many interpretations of it. However, if many interpretations exist, people experience uncertainty and tend to avoid additional interpretations (Hewes, Graham, Monsour, & Doelger, 1989).

This analysis suggests that information is important to relationships but may not be enough to maintain them. Indeed, Duck (1985) contended, new information may actually harm rather than help relationships. Uncertainty has its place in the management of relationships, but what also counts is the ability of persons to persuade one another to improve, maintain, or dissolve a relationship.

What people think of one another affects how they act toward each other and how they plan to communicate with each other. The ability to know each other as well as develop and execute successful communication plans is vital to persons being socially competent. To understand this process requires an examination of the intellectual foundations of social cognition.

INTELLECTUAL ORIGINS OF SOCIAL COGNITION

One intellectual ancestor of social cognition is information theory, which was discussed in chapter 3. That discussion explained that a motive for obtaining and using information is to reduce uncertainty; information increases or decreases the degree of uncertainty a person feels in a given situation.

Another intellectual foundation of social cognition was provided by attribution theory that originated in the work of Heider (1958). He reasoned that, in everyday activities, people engage in a relatively unsophisticated version of the kind of observation and analysis that social scientists use when conducting laboratory experiments. This activity he called *naive psychology*. And he reasoned that people make their way through life as *naive psychologists,* because they gather facts and use them to generalize about the character and motivation of one another. His point was that people attempt to assign causation and meaning to the actions of others as well as themselves.

People like to believe they can understand the physical and social world they encounter. They think the world is rational and adheres to fundamental principles, the most essential of which is causation. As people interact, they attempt to make sense of each other's behavior so they know who the other person is, why the person acts as he or she does, and what those actions (including all verbal and nonverbal communication) mean for the relationship. Thus, they attempt to explain their own behavior and that of others by assigning causes to it. Actions of others, as well as stereotypes people hold about each other and about their actions, are used to explain why people do what they do. These means are used to assign motives to people and to make judgments about relationships. This frame of mind assumes that what each person does is purposive, the result of the kind of person he or she is and the circumstances in which the person behaves.

Social cognition assumes that people desire a causal explanation of the world, one that believes that nature is regular and that behavior can be observed, whereas experience is private. Advancing from the principles Heider established, Kelley (1972) argued that insight can be gained into interpersonal perception and interaction by looking for the cognitive schemata or cognitive rules people use when attempting to infer the causes of behavior. When people assign one cause rather than its alternatives to explain behavior, they make assumptions that offer others the chance to gain insight into their cognitive schemata and interpersonal processes. But, he cautioned, it is easy to assume that people are better at attribution than they actually are. They often make incomplete analyses, use small data samples, and are incomplete when looking at trends of data. For instance, a person might attribute personality characteristics to another person based only on the clothing the person wears and his or her appearance. If the clothing is expensive and the person is well groomed, the conclusion could be made that the person is wealthy; based on that reasoning, other conclusions could be drawn. A more complete review of the data could reveal that the person borrowed the trappings of affluence and is a dishonest, untrustworthy fraud.

Observational patterns, Kelley (1972) reasoned, follow a *covariation principle: "An effect is attributed to one of its possible causes with which, over time, it covaries"* (p. 3). Sometimes an individual will be certain that an attribution is accurate because only one reason seems to explain why someone is behaving in a particular manner. (At least the individual can think of only one reason for the behavior.) At other times, the attribution may not be as certain, especially when several causes are present. This Kelley (1973) called the *discounting effect: "The role of a given cause in producing a given effect is discounted when other plausible causes are also present"* (p. 113).

Principles of covariation are useful for explaining social cognition. As people witness combinations of events, situations, and actions occurring at the same time, they tend to conclude that some principle of causation is operating. How people attribute causes in a given situation is a product of their history of attribution. For instance, if they stereotype people and have acted on those stereotypes, they are likely to continue to use those stereotypes to make subsequent attributions. Each instance they witness that confirms the stereotype will be used as evidence of the covariance of the trait and the stereotype; each instance that occurs that could disconfirm the stereotype is likely to be dismissed or ignored.

This kind of analysis brought Kelley (1973) to argue that a few combinations of principles service each person's efforts to attribute causes of behavior. Even if beliefs and judgments are not veridical, they are servicable because people know that they know. These principles he reduced to key combinations: When attributing, people rely on other persons' qualities or perceived intentions, to the time (situation) when the action occurs, to the entities involved in the action, to the interaction between person and entities, or to the circumstances surrounding the behavior.

In the assignment of causation, each individual employs *causal schemata,* his or her unique beliefs about the salience of which entity is producing the causation (Kelley, 1973). Several examples may help you understand the kinds of attributions that result from these combinations. If a person you know well does something, you will probably use the knowledge of the individual to make the attribution. Even then, certain variations might operate. If an acquaintance does well on a test, you might infer that the test was easy (attribution to circumstances). If you do well on a test, it is because you studied (attribution to self). If you do poorly, you may blame the teacher for being too hard, too vague, or deceptive (attribution to circumstances).

Most people take personal credit when things go well for themselves and blame circumstances when they do not go well. If you see someone you don't know very well listening to a kind of music (entity), you probably infer that the person is the kind of person who likes that kind of music. You can attribute a lot about people based on what they like. In making that attribution, you might ignore the possibility that the person is trying to like or understand the music for a test or to impress someone. If you see classmates in the library during most of the semester, you are likely to assume that they are good students. If you see them there only during finals, you are likely to conclude that they are bad students cramming for tests. A person driving an expensive automobile is assumed to be prosperous and to like other expensive things. See how attribution works. If you stop to think for a moment, you are likely to recall many times when your inferences were incorrect.

This view of attribution assumes that people operate as naive scientists, observing behavior, creating categories, and making attributions based on those categories. How are categories and the attributions drawn from them influenced by communication? To answer this question, *constructivism* has been used to explain attribution by drawing on different assumptions than those made by Heider and Kelley.

Rather than believing that people observe behavior, create categories, and make attributions experientially, constructivists reason that attributional categories result from interpretative systems that people erect primarily through communication with individuals to whom they must accommodate. In this sense, people take on perspectives as they learn the language of the people with whom they associate. This theory reasons that people can communicate with one another — and make attributions — only because they have learned interaction and attribution patterns that are relevant to their encounters.

Constructivism assumes that individuals are creative and dynamic. Rather than merely being acted on by their circumstances, people act dynamically to affect changes based on how they think and regulate their activities. Interpersonal behavior is guided by interpretative schemata as well as strategies designed to achieve goals (Delia et al., 1982). For this reason, people can coordinate activities to the extent they recognize and employ strategies that are compatible with those others use to achieve goals.

This means that each of us can talk to others only because we have developed patterns of thought and interaction that are meaningful and that can be used to coordinate social interaction. Recognition of communication intent on the part of interactional partners and creation of communicative strategies depend on how people interpret their world—their social situation.

One of the central concerns of constructivism is to discover the interpretative schemata people use to characterize their physical and social realms by imposing meaningful categories on them. These categories help individuals make holistic sense of what they perceive. For example, if someone flunks a test, breaks a date, or wins an award, those for whom this behavior is meaningful characterize it according to schemata, which for them, make sense.

Once characterizations are in place and are shared by interactants, they guide human action. This, however, does not mean that everyone acts the same way in the same situation. People may act differently from one another because they perceive the situation (make attributions) differently, the people in it, and the strategies that are relevant to it. Any moment of interpersonal behavior reflects both partners' histories in the behavior relevant to the situation and parties involved. Behavior follows, at least to some extent, schemata that allow people to interact because they know what behavior is appropriate to each set of circumstances. Because individuals share schemata, they can coordinate activities. Even though interpretative processes differ in significant ways, enough overlap exists for people to be able to coordinate activities. Through attribution and communication, people join together into a society that is meaningful for them (Delia et al., 1982; O'Keefe & Delia, 1982).

How people make attributions and use them to try to know one another are important factors in interpersonal communication. During interpersonal communication, many attributions are likely to occur. For instance, if a person talks about a topic, you probably assume the person likes and may even be knowledgeable about it. If someone appears to like you, you might conclude that the situation calls for "liking" and the person is just being polite, or you might assume that the person should like you because you are the kind of person other people can like. If you are a good student, and a classmate shows unusual interest in your ability in a class, you may conclude that you have a positive effect on others, the person is like you and is a good student, or the person is merely trying to be nice to get your help in class.

The schemata you employ regarding such matters—and questions or comments you use to seek additional information—can be used to reduce uncertainty about the person's interest. Does the person like you—for yourself—or your class notes? These are the interpersonal quandaries that motivate efforts to understand attribution as a vital part of social cognition. This observation also emphasizes the place that verbal and nonverbal communication have in attribution.

Attribution is a good starting point from which to study interpersonal communication because all people have to go on is what they think others do and say. Kelley (1973) believed that people make attributions even if they are inaccurate. How good are people at attributing causes of behavior? People assume they are quite accurate. What do you think?

Addressing this question, Sillars (1982) cautioned that people are not naive scientists, using primitive covariation to make attributions; rather, they are just naive. His list of reservations about people's ability to make attributions is enlightening because of what the list says about the difficulty or impossibility of making accurate attributions. A brief review of his criticisms will sharpen your insight into the difficulties of understanding how people go about reducing uncertainty.

One significant flaw in attributional schemata results because prior expectations cause people to imagine relationships even when no correlation exists and to overlook relationships that do exist. Sillars made this point to defend his reservation that people actually not use covariation to make attributions; instead, they operate out of schemata that contain stereotypes and prior expectations.

Whereas Kelley (1972, 1973) argued that people use consensus as a vital part of their attribution processes, Sillars contended that they make little use of this principle. They often ignore consensus data and base their attributions on non-normative actions or traits that they observe in others, an inferential bias. Instead of searching for the best explanation, people usually settle on the first sufficient explanation that comes to mind. Stereotypes are typical examples of this kind of bias. This tendency to settle on the first sufficient explanation is likely to result when some degree of emotion is associated with the explanation. For instance, an egocentric athlete may believe a victory was the result of his or her exceptional effort, whereas a player who believes in the importance of team effort may credit that factor for producing victory. Or people who are fearful that they will be cheated are likely to use this as the basis of attribution and therefore find more cheating than do persons who use different schemata.

Kelley's approach to attribution assumes that each day is relatively new and that people are constantly alert to refining their attributional schemata. Sillars disagreed and contended that people do not adequately reevaluate attributions in light of new data. Even when people are aware that new data do not agree with their attributions, they are not likely to be objective. When new information is received that contradicts an attribution, the information is likely to be critically evaluated; however, when information is received that confirms the attribution, it is likely to be accepted uncritically as confirmation.

Sillars contended that the attributional schemata that people use produce many biases. Some of these result from traits that are salient about the person toward whom attribution is being made. A self-serving bias exists because people prefer to deny responsibility for bad outcomes and take credit for good ones. People tend to overestimate the extent to which they have control in a situation. Many people hold a just "world view" that people get what they deserve; this bias would occur if you say that a person who wrecked a car because of careless driving deserved to suffer the accident—but you may not think how unjust the world is to the innocent persons hurt in the accident.

An important bias results from the belief people have that others are like them—having similar feelings and opinions. Often people expect that others think and behave for the same reasons they do. In making attribution, most people prefer to use a linear model of causality, rather than assuming that many "causes" could have operated to lead a person to a particular opinion, judgment, or behavior. Bias in attribution becomes greater during conflict or when the person making the attribution is emotionally involved with the other person. These observations are intended to lead people to be cautious in their efforts to explain attribution processes.

The starting point to understand and appreciate how people reduce uncertainty, in part through attribution, is to realize the shortcomings in the attributional schemata that people use. This kind of analysis reveals the difference between uncertainty reduction and accurate attribution as vital parts of interpersonal communication. The incentive to reduce uncertainty may lead people to make false attributions. If uncertainty reduction (as a part of social cognition) is essential to knowing whether relationships are good or bad and why relational partners are acting as they do, then caution must be used when examining and explaining the processes of social cognition. Can people ever really know one another?

The standards for accuracy may have to be derived through conversation and observation by the parties involved. Can attribution be accurate if the parties involved hold different opinions about what their own traits and actions mean? Person A may think relational Person B is aloof whereas B thinks of him or herself as quiet and unassuming. Person A may think of B as irresponsible whereas B prides his or her carefree spirit in an uptight world. Accurate attribution would seem to require that relationships and the efforts of relational partners depend on whether the partners agree on which elements are salient to the attributions and what these attributes mean. Many relationships struggle because Person A wants B to be "open," whereas Person B does not want to burden A with "all of my thoughts and feelings." Relationships are harmed by one partner who believes in saving for the future whereas the other does not want to be so frugal. As people date, how can they know with any degree of certainty what their partners will be like in 5, 10, 20, or 40 years? How can relational partners be less uncertain (or more certain) in regard to what each other really is like?

These concerns suggest the value in having a coorientation model to help communicators realize that perspectives flow both ways (McLeod & Chaffee, 1973). Accuracy and satisfaction are vital elements of a relationship. Accuracy refers to the extent to which the partners in a relationship see each other in the same way. What each person thinks of the other and how accurately each person knows the other as that person knows him or herself determines whether people deal with each other in similar or dissimilar ways. Satisfaction refers to the extent to which the participants are pleased by what they know about each other and about the relationship. People could agree and be dissatisfied; both parties might agree that one of them is selfish—but only one person might be satisfied by this fact.

After this summary of the origins of attribution theory and problems of social cognition, it is useful to discuss whether some people are better at cognition than others. If all people are equally good or bad at making attributions, the study of communication would be quite different. How do people make attributions and how skilled are they? Research indicates that some people are better than others. Sensitive people listen differently than people do who are less sensitive. Sensitive listeners make more high-level inferences; they divide conversation elements into small units, store conversation characteristics in their memories, and make more self-references about conversations. Sensitive listeners are more likely to self-monitor, be self-conscious, be perceptive, have higher self-esteem, be assertive, exhibit empathy, and enjoy better social skills. Sensitive listeners are less likely to suffer communication apprehension, receiver apprehension, and anxiety about social relationships (Daly, Vangelisti, & Daughton, 1987).

This review of the intellectual origins of social cognition emphasizes the important role information plays in the process. It also demonstrates that how each person makes attributions—applying his or her idiosyncratic schemata—may produce inaccurate and biased attributions, even though the individual is likely to be blind to those problems. Patterns of attribution exist; these patterns are useful in efforts to get to know one another. Even biases indicate patterns that can be observed and become the basis of conversation. In the effort to make attributions, some people are more competent that others, and coorientation supplies a model by which each of us can look on our communication partner's patterns of attributions as we look on our own. To get to know one another—that is the incentive to reduce uncertainty, a motive for communication.

UNCERTAINTY REDUCTION

Chapter 3 explained how information affects uncertainty. Because uncertainty is uncomfortable, people seek and process information. Sometimes information comes when it is unexpected; even so, it can increase or decrease certainty. This quick review shows how information is vital to social cognition. As people interact, they try to get to know one another. People "read" nonverbal cues and assess personality and behavioral traits to determine who other persons are and why other persons behave as they do. Not only do people obtain information from and about others, but they also want information about themselves that will help reduce their uncertainty in regard to whether they are socially competent. They want to know what others think of them.

As you encounter others, you may wonder, "Is this person friendly?" "Does this person like me?" "Can I talk this person into helping me with my homework?" "Is this person hostile toward me?" If you become romantically interested in a person, you might seek information, such as asking a mutual friend whether the person says nice things about you and indicates any liking toward you. Despite your efforts, you do not get information only because you seek it; some comes accidentally, such as seeing a person you like holding hands with someone else or when a mutual friend comments on how fickle that person is or that the person is involved with someone else. As you encounter others, you only know them from what they appear to be and what they do. This information is used to attribute motives and personality traits that affect how, whether, and why you communicate with them.

Uncertainty reduction, as a theoretical perspective, originated with Berger and Calabrese (1975) who drew on the work of Heider (1958). They reasoned that people seek to make sense of their environment and the people in it. Uncertainty reduction theory is a powerful explanation for communication behavior because it operates in all communication contexts — to help explain why people communicate as they do. Uncertainty is unpleasant and therefore motivational; people communicate to reduce it. But people can also create uncertainty. They withhold information from one another and act mysteriously. They provide information that is biased, untrue, or partially true. They mislead, distort, and tantalize.

Uncertainty occurs in at least two forms in a relationship. It refers to "the number of possible alternative ways of behaving and believing when strangers meet." And it "concerns the ability of each interactant to explain his own and the other's behavior. Each interactant must develop a set of causal attributions in order to answer the question of why he and the other are behaving in particular ways or believing certain things" (Berger, 1975, p. 33).

Berger (1987) observed how difficult it is to interact with a stranger who can behave in many ways—some of which might be quite unpredictable. Moreover, as people begin to interact with strangers, they may encounter personalities, opinions, and communication styles that can be disconcerting. Uncertainty reduction theory has been offered to help explain how individuals obtain enough predictability about one another so that conversations can be conducted smoothly. This requires that people are able to predict how they and others will behave and use the communication repertoire they have acquired. During this interaction, the quality of information exchanged is more important than its quantity. By being able to use context as a starting point to reduce uncertainty and to attribute opinions and judgments, people may be able to decrease uncertainty more quickly. People use many other cues to reduce uncertainty: person prototypes (a version of stereotype), roles, schemas, scripts, and conversation sequences. As you interact with others, the biases they exhibit will be used to figure out who each person is—what he or she likes or dislikes. The role the person assumes can be the foundation of attributions. How the person thinks, what scripted conversational patterns the person uses and how he or she joins (or does not join) in conversations—all of these serve as information to use to make attributions about the person.

As postulated by Berger and Calabrese (1975), uncertainty reduction follows a pattern of developmental stages, especially during initial interaction or when new topics are introduced later in a relationship. The *entry phase* typically consists of information exchanges of demographic information and expressions of attitudes on topics of minimal consequence or low involvement. After this phase, one or both interactants decide whether a relationship seems worth pursuing. The *personal phase* occurs when participants disclose intimate information and discuss topics which involve personal attitudes, feelings, and judgments. This phase is likely to exhibit conversation patterns that are freer of scripted comments and social norms than is typical of the initial phase. The *exit phase* occurs if one or both parties decide to terminate the relationship. As is true of the first two phases, this one is shaped by norms that guide individuals' efforts to signal that a relationship is terminating. In all phases, verbal and nonverbal communication is important, but the last phase may be characterized by nonverbal terminating or leave-taking behaviors, such as refusing invitations, avoiding, or ignoring. This pattern assumes many of the characteristics of social exchange theory including the rewards/costs decision regarding whether a relationship is worth pursuing.

At each of these phases, uncertainty reduction is a primary motive behind communication activities. As Berger and Calabrese (1975) suggested, "when strangers meet, their primary concern is one of uncertainty reduction or increasing predictability about the behavior of both themselves and others in the interaction" (p. 100). One goal of researchers is to determine what norms and schemata guide attempts to obtain information about the communication partner and about one's own competence in the interaction. What do interactants look for in the comments and behavior of others and themselves as they work to reduce uncertainty about the worth of the relationship? The answer to this question needs to be revealed by research. But, in keeping with the tenets of attribution theory, people will make judgments about their performance and that of other participants even if those judgments are inaccurate. In response to the kind of reservations Sillars (1982) raised in regard to people's ability to attribute accurately, Berger and Calabrese (1975) concluded: "Attribution theorists have been quick to point out that such predictions and explanations generally yield *imperfect knowledge* of ourselves and others. However, it is significant that such imperfect knowledge does *guide our total behavior toward others*" (p. 101). Regardless of their ability to attribute accurately, people do so nevertheless, and act accordingly.

To guide research into the ways people attempt to reduce uncertainty, Berger and Calabrese (1975) offered several axioms and theorems.

Axiom 1: *"Given the high level of uncertainty present at the onset of the entry phase, as the amount of verbal communication between strangers increases, the level of uncertainty for each interactant in the relationship will decrease. As uncertainty is further reduced, the amount of verbal communication will increase"* (pp. 101–102).

Axiom 2: *"As nonverbal affiliative expressiveness increases, uncertainty levels will decrease in an initial interaction situation. In addition, decreases in uncertainty level will cause increases in nonverbal affiliative expressiveness"* (p. 103).

Axiom 3: *"High levels of uncertainty cause increases in information seeking behavior. As uncertainty levels decline, information seeking behavior decreases"* (p. 103).

Axiom 4: *"High levels of uncertainty in a relationship cause decreases in the intimacy level of communication content. Low levels of uncertainty produce high levels of intimacy"* (p. 103).

Axiom 5: *"High levels of uncertainty produce high rates of reciprocity. Low levels of uncertainty produce low reciprocity rates"* (p. 105).

Axiom 6: *"Similarities between persons reduce uncertainty, while dissimilarities produce increases in uncertainty"* (p. 106).

Axiom 7: *"Increases in uncertainty level produce decreases in liking; decreases in uncertainty level produce increases in liking"* (p. 107).

By reviewing these axioms, you should understand better the relationship between the quality of relationships, degrees of uncertainty, and communication activities that transpire.

Two primary attribution processes occur during attempts to reduce uncertainty. The first, *proactive attribution,* occurs when individuals use information received verbally and nonverbally, which is considered in the context of a particular situation. As individuals receive information early in an interaction, they make attributions that are tested, as hypotheses, during the conversation. This process includes estimates of opinions the other person has not revealed but may do so as the conversation progresses. The second process is *retroactive attribution,* which occurs when individuals use information they acquire, whether verbal or nonverbal, to explain comments and behaviors that occurred previously in the relationship. One of the obvious occurrences of retroactive attribution is when a person thinks, "So that is why the person said (or did) that."

These processes occur throughout interactions. Retroactive processes often occur when proactive predictions are not affirmed. Retroactive attribution is used when people need to confirm or disconfirm attributions they made earlier in the relationship. One schemata (thought processes) used in proactive attribution is that, when individuals perceive they have similar backgrounds, they will predict they also have similar attitudes. Attitude disagreements appear to be attributed to personality differences, whereas agreements are attributed to similarities of communication style. When persons are engaged in conversations where they experience attitude dissimilarity, they characterize the situation in negative terms, such as unpleasant, cold, active, honest, awful, and complex. Attribution in such situations is made difficult by schemata, which conclude that people are being honest and truthful when they express opinions that differ from those of their interaction partner; expressions of attitude similarity can be truthful or merely attempts to be found acceptable (Berger, 1975). Studies such as this provide keys for unlocking, not only the attribution process, but also the communication strategies employed to reduce uncertainty.

Postulates by Berger and Calabrese prompted more than a decade of research to prove, clarify, and critique uncertainty reduction as a theoretical position explaining how people communicate interpersonally. One of the original assumptions is that people are more likely to engage in question asking to reduce uncertainty when they expect to meet again. However, a test of low, intermediate, and high levels of anticipation revealed that people in the intermediate treatment did more question asking than did those in other treatments. These results suggest that people attempt to avoid negative conversational outcomes (Douglas, 1987).

People appear to experience different levels of apprehension toward the perils of engaging in interactions for the first time and about forming relationships in general, what can be called global uncertainty. Analyzing that concept, Douglas (1991) discovered that people who experience high global uncertainty think of initial interactions in negative ways, prefer to avoid them, and develop less satisfactory long-term relationships. Such persons feel less self-assured and more awkward. During the first moments of interactions with strangers, those persons ask fewer questions and disclose more than persons who do not suffer from global uncertainty. Their more assured counterparts rate them to be less competent communicators.

Uncertainty reduction theory has predicted that during initial interaction, information seeking will occur whether the relationship appears likely to produce negative or positive outcomes. Contrary to that prediction, information seeking increases when individuals predict a positive outcome from initial interaction, whereas a negative prediction leads to less information seeking. The assumption is that people seek information to support their predictions that a relationship will be rewarding. No similar prediction seems to occur when initial predictions are negative (Sunnafrank, 1990).

Do people handle initial interactions differently and, if so, why? One explanation focuses on different levels of self-monitoring—paying attention to oneself as a communicator. High self-monitors are better at initial interactions than are low self-monitors. Self-monitoring is an interaction skill. High self-monitors are more aware of situational demands. They have more of a repertoire of information seeking strategies than do low self-monitors, and do more to direct the flow of conversation. Self-monitoring relates to expression and self-presentation. High self-monitors use more extensive and strategic use of verbal communication, and they use more conversation topics than do low self-monitors (Douglas, 1984).

Tensions exist between persons involved in a relationship because each partner seeks more information than he or she wants to give. How this relationship is negotiated is influenced by the form, content, and value of the information exchanged. *Form* relates to the methods of giving and obtaining information. Form results from desires to interrogate, disclose, demonstrate affect, be involved, and elaborate. How each person satisfies these desires is negotiated as the relationship develops. Content can best be described by polarities such as ambiguous/clear, general/specific, personal/nonpersonal, descriptive/explanatory, accurate/inaccurate, atypical/typical, or negative/positive. Each of these polarities reflects choices made by the person giving information. Value refers to factors related to self-evaluation, evaluation of other and the relationship; this category includes liking, perceived similarity, uncertainty, outcome, and the personality of the people involved (Kellerman, 1987).

Uncertainty reduction theory has been criticized because the stages for reducing uncertainty are not well defined, the causal mechanism that produces changes in levels of certainty has not been specified, and it appears to ignore the environment in which relationships develop. However, Gudykunst, Yang, and Nishida (1985) added support for the postulates by Berger and Calabrese (1975) by comparing uncertainty reduction tactics in acquaintanceships, friendships, and dating relationships in Japan, Korea, and the United States. Under these conditions, uncertainty reduction postulates for initial interaction hold up across different cultures.

Cross-cultural settings offer an opportunity to test uncertainty reduction theory. As researchers delve into the attribution schemata used to reduce uncertainty, they have kept in mind the differences in this process that result when people encounter others of their culture as well as persons from other cultures. When people make positive comparisons of persons from different ethnic groups, they are likely to employ typical uncertainty reduction processes. When people feel good about their own ethnic group, they are more likely to be confident when dealing with persons of another ethnic group. Perceived intimacy level in a relationship will influence the willingness of partners to disclose. These tendencies are more likely to occur when the partner is thought to be typical rather than atypical of his or her ethnic group. These findings not only support uncertainty reduction theory but also social penetration and social identity theories. *Social identity theory* posits that people make sense of their world by seeing themselves and others as members of groups. Such identities are vital to self-concepts. When persons encounter others who are typical of a social group, they experience less uncertainty about them. When people feel better about persons from other ethnic groups, they should be more willing to disclose, as predicted by social penetration theory, eventually improving the quality of the relationship because of rewards gained from it (Gudykunst & Hammer, 1988).

How people communicate, as well as what they say, appears to be a crucial part of the attribution process. Two indices seem useful in attempts to understand this process. One depends on the ratio of different words to all words (a rich vocabulary produces a higher ratio than does a weak vocabulary, which requires that individuals repeat the same words more often) and on the average length of word used during conversation. The other index, verbal immediacy, is a product of the directness of the language—the psychological closeness of the speaker to the topic; this is measured by comparing verb/auxiliary verb ratios, present/future tense ratios, and a range of possibilities. These ratios are used to measure tentativeness that occurs during conversation. As individuals experience uncertainty, they look for signs that can help them know whether the interaction partner is being honest and open. These indices are used to make such attributions, and tentativeness constitutes signs of uncertainty in a conversation (Van Rheenen & Sherblom, 1984).

Greene, O'Hair, Cody, and Yen (1985) reported that people who are being deceptive pause to prepare their statements for shorter periods of time than those who are telling the truth. Deceivers maintain less eye contact and inhibit or control themselves in order not to display behavioral cues of deception. A high degree of control is a sign of deception. Whether or not people are good at spotting deception, they want to believe they are. Research in this regard is devoted to determining how well and by what means people discern deception in their effort to reduce uncertainty.

To increase understanding of processes used to reduce uncertainty, researchers need to examine more than strategies employed by strangers. Much of the communication in which each of us engages occurs with people we know and toward whom we have various feelings of regard and similarity. What happens when events or actions change within existing relationships that cause people to have to deal with new levels of uncertainty?

To better understand this situation, Planalp, Rutherford, and Honeycutt (1988) examined how key events can change relational knowledge when taken-for-granted knowledge is disrupted. These researchers had subjects report their feelings and communication activities following an instance when someone close to them changed in ways that introduced uncertainty into a previously stable relationship. Relationships may go along for some period of time without producing uncertainty, and then something changes to disrupt what had been taken for granted. (Many topics of disclosure were reported in this research, including an announcement that a person was no longer interested in dating the subject and that the person had betrayed a confidence.)

The researchers elicited subjects' reactions to this kind of announcement and event. New information increased uncertainty. Although it decreased after a while, the degree of certainty regarding the quality of the relationship never returned to the level prior to the disclosure. Disclosure resulted in subjects' having negative feelings, but events did not produce negative outcomes. In fact, some of disclosures resulted in stronger relationships. Disclosed information affected relational variables of *trust* (including factors of honesty, confiding, and fairness), *involvement* (such as closeness, companionship, and emotional involvement), and *rules* (such as rewards, freedom, and duties or responsibilities). Disclosure of the information led most subjects to talk over the information rather than to argue about or avoid the issue or the other person. Subjects who talked the matter over with the other person felt the relationship had strengthened. Suggesting the presence of proactive and retroactive attribution, some subjects (41%) reported sensing that the other person had been leading up to an announcement. Whether they were insensitive to relationship changes or whether their partners were not good at signaling changes, most subjects became aware that a serious topic was coming only after it was introduced in conversation. Hints of relational changes that led subjects to suspect the coming information included changes in communication behavior, such as the lack of writing "I love you" in letters. Once the new information was introduced, typical communication reactions to the change included talking, explaining feelings, and information seeking; some subjects reported renegotiating the rules of the relationship. Most subjects reported talking to someone else about the disclosure; these conversations were used to get more information, to understand what was occurring, or to complain or ventilate about the change in the relationship.

Despite these findings, it is unwise to assume that people can easily discuss the quality of their relationships. It may be easier to discuss aspects of the relationship than the total relationship. People have indirect means for discovering information that can be used to reduce uncertainty about the quality of relationships in which they are involved. Berger (1987) argued that three information seeking strategies are used to reduce uncertainty: (a) *passive* strategies, particularly unobtrusive observations of the target person, (b) *active* strategies including asking third parties or creating situations that can be used to test the target individual's responses, (c) and *interactive* strategies whereby the interested party actively engages in communication with the target individual.

Berger (1987) observed that three interactive discovery methods are used widely: question asking, disclosure, and relaxation of the target. He noted that, when people attempt to acquire large amounts of information, they do not necessarily ask any more questions than do persons who are merely having a normal conversation. Rather than the number of questions, the difference seems to be the kind of questions. When persons are in a high information-seeking mode, they ask their relational partners more questions designed to elicit explanations for their partner's behavior, goals, and plans. Strategy selection seems to be guided by (a) the efficiency of the strategy, and (b) its social appropriateness. While seeking information, persons try to get their partners to like them as a means to obtain more information.

One of Berger and Calabrese's (1975) original propositions was that, as uncertainty is reduced, people become more attractive to one another. Reflecting on this proposition, Berger (1987) acknowledged that evidence may show that communication may produce information that increases uncertainty or that triggers dislikes. Either can lead to the person's being viewed as a less attractive relational partner. He reasoned that, if levels of uncertainty are high, relationships are likely to be strained, in part because costs of social exchange may outweigh rewards. Strained relationships are likely to dissolve. Initial interactions may be predicated on information that is obtained at, and based on, superficial levels. Subsequent communication may strengthen, blunt, or negate initial impressions. Although he acknowledged the value of using social exchange as a theoretical underpinning, Berger cautioned that it focuses on outcomes and not on processes. If people are to successfully calculate and exchange what is appropriate to achieve a strong relationship, they must use communication tactics to reduce uncertainty in regard to what conditions produce an equitable social exchange. This process is difficult and fraught with ambiguities and inaccuracies because it is difficult to tell what the relational partner thinks is a fair exchange and whether sufficient exchange has been accomplished. Knowledge of what constitutes equitable exchange can be used as relational power and can lead to conflict.

People employ the following tests in their attempt to check the quality of relationships:

1. *Direct questioning,* whereby one person asks the other about the condition of the relationship.
2. *Asking third parties* about the relationship.
3. *Trial intimacy move,* including becoming physically close or touching, disclosure, or public presentation in which the target individual is put on display or confronted with information to observe his or her reaction.
4. *Taken-for-granted* strategies to see if the other person reveals something about the relationship or merely takes it for granted. (This category includes joking, structuring the situation so the other must assume or reject the burden for the relationship, self-putdown, which challenges the target individual to counter the putdown or take it for granted, and hinting—the target individual is expected to take up the hint if the relationship is serious.)
5. *Endurance tests* which include forced choices ("Either bring me flowers or admit that you don't like me"), physical separation, and testing limits (to see, for instance, what the target individual is willing to give or do to maintain or advance a relationship).
6. *Jealousy tests* to see if the target individual will respond by showing jealousy. (These tests are created by describing alternatives, such as talking about another boy friend or girl friend or initiating alternative behaviors—going out with someone else.)
7. *Fidelity checks* to test whether the person will remain faithful to or violate the relationship.

Females use more tests than males do, and more tests are employed in romantic relationships than in platonic ones. Being able to distinguish between these two kinds of relationships is important because people may want platonic relationships to become romantic (or vice versa), or they may want to prevent romantic relationships from becoming platonic. Separation tests and indirect suggestion tests are more likely to be used when relationships have the potential of becoming romantic than in platonic or romantic relationships. Regardless of the quality of relationships, people have difficulty talking directly about them with one another, particularly aspects that are taboo. Romantic and platonic relationships are characterized by openness, trust, and shared control (Baxter & Wilmot, 1984).

This kind of research extends understanding of uncertainty reduction processes beyond the initial stages of a relationship. It gives us insight into relationships. For instance, at turning points of romantic relationships, participants are more likely to discuss their relationship than at other times. Whether people talk about the turning points in their relationships depends on the kind of turning point that occurs (Baxter & Bullis, 1986).

Uncertainty can also be reduced when partners (romantic partners, for instance) communicate with their partner's friends and family. Moreover, stronger relationships are characterized by open communication and perceived similarity between partners (Parks & Adelman, 1983).

To understand how people make attributions and use communication to reduce uncertainty, researchers need to disclose the schemata they use. People acquire schemata that they use before, during, and after interactions to obtain information and make sense of it. They might, for instance, believe they are more likely to obtain information in social settings rather than formal settings. They use hypotheses as the basis of information seeking and processing. A typical hypothesis might take this form: People who . . . (act in a certain way, for instance) during a conversation are X kind of people.

To this point in the chapter, a case has been made that social cognition involves efforts to gain information about others. Schemata are employed to figure out the character and motives of the relationship and the persons involved. This effort requires that information be interpreted in ways that are meaningful, given the context of the relationship and the goals of the persons involved. Communication strategies – plans – are developed and employed to enact communication episodes in ways thought to be rewarding. All of these factors combine to affect each individual's communication competence.

This review of research and theoretical perspectives points to some universal themes in interpersonal communication research. A common element is that to understand how people attribute and act in regard to one another requires insights into the cognitive schemata by which they come to understand and make sense of their circumstances, especially the people involved in their circumstances. As was discussed in chapter 3, how people characterize one another and the social and physical realms in which they operate depends on perspectives embedded in their idioms, their language. Processes of attribution or characterization are used to understand — to know others, what they know, and the surrounding circumstances. This shared social knowledge helps people to not only know, but to know what others know. The desire to reduce uncertainty motivates individuals to make sense of their physical and social world and to calculate their self-efficacy as communicators.

ACCOMMODATION

Analysis developed to this point suggests that three factors are crucial to interpersonal communication: cognition, planning, and accommodation. Cognition refers to the schemata each person employs during communication. Planning is employed, based on plans learned and schemata utilized, to accommodate to communication partners. Not all conversations are planned; many just happen. Even when they are planned, much that happens is the result of what transpires. For these reasons, an understanding of interactions must encompass a range of actions from the highly planned to the purely spontaneous.

This array of cognitive competencies suggests that individuals involved in communication are busy making many cognitive connections and drawing conclusions. Some people are more mindful than others. Situations may require people to be more mindful than they would be in different circumstances.

Although people can be quite complex and mindful in their communication, much communication is automatic and scripted, at least that is the argument made by *speech accommodation theory*. It assumes that communication competence depends on individuals' ability to perform in ways that enhance interactions in which they participate and achieve their goals (Street & Giles, 1982). This line of research argues that, as people interact, they tend to accommodate to each other; to the extent they do so successfully, they are seen as positive communication partners. Much accommodation occurs through nonverbal cues, such as response latency (time that transpires between a stimulus, a comment, and the response to it), speech rate (how rapidly a person speaks), and turn duration (how long each person talks).

Speech accommodation theory asserts that communication consists primarily of scripted behaviors that are used primarily to present oneself favorably to communication partners. People manage impressions by performing acts designed to get their communication partners to see them in specific ways, especially as desirable, rational partners, and to exert social influence. How people communicate is to a large extent a product of their self-identities, the situation, relationships, goals, and levels of arousal. Throughout interaction, people monitor their behavior and that of their partner. This behavior is evaluated by calculating the extent to which it fits the expectations relevant to the situation (Giles & Street, 1985).

Speech accommodation theory makes quite different assumptions about responses to similar and expected interpersonal behavior than does Cappella and Greene's (1982) discrepancy-arousal theory, which was discussed in chapter 6. Discrepancy-arousal theory postulates that when interactants act in ways that violate the expectations their partners have of them, arousal is created that can negatively affect their interaction and relationship. Street and Giles (1982) believed that three causal links are relevant to the theory: (a) communication patterns one person expects the other to exhibit (such as speaking at an appropriate rate, taking the appropriate amount of time per turn, or matching responses such as nodding approval); (b) arousal which leads to affect; and (c) responses based on the arousal (for instance, if one person speaks too quickly the relational partner might speak more slowly).

Cappella (1985) reasoned that speech accommodation theory can explain what happens in conversations as long as they are going well, but he doubted that it helps explain why they break down. He argued that convergence, reciprocity, and similarity of communication patterns (verbal and nonverbal) lead interactants to evaluate one another positively.

Street and Giles are concerned by the discrepancy-arousal model's prediction that little or no discrepancy can lead to little or no arousal, which is affectively neutral. In contrast to this prediction, speech accommodation theory reasons that if responses are matched, no discrepancy occurs, but the reaction is positive rather than neutral. Similarity produces positive rather than neutral reactions.

Street and Giles (1982) offered speech accommodation theory as an alternative explanation because

> it (1) acknowledges social cognitive processes, (2) has the potential for further scope in those directions, (3) incorporates the social consequences as well as the determinants of speech adjustments, (4) is applicable to many linguistic levels of analysis, from the more intercultural language and dialect switching to the more intracultural conversational and noncontent speech domains, (5) attends to intergroup phenomena and processes, and (6) has had applications to a wide range of speech domain, including those of language and sex. (p. 204)

Seeking to support this theory, Street (1984) examined the extent to which interactants' *noncontent speech* patterns (speech rate, pauses, pitch, intensity, duration, and accent) converge or become similar to one another. Also important in this situation is the *evaluation* each person makes of the other in terms of what transpires during conversation. This theory predicts that as a conversation transpires, participants' noncontent communication patterns should change in ways that mirror one another, what Street called *speech convergence phenomenon.* If convergence occurs, interaction should be more successful and partners should form favorable impressions of each other, even though they may be unaware that is happening. Convergence seems to occur because of several motives: Desire for approval, sensitivity to interpersonal cues, perceived attitudinal similarity, communication effectiveness, competence, social attractiveness, communicator warmth, or desire for social identification.

Speech accommodation theory is based on principles of similarity-attraction, social exchange, attribution, and social identity. According to this theory, people are motivated to adjust their speech styles with respect to one another to foster social identity—shared expression of values, attitudes, and intentions. A key mechanism in the process is the perception one person has of another's speech. Based on what one person perceives as the other's communication patterns, the first person makes evaluations that lead to behavior and further evaluation and subsequent adjustments. The assumption is that intentions, actions, and adjustments will lead to convergence as an expression of a desire for social integration, seeking or showing approval, social identification, or communication competence. Convergence is a employed when one person in an interaction attempts to be like and be liked by another. If convergence is perceived to be intentional rather than accidental, it is likely to be evaluated more positively.

Convergence has many positive benefits. It can result in enhanced perceived intelligibility, supportiveness, predictability, intersubjectivity (shared ideas and views), and smoothness of interaction. It may indicate positive feelings toward the other person involved. Convergence can foster warmth, perceived competence, attraction, and willingness to cooperate.

Convergence is likely to occur when rewards for doing so outweigh costs. It will not occur under the opposite conditions. Convergence depends on participants' communication repertoires and need for social approval. The social identity component of this theory predicts that divergence will occur when people desire to reject or dissociate themselves from people who are perceived to be nongroup members (those who are not part of the person's social, ethnic, economic group, etc.). Divergence will depend on a desire to dissociate from the other person and the communication repertoire available to accomplish this goal.

Speech maintenance occurs when interactants deliberately seek to maintain social distance between themselves and others. In this way, they establish autonomy and independence. Such patterns occur when communication partners are seen as undesirable socially and when differences are to be maintained. Under such circumstances, communicators may even accentuate differences between themselves and their communication partners.

Speech accommodation theory predicts that communication styles of interactants must match to achieve harmony, be successful, and demonstrate competence. For this reason, people who speak quickly are more likely to influence people who think quickly. Likewise, slow decoders are more likely to comply with requests made by slow speakers (Buller & Aune, 1988).

Convergence is likely to occur when the persons involved in communication desire social approval, want the communication to be efficient, have a high incentive to manage their impressions, and have the repertoires needed to accomplish the accommodation. In contrast, convergence is unlikely if (a) the costs outweigh rewards, (b) the patterns required for accommodation have stigmas associated with them, or (c) if one partner desires to change the other's behavior (Giles, Mulac, Bradac, & Johnson, 1987).

COMMUNICATION COMPETENCE AND PLANNING

Some of your friends and acquaintances are probably quite competent communicators, whereas others are not. Do you sometimes feel more competent than at others? This moment of reflection sets the stage to discuss communication competence.

Communication competence requires cognitive and interaction skills needed to exert personal control, the ability to adjust to and affect the environment—including communication episodes. Such skills need not be maximal, merely adequate. Competence occurs at all levels—interpersonal, organizational, and mass-mediated—all of which require the ability to translate thoughts into words from verbal and nonverbal cues. Such cues are organized into sequences ranging in length from sentences to conversational episodes. Control includes the ability to interact in ways that affect relationships and execute programs of action in search of goals. During communication, persons may have to improvise if their initial plans fail (Parks, 1985).

How competent people think they are can affect their willingness and ability to interact with others. Various reasons have been used to explain what impact competence has on the ability to use communication effectively. Studies have concentrated on the communication efforts people make, whether effective or not, to appear competent to others. Three variables are basic to communication competence: motivation, knowledge, and skills. A cost–rewards matrix governs the motivations people have to be competent. People are likely to be more competent if they have knowledge (the information and experience needed for interactions). If their skill level is high, they are likely to be less anxious and show more immediacy, expressiveness, ability to manage interaction, as well as take orientations toward other people (Spitzberg & Hecht, 1984).

A basic issue in the study of communication competence is the degree to which interpersonal communication is strategic and mindful rather than routine and scripted. Rather than performing in ways that are merely mindless and scripted, argued Sypher and Applegate (1984), people apply communication-relevant beliefs that arise from their definition of each situation and their estimation of what communication tactics are most appropriate to achieve their goals.

Favoring a mindful interpretation of this issue, O'Keefe and McCornack (1987) contended that people communicate with one another based on theories of communication each possesses and the relative skill each has to devise and execute an appropriate theory to achieve his/her goals under constraints of each situation. A *theory,* in this sense, is a general plan based on how interactants believe communication transpires. Each person has many theories or plans regarding how to act to be competent in different contexts with many types of communication partners. As their competence develops, people acquire increasingly more sophisticated rationale that can be used to decide which communication means should be employed to achieve each particular set of outcomes. Persons watch the communication behavior of others to learn which message-design logics are more or less effective. Messages that convey the users' communication goals and are designed to save face for the other person involved in the communication are likely to be the most effective.

Because many plans are available, not everyone employs the same one. O'Keefe and McCornack (1987) argued that variety in behavior occurs between partners during communication episodes because people set different goals or use different strategies to achieve goals. People involved in the same communication episode may operate out of different theories or message-design logics regarding which communication tactics are best. Qualities such as egocentrism, rhetorical sensitivity, and person-centeredness account for why people communicate differently. Three kinds of message design logics seem to account for differences in behavior. *Expressive* logic is used when people "dump" their thoughts and feelings on each other. They assume that receivers interpret the messages for what they are. *Conventional* message logic treats communication as a game played cooperatively via rules and conventions; messages are designed to achieve effects. *Rhetorical* message design logic consists of tactics people believe are necessary to portray themselves as they wish to be seen and to influence the outcome of interaction given the circumstances.

O'Keefe and McCornack (1987) contended that people's perceptions of the effectiveness of various message design logics influence which ones they use to achieve their goals. In any situation, various message logics can be equally effective. (Recall the concept of *equifinality,* a term used in systems theory to indicate that each system can obtain the same goal by employing different methods.) Communication competence is enhanced when message logic and goal selection take into consideration what the receiver of the message wants to achieve from the interaction. When the message design logic is well adapted to the receiver, it helps that person to save face and to feel rewarded and competent as a person.

Pursuing the variables central to message design logics, O'Keefe (1988) found two major functional differences between message efforts. The first, *message goal structure,* is a product of the number and types of goals a person is simultaneously pursuing or giving attention to while organizing a message. The second is *message design logic*—this logic reflects the beliefs the person producing a message relies on while deciding which tactics to use to achieve the goals. Cognitive processes, particularly cognitive complexity, rather than personality traits seem to explain the differences in persons' abilities to select goals and message design logics that are appropriate to one another. If people have message design logics that work in one situation, they are likely to use them in other situations.

The kinds of logics people apply may differ in regard to whether they are task or relationship oriented. Males tend to take a task orientation in conversations; this pattern is also likely to be preferred by people who measure high in verbal aggressiveness and low in interpersonal orientation—regardless of sex. Women prefer a relational orientation, as do people who seek interpersonal harmony and to avoid arguments as well as verbal aggressiveness (Hample & Dallinger, 1988).

Some amount of communication is routine, habitual, and scripted, requiring little conscious processing and planning. However, the most important parts of communication are probably those that result from more active planning and processing. Studying communication interaction, persuasion, and conflict resolution, O'Keefe and Shepherd (1987) identified four categories of message strategies that reflect the kinds of plans that can be executed during conflict. These feature the communicative roles persons take as they produce messages, the points of view they take during their turns, the extent to which they explicitly acknowledge conflict, and the manner in which they use strategies to protect the face of their conflict partner and maintain interaction. Planning, in this sense, relates to the ability to select one goal or outcome instead of others, to separate issues, and to integrate efforts as well as achieve reconciliation.

From discussions such as this, it can be assumed that all communication is mindful rather than scripted. Indeed, it is likely that interactions exhibit combinations of both. *Action assembly* is a theory that has been advanced to deal with the fact that communication seems to be patterned and repetitive as well as unique and creative. During a conversation, you may find yourself repeating scripts (words, phrases, or entire conversational passages) that you have used in similar interactions. You may also find that some statements are unique and creative; you may make comments different from any you have made before. Life requires that we periodically create, practice, and employ new communication plans. Such efforts require people to recall scripts used in previous conversations. Factors that influence this process include memory storage, retrieval, and utilization — the ability of communicators to remember, know when and what to recall, and competently utilize what is recalled. Because previously used scripts may be unsatisfactory to achieve an immediate communication outcome, unique versions of conversation may be required (Greene, 1984).

What is recalled and required for each person to participate in a conversation consists both of content (what is or can be said) and procedural protocols (tactics needed to progress through a conversation). These may be stored and recalled in units based on a combination of actions and outcomes (strategies, situations, and goals). Which actions are needed (and perhaps recalled or invented) to achieve the outcomes required in a particular conversation? One of the quickest ways to intuit the process we are discussing here is to recall how, after a conversation, you may think, "I wish I had said . . ." or "I'm glad I remembered to say . . ." In the course of conversation, an individual is expected to recall or invent a wide array of content and procedures. A conversation entails knowing procedures, selecting words and nonverbal cues (to the extent that these are selected rather than merely spontaneous or purely habitual), and identifying conversation goals (Greene, 1984).

This process consists of combinations of actions and outcomes associated with them. How likely a person is to recall any action-outcome unit depends on the recency and frequency with which it is utilized. Activation of any content or procedural script depends on the extent to which the conversational participant recognizes a goal and makes the connection between the goal and a specific message or procedural tactic. Each procedural record is unique to the extent that it relates to one or a combination of several outcomes:

1. Interaction to achieve outcomes specific to a situation, relationship, or identity of the participants.
2. Content.
3. Conversational management — the steps and connections between statements that move the conversation along.

4. Utterances, including word choice, syntax, and articulation.
5. Regulation of the conversation through turn taking and response matching.
6. Need to regulate physiological requirements to participate in the conversation (for instance keep one's temper under control).
7. Coordination of vocal and other nonverbal behaviors needed to affect the conversational partner.

Components of any conversation are not entirely unique, nor are they free from the unique ways participants perceive and characterize themselves and the persons with whom they interact. Each participant is reasonably mindful of what to say and the consequences of what is said (Greene, 1984). The theme of this theory is that individuals "assemble" their conversational "actions" based on predictions of expected or required outcomes.

To explain the action-assembly process, Greene postulated that lower-motor and autonomic processes support-higher order skills such as communication and cognitive processing. This model assumes that several factors are interrelated: (a) expected interaction success, (b) projected self-image, (c) importance of interaction, and (d) interaction success and importance. *Action assembly* postulates that individuals usually can think of social behaviors (especially communication) needed to achieve communication goals, but a problem exists when they think that they have low personal competency and, therefore, anticipate they will be affected negatively by communication outcomes. When they cannot automatically or easily think of the needed behavior, they are likely to experience anxiety. By comparing the communication efforts of high- and low-communication apprehension individuals, Booth-Butterfield (1987) added support to the action-assembly theory, thereby giving additional insights into factors that affect communication planning and competence.

Although speech accommodation and nonverbal convergence may improve rapport between communicators, Hewes and Planalp (1987) argued that shared knowledge is also vital to communication. This view stresses a model of interpersonal communication that assumes more cognitive activity than is typically associated with speech accommodation. To understand communication, insight must be gained into the cognitive processes by which influence and social knowledge are managed. Attributions people make of one another are crucial to explanations of why they act as they do.

Planning results when people seek to know what others know, how they process information, and what their goals are. Such estimations constitute the heart of the planning process by which people seek to achieve communication goals. This process is summarized:

> Speakers are better able to assess and optimize the impact of a message if they know what listeners are focusing on, how they are likely to integrate

information and draw inferences from it, what they are likely to remember, and how they will select and implement their responses. But impact also depends on what the listeners think speakers are focusing on, what inferences they are inviting, and so on. (Hewes & Planalp, 1987, p. 168)

At least to some extent, efforts to reduce uncertainty involve plans and are strategic. When people encounter one another, they formulate and test hypotheses about each other. Reasoning that people gather information out of curiosity and to increase self-efficacy, Hewes and Planalp (1982) contended that efforts to reduce uncertainty require knowledge of prior interactions and attributions. Four factors influence how people go about reducing uncertainty: goals they have for reducing it, communication tools they employ such as asking questions, cognitive functions they utilize to process the information they obtain, and their cognitive capacities. Goals people have for reducing uncertainty in each case guide how they go about doing so. Goals, whether interpersonal or cognitive, are specifiable, even if not explicitly, as part of the process. When people encounter one another, whether for the first time or on subsequent occasions, they do so with a set of goals that govern the kinds of attributions they make. These goals, along with the cognitive capacity of the person who wants to reduce uncertainty, constrain the process of uncertainty reduction. "Interactants' goals determine what social knowledge will be brought to bear, what inferential tasks are needed to reduce uncertainty about the social events, and what cognitive functions and communication tools are needed to accomplish the goals" (Hewes & Planalp, 1982, p. 112). This approach assumes that efforts to reduce uncertainty and to interact depend on strategic and cognitive abilities. Thus, for instance, as you encounter a store clerk for the first time, you estimate the person's ability to help you achieve your purpose for shopping in that store. Is this person competent — as compared with other clerks you have encountered?

To an extent, the cognitive processes involved in uncertainty reduction follow plans. Employing the metaphor of people as naive scientists, Hewes and Planalp argued that the information people receive is meaningless if generalizations ("theories" or "hypotheses") are not used to make sense of it. Four kinds of cognitive processes seem to be employed during efforts to reduce uncertainty: *correlation* (what factors about the other person occur at the same time), *generative* (theories of how stories are structured — interaction happens in narrative form: "I said . . ." and "He/She replied . . ."), *temporal* (in what time order events are observed and what that order says according to the theories individuals hold about others' behavior), and *causality* (assumptions people make about which factors cause what outcomes). All of these factors give interactants a sense of expectation regarding what attributes co-occur, how parts of an episode work together, what events follow one another, and what events are or will be produced by others. Cognitive processes involved in uncertainty reduction are *focusing* (what people pay attention to), *storage/retrieval* (how people "file" and recall information about the targets of their attributions), *integration and inference* (specific cognitive processes people use to process data), and *selection and implementation* (choice and use of specific communication tools and cognitive processes).

Ability to create and execute communication plans is vital to each individual's efforts to initiate and maintain social relationships. "A plan," Berger (1988) claimed, "specifies the actions that are necessary for the attainment of a goal or several goals. Plans vary in their levels of abstraction. Highly abstract plans can spawn more detailed plans. Plans can contain alternative paths for goal attainment from which the social actor can choose" (p. 96). Some plans become scripted, habitual efforts to conduct routine interactions, such as asking about a friend's health, welfare, or weekend activities. As long as the plans used by interactants are appropriate, compatible, and skillfully employed, successful interaction is expected. Plans are likely to reflect not only the means by which to execute an interaction, but also a larger plan as well — the purpose of the interaction. A person applying for a job may have a plan for being successful during an interview, but the larger goal is getting a job and being successful. When plans do not succeed as intended, the individual has to improvise, depending on alternative plans that can be created. This kind of adjustment is likely to require people to have plan repertoires; some will have more plans and be better at improvising than others.

Plans may call for use of various communication activities at different times during a conversation. A person might plan to start a conversation with small talk. This tactic could be used to see if the partner has any interests that can be used as the basis of further discussion, perhaps with the purpose of finding out that both parties share similar tastes in rock music. All of this conversational sequence could be a means one person uses to build up to asking the other for a date (or making oneself available to be asked for a date).

In this process, each individual's perception of self and of the communication partner influences the planning and execution process. Supporting this analysis, Berger and Bell (1988) discovered that plans created to initiate social relationships are better when they are longer and demonstrate greater breadth, thereby offering more possibilities for creating the relationship. Shy and lonely persons are hampered in their ability to create plans to create social relationships.

People are more likely to achieve positive relational outcomes when they have plans that include a wide variety of actions (Berger & Bell, 1988). However, if a plan is too complex, the person employing it may suffer a loss of fluency because he or she cannot decide which variation of the plan to employ at a given moment (Berger, Karol, & Jordan, 1989).

This section has demonstrated an array of views of how people develop and employ communication plans. Such plans are tailored to the situation, the communication partner, and the desired outcomes. They are employed to reduce uncertainty. Although some communication is purely routine and scripted, some of the most important moments require individuals to be competent in their ability to determine what plan is appropriate and to be able to execute it successfully.

CONCLUSION

The research and theory reported in this chapter emphasize cognitive and interactional processes of interpersonal communication. How and why people communicate are influenced by the ways they characterize or make attributions about one another. This theme underpins the social cognition approach to interpersonal communication. Interaction is, in various ways, motivated by uncertainty reduction, which relates not only to others but also to one's own social competence. One of the ways people show their willingness to identify with one another is through speech accommodation. To some extent, such behavior is strategic and mindful. However, higher level and more complex plans seem essential in efforts to communicate strategically in order to achieve communication goals, especially when scripted patterns are inadequate to achieve them.

8 Communication in Organizations

Humans spend their lives in organizations ranging in size from a single family to educational institutions and companies with dozens, hundreds, even thousands of employees world wide. You probably cannot remember a time when you were not part of several organizations. This chapter examines variables and theories that explain why people communicate as they do as a consequence of their membership in organizations. The study of organizational communication centers on means by which people who operate in organizations gain information, shape opinions, make decisions, coordinate efforts, and create rapport to achieve goals that guide the organization and influence individual decisions.

Members of organizations attempt to make rational decisions about their performance, seeking to maximize the rewards for their efforts. Members of organizations communicate to perform tasks and roles on behalf of those organizations and negotiate with other organizational members, including management on how those tasks and roles will be performed.

UNIQUENESS OF ORGANIZATIONAL COMMUNICATION

Early studies of organizational communication limited the key variables to four: organizational structure, messages, media, and communicators (Farace, Stewart, & Taylor, 1978). Advancing beyond that approach, current organizational communication analysis centers on opinions and actions of members, and the dyad has become a focal point of analysis. For this reason, organizational communication should not be studied as something that transpires within a "box" — the organization — but rather what happens between people. Meaning — shared and personal opinions — influences what people do and how they do it in the context — "culture" and "climate" — of each organization. Rather than thinking of an organization communicating, it is appropriate to think of people communicating in an organization and on behalf of an organization.

Although scholars at times stumble in their efforts to define the field of organizational communication (Redding, 1985), the pursuit is necessary because organizational life is an inescapable aspect of human experience (Wiio, Goldhaber, & Yates, 1980). Even what appears to be casual communication in organizations has enormous impact on members' thoughts and actions. Members of organizations tell stories, foster myths, call one another by code names, and enact elaborate rituals. These forms of communication convey each organization's culture and reflect its climate.

Researchers work to discover principles that explain why organizational members perform the way they do. An incentive for such study is to make organizations better and employees happier and more effective. Toward this end, studies focus on the complexity of organizations, seeking to isolate the key factors at all levels: intraindividual, interpersonal, group, organizational, and macrosocietal. Such levels of analysis are easy to conceptualize; however, as Jablin and Krone (1987) concluded, "While researchers have long recognized the theoretical importance of organizing their research around such levels of analysis, as individuals, dyads, small groups, intact organizations, and environments, they have had great difficulty accomplishing this task" (p. 711). Sections of this chapter address issues unique to interpersonal relationships, small group communication (three to seven people, such as a meeting), network — systemwide — communication, and interorganizational communication that involves mass-mediated channels.

As you think about organizations, you might reflect on the following questions. Do you communicate differently in each organization to which you belong because of its unique purpose, structure, climate, and culture? How do you and others use communication to coordinate efforts and shape relationships to work toward shared goals, even though you perform different tasks and have different reasons for being in each organization? Such questions should help you think about topics relevant to the study of organizational communication, which transpires between members of organizations and with persons those organizations affect.

Communication is a means, not an end, of organizations and their members. Even media organizations — a newspaper or broadcast company, for instance — use communication to achieve ends such as entertain, inform, or influence; their goals include earning revenue or raising money (in the case of public television or public radio) through entertainment programming and news.

How an organization operates and whether it is successful depends on two broad sets of variables or functions: task (work activities and roles) and socioemotional (climate). Job performance tasks are functions required for an organization to achieve its goals and for its members to accomplish their private goals (e.g., to earn a living) and organizational objectives (e.g., to sell a product). *Task* refers to what individuals or groups do, and *socioemotional climate* is the psychological state that accompanies those activities. How tasks are performed is influenced by what members of each organization sense as its climate. Socioemotional functions affect the interpersonal relationships in which they operate.

In addition to other job-related tasks in which they must be competent, employees are expected to communicate effectively. If the ability to climb the organizational ladder is a mark of success, then effective communication skills are helpful. Sypher and Zorn (1986) found that people who hold positions at higher levels in companies (as well as those promoted most often) exhibit better cognitive skills and superior communication abilities, as measured by ability to self-monitor, to understand the perspectives other are taking, and to be persuasive.

Studying communication in organizations is different from examining it in interpersonal contexts because of the presence of the organization, along with its norms, goals, and constraints. Outside of organizations, interpersonal episodes often just happen and are negotiated according to skills and purposes of each relational partner. When similar episodes occur in organizations (and on their behalf), they are part of the purpose for which each organization was created and reflect the reasons persons have for being part of it. Communication in an organization, its groups and dyads, happens because of the dynamics of the system itself and its interaction with other systems.

Similar to interpersonal contexts, a lot of communication in organizations is scripted and results from role expectations. For instance, away from a school, a teacher might not intervene in a fight between two children, but at school, a norm attached to the role of teacher would motivate him or her to intervene. Outside of an organization, interpersonal relationships depend on outcomes that participants create and negotiate themselves, whereas in an organization, relationships are substantially influenced by outcomes and meanings prescribed by other members.

As you will note throughout this chapter, information and systems theories have influenced the study of organizational communication. Organizations are treated as systems that use information to achieve goals and maintain equilibrium. According to this paradigm, members of organizations (as well as subgroups in organizations) receive (input) information, process it, and output it. How formation flows between individuals and groups in organizations demonstrates the relationships between them. That conclusion is important to structural-functional analysis which will be examined later in this chapter.

Although information flow is important to the performance of organizations, persuasion also influences organizational processes. Through persuasion, individuals in an organization influence people who are outside, for instance through contract negotiation, public relations, advertising, or sales. Persuasion is pervasive inside organizations; it occurs when supervisors attempt to motivate workers and when workers influence one another. Large organizations employ internal public relations in an attempt to increase employees' commitment to them. Through persuasion, relationships are created, negotiated, and terminated. How organization members interrelate and coordinate their efforts involves persuasion variables such as credibility, as well as message and channel effects. Persuasion theories, especially information integration, involvement, expectancy value, and social learning, explain how people enter, become assimilated, maintain, coordinate, and terminate organizational membership.

Those theories help explain why organization members hold the opinions they do toward work, themselves, the company, and other members. Through persuasion, members negotiate reward systems, role expectations, and relationships that affect organizational structure and power. Leaders of organizations are influenced by actions and statements of their personnel as well as outsiders, such as customers or governmental regulators and legislators. Compliance gaining and conflict resolution are typical organizational communication activities. How people interact involves negotiating relationships to maximize reward/cost outcomes, a concept basic to *social exchange theory*.

In organizations, managers use persuasion to create social realities that influence the perceptions, attributions, judgments, and activities of the members. This social reality provides unobtrusive control over employees' thoughts and behavior once they adopt its assumptions and identify with one another and the organization (Tompkins & Cheney, 1985). Political influence is exerted in an organization when individuals use stories to give unique definitions to roles and relationships (Mumby, 1987). So influential is this shared reality on organizational members' thoughts and behavior that scholars are beginning to study what they call organizational rhetoric and employ a research perspective called *interpretivism*. That organizational analysis assumes that members persuade one another—as well as persons outside of it—to think a particular way about the organization and to act toward it accordingly.

This chapter explores the uniqueness of organizational experience by examining the origins and assumptions of organizational communication research. It considers the systems perspective, communication networks, organizational climate and culture, and levels of analysis—individual, interpersonal, group, organizational, and interorganizational.

PARADIGMS FOR THE STUDY OF ORGANIZATIONAL COMMUNICATION

The origins of organizational communication are timeless, but in this century, it has been studied by social scientific methods since at least the 1920s. Early in this century, the paradigm that guided the study of organizational communication was that managers tell workers what to do, when, and how; organizational communication was viewed as flowing downward, in an autocratic fashion. This view is part of the *classical management philosophy,* which assumes that employees are hired to work, not to think (Morgan, 1986). Although many people have challenged this paradigm, it persists more than it should.

Scholars looking for an alternate paradigm got a substantial boost from the classic Hawthorne studies. While investigating how changes in working conditions affect employees' behavior, researchers conducted thousands of interviews at Western Electric's Hawthorne plant in 1927. Even though working conditions were experimentally made unpleasant, such as dimming the lights to determine the effect on workers' behavior, employees worked harder to compensate for poor lighting. Workers were motivated to strive because they appreciated knowing that someone cared about their opinions and feelings.

In his discussions of organizational behavior in the 1930s, Chester Barnard, president of New Jersey Bell Telephone Company, emphasized the importance of communication among employees. He proposed that communication is best when it achieves understanding, is consistent with personal and company goals, and supports employees' mental and physical tasks. Following these trends, the 1940s and 1950s witnessed an emerging interest in communication, especially two-way flow and network studies. Drawing on prevailing interest in information theory, communication studies began to examine how information is vital to organizations—not just in the sense of something sent from one department to another—but as an essential aspect of their survival. Information theory and systems theory combined to form the dominant paradigm of organizational communication research.

During the 1960s, researchers began to go beyond job satisfaction and motivation studies to explore the intricacies of networks, superior–subordinate relationships, and performance feedback. The 1970s witnessed serious commitment to study climate, patterns of information flow, and message content. That decade felt the influence of humanistic psychology's belief that quality of life could be improved through effective communication; during that era, a relational orientation began to permeate the study of interpersonal communication. Consideration was given to variables such as inclusion–exclusion, similarity, reciprocity, growth, and self-actualization. Relational communication had an impact by arguing for openness in superior–subordinate relationships. Terms such as *acceptance, openness,* and *reciprocation* became popular for explaining employee motivation, job satisfaction, and productivity.

Organizational communication researchers in the 1970s set out to create an enormous database of information that could be used to develop criteria regarding what makes one organization superior to another (Richetto, 1977). The 1980s extended human resource development by giving more attention to organizational climate and culture and by placing less interest in communication networks. The trend is to explore how people negotiate relationships and share meanings needed for the organization to survive and prosper. Much of this research is motivated by the "bottom line," helping managers to know how to increase productivity by involving employees in meaningful decision making.

Management philosophies have conflicting assumptions about the use and flow of communication in an organization. *Classical management philosophy* prevailed in the early part of this century, and still does in some organizations. It assumes that employees work only for tangible rewards, such as money and position. This philosophy assumes that workers need to be directed by managers because they are incapable of making wise decisions about their work; with management status comes the prerogatives of directing others' behavior. According to this philosophy, communication flows downward, primarily in the form of directives. Upward communication is discouraged.

Following the Hawthorne Studies, management philosophy began to emphasize *human relations;* if employees worked harder when management talked with them, then communication could be used as a motive to increase productivity. Some upward communication was encouraged; downward communication was less a matter of directive and more a matter of giving policy and instruction. This management philosophy led to activities, such as company picnics, where employees could get to know one another, which would increase their willingness to produce. If carried too far, this philosophy can turn companies into "country clubs" where managers worry so much whether employees are feeling good that work is deemphasized.

Recent research favors the notion that workers are happiest and most productive when they have some control over their jobs. This principle has lead to the *human resource management philosophy.* This perspective reasons that because employees know how to perform their jobs, they should be involved in task-related decisions to improve work design and job performance. Communication, according to this philosophy, flows in all directions; employees are expected to offer opinion about the way tasks are performed. Managers are expected to be open and responsive to the needs of subordinates. Productivity improves, not only because employees "work smarter," but also because they are involved socioemotionally in their jobs. Supporters believe that this management philosophy encourages openness, trust, and proper distribution of control.

Comparison of these three management philosophies is intended to get you to think about organizations. Your view of organizations must be encompassing enough to include a range from a family to companies with hundreds of employees. It must embrace organizations that have different missions: provide education, satisfy religious needs, deliver governmental services, serve social needs, as well as produce and sell products and services. Toward these ends, organizations need, according to *contingency theory,* to be flexible in their ability to follow one managerial philosophy in preference to others, some of the time or most of the time, depending on what method is best suited to achieve the organization's goals and mission in light of its present circumstances.

To deal with issues vital to management philosophy and focus on appropriate units of analysis, the study of communication in organizations revolves around four paradigms: (a) structural-functionalism, (b) psychological, (c) interpretivism, and (d) systems-interaction (cf. Krone, Jablin, & Putnam, 1987; Putnam, 1982). To some extent, these paradigms overlap and support one another, but they also challenge each other. This wrangle indicates that organizational communication research still lacks an organizational point of view. Analysis of each of these paradigms can give you different orientations for the study of organizational communication.

According to *structural-functionalism,* organizations can be studied by examining the *structure* (arrangement) of people who join to accomplish similar, compatible, or interlocking *functions* (tasks) designed to achieve shared goals. Structures are best described in terms of information flow throughout an organization, including the relationships between superiors and subordinates. Proponents of this paradigm reason that they are studying the dynamic, not static, processes of organizing—rather than the mechanics of organization (Farace, Monge, & Russell, 1977).

This view attempts to account for how people come together for similar, compatible, although not identical goals. Based on systems perspectives and information theory, this approach stresses the need for accurate and rapid transmission of clear and accurate messages. According to this analysis, key concepts are barriers and communication breakdowns. A secretary, for example, might manage the communication of others in an efficient and professional manner—eliminating barriers and breakdowns. Departments are *interlocked* when their goals are complementary; for instance, the persons who work in the exploration department of a major oil company locate (goal) crude oil that the processing department makes (goal) into products such as gasoline that are sold (goal) by the marketing department. Each department has unique, but complementary goals; these support the corporate goal of making a profit, which in turn supports individual employees' goals of earning a living. Goals interlock. For instance, a recalcitrant student has the goal of refusing to learn. His or her goals to avoid school interlock with those of the teacher, principal, school board, and truant officer. In each of these cases, individuals and groups interact with one another through communication, a means by which they seek to achieve their goals. As is seen next, networks are a basic unit of analysis in this model.

In addition to discussing communication networks, scholars address psychological aspects of organizational membership. According to this model, an organization is a *psychological entity*. As each person enters an organization, he or she strives to be assimilated by taking on the organization's expectations for work and performance (Jablin, 1980, 1984). The organization tries to mold each member to norms and roles expected for membership. Each member must acquire "an evolving set of perceptions about what the organization is like as a communication system" (Jablin, 1982a, p. 273). You can appreciate this paradigm by recalling that you have been involved in many organizations, various schools, classes, families, clubs, cliques, and such; in each, you probably felt like a different psychological entity, a "different person." Each entity has a personality, a conception of itself as an organization, the organizations around it, and its members. This view of organizations relies on opinion measures concerning what individuals think about themselves, their role performance, their organization, and the other members in it.

Each organization constitutes a unique social reality — its way of viewing itself, its members, its product or service, and the environment in which it functions, including its competitors and customers. For this reason, organizations can be studied by applying an *interpretive-symbolic perspective* (Pacanowsky & O'Donnell-Trujillo, 1983). This approach views communication as constituting an interpretive process by which people coordinate their efforts by taking roles and sharing meaning — often through stories, myths, rituals, and code names. In this sense, each organization exists as a "symbol" in the minds of its members and others who are affected by it (Daft & Weick, 1984).

Interpretativism relies on the principle that people create their identity and world view through symbolic interaction. For this reason, coordinated management of meaning is a major task of members of organizations; shared meanings are basic units of analysis. As members of organizations, individuals create and live a sense of social reality embedded in their unique idiom—a theme supported by linguistic relativity; each idiom provides "terministic screens" (Burke, 1966; Heath, 1986; Tompkins, 1987). To varying degrees, members take on the social reality of the organizations to which they belong—into which they assimilate.

For instance, a school has a unique sense of reality. Some private schools require that students wear uniforms and adhere to a particular ideology. A large state-supported university may have a different social reality than does a small private, church-supported college. The difference may be the responsibility the organization perceives it has toward the moral development of students. In recent times, major state universities have opted for less moral development of students, whereas many church-supported colleges assume that as a major responsibility. Or, the social reality of one school might include being small, highly selective, and academically superior—even at the expense of athletics. Another school might emphasize athletics and other activities and accept a mediocre academic reputation.

The last of the four paradigms by which organizations can be studied is *systems-interaction*. Viewed this way, an organization is a system. Each system has subsystems (and subsubsystems) that are hierarchically related. This model focuses on organization features such as openness (in varying degrees), system interchange with other systems, balance, wholeness, interdependence, equifinality, and self-regulation through the principles of cybernetics. Organizations take in *(input)* what they need from their environments; this input is processed *(throughput)* and disseminated *(output)*. Schools take in children and educate *(throughput)* them and turn out educated people. Electric utilities take in fuel, which is processed into electricity. As was discussed in chapter 4, organizations take in information that is used to make cybernetic adjustments to the environment based on feedback in regard to how well the organization is meeting its goals by using the tactics it is employing. Newspapers are good examples of how organizations take in, process, and sell information. These principles of interaction not only describe the organization as a whole, but also its components or subsystems. Work groups, relational communication, and decision making are key units of analysis according to this perspective (Krone, Jablin, & Putnam, 1987).

Research efforts become more meaningful if directed at supporting or challenging these encompassing perspectives. For instance, structural functionalism stresses the importance of people using clear and accurate messages. This standard, Eisenberg (1984) contended, is dysfunctional. Ambiguity helps people deal with many situational requirements, develop and pursue multiple and even conflicting goals, and use communication that can be effective, even though ambiguous. He reasoned, "Strategic ambiguity is essential to organizing in that it: (a) promotes unified diversity,

(b) facilitates organizational change, and (c) amplifies existing source attributions and preserves privileged positions" (p. 239). His reasoning is based on the belief that corporations are organized by adhering to key metaphors, a notion compatible with the *interpretive-symbolic* perspective.

This section has demonstrated how managerial philosophies influence assumptions about, and studies of, organizational communication. Competing management philosophies complicate the study of organizations because each suggests a preferable way of viewing the management, performance, and interaction needed to achieve organizational goals. The problems raised by managerial philosophies are compounded by competing paradigms of how to study organizational communication. As frustrating as these competing opinions are, they demonstrate the robustness of the study of organizational communication. To appreciate the efforts of various researchers to explain and prove their perspectives requires that some avenues be explored in more detail.

SYSTEMS RATIONALE FOR ORGANIZATIONAL ANALYSIS

Although systems analysis treats organizations mechanistically, it has been an important paradigm and has supplied a vocabulary for studying organizational communication. A systems perspective is useful as long as it recognizes that organizations must constantly change (Morgan, 1982).

A system, Fisher (1982) defined, is "the 'all' of a thing" (p. 199). It is an organic whole that not only consists of subsystems, but is also part of larger systems, sometimes called environments.

Unique to *systems theory* is an interest in the dynamic properties of wholes and parts, relationships, and hierarchies. Stressing its dynamism, Krippendorff (1977) reasoned that "a *system* consists of a set of states that are chained in time by a transformation. The states take account of the relations between the parts of the system, so that changes over time imply changes in the relations among the system's parts" (p. 150). As any part of a system changes or is affected, so too are its other parts. A major issue in organizational communication is relationship and flow of communication between people. In this way, "parts of a system are often viewed as *integrated* into a whole so that they *serve a common or overriding purpose*" (p. 150).

Cybernetics, the study of regulation and control, explains how units of a system interact by "behaving" to achieve a goal and using feedback to determine whether the action achieved the goal. In this way, cybernetics supplies the rationale for understanding how communicative acts feed back on themselves, thereby providing means of control that communicators can use to determine whether their messages succeed and their information is useful. A systems approach to communication expands the model of sender-to-receiver to feature communication networks, along with mutual causality, to explain how systems adapt to their environments.

This theory treats organizations as systems, each of which is more-or-less open. A continuous variable, openness is vital to a system. Through information obtained via communication, organizations understand and respond to their environments. An *open system* interacts dynamically with its environment and thereby increases its likelihood to survive and prosper. A *closed system* does not interact; it does not take in information from its environment and therefore is likely to atrophy. According to Fisher (1982), "openness is the free exchange of energy between the system and its environment. That is, to the extent that the boundaries are permeable and allow the exchange of information — what energy is to a physical system, information is to a social system — that system is said to be more nearly open than closed" (p. 199). Open systems tend to become increasingly complex. Complexity stresses the connectedness between the system's components. As systems become more complex, they develop more parts or subsystems. For example, as a company expands, it creates new departments, each of which has specialized functions.

Not only can a system be open to its environment and thereby take in information, but it can also generate information and define its environment and establish its boundaries (Fisher, 1982). An open system is not merely a pawn caught within the dynamics of its environment; it can shape its environment. For instance, the oil industry, as we know it today, grew because it took crude oil, a once-abundant but fundamentally worthless substance, and found uses for it; this effort was aided by the invention and mass production of automobiles. Together, the automobile and petrochemical industries dramatically changed our society and have recently brought us as a nation into dramatic interaction with the oil and automobile producing nations of the world. This dynamic quality of systems explains how each system can set goals, forecast whether they will be achieved, change how it seeks to achieve those goals, and even revise the goals.

ORGANIZATIONAL NETWORKS

Information theory and systems theory supply the conceptual underpinnings for using networks as the basic unit of analysis to define and explain the patterns of information flow within an organization. These principles are tempered by contingency theory, which reasons that organizational philosophies and communication strategies are situational; what works in one case may not work in another. According to structural functionalism, the basis of network analysis is the assumption that information flows throughout an organization by taking various pathways, which constitute patterns that can be charted as networks. If information is one of the vital life forces of an organization, then it is important to know how information flows and influence is exerted (Farace, Monge, & Russell, 1977; Monge, 1987).

Concerns addressed by this approach start with the assumption that in any organization there is *absolute information*—all of the information an organization possesses. Information is not concentrated in one part of an organization; rather, it exists as *distributed information* because it is scattered through the organization. One concern is whether the information is distributed so that it is available to the people who need it. This view fits comfortably with the principle that information is needed to reduce uncertainty and to help people be competent in achieving a range of personal and organizational goals.

If an individual has insufficient information, too little to do his or her job adequately, the person suffers information (or communication) *underload*. When persons have so much information (or communication) to process that they are unable to extract what they need, they experience information *overload*. A key principle of the structural-functional approach is that information must be distributed correctly if the organization is to function properly (Farace, Monge, & Russell, 1977).

A *network* is all of the pathways or patterns by which information flows between individuals and groups in an organization. A network consists of person-to-person connections, by which information is exchanged. A set of pathways, such as information flow between accountants in a company, is called a *micronetwork*. When micronetworks are put together, they form a *macronetwork*. To some extent, both types of network correspond to the organization chart, but information also flows through networks that do not correspond to formal organizational structure (Farace, Monge, & Russell, 1977). Whereas macronetworks are systems, micronetworks are subsystems.

Networks consist of people who interact. A person in one micronetwork is a *link* when he or she communicates with a person in another micronetwork, thereby allowing information to flow between the networks. One kind of link is a *bridge,* which results when one person connects two networks; a manager of a department, for instance, is a bridge between his or her department and the vice-president. A slightly different link is a *liaison;* this person connects with several people—not just one—from another network. Some people are *isolates* because they have little interaction with others (Farace, Monge, & Russell, 1977). People are *stars* or *nodes* when, like the hub of a wheel, they receive information from many people and pass it to others. Bridges, liaisons, and stars are gatekeepers who filter, pass, withhold, or distort information. Several types of networks can be found: *line* (one person contacts another, who contacts another and so on), *commune* (open exchange), *hierarchy* (network as organization chart), and *dictator* (super gatekeeper) (Krippendorff, 1977).

Networks are characterized by the number of persons involved and by the relationships between them. These relationships can be described in words such as "talks to," "coordinates with," or "reports to." In this way, analysis not only focuses on the number of people involved but also the *strength* or *intensity* of the relationship between them, which can be estimated by the frequency of contact and the degree of interdependence. Networks exhibit the property of *symmetry,* which describes the direction or flow of information. In this regard, relationships can be one-way or two-way, and they can be symmetrical or asymmetrical. In a one-way asymmetrical relationship, for instance, one person provides information and influence for the other, but does not received much in return. Two-way symmetrical relationships exhibit the most balance because influence and information flows freely between the two parties. Another characteristic of networks is *transitivity,* the ease by which information flows. Typical of a line network, Person A communicates with Person B, who communicates with C, who communicates with D. Person D depends on all of the others for information; for this reason, it may be difficult for A and D to communicate because they depend on B and C. This characteristic can easily be seen in the organizational practice of routing communication; it also refers to communication in a chain of authority (Monge, 1977).

Networks can be static and routine relationships between people within systems and between systems. Networks can also be dynamic, in a constant state of emergence, growth, maintenance, and decline. They grow when contacts become frequent and interdependent. They decline when people cease to have contact with one another. They emerge when they have not been in place before. A classic example of emerging networks is the creation of new sales contacts. Many salespeople "prospect" to make new contacts. If they succeed, a network is established, and two systems begin to interact, a process called *boundary spanning.*

The degree to which information flow is routine depends on demands created for the system by its environment. When a system is beginning (emerging), such as the spawning of a new department, information flow is likely not to be routine. The structures by which information flows are emerging. Over time, these become more routine. For this reason, Monge and Eisenberg (1987) stressed that networks are best thought of as dynamic, emerging. The degree to which each network is dynamic and changing, or routine and static may indicate the health of an organization. According to *contingency theory,* the status of network development is a function of whether any network is adequate given the requirements of its circumstances (Morgan, 1986; Poole & Roth, 1989).

Although it is difficult to determine which is cause and which is effect, the extent to which members are involved (identify) with an organization is associated with whether they believe they have sufficient information for their needs. Increased job involvement decreases turnover and absenteeism and increases job satisfaction (Penley, 1982). Even when employees are not involved in their jobs, they may become more committed to a company when they are involved in the communication networks associated with their jobs. This effect is likely to be seen in employees who have low job involvement, but it does not manifest itself in employees who are moderately or highly involved with their jobs (Eisenberg, Monge, & Miller, 1984). For instance, a receptionist may be committed to a company merely because of his or her level of involvement in the organization's communication network. But an employee who is isolated (not involved in the communication network), such as a pumping station operator for a gas pipeline company, may nevertheless feel high job involvement and high levels of commitment to the company.

In this way, systems and network analysis have produced many interesting and useful research findings. For instance, persons who are links can use information to achieve control and exert power. Links are most effective when they strive to reduce uncertainty. Because of their role and their access to information, links tend to identify closely with their jobs. Their position leads them to think in terms of teamwork and group effectiveness (Albrecht, 1984). This study demonstrates that network analysis and information flow are useful means for analyzing the health and productivity of organizations and their members. However, as important as these findings are, they do not give the entire picture regarding how and why people perform as they do in organizations.

ORGANIZATIONAL CLIMATE AND CULTURE

The previous section demonstrated how network analysis treats organizational communication as information flow patterns throughout subsystems of an organization. However helpful this analysis is, it fails to capture all of what accounts for the effectiveness of organizations and their members' performance. Two other concepts—climate and culture—are used to explain why members of organizations know what is expected of them and feel motivated (or unmotivated) to support an organization's goals. These terms are similar enough so that some researchers treat them as synonymous. However, *climate* can be used to refer to quality of relationships in an organization, whereas *culture* depends on meanings that members share about an organization. We are interested in the communication variables that create and result from climate and culture.

Climate is easy to conceptualize, but difficult to define and study. You have experienced many organizational climates. Recall the "feeling" you have had in different organizations (even different friends' homes or different teachers' classrooms) or how climate changes when a new boss is hired, new members are added, old ones leave, or new tasks, goals, or rewards are implemented. One boss is friendly, open, and helpful, taking the time to explain what subordinates need to know to perform effectively. In contrast, another boss manages by "guerrilla tactics" — explosions, sabotage, secrecy, and sneak attacks. The climate of a group changes when too much work is expected for the time available or skills and capacity of its members. Climate is different — at least perceived so — on the first days on a job when a member really likes what he or she is doing than it is later when boredom has set in and the person has learned the unpleasant aspects of the organization.

What then is organizational climate? One view of climate reasons that it consists of traits that are the product of the structure and operations of an organization, not of the people in the organization. Climate, according to this view, endures even if personnel change. In this regard, the climate of an organization exists even when its membership changes (Tagiuri, 1968). This is an *organizational trait* view of climate.

Another perspective reasons that climate is a product of the perceptions collectively held by the members of the organization; climate exists in their minds. An organization is "open and trusting" if they believe it is. This view reasons that most members in an organization have a similar view of its climate; otherwise, they would not be readily coordinated. This approach to climate is operationalized by surveying employees to determine their opinions of the organization's climate. This view of climate depends on the consensus of members' opinions.

As an advance on other views of climate, Falcione and Kaplan (1984) offered the *perceptual measurement-individual attribute* model, which treats climate more individually, the result of the contact each individual has with a particular organization. Thus, climate is an individual matter, not the consensus of the members of the organization. Although climate depends on the perceptions of each employee, it is based on traits of the company that are revealed by what occurs during its activities — how people act toward and react to one another — and the relationships between them. Based on the traits they perceive a company to exhibit compared to the kind of climate they prefer, people prefer organizations that have climates that match their personalities and needs. Likewise, they seek to associate with members who share their views of climate. This view of climate refines the consensus model and stresses communication variables.

What variables should be used to study climate and its effect on individual task performance, personal satisfaction, and communication interaction? Variables typical of interpersonal relationships are often used in this regard. Thus, Redding (1979) reasoned that climate depends on (a) the extent to which an organization is supportive of its members; (b) whether members are allowed to participate in decision making, a variation of relational control; (c) levels of trust, confidence, and credibility—criteria by which members assess persons who are in leadership positions; (d) amount of openness and candor, and (e) effect the organization has on individual performance goals—a version of commitment. In this vein, Downs (1979) discovered that climate, the quality of feedback members receive, and supervisor communication styles are closely related. Job satisfaction and performance correlate with the quality of communication in an organization. Members' perception of communication quality depends on supervisor communication, communication climate, and personal feedback (Pincus, 1986).

Members of an organization assess the performance of others, including their superiors. Supervisory and communication style differences affect how much satisfaction members experience in an organization. For example, when asked about their impressions of supervisory nurses who managed in "masculine" versus "feminine" styles, nurses reported experiencing greater morale and job satisfaction when their female supervisors used "feminine" rather than "masculine" management styles. Preferred traits were those that promote happy relations, lead to reception of new ideas, encourage effort, as well as show concern, attentiveness, friendliness, and approval. Supervisors who were liked least controlled the conversations in which they engaged as well as were dominant and quick to challenge (Camden & Kennedy, 1986).

Jablin (1982b) found that where members are located within the hierarchy of organizations leads them to perceive different amounts of openness in superior-subordinate relationships. The lower people are in an organization, the less they believe these relationships are open. Employees in large organizations believe less openness exists than do their counterparts in small organizations.

These research findings on communication and supervisory style should help you realize that climate arises from relationships and actions that occur outside each individual, but how each individual characterizes and is affected by these factors is a product of attributional schemata that person uses to define climate. Thus, climate is employee attitudes regarding relationships produced by interactions and perceptions that arise when they interact to achieve their goals. Relationships members have with one another, particularly their superiors, shape climate. How they affect each member depends on his or her idiosyncratic perceptions. For instance, some people like a disciplined, authoritarian climate, whereas others hate that climate. Because people in an organization have similar relational experiences, climate generalizes beyond individual opinions so that outsiders to an organization sense its "common" climate.

Climate and organizational structure interrelate. Structure is enacted as people adjust to one another. Viewed this way, structure—a product of relationships between members—is not static—not the result of a rigid organization chart, but is ever changing—a product of members' values, needs, and interactions. Called *structuration,* this model postulates that "organizational climates are continually being structured through organizational practices" (Poole, 1985, p. 97).

Structure results, not from organizational charts, but from practices or procedures, interpersonal behavior, and superior-subordinate relationships, as well as the meaning (interpretation) people assign to the structure of an organization. The structure of each organization exists in the minds of its members and is the product of the values they enact through communication and compliance. If an organization is autocratic, such is the case only because members verify autocracy by yielding to authority. For instance, you have undoubtedly been in a classroom where a teacher tries to exert direct control over students' behavior; if the students do not yield to this control, the teacher fails to achieve control. Likewise, if the structure of an organization is democratic but the members do not accept the responsibilities of democracy, the structure will fail.

Members of each organization create its climate by their actions, which, in turn, reflect their values and perceptions. The relationship between climate and structure is dialectical; each shapes the other. The structuration of climates is affected by "(1) structural properties of the organization, (2) apparatuses that directly produce and reproduce climates, and (3) members' knowledge and skills" (Poole, 1985, p. 102).

Principles of social exchange theory support this analysis. Each individual attempts to become assimilated by negotiating which of the organization's task and role expectations are acceptable given the reward/cost ratio. Each member negotiates—to the extent possible—a workable relationship with others (superiors and subordinates), task groups, and the total organization. Members expect an organization to be personally rewarding—including tangible outcomes, such as money, or intangibles, such as esteem. If the relationship is rewarding, the member fosters it; if not, the member seeks to change it, reluctantly accommodates to it, or decides to leave. If the person cannot leave, the climate is likely to have negative effects on his or her performance—communication and task—as well as esteem. In turn, the person may have a negative influence on the organization.

Individual perception, values, and actions in an organization reflect each member's view of climate. This process involves attribution and uncertainty reduction. Members of an organization seek to know (assign meaning) what the climate and structure are, how they should perform to achieve reward, and what relational communication variables are typical of, and important to, the organization. They want to know whether their efforts are successful — whether how they manage, work, and communicate leads to positive or negative outcomes. They check to see whether others' views of their competence matches their own views (a coorientation model). Because of these perceptions as well as the attitudes, values, and beliefs associated with them, members develop views of the organization, work, role, and competence. But the individual is not the only unit of analysis. How a member obtains and maintains views of an organization's climate is influenced by interpersonal relationships, policies, group memberships, and actions by people at various levels in the organization, especially those in management.

Because experiences of members differ throughout an organization, the organization will have many climates. Falcione, Sussman, and Herden (1987) argued that the climate in each task group is not identical to that of the total organization. Nor is the climate in each interpersonal relationship the same as that in either the organization or the groups in which its members operate. The climate of the total organization is a product of interactions at each level of analysis: organization, group, and dyad.

Your experience can help you appreciate this point. In some organizations, such as a class, you cooperate because you like the teacher. In another class, you may try to undermine that teacher's authority. Or, you may sabotage efforts of students who are trying to ingratiate themselves with a teacher to get undeserved rewards. The climates of these relationships will reflect and produce your view of the climate of the entire organization. But your view of climate and that of others (inside and outside) is not identical, even though it may be similar.

Communicative contact with other members, groups, and the organization gives individuals an opportunity to form attributions and match them against those held by other members. Differences occur; some members of an organization think it is open and fair and that members participate in decisions; other members of the same organization may think the climate is closed and unfair. An important use of communication in an organization is to share, match, and form impressions of climate. You probably have evidence of this situation by having talked with others in an organization, each of whom has a different opinion of whether it is open or closed, supportive or not.

The creation, negotiation, and use of climate is a product of each individual's efforts to exercise autonomy, seek structure, and obtain rewards, as well as receive consideration, warmth, and support. How these climate variables operate is the result of rules and resources. Individual schemata define what the climate is and ought to be as well as how interaction, communication, and task efforts result in structuration—the ongoing efforts to create an operable system to achieve goals. As Falcione, Sussman, and Herden (1987) concluded, "structuration then serves as the basis of psychological climate, the individual's unique and idiosyncratic perceptions of what is happening in the organization and to him or her" (p. 220). People act in an organization and thereby create its structure in ways that fit their impressions of what the structure is and should be and what performance in that structure is likely to cost versus the rewards it offers.

Once these impressions become translated into comments members make, especially the stories they tell, climate has become embedded in the organization's culture. What role does organizational culture play in the creation of climate? Or is the relationship the opposite—climate shapes culture? One view is that the climate in each organization is instrumental to its culture. Schein (1985) concluded that in this way, culture is "a pattern of basic assumptions—invented, discovered, or developed by a given group as it learns to cope with its problems of external adaptation and internal integration—that has worked well enough to be considered valid and, therefore, to be taught to new members as the correct way to perceive, think, and feel in relation to those problems" (p. 9).

Culture provides employees with assumptions, Morgan (1986) reasoned, because it is "shared meaning, shared understanding, and shared sense making" (p. 128). Culture consists of "significant symbols and modes of legitimated social action that enables selective responses" by organizational members to the requirements of daily activities (Pilotta, Widman, & Jasko, 1988, p. 317). According to this view of culture, employees enact the culture of each company (what they think is expected of them) as actors perform the script of a play (Morgan, 1986).

Treated as a global construct, culture includes everything about a company, such as its image, size, values, place in its industry, managerial style, operating philosophies, personnel, and reputation. Culture consists of an organization's values, norms, beliefs, and structures. Whereas culture exists over longer periods of time, climate is to some extent a moment-by-moment matter that results from members' contact with the organization and others in it. According to this view, "*climate* would become an indicator of the goodness of fit between an organization's *culture* and its people" (Falcione & Kaplan, 1984, p. 301). Whereas climate, according to Krone et al. (1987), is a psychological variable, culture is a focal point for interpreting the meaning of the actions and symbols used by organizational members (Pacanowsky & O'Donnell-Trujillo, 1983).

Culture of each organization is contained in its artifacts. It is conveyed in stories (such as how the company was founded or the "characters" who have worked in a department), legends, and myths, as well as physical attributes of an organization, such as its architecture, furnishings, properties, and accomplishments. Schools, for instance, have a culture that consists of their athletic and academic traditions as well as student life. Culture allows members of an organization to describe and share views of reality, including the unique character of the organization, its members, and its environment (Smircich & Calas, 1987). Stories portray versions of reality, and as such convey a sense of what is appropriate or inappropriate. Those definitions are vital to the politics and power that operate in an organization (Mumby, 1987).

Archetypes are means by which climate and culture are shared between members. For instance, managerial styles are expressed as archetypal characters in the stories members tell. Some managers, Mitroff (1983) observed, are "Sherman Tanks," whereas others are "complainers," "wet blankets," or "innovators." Similarly, companies can be characterized as "fly-by-night," "We'll get back to you," or "The check is in the mail." On the positive side, the culture of an organization might be "service first" or "Customers know best" (Heath, 1988).

According to this analysis, organizations change when their members change the key metaphors by which they think about themselves and the organization. For instance, the structure, functions, and climate of a company will change if the "military metaphor" (highly structured, top-down, autocratic) in its culture is abandoned in favor of a "family metaphor" (open, supportive, shared power). In terms of a climate condu-cive to organizational rapport with its community, a company might abandon a metaphor of privileged self-interest and adopt a metaphor of responsiveness. This use of ambiguity, Eisenberg (1984) reasoned, "is not a kind of fudging, but rather a rational method used by communicators to orient toward multiple goals. It is easy to imagine the ethical problems that might result from the misuse of ambiguity. In the final analysis, however, both the effectiveness and the ethics of any particular communicative strategy are relative to the goals and values of the communicators in the situation" (p. 239). Organizations state ambiguous goals that are imple-mented with ambiguity. Total ambiguity would lead to organizational chaos. However, when employees share principles regarding what perfor-mance is expected, those principles constitute unobtrusive control over employees' choices and actions (Tompkins & Cheney, 1985). Persons can achieve the same corporate goals by employing different individual means, but they need to share common themes so that they can coordinate their activities.

In these ways, climate and culture affect the lives of an organization's members. An organization's climate may even encourage or discourage romantic relationships between its employees. Such relationships are more likely when climate is less formal, less likely in small or large organizations, and more likely to occur in medium-sized organizations (curvilinear relationship). Women who became involved with co-workers are likely to be young, have less tenure in the company, and work in lower ranks (Dillard & Witteman, 1985).

Climate and culture assist each individual's ability to make self-attributions, as well as to attribute traits and motives to others in the organization. These factors assist members' efforts to reduce personal uncertainty and to learn what is expected in order to be productive. But impressions of climate are not universal throughout an organization. Management tends to believe that the climate of the organization is more positive than subordinates do. Management feels more involved in the organization and believes communication is more open than do subordinates. Subordinates do not believe managers are as effective as they think they are (Glaser, Zamanou, & Hacker, 1987).

With this understanding of structure, climate, and culture in mind, we can turn attention to the levels of analysis needed to understand how individuals are affected by and shape the organizations in which they function.

INDIVIDUAL LEVEL OF ANALYSIS

Part of the difficulty of studying organizational communication is knowing whether the appropriate unit of analysis is the individual, dyad, small group, or total organization (system, subsystems, or sub-subsystems). A stress on any one of these can distort research and theory building. By the same token, keeping these factors separate but integrated challenges systematic research.

This section focuses the discussion started previously—networks, climate, and culture—on efforts each person makes to understand and cope with role expectations of organizational membership. The theme is individual efforts to be efficacious in an organization, to serve its goals, and to obtain rewards in exchange. Network members are connected by interpersonal and organizational bonds. Each person's performance depends on his or her perception of the organization, climate, structure, and the other members. Members develop organizational self-concepts, make reward/cost estimates, as well as understand and transmit the organization's culture.

To what extent are people who compose an organization thoughtful—cognitively aware of themselves and the organization? Weick (1979a, 1979b) and Jablin (1982a, 1984) argued that researchers should view organizations as consisting of thinking people. However, Jablin (1982a) doubted that much research operationalizes this assumption to explain "*how* social cognition affects and is affected by organizational communication" (p. 255). How people function in a company depends on how they conceptualize themselves, their task group, climate, and the entire organization. A crucial factor in this social cognition is *organizational assimilation*.

One reality in the organizational life of each person is to become assimilated, not only as a new member of an organization but also as a member of new departments or groups within an organization. Communication is vital to this process. Jablin (1985) believed that each member's efforts to become assimilated are influenced by his or her life perceptions, acknowledged role expectations, and self-assessments as well as external forces.

Individuals acquire role definitions and expectations from those with whom they have close contact. Families and educational institutions are not only "organizations" into which people are assimilated, but they also shape how individuals become assimilated into subsequent organizations — such as those related to occupations. In addition to their families and schools, individuals are influenced in their socialization process by media, peers, and part-time jobs. This background prepares each person, in various ways and to different degrees, for the transition into an organization; this critical moment begins with employment interviews (Jablin & McComb, 1984).

"Organizational assimilation refers to the process by which organizational members become a part of, or are absorbed into, the culture of an organization" (Jablin, 1982a, p. 256). Through this process, they learn what is expected of them and what efforts and attitudes will be required for them to be accepted as meaningful participants who can predictably obtain the rewards of membership. This process, Jablin (1982a) contended, has two interlocking sets of activities and goals: (a) an organization's efforts to integrate the individual into its corporate culture by teaching appropriate attitudes, values, and behaviors, and (b) personal efforts to become part of that culture while maintaining individuality.

To explain this process, Katz and Kahn (1966) contended that membership in a company is a role-taking process. People take on (or are expected to) specific roles unique to the goals and climate of each organization to which they belong. The price of membership is the ability and willingness to comply with and follow the roles the organization prescribes. But, Jablin (1982a) reasoned, Katz and Kahn fail to acknowledge that each member, including new recruits, negotiates the nature of the expected role. By taking an assimilation approach, Jablin is able to study efforts individuals make to understand and negotiate the roles organizations expect them to take. This phenomenon can be observed by looking at the communication organizations use to help members understand and accept their roles. This process is dynamic, not static. Members either confirm or disconfirm an organization by adopting the roles it prescribes.

Assimilation, Jablin (1984, 1985) contended, is a developmental process that consists of three stages: anticipatory socialization, encounter, and metamorphosis. The first phase, *anticipatory socialization,* occurs prior to a recruit's entry into an organization or when entering a different group in an organization. Prior to entry, the individual makes role choices by selecting an occupation or position and deciding to adopt relevant role expectations. This phase has two distinct aspects, vocational and organizational socialization. The first set of cognitions relates to the ability to perform the job whereas the second set of cognitions focuses on how the individual sees himself or herself fitting into and influencing the company.

The second phase, *encounter,* involves actual efforts to "break into" the organization—after being hired. At this time, the new member develops an impression of the new work environment. During this phase, the person relies on scripts and schemata that were acquired before coming to the organization, but must learn new ones that fit his or her view of the particular organization. The best case occurs when the social reality of the individual fits that of the organization. But you need not think very long to realize that whatever the "reality" of the organization is, it differs based on who is describing or thinking about it at a given moment. In this way, the organization really does exist in people's minds. What the new member thinks about this organization will be shaded by his or her personality, values, job experience, and information provided by superiors, peers, and the organization through its many forms of communication, including orientation sessions and company publications, such as newsletters and annual reports.

What happens during the encounter phase, Jablin (1985) reasoned, will affect members' *metamorphosis.* At this point, the individual becomes aware of discrepancies and agreements between his or her attitudes and values and those prevailing in the organization. Metamorphosis occurs if the individual adapts to the organization. Communication plays a major role in the individual's effort to learn appropriate attitudes, values, and behaviors. Information is received from documents. It is obtained through superior–subordinate relationships and from fellow members. Part of what the member learns is how the organization communicates, what is communicated and to whom, and how decisions are made. The organization, brought to life by people who are responsible for and needful of the person making the metamorphosis, expects new members to adopt appropriate patterns of thinking and behaving. As part of successful metamorphosis, the member acquires a sense of the company's reward system and from that derives an understanding of how satisfying the job is. All of this can affect work motivation.

Assimilation, Jablin and Krone (1987) reasoned, is a concept that is central enough to provide the focus for many communication activities—by the member, superiors, peers, and the organization. Assimilation is an excellent way to compare the member's perceptions, sense of expectations, and values against those of others, especially those in authority. In this sense, each member's social reality is pitted against the collective reality of all the individuals of the organization. Roles are building blocks of an organization, and how a person assimilates reflects his or her willingness and ability to take a role.

Personal constructions of social reality about role expectations of participating in organizations begin early in life. Children play "school" and "work." They observe those around them—parents, siblings, and acquaintances—who engage in various roles. The media portray versions of role expectations that viewers use to create conceptions of roles in many organizations in which they might participate. Role definition and expectation may lead to subsequent activities such as obtaining education, training, or apprenticeships. It entails internalizing expectations, values, communication behaviors, and reward/cost matrices.

As individuals begin the process of entering a role, they may experience problems with their self-perception, role expectation, or role reality that comes from testing their skills in the performance of the role and their ability to process a lot of new information. During the encounter phase, the new member may experience difficulties of fitting in. The cognitive processes involved in this effort can be explained by social learning theory (Bandura, 1986), information integration-expectancy value theory (Ajzen & Fishbein, 1980), and involvement theory (Petty & Cacioppo, 1986a). Cognitive processes such as these interrelate with personality factors such as locus of control, independence, and dogmatism as well as relationships with peers, superiors, and subordinates (Jablin & Krone, 1987).

INTERPERSONAL LEVEL OF ANALYSIS

Whenever you think of the flow of information and influence exerted within an organization, you should keep in mind that these transpire, in most cases, between two people—a dyad. For this reason, as Weick (1987) observed, "Interpersonal communication is the essence of organization because it creates structures that then affect what else gets said and done and by whom" (p. 97). You would be incorrect if you think of organizations only as units or groups, such as departments or divisions. A moment's reflection should remind you of the dyads—two people talking or exchanging memos or letters—that occur each day in an organization. Many activities occur interpersonally: telephone conversations, interviews, supervisors assigning and checking on the work someone is doing, negotiations, conversations at water fountains, and sales presentations—to mention only a few.

Communication in superior–subordinate dyads is essential to the success of a company. These relations are affected by communication styles of superiors and subordinates. Classical management style, for example, reasons that influence and instructions on how to perform jobs flow downward, and by this rationale, the quality of a manager depends on the ability to give clear, accurate, and firm instruction. A more vital, albeit more complicated, model assumes that superiors and subordinates use communication to define and operationalize their relationship and negotiate how the work will be performed. Moreover, many of the instructions on how to do a job come from peers rather than from superiors. Members use their contacts with superiors to negotiate their assimilation into organizations.

The quality of the relationship between dyadic partners is essential in understanding superior–subordinate interaction. Because of the need for supervision, dominance can be an important communication style. Studying this issue, Fairhurst, Rogers, and Sarr (1987) were interested in the effect manager dominance has on subordinate performance. At the heart of the issue is the extent to which managers prescribe or negotiate role and work expectations. When subordinates perform poorly, managers are likely to exert dominance. This can hamper the quality of their exchanges with subordinates. Subordinates whose superiors dominate feel uninvolved in decisions. Managers who are dominant believe that their subordinates desire little involvement in decisions and therefore tend to give their subordinates lower performance ratings. Managers who are dominant are more likely to misunderstand the relationship they have with subordinates than less dominant managers.

For these reasons, superiors must be skillful when they attempt to change the performance of their subordinates. Subordinates tend to view such efforts by superiors negatively. This in turn leads subordinates to become dissatisfied (Richmond, Davis, Saylor, & McCroskey, 1984).

Efforts to influence subordinate performance may involve compliance-gaining tactics. What happens if these tactics are countered by noncompliance? In that situation, the superior is likely to use compliance-gaining tactics of reward and punishment. Women are more prone to select this strategy than are men (deTurck, 1985). As predicted by social exchange theory, people employ rewards and constraints to define and negotiate their relationships.

Managers' communication styles affect the opinions subordinates hold about them; these opinions influence employees' productivity. If managers use positive approval when dealing with subordinates, employee performance increases; the amount of positive approval correlates positively with the increase in performance. When supervisors give their subordinates autonomy to correct mistakes in ways the subordinates see fit, the length of time before the problem recurs is lengthened; amount of autonomy correlates positively with the length of time before the problem recurs (Fairhurst, Green, & Snavely, 1984).

Supervisors' credibility affects the way subordinates respond to comments made about their performance. If employees trust their superiors' judgment and believe they have expertise, levels of satisfaction or motivation — or both — will increase. Cusella (1982) found that postperformance feedback from high expertise sources has more impact whether it is positive or negative. But motivation is greatest when individuals receive positive feedback from sources whom they believe have high expertise.

Along with credibility, other traits are important for supervisors' effectiveness: (a) perceptions of openness (willingness to listen and ability to understand), (b) shared attitudes, (c) oral communication apprehension, and (d) self-esteem. These traits lead subordinates to be more satisfied with their supervisors, but not necessarily with their jobs (Falcione, McCroskey, & Daly, 1977).

An open superior–subordinate relationship can foster flow of information and influence within an organization. *Openness* refers to the extent to which members are willing to send and receive information as well as make what could be perceived as negative responses. Openness will affect the content of the message — what can and will be said — and what messages are appropriate (Jablin, 1979). If a boss "blows up" at bad news, subordinates learn what constitutes bad news and avoid those statements, even withholding information the boss needs.

Openness can include willingness and ability to express opinions. Bosses are supposed to have opinions regarding how tasks are performed, but employees like to have some autonomy in performing those tasks. And subordinates like to believe their supervisors can be effective in making a case to their superiors. Supervisory communication style is crucial in this regard. Subordinates are more satisfied with superiors who are argumentative but not verbally aggressive. This kind of boss is perceived to be an effective upward communicator. A boss who is argumentative but not verbally abusive is likely to increase his or her subordinates' career satisfaction and belief that their rights are protected (Infante & Gorden, 1985).

As is the case for all interpersonal communication, people know one another only by their perceptions and attributions of what they see and hear one another do — a central theme of social cognition. Therefore, people assign motives to one another in organizational settings. In this process, supervisors use personal and situational factors when attributing reasons while appraising subordinates' performance. If performance is below expectations, many supervisors attribute the causes to factors internal to subordinates; when positive performance occurs, external factors are used as the basis of the attributions (Green & Mitchell, 1979). These findings are typical of those reported in chapter 7. They should also remind you that even though people are not good at making accurate attributions, they think they are.

Of concern is whether superiors and subordinates accurately understand each other. Coorientation assumes that if people communicate accurately, they will have the same understanding of an object, task, or behavior; this object might be each participant's understanding of self (Person A viewing self) compared to the other person's understanding of that self (Person B viewing Person A). Applying this model, a study found that when supervisors are accurate in their appraisal of subordinate's performance, they are rated higher by the subordinate. When supervisors were seen by subordinates as agreeing with them on rules, subordinates evaluated the supervisors higher. In this relationship, actual accuracy or agreement is not as important as perceived agreement (Eisenberg, Monge, & Farace, 1984).

Interpersonal relationships are a vital link in the process by which individuals assimilate into organizations. This process begins during employment interviews and carries into the orientation phase. Early in their contact with an organization, individuals begin to learn the role expectations others have of them and compare those against their own role expectations. But you should not quickly assume that the parties in these situations have congruent or accurate impressions of one another or of what transpires (including the quality of the relationship) (Jablin & Krone, 1987).

Because employment interviews are important to assimilation, they are studied to determine what transpires. Examining the kinds of questions asked during employment interviews, Babbitt and Jablin (1985) discovered that job applicants ask about one-third of their questions before interviewers explicitly invite inquiries. This invitation by interviewers appears to encourage applicants to ask questions but also suggests that applicants do so even without invitation. Nearly half of the questions asked by applicants seek job-related information. Candidates ask more questions seeking new information (especially on job and organization topics) than questions that seek to clarify or elicit opinions. Applicants tend to ask questions that are closed (versus open), singular (versus multiple), and phrased in the second rather than first person. Candidates who are eventually hired by the interviewer tend to ask fewer questions that seek new information on miscellaneous (irrelevant) topics or about the interview procedures. Successful applicants make fewer self-references and ask relevant rather than miscellaneous questions and demonstrate competence by not asking as many job-related questions, thereby implying that they have done their homework on the interviewer's company.

The mechanics of the interview and communication tactics employed by the persons involved have a great deal to do with whether they accomplish their objectives. The person being interviewed attempts to appraise his or her relationship with the interviewer by looking to see if the person is trustworthy, competent, composed, and organized. Both parties attribute favorable characteristics to one another if they display high rather than low levels of nonverbal immediacy, high vocal activity, and employ "response-response" rather than "question-response" conversation. During an interview, a substantial part of the exchange involves topics related to the organizational climate. Of particular interest are job duties and responsibilities, advancement potential, pay/benefits, supervision, and co-worker relations. Interviewees come away from interviews with high expectations of the interpersonal communication climates in the organization (Jablin, 1985).

After new members have entered an organization, their assimilation continues as they use interpersonal contacts to learn the organization's climate and culture. In this way, they also learn about their job (what it entails) and what about it is positive (interesting or important) or negative (boring or unimportant). Whether workers think a task is "enriched" depends on variables such as feedback, skill variety, autonomy, and task identity. Investigating this situation, Blau (1985) found that subjects who received information about enriched task situations exhibited significantly higher ratings of perceived job scope than did those who received information about unenriched tasks. The study investigated the effects of positive/ negative comments, source credibility, and locus of control (whether people believe they or someone else is in control of a situation). Results reveal that employees are favorably affected when they receive positive social cues from competent (credible) co-workers, and if they believe they have some control rather than being controlled by others. "External locus of control people" believe events happen because of external forces over which they have little or no control.

The kinds of information people seek and the persons they ask for information often are a function of the communication skills of the person and the rewards/cost ratios of seeking the information. For instance, people may not ask questions directly if they believe that tactic would lead them to appear "dumb." Some indirect communication tactics are employed, especially if risks of direct tactics appear high (Miller & Jablin, 1991).

Interpersonal communication in organizations is influenced by attribution processes, relationship development, discrepancy arousal, speech accommodation, and uncertainty reduction. To reduce uncertainty, employees seek information via interpersonal contacts and respond best when they encounter superiors who are credible and open, but not dominant.

How they seek this information, which persons they seek it from, and how the information is interpreted by the person providing it and the one receiving it — these factors influence the ways persons become assimilated into organizations (Jablin & Krone, 1987).

As well as using communication tactics to enter an organization, people also seek and give information when they are transferring from one department to another. This process entails three phases: loosening, transition, and tightening. Loosening involves comments about leaving, including helping those who are staying behind. Transition occurs when the physical move leads the individual to develop new links while maintaining old ones. The tightening phase is similar to assimilation, whereby the person becomes part of a new unit (Kramer, 1989).

Despite generalizations such as these regarding interpersonal effectiveness, organizational communication researchers have not discovered why some individuals succeed by using communication tactics that fail for others. Differences in this regard relate to a host of variables including gender, situations, and the skills of the persons using the tactics. Jablin (1985), for one, doubted "that supervisors or managers possess an 'average' communication style" (p. 630). No standard exists that people can apply to always be effective.

By examining research findings, this section has demonstrated how important interpersonal relationships are to the climate of an organization and that interpersonal relationships are focal points by which information and influence flow throughout an organization.

GROUP LEVEL ANALYSIS

Each day across corporate America, thousands of meetings transpire during which personnel share information and make decisions. Those meetings cost millions of dollars in personnel time. Are these dollars well spent? Because of the cost and the belief that meetings are useful, researchers study small group processes to learn how groups perform their tasks effectively and how satisfied members are by their involvement in groups.

One of the basic models of group dynamics is input–process–output, typical of systems theory. According to this model, members bring in information (input) which is processed and used to make decisions (output). Another model focuses on process and features communication activities as independent variables: gives opinion, gives information, creates solidarity, draws attention, and makes procedural suggestions. Groups that follow the input–process–output model generate decisions that their members believe are superior. However, groups that experience more processing — have more time to converse and comment (engage in more communication) — are more satisfied with group procedures. When the emphasis is on task, the quality of outcome seems higher, and when it is on process, climate or socioemotional feelings are higher (Jarboe, 1988).

This study addresses one of the controversies regarding small group (and meeting management) processes. Do groups produce better decisions and are members more pleased by what they accomplish if they have extensive communication? One assumption is that, through communication, small group members voice opinions and scrutinize ideas; the opposite view is that too many comments bore members because a few people dominate the group, thereby lessening the likelihood that group decisions are superior to individual decisions. One study found that open discussion and exchange of information and ideas produces better and more satisfying decisions than do group interactions, which limit the amount of communication. In addition, the quality of each members' decision increased as did the amount of interaction (Burleson, Levine, & Samter, 1984).

Does all communication help groups or are some types of communication more important than others? Viewed along the lines proposed by the *functional* view of group processes, the answer seems to be that certain types are valuable whereas others are not. Communication is effective when it provides means the group needs to achieve its tasks. Studying how groups make sound decisions, Hirokawa (1985, 1988) found that the quality of group interaction depends on whether members use communication to analyze problems as well as evaluate positive and negative qualities of alternative decisions. A group must exhibit decision skills. Communication is valuable to a group only when it helps members understand the problem, develop and share requirements for an acceptable choice, and assess positive and negative qualities of alternative choices. In their efforts, groups demonstrate a rational ability to adapt their decision processes to the contingencies of the decision (Poole & Roth, 1989).

Part of the impact communication has on the quality of group decisions results from the kind of feedback members receive from one another in regard to their comments. Feedback in task groups has more impact when it is clear, trustworthy, and presented dynamically as well as when it fits the mood of the group. Group members give feedback differently. Feedback has the most effect when it is expressed in dynamic, assertive language (Ogilvie & Haslett, 1985). But even then, group members may not accurately understand one another's views, even when they think they do (Steeves, 1984).

Although evidence supports the claim that group decisions produce an *assembly effect,* which leads collective decisions to be superior to individual ones, not everyone believes such is the case. One critic of group processes is Janis (1972), who asserted that decisions often suffer from what he called groupthink. *Groupthink* is used to explain why decisions, especially those made in an attempt to avoid losses, can lead to fiascoes. Under this condition, groups can become so cohesive that their members avoid dissenting opinions.

Groupthink is thought to occur for several reasons:

1. Group members limit rather than increase the number of alternatives they consider.
2. If a position is initially favored by many group members, it is likely to prevail with little or no challenge.
3. If the majority of a group does not favor alternatives early in the decision-making process, those alternatives are unlikely to receive consideration in later deliberations.
4. Rarely do highly cohesive groups seek outside opinions, unless the members believe their ideas will be confirmed.
5. If the group comes to like the opinions that have emerged, it is unlikely to seek ways to disconfirm them.
6. The group can believe that it is invulnerable (Janis, 1972).

Reexamining groupthink, Whyte (1989) argued that these group dynamics are mediating variables, not independent variables. They reinforce faulty decision processes rather than prompt them. According to Whyte, groupthink results because of *prospect polarization*. In addition to conformity pressures, group members develop and employ decision perspectives to assess the subjective magnitude of losses posed by a decision they must make. In such circumstances, polarization leads group members to attempt to avoid losses even if their decision entails selecting high risk alternatives which are unlikely to be successful.

Another challenge to the proposition that groups suffer from groupthink resulted from a body of studies originally called *risky shift*, but later referred to as *choice shift*. The findings of this series of studies focused on a simple, important question: Is the final decision of the group merely an average of the opinions the members held before discussion began, or can the outcome differ from this average by being either more risky or conservative? The answer: the choice can differ from the average of the members' opinions prior to discussion. Let's think through the situation this way. Imagine that you could calculate what each member of a group thought about some issue that was going to be discussed. (Researchers do this by having subjects mark a scale; the responses are summed and averaged.) Is it not reasonable to predict that group decisions will be the average of all opinions — a kind of predetermined consensus? But research indicates that the final decision can be either more risky or more conservative.

Shift may occur for many reasons:

1. Members' opinions change because of group leaders' efforts (Boulanger & Fischer, 1971).
2. Social comparison and risk taking (people like to be thought of as risk takers) (Blascovich & Ginsburg, 1974; Vinokur & Burnstein, 1974).
3. Diffusion of responsibility ("If this decision goes bad, don't blame me; I only went along with the group.") (Yinon, Jaffe, & Feshback, 1975).
4. Subjective expected utilities (through discussion, group members get a better view of the reward/cost ratio) (Kahan, 1975; Vinokur, Trope, & Burnstein, 1975).

This research challenged the assumption that group decisions are necessarily more cautious, the lowest common denominator that group members will tolerate. Indeed, groups are capable of a range of alternatives, whether conservative or risky. Kellermann and Jarboe (1987) reasoned that groups help individuals check decisions by generating new arguments that they had not thought of by themselves. In this process, members become persuaded to shift their choice. The best indicator of shift is repetition of argument and voiced agreements with arguments. In this way, the group builds consensus.

Because groups continue to demonstrate their usefulness, a small-group technique, utilizing what are called quality circles has been developed to foster employee participation in decision making to increase innovation. A *quality circle* is created when management mandates a select group of employees to suggest ways for improving work design or climate. Examining how quality circles can be successful, Stohl (1987) discovered that they are likely to serve an organization best if they are integrated into the organization and are flexible. Circles that span boundaries and reach broadly by drawing members and suggestions from throughout an organization are likely to have their recommendations accepted. Quality circle members are more likely to believe their efforts are effective if the group is cohesive; this factor is more important for fostering a sense of involvement and participation than is the circle's location in the organization. Managers are most likely to favor recommendations by circles whose members have more tenure and when the circle is integrated into the decision network. Stohl (1986) found that employees who are members of quality circles like the climate and feel more integrated into the organization. Circles offer a flexible structure that encourages communication and innovation. They bring people into the problem-solving system of the organization and span departmental boundaries.

Although quality circles offer many advantages, they cannot correct deeply embedded organizational problems. They improve members' communication and decision-making skills and offer opportunities for advancement, but they do not guarantee increased employee satisfaction (Marks, 1986). They seem to work best when they grow out of an otherwise effective organization, one that has proper structure, supportive management, established decision-making processes, adaptability to change, open communication, and good labor relations (Smeltzer & Kedia, 1985).

Groups do more than merely make decisions. They also help assimilate new members into an organization by teaching the scripts and schemata unique to an organization (Jablin, 1982a). In this way, groups help their members develop a sense of the social reality unique to the organization. Groups are a system (a subsystem of the total organization). Consequently, they exhibit system characteristics. They serve as means for obtaining information about the organization (the group's environment). This information is used by group members to understand the corporate culture (Jablin, 1985) including the organization's reward/punishment system and the means by which rewards are obtained and punishment avoided (Hackman, 1976). For this reason and others previously noted, small groups are useful to organizations.

ORGANIZATION LEVEL ANALYSIS

To this point, emphasis has been placed on subsystems of the organization. But communication efforts can be studied at the organizational level by looking at macronetworks and company-wide symbols. This level of analysis also includes discussions of events that transpire outside the organization and beyond the direct contact of the individual. It can encompass efforts, including mediated messages, the organization makes to communicate with its members. This point of analysis would include means of communication such as employee newsletters.

As Jablin and Krone (1987) observed, "From an organizational assimilation perspective the study of communication at the network or organizational level of analysis focuses on how formal and informal organizational communication structures affect and are affected by the organizational socialization and employee individualization processes" (p. 726). Network analysis treats communication as a dependent variable; the size and kind of network affects communication outcomes. This perspective, Jablin and Krone reasoned, can emphasize the structure so much that researchers lose sight of the fact that it is less of a factor than is the individual's perception of it. For this reason, researchers can consider how communication affects the assimilation process from two viewpoints: "(1) as a process that may vary as a result of formal organizational structure, and (2) as an emergent structuring process that may promote variation in assimilation outcomes (including formal structures)" (p. 727).

From a network perspective, research might attempt to understand how kinds and sizes of networks affect the work socialization and assimilation efforts of members. Viewed from this perspective, the focus would be more on factors that influence each worker's efforts and views of the organization—the efforts required for assimilation, along with their costs and rewards.

How effectively individuals become assimilated into networks is likely to affect whether they assume roles as "linkers" in the network or as "nonlinkers" (Jablin, 1985). Linkers tie networks together, nonlinkers do not. Where individuals are located in organizational hierarchies can affect their perceptions of factors such as *openness*. Employees at the lower levels of organizations are likely to believe superior-subordinate relationships are less open than do employees at higher levels of the organization (Jablin 1982b).

Throughout networks, information is shared and influence is exerted in many directions: upward, downward, and horizontally. Distortion occurs during information transmission. *Serial transmission effects* occur when information is altered at each point of exchange. Each person who receives and sends a message may alter or distort it in several ways, especially by adding or removing detail, or by making it more positive or negative. Sometimes employees perceive information differently, and they may withhold some or all of it.

Superior-subordinate relationships are key focal points for studying distortion of information during transmission. Several variables predict whether distortion is likely to occur as people pass information upward or downward. These include supervisor's power, amount of upward influence the supervisor has, subordinate's aspiration for upward mobility, and whether the subordinate trusts the supervisor. In addition to these factors, the relationship between superior and subordinate as well as the supervisor's communication style are factors. Supervisors who suffer from role conflict (cannot resolve the conflicts in their job) are likely to withhold information from subordinates. If the superior communicates frequently and openly, so does the subordinate. Supportive superiors promote open and undistorted information, as is the case when they are friendly, approachable and considerate of subordinates' needs (Fulk & Sirish, 1986).

INTERORGANIZATIONAL/MEDIATED COMMUNICATION

Research focuses on how communication transpires across boundaries of a system as well as within it. This research can examine the information and influence that flow from organizations as well as that which comes from forces outside of organizations members. Chapter 4 discussed this issue in terms of the effort required to span the boundary of one system or organization to obtain information from outside, from the environment. This environment consists of individuals and other organizations who provide information a system needs to guide and regulate itself. Sometimes the information environment is turbulent, meaning that so much information and change are occurring that organization members have difficulty making sense of what is going on. Turbulent situations require people and systems who have a high information processing capacity (Huber & Daft, 1987).

An organization's ability to achieve its goals depends on its ability to obtain information from outside and process and use this information to correct its plans. Adaptations may include changing goals or selecting new means for achieving them. Without information regarding what is going on outside of itself, an organization might have a false sense of certainty. As the environment becomes more turbulent, more effort is likely to be exerted to reduce uncertainty (Dutton & Duncan, 1987; Dutton & Ottensmeyer, 1987).

Most organizations communicate outwardly, to solicit business, raise funds, notify members of a community, along with many other purposes. As organizations communicate outwardly, they provide information and influence aimed at shaping judgments and behaviors of people who are not their members. Informational and persuasive campaigns often involve mediated communication, such as print or electronic ads regarding products or services. In this way, organizations affect persons outside and improve or damage relationships that are instrumental to the organization's goals.

The nature of the environment can affect how the organization operates. For instance, at one time, air pollution was virtually uncontrolled; then recognition of the health hazards associated with it brought activist group and governmental efforts to impose clean air standards. In its boundary spanning activities, an organization may need to observe early in a public policy debate that efforts are being made to change the way the organization is allowed to function (Crable & Vibbert, 1985). To avert unreasonable regulations of their activities, organizations may respond in ways that can help shape the social reality by which people outside the organization view it and the standards by which it can operate (Cheney & Vibbert, 1987; Heath, 1988; Heath & Nelson, 1986). For instance, debates waged over air quality bring together companies, activist groups, governmental agencies, and media reporters and editorialists. From this dynamic interaction emerge the standards by which companies are allowed to operate.

Organizations' efforts to interact with individuals and other organizations may be better served if they employ a two-way symmetrical flow of communication (Grunig & Hunt, 1984). Communication flows from companies to inform and influence others, but companies also take in information and yield to the influence of others. If an organization fosters two-way communication, it is likely to increase trust that it is acting in the interests of others and thereby foster their willingness to act in the interest of the organization. Whether the leadership of an organization adopts two-way communication depends on its ideology and the extent to which any set of strategies seems most useful. Only when public relations practitioners are part of the dominant coalition of an organization can they foster two-way communication (Grunig & Grunig, 1989).

As organizations attempt to communicate with external publics, several factors influence their ability to do so. Persons are likely to become activists (whether for or against a company's interests) when they recognize problems that need to be solved, experience high levels of involvement regarding the issue, and believe that rewards of activism outweigh its costs (Grunig, 1989). High levels of involvement lead individuals to be more willing to communicate (talk, read, and teleview) about the topic. Persons who are highly involved tend to have more messages about those topics. This is true whether the persons favor or disfavor the issue affecting a company's interests (Heath & Douglas, 1990).

In conceptualizing organizational communication at this level, you may want to remember that organizations attempt to assimilate into the values, institutions, and expectations of society at large. And organizations attempt to get people who are not its members to support its goals, whether to buy products, donate funds, support public education or whatever. Organizations are not likely to last long if they attempt to stand alone.

CONCLUSION

At first thought, the notion of organizational communication seems to imply a set of activities that organizations do. As Jablin and Krone (1987) observed, however,

> the study of communication phenomena at the network or organizational level is inherently a multilevel form of analysis. In other words, since communication networks are composed of individual communicators (nodes) interpersonally linked to other communicators, it is essentially impossible to examine organizational structures without also considering intrapersonal and interpersonal level communication factors. (p. 739)

For this reason, effort is made to describe the variables and points of analysis that can define communication at all levels of analysis in organizations. Through communication, members of organizations — as well as external persons whom organizations affect — form meaning regarding the organization and the quality of their relationship with it. The meaning that is derived will affect behavior of people in regard to and in behalf of the organization. To alter reactions to each organization requires changing what it means for the people it affects.

9 Mass Communication

In chapter 2, you were asked to jot down your definition of communication and then reexamine that definition after reading the chapter. No doubt your perception of the term was somewhat altered after being exposed to the various concepts, models, and theories that are involved in the communication process. You quickly realized that there is no one definition of communication that can be agreed on, nor one process that can be applied to all types of interaction. The same can be said when trying to conceptualize the term *mass communication*. DeFleur (1970) reminded us that "in the past, the content of the field of mass communication and the directions of its inquiry have been defined by whatever happened to be currently capturing the attention of its more prominent students" (p. xiii). However, we will attempt to provide a working definition of mass communication or at least provide you with characteristics that are generally recognized as unique in the process of mass communication. It may be easier to understand by contrasting mass communication with something you are already familiar with—interpersonal communication. You will also notice that many of the theories and paradigms found in chapters 1 and 2 relate directly to our understanding of the mass communication process.

In chapters 6 and 7, we examined how people use communication to shape interpersonal relationships and emphasized the interactional nature of interpersonal communication. Recall that interpersonal communication was defined as dyadic interaction, in which people engage to negotiate relationships by using direct and indirect communication that becomes personally meaningful as they attempt to reduce uncertainty about themselves, their partners, and their relationships. Interpersonal communication usually involves a single source (the encoder) and a single receiver (the decoder), and feedback (verbal and nonverbal) that can occur between both parties immediately. There is interaction. The roles of source and receiver alternate between parties; what one person says can influence future messages. In addition, there is a level of homogeneity between the source and receiver, a common bond or need to communicate.

In its most basic form, the term mass communication most commonly refers to the process of communicating through a medium to an audience. When you think of the term mass communication, what immediately comes to mind? Do you think about television, radio, motion pictures, newspapers, magazines, and books? Wright (1986) reminded us that, while these are often essential in the process of mass communication, they represent the technological instruments or media used to convey messages and do not constitute the processes involved. Any device that is capable of carrying messages between people can be considered a medium. This would include the telephone, a personal letter, an electronic bulletin board, and so on. For example, a telecast of the popular show "60 Minutes" or the latest issue of *Time Magazine* is an instance of mass communication; a closed-circuit security camera in a retail store or an interoffice memo is not. Mass communication involves distinctive characteristics concerning each element within the communication process.

Recall that interpersonal communication involves a single source; the communicator in mass communication usually involves a complex and highly organized media entity such as a national television network like ABC, NBC, CBS, or FOX, or large publishing concerns such as Gannett or Knight-Ridder. Public access to these media is often restricted, and messages (television programs, for instance) are usually very expensive to produce and distribute, requiring the sale of either air time or space to keep the organization functioning.

The audience for mass-mediated messages is usually large, involving too many people for the communicator to interact with personally. Unlike interpersonal communication, there is little or no interaction or feedback from the audience back to the communicator. Audience members are heterogeneous in that the receivers of messages are demographically diverse and are usually anonymous or unknown to the communicator.

The mass communication experience can further be defined with the following terms: *public*—messages are not addressed to particular individuals; rapid—messages are delivered simultaneously or in minimal time; and transient—messages are usually consumed immediately but can be stored (e.g., in video tape, libraries, or newspaper "morgues").

In discussing the functions that the mass media serve, many theorists rely on a set of four propositions stated by Lasswell (1948) and expanded by Wright (1986). They postulated that media serve the following functions:

1. Surveillance—surveying the environment and providing news-worthy information.
2. Correlation—interpreting information about the environment and editorializing or prescribing how people should react to those events.
3. Transmission of culture—binding time across generations by educating people about information, values, and social norms.
4. Entertainment—amusing people without necessarily offering any other functional values.

Wright (1986) added that these four functions can also be seen to have negative effects or dysfunctions for both the individual and society. For example, "mass communicated news about impending danger, broadcast to the general public without local mediation and interpretation by someone, may lead to widespread panic (surveillance)" (p. 18). Hearing numerous alternative political or commercial messages may bring about sophistication or become confusing and lessen the individual's ability to think independently (correlation). "The presentation on a more or less standardized view of culture through mass communication could result in a loss of regional, ethnic, and other subcultural variety and could discourage cultural diversity and creativity (transmission of culture)" (p. 21). And finally, spending too much time on nonproductive entertaining diversions can distract people from useful social participation and interactions and result in their becoming dependent on a medium for all entertainment needs (entertainment).

As we begin our discussion of mass communication theory, remember that these theories are complex and involve many volumes of studies conducted over several decades by diverse researchers. Every theory has its proponents and critics. This chapter focuses on the basic characteristics of the most prevalent theories and processes of mass communication.

The study of mass communication is developing at a rapid pace. In this, the information age, it is difficult for researchers to keep up with the ever-changing media environment and how it may effect individuals or our society as a whole. However, with a basic knowledge of the theoretical developments thus far, you will be able to better understand the opportunities and limitations of mass communication study.

PREMATURE PERSPECTIVES ON MASS COMMUNICATION THEORY

Prior to the 1930s, most mass communication theorists assumed that mass media messages were immensely powerful and capable of directly influencing the values, opinions, and emotions of people within the audience. They embraced the concept of *mass society* that emerged from the study of the fundamental social changes that had taken place over the last two centuries. Lowery and DeFleur (1983) explained that "mass" in this context refers not to numbers but to a distinctive process or pattern of social organization that occurs when industrialization, urbanization, and modernization increasingly modify the social order. It was thought that, as the populace of the 19th century and early 20th century moved from a rural, agricultural-based society to an urban-industrial society, open communication as a basis of social solidarity between members became more difficult. Psychological alienation and the erosion of traditional social groups resulted in an independent and culturally isolated mass of people. Early theorists assumed that, if individuals were not influenced by social variables but shared the same psychological and emotional makeup, then mediated messages would presumably have a powerful, predictable, and uniform effect on all the members. Tan (1985) added that the audience was best thought to be classified by demographic characteristics such as age, sex, socioeconomic status, and education rather than as members of a social group.

This argument of uniform and powerful direct media effects has, in retrospect, been labeled the "bullet theory" or "hypodermic needle theory," and even later was known as the stimulus–response theory or the theory of uniform influences. Studies conducted after World War I indicated that propaganda and advertising campaigns in newspapers were highly effective in shaping the attitudes, beliefs, and consumer behavior of their audiences. Messages had only to be loaded, directed to the target, and fired; if they hit their target, then the expected response would be forthcoming. Audiences were assumed to act on impulse, emotion, instinct, and basic human nature rather than on reason. In retrospect, the results of these studies may have been tainted by the lack of rigorous methodology and the absence of accumulated empirical evidence; or, the results may have come about because of the naivete of the mass audience, whose members were unaccustomed to mediated messages. Regardless, proponents of the bullet theory are with us even today. Critics of the mass media continue to claim that the highly institutionalized and omnipotent mass media exercise a powerful influence over a passive, trusting, and vulnerable consumer, despite decades of research evidence that indicates that the relationships between mass media messages and audiences are seldom simple and direct.

Television is perhaps the favorite target of such critics today. Television has been accused of inciting riots, promoting crime and violence, encouraging illicit sex, promoting alcohol and drug abuse, reducing the populace to a nation of mindless "couch potatoes," creating a nation of obese and passive illiterates, and breaking up the nuclear family. Granted, television may have some influence on some people some of the time, but television and other mass media obviously do not effect all people in the same manner all of the time.

It is, in fact, this realization that prompted psychologists and social psychologists in the 1930s and 1940s to focus their research attention on the widely divergent reactions of individuals to the same media content. It was soon discovered that audience members were not passive receivers of information, but rather they were active, and various intervening variables affected their reactions to messages. Researchers began to emphasize the individual differences in audience needs, attitudes, values, motivations, and moods, as well as the psychologically oriented personality variables of audience members. It was found that these differences as well as environmental factors greatly influenced individuals' perceptions of the world and caused them to react in distinctly individual ways (DeFleur, 1970). Although mediated messages were believed to influence the individual, the effects were not as powerful, indiscriminate, and predictable as once thought. Human nature was not uniform; rather it was comprised of diverse, complex, and highly integrated psychological characteristics. The question before researchers was not only what were the effects of mass-mediated messages, but how and why were particular media selected, and what factors influenced the selection of one media or message over another?

Much of the early theory building at this time came from the then rapidly growing field of psychology. Experiments in behaviorism, motivation, persuasion, and conditioning led researchers to examine the processes of habit formation and learning. Differences among individual personality traits and psychological organization were found to be affected by the social environment in which people were raised. Moreover, studies in human perception showed that an individual's values, needs, beliefs, and attitudes were instrumental in determining how stimuli are selected from the environment and the way meaning is attributed to those stimuli within an individual's frame of reference (DeFleur, 1970).

From these findings, the concept of selective attention or exposure, selective perception, and selective retention were formulated to explain how individuals contend with the multiplicity of mediated messages that are available. DeFleur concluded that selective attention and perception are intervening psychological mechanisms that modify the stimulus–response model of mass communication. Individual audience members were found to selectively attend to messages, "particularly if they were related to his interests, consistent with his attitudes, congruent with his beliefs, and supportive of his values" (p. 122). Similarly, it was found that individuals tended to avoid communication that was contrary to their interests, attitudes, beliefs, and values. For example, if you were an avid sports fan and were given the opportunity to watch either the Super Bowl or a PBS documentary on the migration of the snow goose, you would probably be inclined to watch the football game. Message selection was not found to be random; in fact, much media selection was quite purposeful and deliberate.

Selectivity continues after the individual chooses which messages will be selected. *Selective perception* is the tendency for people to adapt mediated messages to fit their own preferences. *Perception* has been defined as a "complex process by which people select, organize, and interpret sensory stimulation into a meaningful and coherent picture of the world" (Berelson & Steiner, 1964, p. 88). Perception can be influenced by a myriad of psychological factors, including predispositions based on past experience, cultural expectations, motivations, moods, and attitudes. These factors can cause individuals to misperceive and misinterpret messages, so the communicator cannot assume that all receivers will extract the same meaning from the same message.

The process of selective retention or recall reveals that people tend to remember messages they consciously perceive and accept rather than those they consciously reject. Factors that influence this include: whether the messages are consistent with prior attitudes and experience, the importance of the message for later use, the intensity of the message, and the medium used to transmit the message. As with selective perception, selective retention also involves the distortion of the intended message. The audience may adapt the message and retain it in a form that best suits individual member needs.

Concurrent with the studies of selectivity and perception of individuals in the field of psychology, another group of social scientists, primarily sociologists, began to look at the various characteristics in common with people within social groups. Called the *social categories perspective,* it assumed that people in various positions of the social structure shared the same demographic characteristics and would have similar reactions to mediated messages. Variables such as age, sex, income, education, religious affiliation, and ethnic background seemed to have a powerful influence on the type of communication content selected from the various media options available. For example, most prosperous urban males may prefer reading *The New York Times,* whereas most adolescent girls may prefer reading magazines like *Seventeen.*

AN EARLY INTERPERSONAL TWIST IN MASS COMMUNICATION RESEARCH

However, sociologists continued to assume that members of any given social group were isolated from each other and that interaction occurred only indirectly via the media. Public opinion or mass behavior was considered the summation of individual decisions of persons within each social group. Although they produced a substantial number of studies categorizing the usage patterns and knowledge acquisition of various social groups, researchers did not consider other variables that were affecting the communication process (Black & Bryant, in press).

This was to change with a 1940 voting study conducted by Lazarsfeld, Berelson, and Gaudet in Elmira, New York, published under the title *The People's Choice* (1948). Originally the researchers had set out to compare the effectiveness of radio to that of newspapers and magazines in influencing public opinion during the 1940 presidential campaign. After several months of conducting personal interviews, it became apparent that, whereas newspapers and radio had some influence on public opinion, it was through interpersonal contacts that most people received most of their influence.

This accidental finding was significant in that it indicates that interpersonal communication about mass media messages was taking place and was modifying media effects. Recall that, in the original stimulus–response model, mediated messages were communicated from the source to an independent receiver in what was perceived as a single, linear process. Now it appeared that, not only were people talking about the election, but certain individuals began to surface as "opinion leaders." These opinion leaders were heavy users of the available media who would pass information along to their peers who had lesser or no media exposure or less expertise on the topic in question. These opinion leaders, in retransmitting the media messages to their associates, often included, gratis, their own interpretation of the information they had received. Thus was born the concept of the *two-step flow of mass communication.*

Prominence in the community was not a requisite qualification for opinion leaders; they were found at all levels of the social structure. Friends' and acquaintances' perceptions of one's expertise of a subject and the confidence of peers were key characteristics of opinion leaders. Subsequently, the role of opinion leader could change with any given topic. Lowery and DeFleur (1983) added that "personal influence from opinion leaders was more likely to reach the undecided and the uninterested voter, both of whom were all but impervious to the political campaign presented via the media. . . . Opinion leaders were also likely to be trusted as a nonpurposive source of information and interpretation" (p. 109). In addition, because the exchange of information was likely to take place in a social situation, the opinion leader was able to respond to questions and make counterarguments throughout the discussion; something that the mass media was unable to do.

The concept of two-step flow and other findings contained in *The People's Choice* were instrumental in guiding future research into the limited effects model of mass communication and the role of interpersonal processes in communication. However, the recognition of several shortcomings would later expand the two-step flow into a multi-step flow. One limitation is that the study was conducted over a relatively short period of time and dealt exclusively with a highly political matter. Also, access to the mass media was limited, and the introduction of television, our most prevalent mass medium today, was still years away.

Later studies concluded that the influence of opinion leaders was not always "downward," as in the interpretation of news events for a less-informed audience. Opinion leaders were found to communicate "upward" to the media gatekeepers (i.e., newspaper editors and radio programmers) as well as share information "sideways" with other opinion leaders. Further studies of interpersonal communication showed that an individual's personal identification with an organization, religion, or other social group has a strong influence on the type of media content selected (recall selective attention, perception, and retention). Group norms apparently provide a type of "social reality" check built on similar and shared beliefs, attitudes, opinions, and concerns that tend to form barriers against mediated messages contrary to the group's point of view. Likewise, mediated messages in agreement with the group or provided by the group are usually attended to and utilized to reinforce the status quo.

In addition, research conducted by Merton in the late 1940s sought to determine the characteristics of "community influentials" or opinion leaders in a small eastern community. Merton identified two types of opinion leaders: the local and the cosmopolitan influential (Wright, 1986, p. 91). The local influential was usually found to be born in or near the community, interested in local activities, concerned with knowing a wide variety of townspeople, have membership in voluntary associations, and take an interest in local newspapers and radio broadcasts. In contrast, the cosmopolitan influential was usually a newcomer to the town, was interested in national and international affairs, had a restrictive circle of friends on the same status level, belonged to specialized or professional associations, and sought media messages that reduced feelings of cultural isolation and helped maintain expertise on nonlocal matters.

Merton found that local influentials are most likely to have influence over a wide variety of people in various topics, whereas cosmopolitan influentials are restricted to a specific field in which they are considered expert.

Social Learning Theory

Social learning theory (also referred to as observational learning or modeling theory) was primarily developed by Bandura and his associates in the 1960s and remains one of the most widely used theories of mass communication today. (See Chapter 5, this volume, for an extensive discussion of this theory.) Tan (1985, p. 244) stated that social learning theory explains how we learn from direct experience as well as by observing and modeling individuals and events we see in the mass media; behavior is the result of both environmental and cognitive factors. Bandura's original studies found that, under certain circumstances, children can learn aggressive behavior on television. If aggressive behavior is attended to, cognitively retained, and perceived as beneficial, it increases the probability that the children may model this behavior at a future time. Although commonly used to study how children learn aggressive behavior from watching television, learned prosocial behavior has also been observed.

There are several components to the social learning process (e.g., Bandura & Walters, 1963; Tan, 1985). An individual must first be exposed to and attend to an event or the behavior of an individual, either directly or symbolically via television or other media. Events or behavior that are simple, distinctive, elicit positive feelings, and are observed repeatedly are most likely to be modeled. Several characteristics of the observer may also influence attention (see Fig. 9.1). These are the capacity to mentally process information, usually related to age and intelligence; perceptual set as determined by needs, moods, values, and previous experiences; past reinforcement, both positive and negative, from attending to the same or similar events; and often the arousal level of the individual.

Next, an individual must be capable of mentally retaining the observed behavior or event. This is accomplished by visual imagery or the storing of mental pictures of observations, and by representing symbolically events using verbal codes or a common language. In addition, because most behaviors that are learned are not immediately performed, an individual must be able to cognitively rehearse the experience before actively repeating it.

The third step is behavioral enactment. An individual must possess the cognitive and motor skills necessary to initiate the learned behavior. Repetition, self-observation, and feedback from others are helpful in refining an accurate reproduction of the desired behavior.

Finally, the individual must be motivated to perform the learned behavior (see Fig. 9.2). Bandura stated that reinforcement is the key to motivation and will increase the probability that a behavior will be modeled. External reinforcements are the actual rewards or the expectation of rewards such as praise, social approval, and prestige. Vicarious reinforcement or observing others being reinforced for certain behavior can also motivate similar behavior. Lastly, self-reinforcement can occur by internal rewards such as self-satisfaction.

Lowery and DeFleur (1983, p. 333) pointed out an important distinction between the acquisition of new behavior and the acceptance of new

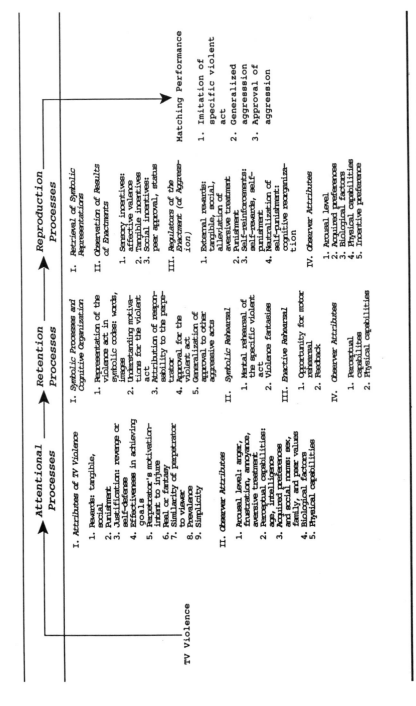

FIG. 9.1. A model of social learning of aggression from television (from Tan, 1986. Reprinted by permission).

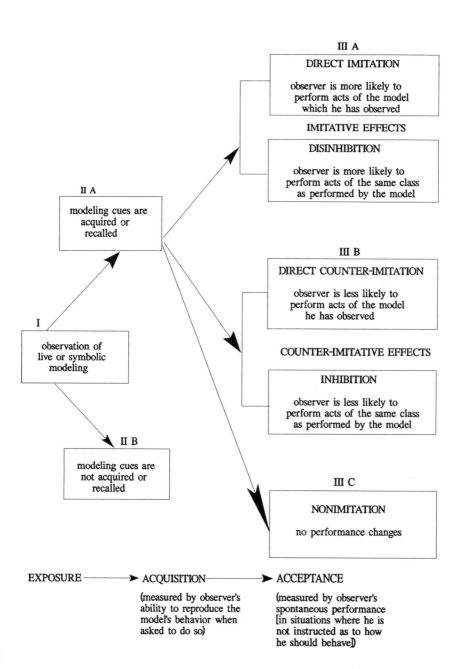

III A

DIRECT IMITATION

observer is more likely to
perform acts of the model
which he has observed

IMITATIVE EFFECTS

DISINHIBITION

observer is more likely to
perform acts of the same class
as performed by the model

II A

modeling cues are
acquired or
recalled

III B

DIRECT COUNTER-IMITATION

observer is less likely to
perform acts of the model
he has observed

COUNTER-IMITATIVE EFFECTS

INHIBITION

observer is less likely to
perform acts of the same class
as performed by the model

I

observation of
live or symbolic
modeling

II B

modeling cues are
not acquired or
recalled

III C

NONIMITATION

no performance changes

EXPOSURE ─────▶ ACQUISITION ─────────▶ ACCEPTANCE

(measured by observer's
ability to reproduce the
model's behavior when
asked to do so)

(measured by observer's
spontaneous performance
[in situations where he is
not instructed as to how
he should behave])

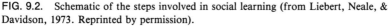

FIG. 9.2.   Schematic of the steps involved in social learning (from Liebert, Neale, &
Davidson, 1973. Reprinted by permission).

275

behavior. *Acquisition* is the ability to reproduce previously unfamiliar response, whereas *acceptance* is the actual performance of the same or similar response.

Stalagmite Theories

With the decline of hypodermic needle theories and the inclusion of more interpersonal and social group considerations into mass communication theories, social scientists began to look to more complicated theoretical models to explain the effects of mass media messages on their audiences. One of the dominant perspectives on media effects during the 1970s and 1980s was that the impact of consuming media messages is very real and, potentially, of critical psychological and social consequence, but the effects are cumulative and transpire unnoticeably over a long period of time. Black and Bryant (in press) referred to such perspectives via the metaphor of *stalagmite theories,* suggesting that media effects occur analogously to the slow buildup of formations on cave floors, which take their interesting forms after eons of the steady dripping of limewater from the cave ceilings above. The most popular "name brand" theory that fits this perspective is *cultivation theory.* Several formulations of *socialization theories* also seem to fit this category.

Cultivation Theory. The prototypical "stalagmite" perspective concerning the societal impact of the mass media can be found in the work of Gerbner and his associates (e.g., Gerbner, Gross, Morgan, & Signorielli, 1986). Cultivation theory or cultivation analysis in its most basic form suggests that television is responsible for shaping or "cultivating" viewers' conceptions of social reality. Cultivation theory is not concerned with any one type of media content or with a specific immediate effect. The theory states that concentrating on individual differences and immediate change misses the main point of television: the absorption of divergent currents into a stable and common mainstream (1986, p. 20). Rather, "the pattern that counts is that of the total pattern of programming to which entire communities are regularly exposed over long periods of time" (p. 19). The combined effect of massive television exposure by viewers over time subtly shapes the perception of social reality for individuals and, ultimately, for our culture as a whole. The highly stylized, stereotyped, and repetitive messages and images portrayed by television have become our most common source of socialization and everyday information. "Television provides a daily ritual of highly compelling and informative content that forms a strong cultural link between elites and the rest of the population" (p. 18). Gerbner called this effect "mainstreaming," or the homogenization of our perceptions of social reality, and argued that it results in significant personal and social consequences. In the words of Gerbner et al. (1986), "Mainstreaming means that television viewing may absorb or override differences in perspectives and behavior that stem from other social, cultural, and demographic influences. It represents a homogenization of divergent views and a convergence of disparate viewers" (p. 31).

Through content analysis of prime-time television, Gerbner and his associates found that the television world does not necessarily mirror the real world. Discrepancies included: three times more male characters than female; few minority characters, usually portrayed in minor roles; misrepresentation of various social groups such as the elderly; and a preponderance of violent media content. Gerbner argued that repeated viewing of such portrayals contributes to the development of particular beliefs about the world and reinforces those beliefs once they are established. One such belief was termed the *mean world syndrome,* or the belief, acquired by massive exposure to violent media fare, that the world is a mean and dangerous place, which can instill in people a fear of violent crime (Gerbner et al., 1986, p. 28).

Cultivation analysis recognizes the "cultivation differential" between light viewers and heavy viewers. Heavy viewers are more likely to be influenced by television viewing than are light viewers. In addition, Gerbner and his colleagues "observed a complex relationship between the cultivation of general orientations or assumptions about facts of life and more specific personal expectations . . . Television may cultivate exaggerated notions of the prevalence of violence and risk out in the world, but the cultivation of expectations of personal victimization depends on the neighborhood of the viewer" (p. 29). Likewise, social interaction and prior knowledge of the subject matter can also influence the acceptance of television reality.

In spite of its prominence, cultivation theory has not been without its critics. Some researchers have attempted to replicate cultivation studies and failed to support their findings; others have questioned the dominant methodologies of cultivation research. For example, Hirsch (1979) questioned the differences found between heavy and light viewers when controls for demographic and social characteristics are used. Gerbner and his associates, of course, disagreed with this criticism.

Regardless of the debate, cultivation theory has made a valuable contribution by emphasizing the totality of the television viewing experience. Rather than focusing on the impact of a single mass mediated message, concentration is placed on the effect of the cumulative exposure pattern and the homogeneity of media fare.

Socialization Theories.   Numerous other scholars have conducted research that has shared, either explicitly or implicitly, many of the perspectives of what we are calling stalagmite theories. Some of this research might be identified rather generically as socialization theories.

One important and expansive body of literature that tends to fit under this rubric looks at the effects of advertising on young children. A descriptive title from one volume in this tradition is *How Children Learn to Buy* (Ward, Wackman, & Wartella, 1977). For obvious reasons, most of the research in this tradition has focused on television.

A glance at several of the assumptions that distinguish this literature indicate why it fits under the category of stalagmite theories. First, children have been considered to be a special audience, particularly vulnerable to media effects (Adler, 1980), primarily because they have been assumed not to have the cognitive capacity to recognize, as well as to resist, various effects derived from repeated exposure to television advertisements. Secondly, it has been alleged that much of the content of advertising directed to children is for unhealthy or otherwise undesirable products and is, at least, somewhat misleading in the way it is presented (Barcus, 1980). And, finally, it has been first presumed and then substantially demonstrated that children's repeated exposure to the vast number of advertising messages they watch has subtle but powerful effects over their requests for products, on their rate of consumption of products, on their emotional state, and even on the way they interact with their parents (Atkin, 1980). By and large, once children reach the level of cognitive and emotional maturity whereby they can consciously determine the validity of advertising claims and recognize their intent, social and policy concerns, as well as research interest, have greatly diminished. Given the findings in other stalagmite theory domains, it may be invalid to assume that the effects of long-term exposure to advertising will be inconsequential once an individual reaches cognitive maturity.

Many similar perspectives undergird the area of mass communication theory known as *political socialization*. This category of socialization theory has examined the role of the mass media in creating political awareness and political values among children and adolescents. Because political ideas and values begin rather early in childhood, communication scholars and political scientists have examined the relationships between the content of media message systems used by children and the political norms, values, attitudes, and beliefs to which they adhere (Van Evra, 1990). It has been found that the mass media provide a great deal of the political information children and adolescents receive; moreover, children frequently cite the media as their most important sources of political information and opinion (e.g., Nimmo, 1978).

> Most of the studies are necessarily of long-term nature, for only a reckless scientist would claim a direct cause–effect relationship between a particular media message and a specific subsequent political behavior. Nevertheless, evidence is accumulating that the media are an important, though subtle, influence in children's definitions of political reality and subsequent political behavior. (Black & Bryant, in press, p. 52)

Following an extensive review of the media socialization literature, Van Evra (1990) posited a developmental model of *media socialization effects*. Her model, which can be seen in Fig. 9.3, predicts a range of effects dependent on the use youngsters make of media content, their perceptions of the reality of the content they consume, their amount of media consumption, and the number of information alternatives available in the child's environment. Van Evra predicted maximal stalagmite effects, which she refers to as "drip" effects, when children (a) view for diversion, (b) perceive the media content to be realistic, (c) are heavy viewers, and (d) have few information alternatives available. Empirical tests of complex socialization models, such as Van Evra's, are sorely needed.

A provocative but untested socialization hypothesis has recently been advanced by Meyrowitz (1985). This author presumed that, for some time now, mass media has been a major force of socialization for children. Two suppositions form the basis for his argument: (a) ". . . book [print] information is still thick and strong, but television now provides children with a large keyhole through which to view the adult world" (p. 151); and (b) "now, children of every age are presented with 'all age' social information through electronic media" (p. 151). He sees the results as an "homogenization of socialization stages" (p. 152). These arguments are closely related to Postman's thesis that modern mass-mediated reality has led to *The Disappearance of Childhood* (1982). Although such claims by Postman and Meyrowitz are for potent media effects, they too seem to presume a cumulative, gradual buildup of media impact rather than a "big bang" effect from single exposures to media messages. In this way, they too are stalagmite theorists, although it might be argued that, in their views, the monuments of Mammoth Cave were created more rapidly than many of their contemporary spelunkers might imagine, and some might argue that Postman and Meyrowitz see these fascinating stalagmites as more central to the keystone of our "caverns' structures" than do most of us.

Agenda Setting

Another influential mass communication theory that deals with media and political behavior, broadly defined, that also rests its case on relatively subtle media effects, is that of agenda setting. McCombs and Gilbert (1986) defined the agenda-setting function of mass communication as the "ability of the mass media to structure audience cognitions and to effect change among existing cognitions" (p. 4). More simply put, agenda-setting is the creation of public awareness and concern of salient issues by the news media. The agenda-setting role of the news media has frequently been traced back to the publication of Walter Lippmann's *Public Opinion* (1922) and his argument that the public responds, not to actual events in the environment, but to a pseudo-environment or, as Lippmann described it,

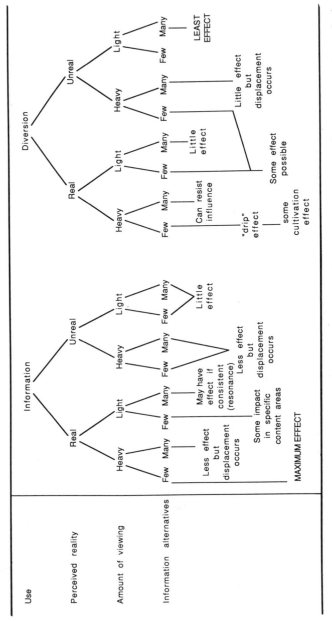

FIG. 9.3. A developmental model of media socialization effects. Interactions among use and amount of viewing with perceived reality and information alternatives. Developmental level, socioeconomic level, race, gender, and other factors determine use made of television, reality perceived, amount viewed, and informational alternatives (from Van Evra, 1990. Reprinted by permission).

"the pictures in our heads" (p. 271). However, it was not until after the 1968 presidential election that this concept was empirically tested by McCombs and Shaw (1972).

Many commentators on agenda-setting have stated that the process occurs because the press must be selective in reporting the news. The media employ professional "gatekeepers" who daily make informal choices about what to report and how to report it. In addition, the media "cue" the public as to which news items are deemed most important. Such cues include the frequency with which the item is repeated, the prominence with which items are displayed (front page or lead story), the length or time allotted for the item, and the framing (in what context and on what occasion the media give attention to an item).

McCombs and Gilbert (1986) stated that "one of the most critical aspects in the concept of an agenda-setting role of mass communication is the time frame for this phenomenon" (p. 8). Determinants of the time frame include: (a) the overall time frame, which is the total period of time under consideration; (b) the time lag, which is the elapsed time between the appearance of an item on the media agenda and its appearance on the public agenda; (c) the duration of the media agenda; (d) the duration of the public agenda measure; and (e) the optimal effect span, which is the peak association between media emphasis and public emphasis of an issue (p. 8).

In addition, there is evidence that, over time, different media have different agenda-setting potential. Shaw and McCombs (1977) found that, in a 1972 political campaign, newspapers were initially more effective in agenda-setting than in influencing public opinion. However, television supplanted newspapers as election day grew closer. McCombs concluded that "Technological and stylistic differences between the media accounted for the different functions during distinct phases over time . . . Television news is more like the front page of a newspaper, so that readers have a longer period of experience with an issue than do viewers. But once an issue is on television, the treatment tends to be more intensive and its salience is more apparent" (McCombs & Gilbert, 1986, p. 9).

Lowery and DeFleur (1983) stated that another issue associated with the agenda-setting function of the media is "the degree to which the meanings attached to issues by the public (e.g., perceived importance) play a part in formulating public policy . . . If the press emphasizes a given topic to a point where the public comes to believe that it is truly important, do political leaders then take action to 'do something' about the issue?" (p. 381). It appears that this may be true, although empirical evidence regarding this complex effect is only beginning to be marshalled in a useful way.

Invariably, when discussing the concept of agenda-setting, one is reminded of Bernard Cohen's (1963) statement to the effect that the press may not be successful much of the time in telling people what to think, but it is stunningly successful in telling its readers *what to think about.*

Uses and Entertainment

Uses and Gratifications. A number of classic and recent media theories have focused, not on what media messages do to audiences, but what media users do with media. The most prominent of those is uses and gratifications. Uses and gratifications research assumes that individuals take an active role in the communication process and are goal directed in their media behavior (from which we derive the term *uses*). This approach also assumes that alternate choices are available to gratify the needs or motives of the individual (gratifications or rewards) (Rubin & Windahl, 1986).

In an historical perspective, uses and gratifications research began under other rubrics in the 1940s in the few social scientific areas concerned with mass communication (McQuail, 1984). Throughout that decade, empirical mass communication research centered on studying the "effects" of media content, rather than differences in individual gratifications. "Researchers were investigating 'why' people engaged in various kinds of mass communications behavior, such as listening to radio quiz programs and daytime serials, reading comic books, and reading the newspaper" (Tan, 1985, p. 233). Early descriptive research was hindered by both conceptual and methodological limitations. One serious limitation was an inability to determine whether the gratifications sought and the gratifications received were one and the same. Researchers were able to tell who the heavy users were but often were unable to determine what precise gratifications they were receiving from their communication experience. However, these surveys, case studies, and other forms of audience analysis did provide an empirical base from which to build (Black & Bryant, in press).

In the late 1950s and early 1960s, researchers became disappointed with results of measuring the short-term effects from exposure to mass media campaigns. "It reflected a desire to understand audience involvement in mass communications in terms more faithful to the individual user's own experience and perspective than the effects tradition could attain" (Blumler, 1979, p. 10). Katz (1959) summarized when he stated the following:

> Less attention (should be paid) to what media do to people and more to what people do with the media. Such an approach assumes that even the most potent of mass media content cannot ordinarily influence an individual who has no "use" for it in the social and psychological context in which he lives. The "uses" approach assumes that people's values, their interests, their associations, their social roles, are pre-potent and that people selectively "fashion" what they see and hear to these interests. (p. 2)

It is important to note that, during this time, television was fast becoming the dominant mass medium that it is today. Naturally, as with any developing mass media, much skepticism and conjecture concerning television's potential for "good" or "evil" spawned a flurry of scholastic attention.

Throughout the 1970s, many assumptions of the uses and gratifications approach were revised as researchers began to work toward theoretical integration. There are several widely accepted approaches to identifying and measuring audience needs and the functions mass media serve, but most of them adhere to a set of basic assumptions found in Blumler and Katz's (1974) volume, *The Uses of Mass Communication: Current Perspectives on Gratifications Research*. This book was extremely instrumental in conceptualizing the focus of uses and gratifications research. The authors proposed that the uses and gratifications approach concerns:

1. the social and psychological origins of
2. needs, which generate
3. expectations of
4. the mass media or other sources, which lead to
5. differential patterns of media exposure (or engagement in other activities), resulting in
6. needs gratification and
7. other consequences, perhaps mostly unintended ones. (p. 20)

More recently, Palmgreen, Wenner, and Rosengren (1985) provided a more contemporary view of uses and gratifications research. Eight important assumptions they mentioned are:

1. the audience is active, thus
2. much media use can be conceived as goal directed and
3. competing with other sources of need satisfaction, so that when
4. substantial audience initiative links needs to media choice,
5. media consumption can fulfill a wide range of gratifications, although
6. media content alone cannot be used to predict patterns of gratifications accurately because
7. media characteristics structure the degree to which needs may be gratified at different times, and further, because
8. gratifications obtained can have their origins in media content, exposure in and of itself, and/or the social situation in which exposure takes place (p. 14).

While audience activity is a central theme throughout uses and gratifications research, researchers no longer regard audience members as universally active. Rubin (in press) analyzed the work of several researchers and suggested several influences:

> Activity depends, to a large extent, on the social context and potential for interaction. Elements such as mobility and loneliness are important. Reduced mobility and greater loneliness, for example, result in ritualized media orientations and greater reliance on the media. Attitudinal dispositions such as affinity and perceived realism are also important. Attitudes filter media and message selection and use . . . These attitudes, which result from past experiences with a medium and produce expectations for future gratification-seeking behavior, affect meaning.

In the study of uses and gratifications, the seeking of gratifications is seen as a significant determination of an individual's exposure to mass communication.

> Early uses and gratifications research indicated that newspapers, radio, and television seemed to connect individuals to society, whereas books and cinema appeared to cater to more "selfish" needs such as those dealing with self-fulfillment and self-gratification. Further research, however, led to the argument that the same set of media materials was capable of serving a multiplicity of audience needs. The contemporary view is that the relationship between the content of specific media and the needs of audience is rather complex. . . . Experiences with the media are probably highly individualized, and the utility of particular media content is unique to the consumer. (Black & Bryant, in press)

Tan (1985) stated that "the uses and gratifications model begins by attempting to classify human needs into distinct and theoretically meaningful categories" (p. 235). Rather than focus on a lengthy list of specific needs, he cited a typology of media-related needs that groups specific needs into five categories.

1. Cognitive Needs. Needs related to strengthening of information, knowledge, and understanding of our environment. They also satisfy our curiosity and exploratory drives.
2. Affective Needs. Needs related to strengthening aesthetic, pleasurable, and emotional experiences. The pursuit of pleasure and entertainment is a common motivation that can be satisfied by the media.
3. Personal Integrative Needs. Needs related to strengthening credibility, confidence, stability, and status of the individual. They are derived from the individual's desire for self-esteem.

4. Social Integrative Needs. Needs related to strengthening contact with family, friends, and the world. These are based on an individual's desire for affiliation.

5. Escapist Needs. Needs related to escape, tension release, and desire for diversion (pp. 235–236).

One approach that has advanced the understanding of why people use mass media the way they do integrates expectancy-value theories within the uses and gratifications framework. (Recall that this theory was discussed in chapter 5, this volume; there it was applied to a broad array of decisions, whereas here it is used to explain media selection.) In regard to this, Rayburn and Palmgreen (1984) stated the following: "The concept of audience expectations concerning the characteristics of the media and potential gratifications to be obtained is essential to the uses and gratifications assumption of an active audience. If audience members are to select from among various media and nonmedia alternatives according to their needs, they must have some perception of the alternatives most likely to meet those needs" (p. 538).

Expectancy-value theory suggests that "people orient themselves to the world according to their expectations (beliefs) and evaluations" (Littlejohn, 1989, p. 275). Utilizing this approach, behavior, behavioral intentions, or attitudes are seen as a function of "(1) expectancy (or belief)—the perceived probability that an object possesses a particular attribute or that a behavior will have a particular consequence; and (2) evaluation—the degree of affect, positive or negative, toward an attribute or behavioral outcome" (Palmgreen, 1984, p. 36).

From an expectancy-value perspective, Palmgreen has constructed a process model of gratifications sought and gratifications obtained that states that "the products of beliefs (expectations) and evaluations influence the seeking of gratifications, which, in turn, influence media consumption. Such consumption results in the perception of certain gratifications obtained, which then feed back to reinforce or alter an individual's perceptions of the gratification-related attributes of a particular newspaper, program, program genre, or whatever" (pp. 36–37). Palmgreen's formula for this generalized orientation to seek various gratifications parallels that of the general expectancy-value formula (see p. 146) and is stated:

$$\sum_{i=1}^{n} GS_i = \sum_{i=1}^{n} b_i e_i$$

In other words, if an individual evaluates information about football and believes (expects) that the Entertainment Sports Programming Network (ESPN) would best supply that information, he or she will be motivated to

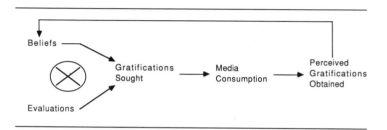

FIG. 9.4. Schematic model of expectancy-value theory (from Palmgreen, 1984. Reprinted by permission).

seek such information from ESPN, as is explained in Fig. 9.4. If the individual obtains the expected information about football (gratifications obtained), it should feed back in a cyclical process to reinforce previous beliefs about ESPN being a good source of information. In addition, if the individual obtains football information at a higher or lower level than expected, it should produce a subsequent change in beliefs about ESPN as well as affect the motivation to seek football information from that source. Thus, the combination of beliefs and evaluations developed via this process about a program, a program genre, the content, or a specific medium could be either positive or negative. If positive, it is likely that the individual would continue to use that media choice; if negative, then one would avoid it.

However, although expectancy value theory can be used to explain central concepts in uses and gratifications research, there are other factors that influence the process. Palmgreen (1984) devised a schematic model that

> integrates what is known about media consumption on the basis of uses and gratifications research and research in other social science disciplines. . . . The integrative model, while taking into account the feedback from gratifications obtained to those sought, also considers (among other things) the social and psychological origins of needs, values, and beliefs, which give rise to motives for behavior, which may be guided by beliefs, values, and social circumstances into seeking various gratifications through media consumption and other nonmedia behaviors. (p. 46)

No single element or concept dominates the model, but, as is indicated in Fig. 9.5, it shows that gratifications sought cannot be viewed in isolation, connected as they are in both antecedent and consequent fashion to a host of media, perceptual, social, and psychological variables. In addition to the expectancy-value approach, several other categories of uses and gratifications research are currently being pursued. Rubin (in press) listed six active research directions:

1. Links among media-use motives and their associations with media attitudes and behaviors.

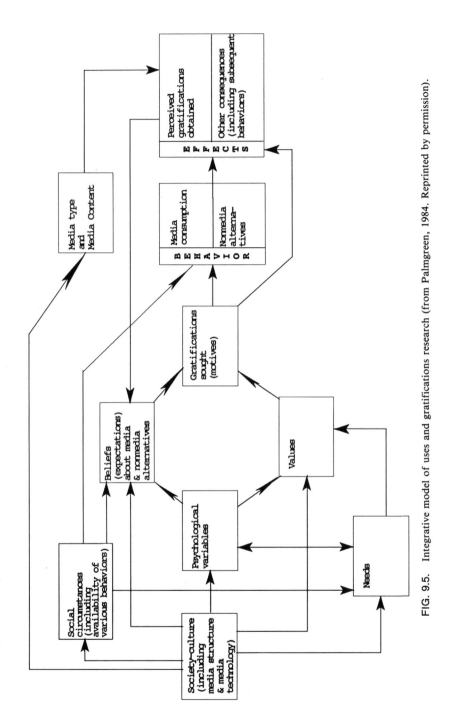

FIG. 9.5.　Integrative model of uses and gratifications research (from Palmgreen, 1984. Reprinted by permission).

287

2. Comparing motives across media or content.
3. Examining social and psychological circumstances of media use.
4. Links between gratifications sought and obtained when using media or their content.
5. Assessing how variations in background variables, motives, and exposure affect outcomes such as the effects of exposure or motivation on relational perceptions, cultivation, involvement, parasocial interaction, satisfaction, and political knowledge.
6. Methods for measuring and analyzing motivation including reliability and validity.

While the study of uses and gratifications has gained momentum in recent years, it has been criticized from its beginning by a host of mass communication scholars. One recurring complaint, voiced by McQuail (1984), is that "no common model, set of procedures or purposes informs the tradition . . . It is essentially lacking in theory and such theory it has is inadequate and confused" (pp. 181–182). That critique seems "dated" in light of current theory development in this area. Another criticism focuses on social and political objections from the perspective of critical theory, which has depicted uses and gratifications research as "pollyanaish," in that it tends to view media consumption almost exclusively in positive terms. By focusing on the fact that media meet people's needs, the criticism tends to ignore the overall negative effects of media on the culture.

A final common criticism of uses and gratifications research is that it offers a more rational view of media users than is realistic. This criticism notes that people frequently use media without thinking about their needs and gratifications, operating "mindlessly" or ritualistically. Then when asked to complete a questionnaire, they "rationalize" their viewing in ways that may not accurately reflect their true motives. Rubin (1986, in press) has addressed these criticisms rather convincingly.

Play Theory and Entertainment Theories. Closely related to uses and gratifications research is play theory and entertainment theory. As previously stated, many mass communication theories have originated in other social scientific disciplines. For example, psychological theories, such as learning theories, have been extended and generalized to include media socialization. Freud's *pleasure principle,* an early theory of psychological gratifications, has been applied to the consumption and enjoyment of media messages. Freud stated that all activities, psychological and social, are the product of a fundamental need to reduce emotional tension. People are motivated to alleviate disagreeable states that they experience consciously and painfully. Pleasure is a means of tension reduction, and humans seek pleasure from both internal and external sources. The mass media are one source of pleasure readily available in our everyday environment. These pleasure-gratifying situations become learned and recognized, which increases the likelihood of repeating the pleasurable situation. You will recognize that this principle has been incorporated in some of the theories described thus far.

Drawing on Freud's principles, Stephenson (1967) proposed and empirically supported a mass communication theory based on such concepts of pain and pleasure, work and play. Stephenson's *play theory* maintains that audiences, whenever they are given the chance, will manipulate their media to serve their own needs. In addition, he stated that when pursuing media in their daily lives, audiences are engaged in pleasurable, ritualistic, and self-serving activities that are essentially playlike in nature. Enjoyment and contentment are inherent in activities that allow freedom of choice rather than social control. Play theory and the psychological principles on which it is based posit that individuality is preferable to being forced to work and to conform to the expectations of someone else. In a similar vein, Mendelsohn (1966) added that "when most people are confronted with a choice between deriving pleasure from 'serious' non-entertainment fare or from non-serious entertainment fare, they will choose the latter in much greater proportions than the former" (p. 143).

However, not all communication is characterized by play and pleasure. Purposeful activities expected to elicit a specific reaction from us, according to Stephenson, incorporate elements of work, pain, and social control. The distinction between play and pain rests, not in the communication per se nor in the motivations of the communicators and gatekeepers, but rather in the minds and behaviors of the audiences. For example, a medical student may derive much pleasure from viewing a television drama that includes a scene with a particularly complex operation. In contrast, a humanities student may find the experience distasteful and psychologically painful. Thus, it is the psychological orientation of the consumer that is critical in determining the extent to which that consumer is able to enjoy media content.

An emerging area that shares some concepts with play theory has been labeled *entertainment theory* (e.g., Zillmann & Bryant, 1986). The research focuses on message and audience variables in attempting to build more cohesive theories of mass entertainment. Such studies have examined the elements within media messages and the psychological and personality factors that, for example, cause viewers to ultimately enjoy a movie after the strain of watching 90 minutes of agonizing suspense sequences capped off with a mere 5-minute "happy ending" (or suspense resolution). A combination of physiological factors (such as varying levels of excitation experienced), and cognitive factors (such as how well the viewer like the resolution of the suspense), help determine the moviegoers' ultimate level of enjoyment of the presentation. Other related entertainment theories have been applied to understanding and predicting enjoyment from televised sporting events, horror movies, music videos, humor and comedy, and various other genres of media fare. Over 25 years ago, Mendelsohn (1966) stated:

> What is essential in the psychological study of mass entertainment is the precise discernment of those psychological needs that impel individuals to seek mass entertainment rather than other available sources of satisfaction. Nor will a mere cataloguing of such needs—either a priori or post hoc—suffice. What is called for here is a series of studies that first ascertain specific psychological needs via testing and clinical observation; second, trace the specific pathways, including the mass media, through which these explicitly stated needs are satisfied both temporarily and over relatively long time periods; third, weigh the relative importance of mass entertainment vis-à-vis other "outlets" in satisfying these specific needs; and fourth, determine the over-all consequence of these experiences to the totality of the individual's psyche. (pp. 172–173)

This is a rather tall order that should keep mass communication scholars busy for some time. Nonetheless, entertainment theory seems to be taking some important first steps in this direction.

Semiotics and Meaning Theories in Mass Communication

Throughout our discussion of the various concepts and theories of mass communication, two assumptions have been made. We have assumed that the audience is an active participant in the mass communication process (e.g., selective attention, perception, and retention; uses and gratifications research) and that mediated messages do have some "affect" on the audience (e.g., cultivation analysis, cultural and critical studies, social learning theory, or entertainment effects). Hall (1980) stated that contemporary research in mass communication concentrates on behavior manifestations of communication. It is assumed that meaning is constituted behaviorally or that behavior is meaning made manifest. Hall argued that "before a message can have an 'effect,' satisfy a 'need,' or be put to a 'use,' it must first be appropriate as a meaningful discourse and be meaningfully decoded" (p. 130). He called for increased research into the processes through which mediated messages become meaningful to audiences. Similarly, other researchers have questioned how identical mediated messages may be interpreted differently or in unintended ways by individuals. Such research postulates are not new but are being examined with fresh approaches utilizing both centuries-old and new methods.

Semiotics, or the analysis of signs and symbols, especially in language, has been used extensively in advertising and public relations research. One branch of semiotics attempts to decipher hidden messages and the system of codes through which people communicate both verbally and nonverbally, consciously and unconsciously. Charles Sanders Peirce is recognized as one of the great figures in the history of semiotics and as the founder of the modern theory of signs. Combining the work of Peirce at the turn of the century with more contemporary research by Umberto Eco, Fry and Fry (1986) attempted to reconceptualize the process of mass communication by utilizing the principles of semiotics. They merge Peirce's concepts of sign and interpretant with Eco's theory of semiotics "in which the process of signification is explained in terms of codes and the production of new signs" (Fry & Fry, 1986, p. 444). Fry and Fry's synthesis and extension of this research attempts to "account for both the media text and the audience's interpretation without reducing the importance of either" (p. 444). Fry and Fry stated:

> It is necessary to adopt an orientation that places total power neither in the media text (as has been implicit in some semiotic textual analyses) nor in the interpretive capacities of the audience member (a position that has been often implicit in the uses and gratifications approach). Thus, a semiotic model must address the question of the relative power of both the text and audience in determining the meaning of media texts. (p. 444)

The following postulate is essential to Fry and Fry's (1986) developing semiotic model: "Mass media messages are textual resources capable of engendering multiple levels of potential meanings. Because signs convey numerous intertwined meanings, that which is normally called a mass media message is, more appropriately, a text capable of producing multiple levels of meaning" (p. 445). Such applications of semiotic theory would seem to hold substantial promise if they retain their focus on the interplay of audiences and the meaning of media messages.

Other Modern Mass Communication Theories

Recently, mass communication theory has taken many interesting turns. It is beyond the potential of this chapter to represent all the perspectives and theories that currently comprise the body of knowledge of contemporary mass communication theory. Instead, we have selected and will present three emerging formulations that we think characterize fruitful lines of representative theory development in mass communication today.

Integrated Theories.   One potentially significant development in mass communication theory construction features attempts to consolidate various research perspectives and traditions into more integrated theories. Perhaps the outstanding exemplar in this tradition is DeFleur and Ball-Rokeach's (1989) media system *dependency theory* of mass communication. This theory is integrative in many ways: First, it combines perspectives from psychology with ingredients from social categories theory. Second, it integrates systems perspectives with elements from more causal approaches. Third, it combines elements of uses and gratifications research with those of media effects traditions, although its primary focus is less on effects per se than on rationales for why media effects typically are limited. Representative of this perspective are statements such as, "The surrounding sociocultural context provides controls and constraints not only on the nature of media messages but also on the nature of their effects on audiences" (p. 234). And, finally, a contextualist philosophy is incorporated into the theory, which also features traditional concerns with the content of media messages and their effects on audiences.

To date, research generated by this model has tended to be more descriptive than explanatory or predictive. Nonetheless, although "the jury is still out" on the place of dependency theory in the annals of mass communication theory, it continues to serve a useful role in casting researchers' gazes upon some of the more molar sociocultural issues that surround concerns with media effects.

Cognitive Theories. A second interesting turn in mass communication theory construction has been an increased emphasis on cognitive dimensions of mass communication. The 1970s and 1980s bore witness to extensive and seemingly productive inquiry into the "black box" of human cognition. Cognitive psychologists and sociologists joined forces with specialists in computer modeling and artificial intelligence to explore more carefully what might be going on in the minds of viewers, readers, and listeners of mass media messages. With this cognitive emphasis came a shift from an examination of effects to a focus on processes—a regular feature of our first mass communication formulations that seems to have been lost during the period of radical behaviorism during which much early mass communication theory developed. With this new focus on cognition came a shift in the nature of researchers' perceptions of communicators. Specifically, that portion of our theories that had been passive audiences during the period of the "magic bullet" gradually began to be reconceptualized as active users of media fare—users who have sometimes emerged as the "Sovereign Consumers" of media messages in today's rich media environments.

One common concern of the cognitive media theorists has been to identify and examine the place of purposeful or goal-directed media use. For example, one cognitive psychologist (Bargh, 1988) concluded that the nature of the media users' cognitive goals are critical in determining more than just what information they receive from media messages: "The type of information one attends to, how much attention one pays to it, how one encodes and interprets it, and consequently how one remembers it all are greatly influenced by one's processing goals while encountering the information" (p. 18). Furthermore, cognitive scientists have posited mental analogs, such as *schemas,* to explain why we process different types of media fare differently. For example, it has been claimed that well-developed cognitive schemas allow us to process highly repetitive media fare with minimal effort — so-called "top-down" processing; while exposure to novel or highly complex mediated information or entertainment requires a qualitatively different sort of process if such fare is to be mastered. Compare, for example, the simplicity of the schema required to follow your 100th episode of "The Beverly Hillbillies" with that required for fully comprehending "Mystery" on public television.

Like Van Evra's (1990) model of developmental socialization and De-Fleur and Ball-Rokeach's (1989) dependency theory, more recent cognitive models of mass communication processes have exhibited considerable complexity and elegance. For example, as expressed in Fig. 9.6, Thorson (1989) presented a model for the cognitive processing of television commercials that includes consideration of goal specification, memory mechanisms, language structure, emotional state, and distraction. Although complexity for complexity's sake certainly is not desirable, what we have learned in recent years about the cognitive processing of mass communication suggests that our models must be complex if they are to fairly and accurately represent the processes undergirding the complex behaviors involved in selecting and using media messages.

Cultural and Critical Studies. Another set of approaches to mass communication theory that has received considerable scholarly attention of late are cultural and critical studies. These approaches to mass communication theory were spawned by European researchers in the 1950s, but it has only been during the past decade that they have captured much of the interest of American communication scholars. Many of these theoretical perspectives have their roots in the Marxist critical tradition, which typically has been seen as having two main areas of focus: the "politics of textuality" and the "problematic of cultural studies." Grossberg (1983) made this statement: "The politics of textuality concerns the ways in which media producers encode messages, the ways in which audiences decode those messages, and the power domination apparent in these processes . . . The problematic of cultural studies examines more closely the relation among media, other institutions in society, and the ideology of culture" (p. 52). These traditions frequently are concerned with the evils and injustices of a

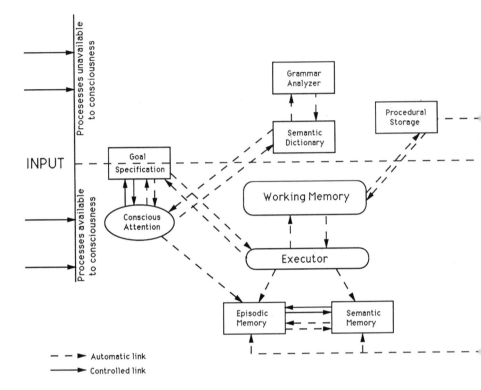

FIG. 9.6. A cognitive model of information processing of television commercials (from Thorson, 1989. Reprinted by permission).

ruling elite and a social class system, as well as how the social structure is formed and reinforced via the actions of individuals, groups, and institutions. It is important to note that although proponents of these traditions view the mass media as important and powerful institutions, the media are perceived to be but one influence in a complex social structure that attempts to dominate the ideology of a people. Other influences include education, government, and religion.

One of the prevalent traditions to emerge in this domain is that of British Cultural Studies. Many scholars adhering to this approach have sought to change or reform western society via their scholarship. This change is said to occur by identifying contradictions in society and suggesting resolutions that will lead to positive change.

Many American cultural theorists have also seen themselves as agents of social change. For example, via detailed scholarship, they have first identified and publicized how the agents of control—media for example—have sustained the dominant ideology of capitalism. Such revelations are intended to help people realize how media are instruments of a power struggle controlled by an elite group. Another step that has been taken quite frequently has been to point out to the populace what can be done to shift power back to them. Becker (1984) articulated this role clearly: "These communication scholars want to keep jarring both the audience and the workers in the media back from becoming too accepting of their illusions or existing practices so they will question them and their conditions" (p. 67).

The usefulness of the cultural studies tradition to American mass media studies is evidenced by its growth in prominence. As we have suggested, it is substantially different from the other theories we have discussed. A primary reason for this is that most of its roots are in the humanities, whereas those of the other theories we have reviewed are in the social and behavioral sciences. To some people, this makes cultural studies incompatible with mass communication theory construction. We do not see it that way. We find these diverse positions complementary and ideally reflective of the complexity of the contemporary mass communication milieu. As Grossberg (1983) indicated, cultural studies, "as a theory of communication . . . opens new possibilities for the discipline by interrogating the place of communication within the production of the real, a place that we recently have begun to take for granted" (p. 70).

NEW MODELS DICTATED BY NEW MEDIA

To this point, our treatment has focused on mass communication without featuring a great deal of discussion about the evolving nature of the mass communication process. In reality, mediated communication with large, heterogeneous, and anonymous audiences is becoming a thing of the past. One of the important trends of the 1980s was the fragmentation of media audiences into smaller and more homogeneous mini-audiences whose essential characteristics were rather well known by editors, programmers, media planners, and other gatekeepers. This period in media development was a time of audience fragmentation and audience segmentation. In order to survive, media entities have gradually changed form to suit the needs and interests of their consumers (e.g., general interest magazines have died or altered their form and mission substantially, radio has sought niche formats), or have lost sizeable portions of their audience (e.g., network television has lost many of its viewers to specialized cable programming).

The 1990s promise even more radical shifts in perspectives and processes, shifts that our communication theories and models must reflect if they are to remain veridical and, thereby, useful. It is almost certain that the decade of the 1990s will yield a generation of addressable users of micro-multimedia. Each element of that emphasized phrase warrants far more explication than can be provided in this text, but we would be remiss if we did not offer just a few words of annotation.

First, *addressable;* by this we mean that, in the near future, media messages will no longer be sent "to whom it may concern." Indeed, they will be selected and "downloaded" by parties whose name, address, identification number, and demographic and marketing profile is a part of the media distributor's data base. Communication systems such as this already are operational in places like The Woodlands, Texas, and Santa Monica, California. The degree of efficiency and profitability such communication systems will provide surely will make them commonplace by the turn of the century, despite the increased expenses of initial installation and start-up.

Secondly, why the shift from audiences to *users?* How can we call "an audience" an active aggregate of media users who can and will, by programming a scanner, actively select from thousands of informational, educational, and entertainment options? We cannot. Some have called him or her "the sovereign consumer of the information age." We prefer the less pretentious label of "media user."

Finally, what do we mean by *micro-, multimedia?* The changes that support this seemingly innocent term are revolutionary. They are also multidimensional. At the core are essential alterations to the communications skeleton of our nation (and, indeed, our world!), a backbone of which many of us are not even aware. But the technological, operational, and functional shifts that are taking place in the communications infrastructure of modern society soon will be felt by every citizen. In the future, albeit still some years away, is an intelligent network. This advanced information system will be supported by a spinal column comprised of a fiber optic-based, broadband integrated services digital network (B-ISDN). The technology is not our present concern, but its potential to deliver diverse, customized functions and incredibly specialized media messages is our concern. When media messages are encoded into a digital format, video, audio, and textual messages can be combined in an almost unlimited way. As Brand (1988) wrote quite poetically in *The Media Lab: Inventing the Future at MIT:*

> With digitalization all of the media become translatable into each other — computer bits migrate merrily — and escape from their traditional means of transmission. A movie, phone call, letter, or magazine article may be sent digitally via phone line, coaxial cable, fiber optic cable, microwave, satellite, the broadcast air, or a physical storage medium such as tape or disk. If that's not revolution enough, with digitalization the content becomes totally plastic — any message, sound, or image may be edited from anything into anything else. (p. 19)

This plastic translation of message form is what we refer to as a multimedia format. The fact that the form can readily be shaped to suit the desires of an individual user is signalled by the term *micromedia*. Certainly the prototypical scenario for typical media use under the micro-, multimedia environment is miles removed from what our intellectual ancestors meant by mass communication.

Rogers (1986) made many of the same points, and some additional ones, using a different vocabulary. He noted the following:

> What is different about human communication as a result of the new technologies?
>
> 1. All of the new communication systems have at least a certain degree of *interactivity*, something like a two-person, face-to-face conversation. . . .
>
> 2. The new media are also *de-massified,* to the degree that a special message can be exchanged with each individual in a large audience. . . .
>
> 3. The new communication technologies are also *asynchronous,* meaning they have the capability for sending or receiving a message at a time convenient for an individual. . . .
>
> Many changes can indeed be traced to the new technologies, but the way in which individuals *use* the technologies is driving the Information Revolution . . . (pp. 4–8)

Attempts to build comprehensive communication theory that would account for these significant shifts have occurred at two different levels. Macro-analytical models have been offered to guide our understanding of the relationships between communications infrastructure, technologies, communication policies, and society. For example, in an extremely comprehensive and useful report entitled *Critical Connections: Communication for the Future,* the Office of Technology Assessment (1990, p. 35) of the U.S. Congress proposed this "Interactive Model of Communication and Society." In Fig. 9.7, 1a. represents the effect of all social, economic, political, and cultural activities engendered by the activities of the "communication regime" (1); 1b. plots the effects of the communication regime on the values and positions of key decisionmakers; and 1c. indicates how activities within the communication regime will also affect the level and direction of technological development. All of the "operations" associated with 2 refer to the interaction of social forces and technological advances. 2a. indicates that their interaction will create new ways of carrying out economic, political, cultural, and social activities as well as new opportunities and constraints. That these same interactions also create new communication needs and desires and change the key parties' perceptions of their interests is indicated in 2b. The potential opportunities and constraints posed by new technology is presented as 3. 3a. shows that these opportunities and constraints may alter the position and status of the key participants (e.g, opinion leaders) in the process-the so-called stakeholders,

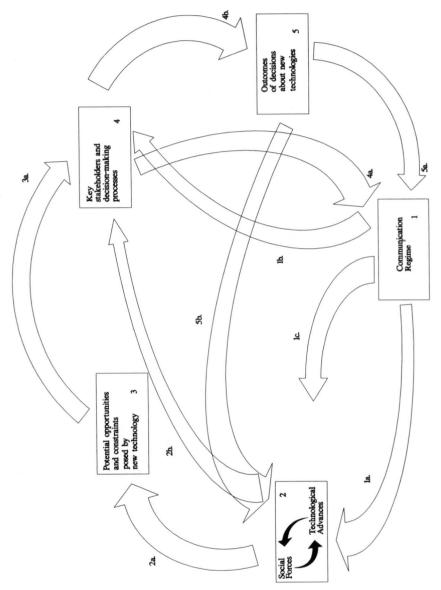

FIG. 9.7. An interactive model of media and society (from Office of Technology Assessment, 1990).

represented in 4. 4a. is the pathway for stakeholders to influence the communication regime via their decisions; 4b. represents how the stakeholders' decision-making processes affect the outcomes of decisions about new technologies in society (5). Finally, 5a. plots the pathway by which outcomes of decisions about new technologies affect the communication regime.

This molar model is useful if it accurately describes the overarching "players" and essential relationships in the realm of communication and society, and if it guides research that explains and predicts how technology changes society and vice-versa. Nonetheless, it is presented at a much more macroanalytic level than most of the models and theories we have considered in this chapter. Those models that have focused on the human and message elements of the new multimedia environment have also tended to depart rather radically from orthodoxy — for example, the Shannon-Weaver paradigm. (Recall this discussion in chapters 2 and 3 of this volume.) If they are to be accurate representations of the new media environment and the communication processes of the users of new media, they must depart radically from orthodoxy. As Rogers (1986) indicated:

> The new media are having a powerful influence on the nature of communication research, unfreezing this field from many of its past assumptions, prior paradigms and methods. As we have stated previously, the predominant linear models of one-way communication effects must give way to convergence models of communication as a two-way process of information exchange, due to the interactivity of new media. (p. 213)

The Office of Technology Assessment (1990) report offered a slightly different slant but reflects similar concerns:

> The sender/receiver model is also much too orderly to describe many of today's mediated communication processes. It assumes that communication takes place as a consistent, linear sequence of events — an assumption that is not supportable in today's technology-mediated information environment. With a computerized bulletin board, for example, how does one identify and distinguish between who is the sender and who is the receiver? And, similarly, who is considered the sender when the receiver can now access information on demand? (pp. 31–32)

The Office of Technology Assessment (1990, p. 33) offered the following simple model (Fig. 9.8) to indicate the transactional nature veridical communication theories must assume in the multimedia environment. Their model "highlights interrelationships and interdependencies and institutions" (p. 32) and brings a multidimensional approach to communication, which is

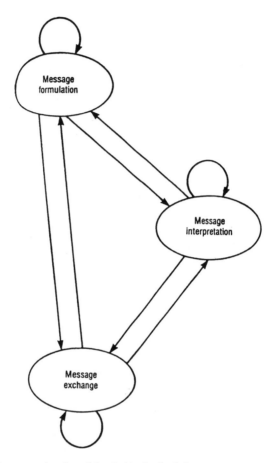

FIG. 9.8.   A transactional model suitable for both interperson communication and interactive mediated communication (from Office of Technology Assessment, 1990).

defined in the context of this model as *"the process by which messages are formulated, exchanged, and interpreted"* (p. 31).

One of the appropriate things that this definition does is bring this chapter full circle. We began with interpersonal communication; we end with a definition that spans interpersonal and multimedia communication. That is most appropriate, because as far as theory construction in the new mediated environment is concerned, "we've only just begun." May our journey be happy and rewarding.

References

Adler, R. P. (1980). Children's television advertising: History of the issue. In E. L. Palmer & A. Dorr (Eds.). *Children and the faces of television: Teaching, violence, selling* (pp. 237–249). New York: Academic Press.

Ajzen, I., & Fishbein, M. (1980). *Understanding attitudes and predicting social behavior.* Englewood Cliffs, NJ: Prentice-Hall.

Allen, M., Hale, J., Mongeau, P., Berkowitz-Stafford, S., Stafford, S., Shanahan, W., Agee, P., Dillon, K., Jackson, R., & Ray, C. (1990). Testing a model of message sidedness: Three replications. *Communication Monographs, 57,* 275–291.

Alberts, J. K. (1988). An analysis of couples' conversational complaints. *Communication Monographs, 55,* 184–197.

Albrecht, T. L. (1984). Managerial communication and work perception. In R. N. Bostrom & B. H. Westley (Eds.), *Communication yearbook 8* (pp. 538–557). Newbury Park, CA: Sage.

Allport, G. E. (1935). Attitudes. In C. Murchison (Ed.), *Handbook of social psychology* (Vol. 2, pp. 798–844). Worcester, MA: Clark University Press.

Alper, S. W., & Leidy, T. R. (1969). The impact of information transmission through television. *Public Opinion Quarterly, 33,* 556–562.

Altman, I., & Taylor, D. A. (1973). *Social penetration: The development of interpersonal relationships.* New York: Holt, Rinehart & Winston.

Altman, I., Vinsel, A., & Brown, B. B. (1981). Dialectic conceptions in social psychology: An application to social penetration and privacy regulation. In L. Berkowitz (Ed.), *Advances in experimental social psychology* (Vol. 14, pp. 107–160). New York: Academic Press.

Andersen, P. A. (1985). Nonverbal immediacy in interpersonal communication. In A. W. Siegman & S. Feldstein (Eds.), *Multichannel integrations of nonverbal behavior* (pp. 1–36). Hillsdale, NJ: Lawrence Erlbaum Associates.

Anderson, J. D. (1985). Indexing systems: Extensions of the mind's organizing power. In B. D. Ruben (Ed.), *Information and behavior* (Vol. 1, pp. 287–323). New Brunswick, NJ: Transaction Books.

Andrews, P. H. (1987). Gender differences in persuasive communication and attribution of success and failure. *Human Communication Research, 13,* 372–385.

Aristotle (1954). *Rhetoric* (W. R. Robert, Trans.). New York: Modern Library.

Ashby, W. R. (1963). *An introduction to cybernetics.* New York: Science Editions.

Atkin, C. K. (1980). Effects of television advertising on children. In E. L. Palmer & A. Dorr (Eds.), *Children and the faces of television: Teaching, violence, selling* (pp. 287–304). New York: Academic Press.

Austin, J. L. (1962). *How to do things with words.* Cambridge: Harvard University Press.

Austin, J. L. (1964). *Philosophy of language.* Englewood Cliffs, NJ: Prentice-Hall.

Babbitt, L. V., & Jablin, F. M. (1985). Characteristics of applicants' questions and employment screening interview outcomes. *Human Communication Research, 11,* 507–535.

Babrow, A. S., & Swanson, D. L. (1988). Disentangling antecedents of audience exposure levels: Extending expectancy-value analysis of gratifications sought from television news. *Communication Monographs, 55,* 1–21.

Baglan, T., Lalumia, J., & Bayless, O. L. (1986). Utilization of compliance-gaining strategies: A research note. *Communication Monographs, 53,* 289–293.

Bandura, A. (1977). *Social learning theory.* Englewood Cliffs, NJ: Prentice-Hall.

Bandura, A. (1986). *Social foundations of thought and action: A social cognitive theory.* Englewood Cliffs, NJ: Prentice-Hall.

Bandura, A., & Walters, R. (1963). *Social learning and personality development.* New York: Holt, Rinehart & Winston.

Barcus, F. E. (1980). The nature of television advertising to children. In E. L. Palmer & A. Dorr (Eds.), *Children and the faces of television: Teaching, violence, selling* (pp. 283–285). New York: Academic Press.

Bargh, J. A. (1988). Automatic information processing: Implications for communication and affect. In L. Donohew, H. E. Sypher, & E. T. Higgins (Eds.), *Communication, social cognition, and affect* (pp. 9–32). Hillsdale, NJ: Lawrence Erlbaum Associates.

Bauchner, J. E., Brandt, D. R., & Miller, G. R. (1977). The truth/deception attribution: Effects of varying levels of information availability. In B. D. Ruben, (Ed.), *Communication yearbook 1* (pp. 229–243). New Brunswick, NJ: Transaction Books.

Baxter, L. A. (1982). Strategies for ending relationships: Two studies. *Western Journal of Speech Communication, 46,* 223–241.

Baxter, L. A. (1990). Dialectical contradictions in relationship development. *Journal of Social and Personal Relationships, 7,* 69–88.

Baxter, L. A., & Bullis, C. (1986). Turning points in developing romantic relationships. *Human Communication Research, 12,* 469–493.

Baxter, L. A., & Wilmot, W. W. (1984). "Secret tests" social strategies for acquiring information about the state of the relationship. *Human Communication Research, 11,* 171–201.

Beatty, M. J., & Payne, S. K. (1985). Is construct differentiation loquacity? A motivational perspective. *Human Communication Research, 11,* 605–612.

Becker, S. L. (1984). Marxist approaches to media studies: The British experience. *Critical Studies in Mass Communication, 1,* 66–80.

Bell, R. A., Buerkel-Rothfuss, N. L., & Core, K. E. (1987). "Did you bring the yarmulke for the Cabbage Patch Kid?" The idiomatic communication of young lovers. *Human Communication Research, 14,* 47–67.

Bell, R. A., & Daly, J. A. (1984). The affinity-seeking function of communication. *Communication Monographs, 51,* 91–115.

Bem, D. J. (1965). An experimental analysis of self-persuasion. *Journal of Experimental Social Psychology, 1,* 199–218.

Bem, D. J. (1968). Attitudes as self-descriptions: Another look at the attitude-behavior link. In A. G. Greenwald, T. C. Brock, & T. M. Ostrom (Eds.), *Psychological foundations of attitudes* (pp. 197–215). New York: Academic Press.

Bem, D. J. (1970). *Beliefs, attitudes, and human affairs.* Belmont, CA: Brooks/Cole.

Bem, D. J. (1972). Self-perception theory. In L. Berkowitz (Ed.), *Advances in experimental social psychology* (Vol. 6, pp. 2–63). New York: Academic Press.

Berelson, B. (1959). The state of communication research. *Public Opinion Quarterly, 23,* 1–6.

Berelson, B., & Steiner, G. A. (1964). *Human behavior: An inventory of scientific findings.* New York: Harcourt, Brace & World.

Berger, C. R. (1975). Proactive and retroactive attribution processes in interpersonal communications. *Human Communication Research, 2,* 33–50.

Berger, C. R. (1977a). The covering law perspective as a theoretical basis for the study of human communication. *Communication Quarterly, 25,* 7–18.

Berger, C. R. (1977b). Interpersonal communication theory and research: An overview. In B. D. Ruben (Ed.), *Communication yearbook 1* (pp. 217–228). New Brunswick, NJ: Transaction Books.

Berger, C. R. (1985). Social power and interpersonal communication. In M. L. Knapp & G. R. Miller (Eds.), *Handbook of interpersonal communication* (pp. 439–499). Newbury Park, CA: Sage.

Berger, C. R. (1987). Communicating under uncertainty. In M. E. Roloff & G. R. Miller (Eds.), *Interpersonal processes: New directions in communication research* (pp. 39–62). Newbury Park, CA: Sage.

Berger, C. R. (1988). Planning, affect, and social action generation. In L. Donohew, H. E. Sypher, & E. T. Higgins (Eds.), *Communication, social cognition, and affect* (pp. 93–116). Hillsdale, NJ: Lawrence Erlbaum Associates.

Berger, C. R., & Bell, R. A. (1988). Plans and the initiation of social relationships. *Human Communication Research, 15,* 217–235.

Berger, C. R., & Bradac, J. J. (1982). *Language and social knowledge: Uncertainty in interpersonal relations.* London: Edward Arnold.

Berger, C. R. & Calabrese, R. J. (1975). Some explorations in initial interaction and beyond: Toward a developmental theory of interpersonal communication. *Human Communication Research, 1,* 99–112.

Berger, C. R., & Douglas, W. (1982) Thought and talk: "Excuse me, but have I been talking to myself?" In F. E. X. Dance (Ed.), *Human communication theory: Comparative essays* (pp. 42–60). New York: Harper & Row.

Berger, C. R., Karol, S. H., Jordan, J. M. (1989). When a lot of knowledge is a dangerous thing: The debilitating effects of plan complexity in verbal fluency. *Human Communication Research, 16,* 91–119.

Berger, C. R., Weber, M. D., Munley, M. E., & Dixon, J. T. (1977). Interpersonal relationship levels and interpersonal attraction. In B. D. Ruben (Ed.), *Communication yearbook 1* (pp. 245–261). New Brunswick, NJ: Transaction Books.

Berger, P., & Luckmann, T. (1966). *The social construction of reality.* Garden City, NY: Doubleday.

Berlo, D. K. (1960). *Communication: An introduction to theory and practice.* New York: Holt, Rinehart & Winston.

Berlo, D. K. (1977). Communication as process: Review and commentary. In B. D. Ruben (Ed.), *Communication yearbook 1* (pp. 11–27). New Brunswick, NJ: Transaction Books.

Berlo, D. K., Lemert, J. B., & Mertz, R. J. (1969). Dimensions for evaluating the acceptability of message sources. *Public Opinion Quarterly, 33,* 563–576.

Bertalanffy, L. (1968). *General system theory: Foundations, development, applications.* New York: Braziller.

Bineham, J. L. (1988). A historical account of the hypodermic model of mass communication. *Communication Monographs, 55,* 230–246.

Black, J., & Bryant, J. (in press). *Introduction to mass communication* (3rd ed.). Dubuque, IA: Brown.

Blankenship, J. (1974). The influence of mode, sub-mode, and speaker predilection on style. *Speech Monographs, 41,* 85–118.

Blascovich, J., & Ginsburg, G. P. (1974). Emergent norms and choice shifts involving risk, *Sociometry, 37,* 205-218.

Blau, G. J. (1985). Source-related determinants of perceived job scope. *Human Communication Research, 11,* 536-553.

Blumler, J. G. (1979). The role of theory in uses and gratifications studies. *Communication Research, 6,* 9-36.

Blumler, J. G., & Katz, E. (Eds.). (1974). *The uses of mass communications: Current perspectives on gratifications research.* Newbury Park, CA: Sage.

Booth-Butterfield, S. (1987). Action assembly theory and communication apprehension: A psychophysiological study. *Human Communication Research, 13,* 386-398.

Bormann, E. C. (1983). Symbolic convergence: Organizational communication and culture. In L. L. Putnam & M. E. Pacanowsky (Eds.), *Communication and organizations: An interpretive approach* (pp. 99-122). Newbury Park: Sage.

Boster, F. J., & Mongeau, P. (1984). Fear-arousing persuasive messages. In R. N. Bostrom (Ed.), *Communication yearbook 8* (pp. 330-375). Newbury Park, CA: Sage.

Boster, F. J., & Stiff, J. B. (1984). Compliance-gaining message selection behavior. *Human Communication Research, 10,* 539-556.

Boulanger, F., & Fischer, D. G. (1971). Leadership and the group-shift phenomenon. *Perceptual and Motor Skills, 33,* 1251-1258.

Bowers, J. W. (1963). Language intensity, social introversion, and attitude change. *Speech Monographs, 30,* 345-352.

Bowers, J. W., & Bradac, J. J. (1982). Issues in communication theory: A metatheoretic analysis. In M. Burgoon (Ed.), *Communication yearbook 5* (pp. 1-27). New Brunswick, NJ: Transaction Books.

Boyanowsky, E. O. (1977). Film preferences under conditions of threat. *Communication Research, 4,* 133-144.

Bradac, J. J., Bowers, J. W., & Courtright, J. A. (1979). Three language variables in communication research: Intensity, immediacy, and diversity. *Human Communication Research, 5,* 257-269.

Bradac, J. J., & Mulac, A. (1984). A molecular view of powerful and powerless speech styles: Attributional consequences and specific language features and communicator intentions. *Communication Monographs, 51,* 307-319.

Brand, S. (1988). *The media lab: Inventing the future at MIT.* New York: Penguin.

Brenders, D. A. (1987). Fallacies in the coordinated management of meaning: A philosophy of language critique of the hierarchical organization of coherent conversation and related theory. *Quarterly Journal of Speech, 73,* 329-348.

Broadhurst, A. R., & Darnell, D. K. (1965). An introduction to cybernetics and information theory. *Quarterly Journal of Speech, 51,* 442-453.

Bryant, J. (1990). *Television and the American family.* Hillsdale, NJ: Lawrence Erlbaum Associates.

Bryant, J., & Street, R. L., Jr. (1988). From reactivity to activity and action: An evolving a concept and *Weltanschauung* in mass and interpersonal communication. In R. P. Hawkins, J. M. Wiemann, & S. Pingree (Eds.), *Advancing communication science: Merging mass and interpersonal processes* (Vol. 16, pp. 162-190). Newbury Park, CA: Sage.

Buller, D. B., & Aune, R. K. (1988). The effects of vocalics and nonverbal sensitivity on compliance: A speech accommodation theory explanation. *Human Communication Research, 14,* 301-332.

Buller, D. B., & Burgoon, J. K. (1986). The effects of vocalics and nonverbal sensitivity on compliance: A replication and extension. *Human Communication Research, 13,* 126-144.

Buller, D. B., Strzewski, K. D., & Comstock, J. (1991). Interpersonal deception: I. Deceivers' reactions to receivers' suspicions and probing. *Communication Monographs, 58,* 1-24.

Burggraf, C. S., & Sillars, A. L. (1987). A critical examination of sex differences in marital communication. *Communication Monographs, 54,* 276–294.

Burgoon, J. K. (1975). Conflicting information, attitude, message variables as predictors of learning and persuasion. *Human Communication Research, 1,* 133–144.

Burgoon, J. K. (1985). Nonverbal signals. In M. L. Knapp & G. R. Miller (Eds.), *Handbook of interpersonal communication* (pp. 344–390). Newbury Park, CA: Sage.

Burgoon, J. K., & Aho, L. (1982). Three field experiments on the effects of violations on conversational distance. *Communication Monographs, 49,* 71–88.

Burgoon, J. K., Birk, T., & Pfau, M. (1990). Nonverbal behaviors, persuasion, and credibility. *Human Communication Research, 17,* 140–169.

Burgoon, J. K., Buller, D. B., Hale, J. L., & deTurck, M. A. (1984). Relational messages associated with nonverbal behaviors. *Human Communication Research, 10,* 351–378.

Burgoon, J. K., Pfau, M., Parrott, R., Birk, T., Coker, R., & Burgoon, M. (1987). Relational communication, satisfaction, compliance-gaining strategies, and compliance in communication between physicians and patients. *Communication Monographs, 54,* 307–324.

Burgoon, J. K., Coker, D. A., & Coker, R. A. (1986). Communicative effects of gaze behavior: A test of two contrasting explanations. *Human Communication Research, 12,* 469–493.

Burgoon, J. K., & Hale, J. L. (1984). The fundamental topoi of relational communication. *Communication Monographs, 51,* 193–214.

Burgoon, J. K., & Hale, J. L. (1987). Validation and measurement of the fundamental themes of relational communication. *Communication Monographs, 54,* 19–41.

Burgoon, J. K., & Hale, J. L. (1988). Nonverbal expectancy violations: Model elaboration and application to immediacy behaviors. *Communication Monographs, 55,* 58–79.

Burgoon, J. K., & Koper, R. J. (1984). Nonverbal and relational communication associated with reticence. *Human Communication Research, 10,* 601–626.

Burgoon, M., & King, L. B. (1974). The mediation of resistance to persuasion strategies by language variables and active-passive participation. *Human Communication Research, 1,* 30–41.

Burke, K. (1934, May 2). The meaning of C. K. Ogden. *New Republic, 78,* 328–331.

Burke, K. (1952). "Ethan Brand": A preparatory investigation. *Hopkins Review, 5,* 45–65.

Burke, K. (1958). The poetic motive. *Hudson Review, 40,* 54–63.

Burke, K. (1961). *Attitudes toward history.* Boston: Beacon Press. (Original work published 1937)

Burke, K. (1964). On form. *Hudson Review, 17,* 103–109.

Burke, K. (1965). *Permanence and change.* Indianapolis: Bobbs-Merrill. (Original work published 1935)

Burke, K. (1966). *Language as symbolic action.* Berkeley: University of California Press.

Burke, K. (1969a). *A grammar of motives.* Berkeley: University of California Press. (Original work published 1945)

Burke, K. (1969b). *A rhetoric of motives.* Berkeley: University of California Press. (Original work published 1950)

Burleson, B. R., Levine, B. J., & Samter, W. (1984). Decision making procedure and decision quality. *Human Communication Research, 10,* 557–574.

Burleson, B. R., Wilson, S. R., Waltman, M. S., Goering, E. M., Ely, T. K., & Whaley, B. B. (1988). Item desirability effects in compliance-gaining research: Seven studies documenting artifacts in the strategy selection procedure. *Human Communication Research, 14,* 429–486.

Cacioppo, J. T., Harkins, S. G., & Petty, R. E. (1981). The nature of attitudes and cognitive responses and their relationships to behavior. In R. Petty, T. Ostrom, & T. Brock (Eds.), *Cognitive responses in persuasion* (pp. 31–54). Hillsdale, NJ: Lawrence Erlbaum Associates.

Cacioppo, J. T., & Petty, R. E. (1979). Effects of message repetition and position on cognitive responses, recall, and persuasion. *Journal of Personality and Social Psychology, 37,* 97–109.

Camden, C. T., & Kennedy, C. W. (1986). Manager communicative style and nurse morale. *Human Communication Research, 12,* 551–563.

Cappella, J. N. (1977). Research methodology in communication: Review and commentary. In B. D. Ruben (Ed.), *Communication yearbook 1* (pp. 37–53). New Brunswick, NJ: Transaction Books.

Cappella, J. N. (1985). The management of conversations. In M. L. Knapp & G. R. Miller (Eds.), *Handbook of interpersonal communication* (pp. 393–443). Newbury Park, CA: Sage.

Cappella, J. N. (1987). Interpersonal communication: Definitions and fundamental questions. In C. R. Berger & S. H. Chaffee (Eds.), *Handbook of communication science* (pp. 184–238). Newbury Park, CA: Sage.

Cappella, J. N., & Greene, J. O. (1982). A discrepancy-arousal explanation of mutual influence in expressive behavior for adult-adult and infant-adult interaction. *Communication Monographs, 49,* 89–114.

Cassirer, E. (1946). *Language and myth* (S. K. Langer, Trans.). New York: Harper & Brothers.

Cassirer, E. (1953). *The philosophy of symbolic forms. Vol I, Language* (R. Manheim, Trans.) New Haven: Yale University Press.

Chaffee, S. H. (1988). Differentiating the hypodermic model from empirical research: A comment on Bineham's commentaries. *Communication Monographs, 55,* 247–249.

Chaffee, S. H., & Roser, C. (1986). Involvement and the consistency of knowledge, attitudes, and behaviors. *Communication Research, 13,* 373–399.

Chaffee, S., & Wilson D. G. (1977). Media rich, media poor: Two studies of diversity in agenda-holding. *Journalism Quarterly, 54,* 466–476.

Cheney, G., & Vibbert, S. L. (1987). Corporate discourse: Public relations and issue management. In F. M. Jablin, L. L. Putnam, K. H. Roberts, & L. W. Porter (Eds.), *Handbook of organizational communication* (pp. 165–194). Newbury Park, CA: Sage.

Cherry, C. (1978). *On human communication* (3rd ed.). Cambridge, MA: MIT Press.

Cialdini, R. B., Petty, R. E., & Cacioppo, J. T. (1981). Attitude and attitude change. *Annual Review of Psychology, 32,* 357–404.

Cody, M. J., & McLaughlin, M. L. (1980). Perceptions of compliance-gaining situations: A dimensional analysis. *Communication Monographs, 47,* 132–148.

Cody, M. J., & McLaughlin, M. L. (1985). The situation as a construct in interpersonal communication research. In M. L. Knapp & G. R. Miller (Eds.), *Handbook of interpersonal communication* (pp. 263–312). Newbury Park, CA: Sage.

Cohen, B. (1963). *The press and foreign policy.* Princeton, NJ: Princeton University Press.

Coker, D. A., & Burgoon, J. K. (1987). The nature of conversational involvement and nonverbal encoding patterns. *Human Communication Research, 13,* 463–494.

Conant, R. C. (1979). A vector theory of information. In D. Nimmo (Ed.), *Communication yearbook 3* (pp. 177–194). New Brunswick, NJ: Transaction Books.

Crable, R. E., & Vibbert, S. L. (1985). Managing issues and influencing public policy. *Public Relations Review, 11*(2), 3–16.

Craig, R. T. (1979). Information systems theory and research: An overview of individual information processing. In D. Nimmo (Ed.), *Communication yearbook 3* (pp. 99–121). New Brunswick, NJ: Transaction Books.

Cronen, V. E., & Davis, L. K. (1978). Problems in the laws-rules-systems trichotomy. *Human Communication Research, 4,* 120–128.

Cronen, V. E., Pearce, W. B., & Harris, L. M. (1982). The coordinated management of meaning: A theory of communication. In F. E. X. Dance (Ed.), *Human communication theory: Comparative essays* (pp. 61–89). New York: Harper & Row.

Cronkhite, G., & Liska, J. R. (1980). The judgment of communicant acceptability. In M. E. Roloff & G. R. Miller (Eds.), *Persuasion: New directions in theory and research* (pp. 100–139). Newbury Park, CA: Sage.

Cusella, L. P. (1982). The effects of source expertise and feedback valence on intrinsic motivation. *Human Communication Research, 9,* 17–32.

Daft, R. L., & Weick, K. E. (1984). Toward a model of organizations as interpretive systems. *Academy of Management Review, 9,* 284–295.

Daly, J. A., Vangelisti, A. I., & Daughton, S. M. (1987). The nature and correlates of conversational sensitivity. *Human Communication Research, 14,* 167–202.

Dance, F. E. X. (1967). Toward a theory of human communication. In F. E. X. Dance (Ed.), *Human communication theory* (pp. 288–309). New York: Holt, Rinehart & Winston.

Dance, F. E. X. (1970). The "concept" of communication. *Journal of Communication, 20,* 201–210.

Dance, F. E. X. (1978). Human communication theory: A highly selective review and two commentaries. In B. D. Ruben (Ed.), *Communication yearbook 2* (pp. 7–22). New Brunswick, NJ: Transaction Books.

Dance, F. E. X. (1985). The functions of human communication. In B. D. Ruben (Ed.), *Information and behavior* (Vol. 1, pp. 62–75). New Brunswick, NJ: Transaction Books.

Danes, J. E. (1978). Communication models of the message-belief change process. In B. D. Ruben (Ed.), *Communication yearbook 2* (pp. 109–124). New Brunswick, NJ: Transaction Books.

Darnell, D. (1971). Toward a reconceptualization of communication. *Journal of Communication, 21*(1), 5–16.

Deetz, S. (1973). Words without things: Toward a social phenomenology of language. *Quarterly Journal of Speech, 59* 40–51.

Deetz, S., & Mumby, D. (1985). Metaphors, information, and power. In B. D. Ruben (Ed.), *Information and behavior* (Vol. 1, pp. 369–386). New Brunswick, NJ: Transaction Books.

DeFleur, M. L. (1970). *Theories of mass communication* (2nd ed.). New York: David McKay.

DeFleur, M. L., & Ball-Rokeach, S. (1989). *Theories of mass communication* (5th ed.). New York: Longman.

Delia, J. G. (1977). Constructivism and the study of human communication. *Quarterly Journal of Speech, 63,* 66–83.

Delia, J. G., O'Keefe, B. J., & O'Keefe, D. J. (1982). The constructivist approach to communication. In F. E. X. Dance (Ed.), *Human communication theory: Comparative essays* (pp. 147–191). New York: Harper & Row.

Derlega, V. J., Winstead, B. A., Wong, P. T. P., & Greenspan, M. (1987). Self-disclosure and relationship development: An attributional analysis. In M. E. Roloff & G. R. Miller (Eds.), *Interpersonal processes: New directions in communication research* (pp. 172–187). Newbury Park, CA: Sage.

Desmond, R. J., Singer, J. L., Singer, D. G., Calam, R., & Colimore, K. (1985). Family mediation patterns and television viewing: Young children's use and grasp of the medium. *Human Communication Research, 11,* 461–480.

deTurck, M. A. (1985). A transactional analysis of compliance-gaining behavior: Effects of noncompliance, relational contexts, and actors' gender. *Human Communication Research, 12,* 54–78.

deTurck, M. A. (1987). When communication fails: Physical aggression as a compliance-gaining strategy. *Communication Monographs, 54,* 106–112.

deTurck, M. A., & Miller, G. R. (1985). Deception and arousal: Isolating behavioral correlations of deception. *Human Communication Research, 12,* 181–201.

Devito, J. A. (1986). *The communication handbook: A dictionary.* New York: Harper & Row.

Dillard, J. P., & Burgoon, M. (1985). Situational influences on the selection of compliance-gaining messages: Two tests of the predictive utility of the Cody-McLaughlin typology. *Communication Monographs, 52,* 289–304.

Dillard, J. P., Hunter, J. E., & Burgoon, M. (1984). Sequential-request persuasive strategies: Meta-analysis of foot-in-the-door and door-in-the-face. *Human Communication Research, 10,* 461–488.

Dillard, J. P., & Witteman, H. (1985), Romantic relationships at work: Organizational and personal influences. *Human Communication Research, 12,* 99–116.

Dindia, K. (1987). The effect of sex of subject and sex of partner on interruptions. *Human Communication Research, 13,* 345–371.

Dizard, W. P., Jr. (1982). *The coming information age: An overview of technology, economics, and politics.* New York: Longman.

Doelger, J. A., Hewes, D. E., & Graham, M. L. (1986). Knowing when to "second-guess": The mindful analysis of messages. *Human Communication Research, 12,* 301–338.

Donohue, W. A., & Diez, M. E. (1985). Directive use of negotiation interaction. *Communication Monographs, 52,* 305–318.

Donohue, W. A., Weider-Hatfield, D., Hamilton, M., & Diez, M. E. (1985). Relational distance in managing conflict. *Human Communication Research, 11,* 387–406.

Douglas, D. F., Westley, B. N., & Chaffee, S. H. (1970). An information campaign that changed community attitudes. *Journalism Quarterly, 47,* 479–487, 492.

Douglas, W. (1984). Initial interaction scripts: When knowing is behaving. *Human Communication Research, 11,* 203–219.

Douglas, W. (1987). Question-asking in same- and opposite-sex initial interactions: The effects of anticipated future interaction. *Human Communication Research, 14,* 230–245.

Douglas, W. (1991). Expectations about initial interaction: An examination of the effects of global uncertainty. *Human Communication Research, 17,* 355–384.

Downs, C. (1979). The relationship between communication and job satisfaction. In R. Huseman, C. Logue, & D. Freshley (Eds.), *Readings in interpersonal and organizational communication* (pp. 363–376). Boston: Allyn & Bacon.

Duck, S. (1982). A topography of relationship disengagement and dissolution. In S. Duck (Ed.), *Personal relationships 4: Dissolving personal relationships* (pp. 1–30). London: Academic Press.

Duck, S. (1985). How to lose friends without influencing people. In M. E. Roloff & G. R. Miller (Eds.), *Interpersonal processes: New directions in communication research* (pp. 278–298). Newbury Park, CA: Sage.

Duck, S. (1990). Relationships as unfinished business: Out of the frying pan and into the 1990s. *Journal of Social and Personal Relationships, 7,* 5–28.

Duck, S., & Miell, D. E. (1986). Charting the development of personal relationships. In R. Gilmour & S. Duck (Eds.), *The emerging field of personal relationships* (pp. 133–143). Hillsdale, NJ: Lawrence Erlbaum Associates.

Dutton, J. E., & Duncan, R. B. (1987). The creation of momentum for change through the process of strategic issue diagnosis. *Strategic Management Journal, 8,* 279–295.

Dutton, J. E., & Ottensmeyer, E. (1987). Strategic issue management systems: Forms, functions, and contexts. *Academy of Management Review, 12* (2), 355–365.

Eisenberg, E. M. (1984). Ambiguity as strategy in organizational communication. *Communication Monographs, 51,* 227–242.

Eisenberg, E. M. (1986). Meaning and interpretation in organizations. *Quarterly Journal of Speech, 72,* 88–97.

Eisenberg, E. M., Monge, P. R., & Farace, R. V. (1984). Coorientation on communication rules in managerial dyads. *Human Communication Research, 11,* 261–271.

Eisenberg, E. M., Monge, P. R., & Miller, K. I. (1984). Involvement in communication networks as a predictor of organizational commitment. *Human Communication Research, 10,* 179-201.

Ekman, P., & Friesen, W. V. (1974). Detecting deception from the body or face. *Journal of Personality and Social Psychology, 29,* 288-298.

Fairhurst, G. T., Green, S. G., & Snavely, B. K. (1984). Face support in controlling poor performance. *Human Communication Research, 11,* 273-295.

Fairhurst, G. T., Rogers, L. E., & Sarr, R. A. (1987). Manager-subordinate control patterns and judgments about the relationship. In M. L. McLaughlin (Ed.), *Communication yearbook 10* (pp. 395-415). Newbury Park: Sage.

Falcione, R. L., & Kaplan, E. A. (1984). Organizational climate, communication, and culture. In R. N. Bostrom & B. H. Westley (Eds.), *Communication yearbook 8* (pp. 285-309). Newbury Park, CA: Sage.

Falcione, R. L., McCroskey, J. C., & Daly, J. A. (1977). Job satisfaction as a function of employees' communication apprehension, self-esteem, and perceptions of their immediate supervisors. In B. D. Ruben (Ed.), *Communication yearbook 1* (pp. 363-375). New Brunswick, NJ: Transaction Books.

Falcione, R. L., Sussman, L., & Herden, R. P. (1987). Communication climate in organizations. In F. M. Jablin, L. L. Putnam, K. H. Roberts, & L. W. Porter (Eds.), *Handbook of organizational communication* (pp. 195-227). Newbury Park, CA: Sage.

Farace, R. V., Monge, P. R., & Russell, H. (1977). *Communicating and organizing.* Reading: Addison-Wesley.

Farace, R. V., Stewart, J. P., & Taylor, J. A. (1978). Criteria for evaluation of organizational communication effectiveness: Review and synthesis. In B. Ruben (Ed.), *Communication yearbook 2* (pp. 271-292). New Brunswick, NJ: Transaction Books.

Festinger, L. (1957). *A theory of cognitive dissonance.* Stanford, CA: Stanford University Press.

Festinger, L., & Carlsmith, J. M. (1959). Cognitive consequences of forced compliance. *Journal of Abnormal and Social Psychology, 58,* 203-210.

Finn, S., & Roberts, D. (1984). Source, destination, and entropy: Reassessing the role of information theory in communication research. *Communication Research, 11,* 453-476.

Fishbein, M., & Ajzen, I. (1975). *Belief, attitude, intention, and behavior: An introduction to theory and research.* Reading: Addison-Wesley.

Fishbein, M., & Ajzen, I. (1981). Acceptance, yielding and impact: Cognitive processes in persuasion. In R. E. Petty, T. M. Ostrom, & T. C. Brock (Eds.), *Cognitive responses in persuasion* (pp. 339-359). Hillsdale, NJ: Lawrence Erlbaum Associates.

Fisher, B. A. (1978). Information systems theory and research: An overview. In B. D. Ruben, (Ed.), *Communication yearbook 2* (pp. 81-108). New Brunswick, NJ: Transaction Books.

Fisher, B. A. (1982). The pragmatic perspective of human communication: A view from system theory. In F. E. X. Dance (Ed.), *Human communication theory: Comparative essays* (pp. 192-219). New York: Harper & Row.

Fitzpatrick, M. A. (1977). A typological approach to communication in relationships. In B. D. Ruben (Ed.), *Communication yearbook 1* (pp. 263-275). New Brunswick, NJ: Transaction Books.

Folger, J. P., & Poole, M. S. (1982). Relational coding schemes: The question of validity. In M. Burgoon (Ed.), *Communication yearbook 5* (pp. 235-247). New Brunswick, NJ: Transaction Books.

Fry, D. L., & Fry, V. H. (1986). A semiotic model for the study of mass communication. In M. L. McLaughlin (Ed.), *Communication yearbook 9* (pp. 443-462). Newbury Park, CA: Sage.

Fulk, J., & Sirish, M. (1986). Distortion of communication in hierarchical relationships. In M.

L. McLaughlin (Ed.), *Communication yearbook 9* (pp. 483-510). Newbury Park, CA: Sage.

Gerbner, G. (1967). An institutional approach to mass communications research. In L. Thayer, (Ed.), *Communication: Theory and research* (pp. 429-445). Springfield, IL: Charles C. Thomas.

Gerbner, G., Gross, L., Morgan, M., & Signorielli, N. (1986). Living with television: The dynamics of the cultivation process. In J. Bryant & D. Zillmann (Eds.), *Perspectives on media effects* (pp. 17-40). Hillsdale, NJ: Lawrence Erlbaum Associates.

Giles, H., Mulac, A., Bradac, J. J., & Johnson, P. (1987). Speech accommodation theory: The first decade and beyond. In M. L. McLaughlin (Ed.), *Communication yearbook 10* (pp. 13-48). Newbury Park, CA: Sage.

Giles, H., & Powesland, P. F. (1975). *Speech style and social evaluation.* London: Academic Press.

Giles, H., & Street, R. L., Jr. (1985). Communicator characteristics and behavior. In M. L. Knapp & G. R. Miller (Eds.), *Handbook of interpersonal communication* (pp. 205-261). Newbury Park, CA: Sage.

Giles, H., & Wiemann, J. M. (1987). Language, social comparison, and power. In C. R. Berger & S. H. Chaffee (Eds.), *Handbook of communication science* (pp. 350-384). Newbury Park, CA: Sage.

Glaser, S. R., Zamanou, S., & Hacker, K. (1987). Measuring and interpreting organizational culture. *Management Communication Quarterly, 1,* 173-198.

Golden, L. L., & Alpert, M. I. (1987). Comparative analysis of the relative effectiveness of one- and two-sided communication for contrasting products. *Journal of Advertising, 16*(1), 18-25.

Green, S. G., & Mitchell, T. R. (1979). Attributional processes of leaders in leader-member interactions. *Organizational Behavior and Human Performance, 23,* 429-458.

Greene, J. O. (1984). A cognitive approach to human communication: An action assembly theory. *Communication Monographs, 51,* 289-306.

Greene, J. O., O'Hair, H. D., Cody, M. J., & Yen, C. (1985). Planning and control of behavior during deception. *Human Communication Research, 11,* 335-364.

Grossberg, L. (1983). Cultural studies revisted and revised. In M. S. Mander (Ed.), *Communications in transition* (pp. 39-70). New York: Praeger.

Grunig, J. E. (1989). Sierra Club study shows who become activists. *Public Relations Review, 15,* 3-24.

Grunig, J. E., & Grunig, L. S. (1989). Toward a theory of the public relations behavior of organizations: Review of a program of research. In J. E. Grunig & L. S. Grunig (Eds.), *Public relations research annual* (Vol. 1, pp. 27-63). Hillsdale, NJ: Lawrence Erlbaum Associates.

Grunig, J. E., & Hunt, T. (1984). *Managing public relations.* New York: Holt, Rinehart & Winston.

Gudykunst, W. B., & Hammer, M. R. (1988). The influence of social identity and intimacy of interethnic relationships on uncertainty reduction processes. *Human Communication Research, 14,* 569-601.

Gudykunst, W. B., Yang, S., & Nishida, T. A (1985). cross-cultural test of uncertainty reduction theory. *Human Communication Research, 11,* 407-455.

Hackman, J. R. (1976). Group influences on individuals. In M. D. Dunnette (Ed.), *Handbook of industrial and organizational psychology* (pp. 1455-1525). Chicago: Rand McNally.

Hall, S. (1980). Encoding/decoding. In S. Hall, D. Hobson, A. Lowe, & P. Wilis (Eds.), *Culture, media, language: Working papers in cultural studies, 1972-1979* (pp. 128-138). London: Hutchinson.

Hample, D., & Dallinger, J. M. (1988). Individual differences in cognitive editing standards. *Human Communication Research, 14,* 123-144.

Hawes, L. C. (1973). Elements of a model for communication processes. *Quarterly Journal of Speech, 59,* 11–21.

Hawes, L. C. (1975). *Pragmatics of analoguing: Theory and model construction in communication.* Reading, MA: Addison-Wesley.

Heath, R. L. (1976). Variability in value system priorities as decision-making adaptation to situational differences. *Communication Monographs, 43,* 325–333.

Heath, R. L. (1986). *Realism and relativism: A perspective on Kenneth Burke.* Macon, GA: Mercer University Press.

Heath, R. L. (Ed.). (1988). *Strategic issues management: How organizations influence and respond to public interests and policies.* San Francisco, CA: Jossey-Bass.

Heath, R. L., & Nelson, R. A. (1986). *Issues management: Corporate public policymaking in an information society.* Newbury Park, CA: Sage.

Heath, R. L., & Douglas, W. (1990). Involvement: A key variable in people's reaction to public policy issues. In L. A. Grunig & J. E. Grunig (Eds.), *Public relations research annual* (Vol. 2, pp. 193–204). Hillsdale, NJ: Lawrence Erlbaum Associates.

Heider, F. (1958). *The psychology of interpersonal relations.* New York: Wiley.

Heikkinen, K. J., & Reese, S. D. (1986). Newspaper readers and a new information medium: Information need and channel orientation as predictors of videotext adoption. *Communication Research, 13,* 19–36.

Hewes, D. E., Graham, M. L., Doelger, J., & Pavitt, C. (1985). "Second-guessing": Message interpretation in social networks. *Human Communication Research, 11,* 299–334.

Hewes, D. E., Graham, M. L., Monsour, M., & Doelger, J. A. (1989). Cognition and social information-gathering strategies: Reinterpretation assessment in second-guessing. *Human Communication Research, 16,* 297–321.

Hewes, D. E., & Planalp, S. (1982). There is nothing as useful as a good theory . . . The influence of social knowledge on interpersonal communication. In M. E. Roloff & C. R. Berger (Eds.), *Social cognition and communication* (pp. 107–150). Newbury Park, CA: Sage.

Hewes, D. E., & Planalp, S. (1987). The individual's place in communication science. In C. R. Berger & S. H. Chaffee (Eds.), *Handbook of communication science* (pp. 146–183). Newbury Park, CA: Sage.

Hirokawa, R. Y. (1985). Discussion procedures and decision-making performance: A test of a functional perspective. *Human Communication Research, 12,* 203–224.

Hirokawa, R. Y. (1988). Group communication and decision-making performance: A continued test of the functional perspective. *Human Communication Research, 14,* 487–515.

Hirsch, P. (1979). The role of television and popular culture in contemporary society. In H. Newcomb (Ed.), *Television: The critical view* (2nd ed., pp. 249–279). New York: Oxford University Press.

Hocking, J., Bauchner, J. Kaminski, E., & Miller, G. (1979). Detecting deceptive communication from verbal, visual, and paralinguistic cues. *Human Communication Research, 6,* 33–46.

Hoffman, E., & Roman, P. M. (1984). Information diffusion in the implementation of innovation process. *Communication Research, 11,* 117–140.

Honeycutt, J. M., Cantrill, J. M., & Greene, R. W. (1989). Memory structures for relational escalation. *Human Communication Research, 16,* 62–90.

Hovland, C. I., Janis, I. L., & Kelley, H. H. (1953). *Communication and persuasion.* New Haven: Yale University Press.

Hovland, C. I., Mandell, W., Campbell, E. H., Brock, T., Luchins, A. S., Cohen, A. R., McGuire, W. J., Janis, I. L., Feierabend, R. L., & Anderson, N. H. (1959). *The order of presentation in persuasion.* New Haven: Yale University Press.

Huber, G. P., & Daft, R. L. (1987). The information environments of organizations. In F. M.

Jablin, L. L. Putnam, K. H. Roberts, & L. W. Porter (Eds.), Handbook of organizational communication (pp. 130–164). Newbury Park, CA: Sage.

Hunter, J. E., & Boster, F. J. (1987). A model of compliance-gaining message selection. *Communication Monographs, 54,* 63–84.

Infante, D. A., & Gorden, W. I. (1985). Superiors' argumentativeness and verbal aggressiveness as predictors of subordinates' satisfaction. *Human Communication Research, 12,* 117–125.

Innis, H. (1951). *The bias of communication.* Toronto: University of Toronto Press.

Jablin, F. M. (1979). Superior-subordinate communication: The state of the art. *Psychological Bulletin, 86,* 1201–1222.

Jablin, F. M. (1980). Organizational communication theory and research: An overview of communication climate and network research. In D. Nimmo (Ed.), *Communication yearbook 4* (pp. 327–347). New Brunswick, NJ: Transaction Books.

Jablin, F. M. (1982a). Organizational communication: An assimilation theory. In M. E. Roloff & C. R. Berger (Eds.), *Social cognition and communication* (pp. 255–286). Newbury Park, CA: Sage.

Jablin, F. G. (1982b). Formal structural characteristics of organizations and superior-subordinate communication. *Human Communication Research, 8,* 338–347.

Jablin, F. M. (1984). Assimilating new members into organizations. In R. N. Bostrom & B. H. Westley (Eds.), *Communication yearbook 8* (pp. 594–626). Newbury Park, CA: Sage.

Jablin, F. M. (1985). Task/work relationships: A life-span perspective. In M. L. Knapp & G. R. Miller (Eds.), *Handbook of interpersonal communication* (pp. 615–654). Newbury Park, CA: Sage.

Jablin, F. M., & Krone, K. J. (1987). Organizational assimilation. In C. R. Berger & S. H. Chaffee (Eds.), *Handbook of communication science* (pp. 711–746). Newbury Park, CA: Sage.

Jablin, F. M., & McComb, K. B. (1984). The employment screening interview: An organizational assimilation and communication perspective. In R. N. Bostrom & B. H. Westley (Eds.), *Communication yearbook 8* (pp. 137–163). Newbury Park, CA: Sage.

Jacobs, S. (1985). Language. In M. L. Knapp & G. R. Miller (Eds.), *Handbook of interpersonal communication* (pp. 313–343). Newbury Park, CA: Sage.

Janis, I. (1972). *Victims of groupthink: A psychological study of foreign policy decisions and fiascos.* Boston: Houghton Mifflin.

Janis, I. L., Hovland, C. I., Field, P. B., Linton, H., Graham, E., Cohen, A. R., Refe, D., Abelson, R. P., Lesser, G. S., & King, B. T. (1959). *Personality and persuasibility.* New Haven: Yale University Press.

Jarboe, S. (1988). A comparison of input-output, process-output, and input-process-output models of small group problem-solving effectiveness. *Communication Monographs, 55,* 121–142.

Johnson, W. (1946). *People in quandaries.* New York: Harper & Brothers.

Kahan, J. P. (1975). Subjective probability interpretation of the risky shift. *Journal of Personality and Social Psychology, 31,* 977–982.

Kaplan, A. (1964). *The conduct of inquiry.* San Francisco, CA: Chandler.

Katz, E. (1959). Mass communication research and the study of culture. *Studies in Public Communication, 2,* 1–16.

Katz, E., Blumler, J. G., & Gurevitch, M. (1974). Utilization of mass communication by the individual. In J. G. Blumler & E. Katz (Eds.), *The uses of mass communications: Current perspectives on gratifications research* (pp. 19–32). Newbury Park, CA: Sage.

Katz, R. L., & Kahn, D. (1966). *The social psychology of organizations.* New York: Wiley.

Kellermann, K. (1987). Information exchange in social interaction. In M. E. Roloff & G. R. Miller (Eds.), *Interpersonal processes: New directions in communication research* (pp. 188–217). Newbury Park, CA: Sage.

Kellerman, K., & Jarboe, S. (1987). Conservatism in judgement: Is the risky shift-ee really risky, really? In M. L. McLaughlin (Ed.), *Communication yearbook 10* (pp. 259-282). Newbury Park, CA: Sage.

Kelley, H. H. (1972). Attribution in social interaction. In E. E. Jones, H. H. Kanouse, H. H. Kelley, R. E. Nisbett, S. Valins, & B. Weiner (Eds), *Attribution: Perceiving the causes of behavior* (pp. 1-26). Morristown, NJ: General Learning Press.

Kelley, H. H. (1973). The processes of causal attribution. *American Psychologist, 28,* 107-128.

Kelley, G. (1955). *The psychology of personal constructs.* New York: Norton.

Kennamer, J. D., & Chaffee, S. H. (1982). Communication of political information during early presidential primaries: Cognition, affect, and uncertainty. In M. Burgoon (Ed.), *Communication yearbook 5* (pp. 627-650). New Brunswick, NJ: Transaction Books.

Kerlinger, F. N. (1973). *Foundations of behavioral research* (2nd ed.). New York: Holt, Rinehart & Winston.

Kippax, S., & Murray, J. P. (1980). Using the mass media: Need gratification and perceived utility. *Communication Research, 7,* 335-360.

Klapper, J. T. (1960). *The effects of mass communication.* New York: Free Press.

Knapp, M. L. (1978). *Social intercourse: From greeting to goodbye.* Boston: Allyn & Bacon.

Knapp, M. L., Ellis, D. G., & Williams, B. A. (1980). Perceptions of communication behavior associated with relationship terms. *Communication Monographs, 47,* 262-278.

Korzybski, A. (1948). *Science and sanity: An introduction to non-Aristotelian systems and general semantics* (3rd ed.). Lakeville, CT: International Neo-Aristotelian Library.

Kramer, M. W. (1989). Communication during intraorganizational job transfers. *Management Communication Quarterly, 3,* 219-248.

Krippendorff, K. (1975). Information theory. In G. J. Hanneman & W. J. McEwen (Eds.), *Communication and behavior* (pp. 351-389). Reading, MA: Addison-Wesley.

Krippendorff, K. (1977). Information systems theory and research: An overview. In B. D. Ruben (Ed.), *Communication yearbook 1* (pp. 149-171). New Brunswick, NJ: Transaction Books.

Krone, K. J., Jablin, F. M., & Putnam, L. L. (1987). Communication theory and organizational communication: Multiple perspectives. In F. M. Jablin, L. L. Putnam, K. H. Roberts, & L. W. Porter (Eds.), *Handbook of organizational communication* (pp. 18-40). Newbury Park, CA: Sage.

Krull, R., Watt, J. H., & Lichty, L. W. (1977). Entropy and structure: Two measures of complexity in television programs. *Communication Research, 4,* 61-86.

Kuhn, T. S. (1970). *The structure of scientific revolutions.* Chicago: University of Chicago Press.

Langer, S. K. (1951) *Philosophy in a new key* (2nd ed.). New York: New American Library.

LaPiere, R. T. (1934). Attitudes vs. action. *Social Forces, 13,* 230-237.

Lasswell, H. D. (1927). *Propaganda technique in the World War.* New York: Knopf.

Lasswell, H. D. (1948). The structure and function of communication in society. In L. Bryson (Ed.), *The communication of ideas* (pp. 37-51). New York: Harper.

Lazarsfeld, P. F., Berelson, B., & Gaudet, H. (1948). *The people's choice.* New York: Columbia University Press.

Lee, I. J. (1941). *Language habits in human affairs: An introduction to general semantics.* New York: Harper.

Lee, I. J. (1952). *How to talk with people.* New York: Harper.

Lewin, K. (1951). *Field theory in social science.* Westport, CT: Greenwood.

Liebert, R. M., Neale, J. M., & Davidson, E. S. (1973). *The early window: Effects of television on children and youth.* New York: Pergamon.

Lippmann, W. (1922). *Public opinion.* New York: Harcourt Brace.

Littlejohn, S. W. (1989). *Theories of human communication* (3rd ed.). Belmont, CA: Wadsworth.

Lometi, G. E., Reeves, B., & Bybee, C. R. (1977). Investigating the assumptions of uses and gratifications research. *Communication Research, 4,* 321–338.

Lowery, S., & DeFleur, M. L. (1983). *Milestones in mass communication theories and research: Media effects.* New York: Longman.

Marks, M. L. (1986). The question of quality circles. *Psychology Today, 20*(3), 36–46.

Marwell, G., & Schmitt, D. R. (1967). Dimensions of compliance-gaining behavior: An empirical analysis. *Sociometry, 30,* 350–364.

McCombs, M. E., & Gilbert, S. (1986). News influence on our pictures of the world. In J. Bryant & D. Zillmann (Eds.), *Perspectives on media effects* (pp. 1–15). Hillsdale, NJ: Lawrence Erlbaum Associates.

McCombs, M. E., & Shaw, D. L. (1972). The agenda-setting function of the mass media. *Public Opinion Quarterly, 36,* 176–187.

McCornack, S. A., & Levine, T. R. (1990). When lovers become leery: The relationship between suspicion and accuracy in detecting deception. *Communication Monographs, 57,* 219–230.

McGuire, W. J. (1864). Inducing resistance to persuasion: Some contemporary approaches. *Advances in Experimental Social Psychology, 1,* 192–229.

McGuire, W. J. (1968a). Personality and attitude change: An information-processing theory. In A. G. Greenwald, T. C. Brock, & T. M. Ostrom (Eds.), *Psychological foundations of attitudes* (pp. 171–196). New York: Academic Press.

McGuire, W. J. (1968b). Personality and susceptibility to social influence. In E. F. Borgatta & W. W. Lambert (Eds.), *Handbook of personality theory and research* (pp. 1130–1187). Chicago: Rand McNally.

McGuire, W. J. (1981). Theoretical foundations of campaigns: In R. E. Rice & W. J. Paisley (Eds.), *Public communication campaigns* (pp. 41–70). Newbury Park, CA: Sage.

McLaughlin, M. L. (1984). *Conversation: How talk is organized.* Newbury Park, CA: Sage.

McLeod, J. M., Becker, L. B., & Byrnes, J. E. (1974). Another look at the agenda setting function of the press. *Communication Research, 1,* 131–166

McLeod, J. M., & Chaffee, S. H. (1973). Interpersonal approaches to communication research. *American Behavioral Scientist, 16,* 469–499.

McLuhan, M. (1964). *Understanding media: The extensions of man.* New York: New American Library.

McQuail, D. (1984). With the benefit of hindsight: Reflections on uses and gratifications research. *Critical Studies in Mass Communication, 1,* 177–193.

Mead, G. H. (1934). *Mind, self, and society.* Chicago: University of Chicago Press.

Mehrabian, A. (1981). *Silent messages: Implicit communication of emotions and attitudes* (2nd ed.). Belmont, CA: Wadsworth.

Mendelsohn, H. (1966). *Mass entertainment.* New Haven, CT: College and University Press.

Mendelsohn, H. (1973). Some reasons why information campaigns can succeed. *Public Opinion Quarterly, 37,* 50–61.

Meringoff, L. K., Vibbert, M. M., Char, C. A., Fernie, D. E., Bunker, G. S., & Gardner, H. (1983). How is children's learning from television distinctive? Exploiting the medium methodologically. In J. Bryant & D. R. Anderson (Eds.), *Children's understanding of television: Research on attention and comprehension* (pp. 151–179). New York: Academic Press.

Metts, S., & Cupach, W. R. (1990). The influence of relationship beliefs and problem-solving responses on satisfaction in romantic relationships. *Human Communication Research, 17,* 170–185.

Meyer, T. P., Trandt, P. J., & Anderson, J. A. (1980). Nontraditional mass communication research methods: An overview of observational case studies of media use in natural settings. In D. Nimmo (Ed.), *Communication yearbook 4* (pp. 261–275). New Brunswick, NJ: Transaction Books.

Meyrowitz, J. (1985). *No sense of place: The impact of electronic media on social behavior.* New York: Oxford University Press.

Millar, F. E., & Rogers, L. E. (1976). A relational approach. In G. Miller (Ed.), *Explorations in interpersonal communication* (pp. 87–103). Newbury Park, CA: Sage.

Millar, F. E., & Rogers, L. E. (1987). Relational dimensions of interpersonal dynamics. In M. E. Roloff & G. R. Miller (Eds.), *Interpersonal processes: New directions in communication research* (pp. 117–139). Newbury Park, CA: Sage.

Miller, G. R. (1980). On being persuaded: Some basic distinctions. In M. E. Roloff & G. R. Miller (Eds.), *Persuasion: New directions in theory and research* (pp. 11–28). Newbury Park, CA: Sage.

Miller, G. R. (1987). Persuasion. In C. R. Berger & S. H. Chaffee (Eds.), *Handbook of communication science* (pp. 446–483). Newbury Park, CA: Sage.

Miller, G. R., Boster, F. J., Roloff, M. E., & Seibold, D. R. (1987). MBRS rekindled: Some thoughts on compliance gaining in interpersonal settings. In M. E. Roloff & G. R. Miller (Eds.), *Interpersonal processes: New directions in communication research* (pp. 89–116). Newbury Park, CA: Sage.

Miller, G. R., & Burgoon, M. (1978). Persuasion research: Review and commentary. In B. D. Ruben (Ed.). *Communication Yearbook 8* (pp. 29–47). New Brunswick, NJ: Transaction Books

Miller, G. R., & Steinberg, M. (1975). *Between people: A new analysis of interpersonal communication.* Chicago: Science Research Associates.

Miller, M. D., & Burgoon, M. (1979). The relationship between violations of expectations and the induction of resistance to persuasion. *Human Communication Research, 5,* 301–313.

Miller, V. D., & Jablin, F. M. (1991). Information seeking during organizational entry: Influences, tactics, and a model of the process. *Academy of Management Review, 16,* 92–120.

Mitroff, I. I. (1983). *Stakeholders of the organizational mind: Toward a new view of organizational policy making.* San Francisco, CA: Jossey-Bass.

Monge, P. R. (1977). The systems perspective as a theoretical basis for the study of human communication. *Communication Quarterly, 25,* 19–29.

Monge, P. R. (1987). The network level of analysis. In C. R. Berger & S. H. Chaffee (Eds.), *Handbook of communication science* (pp. 239–270). Newbury Park, CA: Sage.

Monge, P. R., & Eisenberg, E. M. (1987). Emergent communication networks. In F. M. Jablin, L. L. Putnam, K. H. Roberts, & L. W. Porter (Eds.), *Handbook of organizational communication* (pp. 304–342). Newbury Park, CA: Sage.

Morgan, G. (1982). Cybernetics and organization theory: Epistemology or technique? *Human Relations, 35,* 521–537.

Morgan, G. (1986). *Images of organization.* Newbury Park, CA: Sage.

Morley, D. D., & Walker, K. B. (1987). The role of importance, novelty, and plausibility in producing belief change. *Communication Monographs, 54,* 436–442.

Morton, T. L., Alexander, J. F., & Altman, I. (1976). Communication and relationship definition. In G. R. Miller (Ed.), *Explorations in interpersonal communication* (pp. 105–125). Newbury Park: Sage.

Moschis, G. P. (1980). Consumer information use: Individual versus social predictors. *Communication Research, 7,* 139–160.

Muehling, D. D. (1987). An investigation of factors underlying attitude-toward-advertising-in-general. *Journal of Advertising, 16*(1), 32–40.

Mumby, D. K. (1987). The political function of narrative in organizations. *Communication Monographs, 54,* 113–127.

Newcomb, T. M. (1953). An approach to the study of communicative acts. *Psychological Review, 60,* 393–404.

Nimmo, D. (1978). *Political communication and public opinion in America.* Santa Monica, CA: Goodyear Publishing.

Office of Technology Assessment (1990). *Critical connections: Communications for the future.* Washington, DC: U.S. Government Printing Office.

Ogden, C. K., & Richards, I. A. (1923). *The meaning of meaning.* New York: Harcourt, Brace Jovanovich.

Ogilvie, J. H., & Haslett, B. (1985). Communicating peer feedback in a task group. *Human Communication Research, 12,* 79–98.

O'Keefe, B. J. (1988). The logic of message design: Individual differences in reasoning about communication. *Communication Monographs, 55,* 80–103.

O'Keefe, B. J., & Delia, J. G. (1982). Impression formation and message production. In M. E. Roloff & C. R. Berger (Eds.), *Social cognition and communication* (pp. 33–72). Newbury Park, CA: Sage.

O'Keefe, B. J., & McCornack, S. A. (1987). Message design logic and message goal structures. *Human Communication Research, 14,* 68–92.

O'Keefe, B. J., & Shepherd, G. J. (1987). The pursuit of multiple objectives in face-to-face persuasive interaction: Effects of construct differentiation on message organization. *Communication Monographs, 54,* 396–419.

O'Keefe, D. J. (1975). Logical empiricism and the study of human communication. *Speech Monographs, 42,* 169–183.

O'Keefe, D. J. (1987). The persuasive effects of delaying identification on high- and low-credibility communicators: A meta-analytic review. *Central States Speech Journal, 38,* 63–72.

Oliver, R. L. (1981). Measurement and evaluation of satisfaction processes in retail settings. *Journal of Retailing, 51,* 25–48.

Osgood, C. E. (1953). *Method and theory in experimental psychology.* New York: Oxford University Press.

Osgood, C. E. (1963). On understanding and creating sentences. *American Psychologist, 18,* 735–751.

Osgood, C. E., Suci, G. J., & Tannenbaum, P. H. (1957). *The measurement of meaning.* Urbana, IL: University of Illinois Press.

Pacanowsky, M. E., & O'Donnell-Trujillo, N. (1983). Organizational communication as cultural performance. *Communication Monographs, 50,* 126–147.

Palmgreen, P. (1984). Uses and gratifications: A theoretical perspective. In R. N. Bostrom & B. H. Westley (Eds.), *Communication yearbook 8* (pp. 20–55). Newbury Park, CA: Sage.

Palmgreen, P., & Rayburn, J. D., II (1982). Gratifications sought and media exposure: An expectancy value model. *Communication Research, 9,* 561–580.

Palmgreen, P., & Rayburn, J. D., II (1985a). A comparison of gratification models of media satisfaction. *Communication Monographs, 52,* 334–346.

Palmgreen, P., & Rayburn, J. D., II. (1985b). An expectancy-value approach to media gratifications. In K. Rosengren, L. Wenner, & P. Palmgreen (Eds.). *Media gratifications research: Current perspectives* (pp. 61–72). Newbury Park, CA: Sage.

Palmgreen, P., Wenner, L. A., & Rayburn, J. D., II. (1981). Gratification discrepancies and news program choice. *Communication Research, 8,* 451–478.

Palmgreen, P., Wenner, L. A., & Rosengren, K. E. (1985). Uses and gratifications research: The past ten years. In K. E. Rosengren, L. A. Wenner, & P. Palmgreen (Eds.), *Media gratifications research: Current perspectives* (pp. 11–37) Newbury Park, CA: Sage.

Parks, M. R. (1985). Interpersonal communication and the quest for personal competence. In M. L. Knapp & G. R. Miller (Eds.), *Handbook of interpersonal communication* (pp. 171–201). Newbury Park, CA: Sage.

Parks, M. R., & Adelman, M. B. (1983). Communication networks and the development of romantic relationships: An expansion of uncertainty reduction theory. *Human Communication Research, 10,* 55–80.

Patterson, M. L. (1982). A sequential functional model of nonverbal exchange. *Psychological Review, 89,* 231–249.

Patterson, M. L. (1983). *Nonverbal behavior: A functional perspective.* New York: Springer-Verlag.

Pavitt, C., & Cappella, J. N. (1979). Coorientation, accuracy in interpersonal and small group discussions: A literature review, model, and simulation. In D. Nimmo (Ed.), *Communication yearbook 3* (pp. 123–156). New Brunswick, NJ: Transaction Books.

Pearce, W. B., & Cronen, V. E. (1980). *Communication, action, and meaning.* New York: Praeger.

Penley, L. E. (1982). An investigation of the information processing framework of organizational communication. *Human Communication Research, 8,* 348–365.

Petronio, S., Martin, J., & Littlefield, R. (1984). Prerequisite conditions for self-disclosing: A gender issue. *Communication Monographs, 51,* 268–273.

Petty, R. E., & Cacioppo, J. T. (1979). Issue-involvement can increase or decrease persuasion by enhancing message-relevant cognitive responses. *Journal of Personality and Social Psychology, 37,* 1915–1926.

Petty, R. E., & Cacioppo, J. T. (1981). *Attitudes and persuasion: Classic and contemporary approaches.* Dubuque, IA: Brown.

Petty, R. E., & Cacioppo, J. T. (1986a). *Communication and persuasion: Central and peripheral routes to attitude change.* New York: Springer-Verlag.

Petty, R. E., & Cacioppo, J. T. (1986b). The elaboration likelihood model of persuasion. In L. Berkowitz (Ed.), *Advances in experimental social psychology* (Vol. 19, pp. 123–205). New York: Academic Press.

Petty, R. E., Cacioppo, J. T., & Goldman, R. (1981). Personal involvement as a determinant of argument based persuasion. *Journal of Personality and Social Psychology, 41,* 847–855.

Petty, R. E., Cacioppo, J. T., & Schumann, D. (1983). Central and peripheral routes to advertising effectiveness: The moderating role of involvement. *Journal of Consumer Research, 10,* 135–146.

Petty, R. E., Kasmer, J. A., Haugtvedt, C. P. & Cacioppo, J. T. (1987). Source and message factors in persuasion: A reply to Stiff's critique of the elaboration likelihood model. *Communication Monographs, 54,* 233–249.

Pilotta, J. J., Widman, T., & Jasko, S. A. (1988). Meaning and action in the organizational setting: An interpretive approach. In J. A. Andersen (Eds.), *Communication yearbook 11* (pp. 310–324). Newbury Park, CA: Sage.

Pincus, J. D. (1986). Communication satisfaction, job satisfaction, and job performance. *Human Communication Research, 12,* 395–419.

Planalp, S. (1985). Relational schemata: A test of alternative forms of relational knowledge as guides to communication. *Human Communication Research, 12,* 3–29.

Planalp, S., Graham, M., & Paulson, L. (1987). Cohesive devices in conversations. *Communication Monographs, 54,* 325–343.

Planalp, S., Rutherford, D. K., & Honeycutt, J. M. (1988). Events that increase uncertainty in personal relationships II: Replication and extension. *Human Communication Research, 14,* 516–547.

Poole, M. S. (1985). Communication and organizational climates: Review, critique, and a new perspective. In R. D. McPhee & P. K. Tompkins (Eds.), *Organizational communication: Traditional themes and new directions* (pp. 79–108). Newbury Park, CA: Sage.

Poole, M. S., & Roth, J. (1989). Decision development in small groups V: Test of a contingency model. *Human Communication Research, 15,* 549–589.

Porat, M. U. (1977). *The information economy.* Washington D.C.: U. S. Department of Commerce.

Postman, N. (1982). *The disappearance of childhood.* New York: Delacorte.

Potter, W. J. (1987). Does television viewing hinder academic achievement among adolescents? *Human Communication Research, 14,* 27–46.

Putnam, L. L. (1982). Paradigms for organizational communication research: An overview and synthesis. *Western Journal of Speech Communication, 46,* 192–206.

Rayburn, J. D., & Palmgreen, P. (1984). Merging uses and gratifications and expectancy-value theory. *Communication Research, 11,* 537–562.

Reardon, K. K. (1981). *Persuasion: Theory and context.* Newbury Park, CA: Sage.

Redding, W. C. (1979). *Communication within the organization: An interpretive review of theory and research.* New York: Industrial Communication Council

Redding, W. C. (1985). Stumbling toward identity: The emergence of organizational communication as a field of study. In P. K. Tompkins & R. D. McPhee (Eds.), *Organizational communication: Traditional themes and new directions* (pp. 15–54). Newbury Park, CA: Sage.

Reeves, B., Chaffee, S. H., & Tims, A. (1982). Social cognition and mass communication research. In M. E. Roloff & C. R. Berger (Eds.), *Social cognition and communication* (pp. 287–326). Newbury Park, CA: Sage.

Reinard, J. C. (1988). The empirical study of the persuasive effects of evidence: The status after fifty years of research. *Human Communication Research, 15,* 3–59.

Reinsch, N. L., Jr. (1974). Figurative language and source credibility: A preliminary investigation and reconceptualization. *Human Communication Research, 1,* 75–80.

Richards, I. A. (1925). *Principles of literary criticism.* New York: Harcourt, Brace Jovanovich.

Richards, I. A. (1936). *The philosophy of rhetoric.* New York: Oxford University Press.

Richetto, G. M. (1977) Organizational communication theory and research: An overview. In B. D. Ruben (Ed.), *Communication yearbook 1* (pp. 331–346). New Brunswick, NJ: Transaction Books.

Richmond, V. P., Davis, L. M., Saylor, K., & McCroskey, J. C. (1984). Power strategies in organizations: Communication techniques and messages. *Human Communication Research, 11,* 85–108.

Richmond, V. P., Gorham, J. S., & Furio, B. J. (1987). Affinity-seeking communication in collegiate female-male relationships. *Communication Quarterly, 35,* 334–348.

Ritchie, D. (1986). Shannon and Weaver: Unravelling the paradox of information. *Communication Research, 13,* 278–298.

Rogers, E. M. (1962). *Diffusion of innovations.* New York: Free Press.

Rogers, E. M. (1986). *Communication technology: The new media in society.* New York: Free Press.

Rogers, E. M., & Kincaid, D. L. (1981). *Communication networks: Toward a new paradigm for research.* New York: Free Press.

Rogers, R. W. (1975). A protection motivation theory of fear appeals and attitude change. *Journal of Psychology, 91,* 93–114.

Roloff, M. E. (1981). *Interpersonal communication: The social exchange approach.* Newbury Park, CA: Sage.

Roloff, M. E. (1987). Communication and reciprocity within intimate relationships. In M. E. Roloff & G. R. Miller (Eds.), *Interpersonal processes: New directions in communication research* (pp. 11–38). Newbury Park, CA: Sage.

Roloff, M. E., & Berger, C. R. (1982). Social cognition and communication: An introduction. In M. E. Roloff & C. R. Berger (Eds.), *Social cognition and communication* (pp. 9–32). Newbury Park, CA: Sage.

Roloff, M. E., & Campion, D. E. (1987). On alleviating the debilitating effects of accountability on bargaining: Authority and self-monitoring. *Communication Monographs, 54,* 145–164.

Roloff, M. E., Janiszewski, C. A., McGrath, M. A., Burns, C. S., & Lalita, A. M. (1988). Acquiring resources from intimates: When obligation substitutes for persuasion. *Human Communication Research, 14,* 364–396.

Roloff, M. E., & Janiszewski, C. A. (1989). Overcoming obstacles to interpersonal compliance: A principle of message construction. *Human Communication Research, 16,* 33–61.

Ruben, B. D. (1985). The Coming of the information age: Information, technology, and the study of behavior. In B. D. Ruben (Ed.), *Information and behavior* (Vol. 1, pp. 3–26). New Brunswick, NJ: Transaction Books.

Rubin, A. M. (in press). Media uses and effects: A uses-and-gratifications perspective. In J. Bryant & D. Zillmann (Eds.), *Media effects: Advances in theory and research.* Hillsdale, NJ: Lawrence Erlbaum Associates.

Rubin, A. M., & Windahl, S. (1986). The uses and dependency model of mass communication. *Critical Studies in Mass Communication, 3,* 184–199.

Salmon, C. T. (1986). Message discrimination and the information environment. *Communication Research, 13,* 363–372.

Saltiel, J., & Woelfel, J. (1975). Inertia in cognitive processes: The role of accumulated information in attitude change. *Human Communication Research, 1,* 333–344.

Samter, W., & Burleson, B. R. (1984). Cognitive and motivational influences on spontaneous comforting behavior. *Human Communication Research, 11,* 231–260.

Schein, E. H. (1985). *Organizational cultures and leadership.* San Francisco, CA: Jossey-Bass.

Schiller, H. J. (1983). The privatization of information. In E. Wartella, D. C. Whitney, & S. Windahl (Eds.), *Mass communication review yearbook* (Vol. 4, pp. 537–568). Newbury Park, CA: Sage.

Schramm, W. (1954). How communication works. In W. Schramm (Ed.), *The process and effects of mass communication* (pp. 3–26). Urbana, IL: University of Illinois Press.

Schramm, W. (1955). Information theory and mass communication. *Journalism Quarterly, 32,* 131–146.

Schramm, W. (1973). *Men, messages, and media.* New York: Harper & Row.

Searle, J. R. (1969). *Speech acts: An essay in the philosophy of language.* Cambridge: Cambridge University Press.

Searle, J. R. (1976). A classification of illocutionary acts. *Language in Society, 5,* 1–23.

Seibold, D. R., & Spitzberg, B. H. (1982). Attribution theory and research: Review and implications for communication. In B. Dervin & M. J. Voigt (Eds.), *Progress in the communication sciences* (Vol. 3, pp. 85–125). Norwood, NJ: Ablex.

Shannon, C. E., & Weaver, W. (1949). *The mathematical theory of communication.* Urbana, IL: University of Illinois Press.

Shapere, D. (1974). Scientific theories and their domains. In F. Suppe (Ed.), *The structure of scientific theories* (pp. 518–589). Urbana, IL: University of Illinois Press.

Shaw, D. L., & McCombs, M. E. (1977). *The emergence of American political issues: The agenda-setting function of the press.* St. Paul, MN: West.

Shepherd, G. J. (1987). Individual differences in the relationship between attitudinal and normative determinants of behavioral intent. *Communication Monographs, 54,* 221–231.

Sherif, C. W., Sherif, M., & Nebergall, R. E. (1965). *Attitude and attitude change: The social judgment-involvement approach.* Philadelphia, PA: Saunders.

Sherif, M., & Cantril, H. (1947). *The psychology of ego-involvement.* New York: Wiley.

Sherif, M., & Hovland, C. I. (1961). *Social judgment; assimilation and contrast effects in communication and attitude change.* New Haven: Yale University Press.

Sherif, M., & Sherif, C. W. (1967). Attitude as the individual's own categories: The social judgment-involvement approach to attitude and attitude change. In C. W. Sherif & M. Sherif (Eds.), *Attitude, ego-involvement, and change* (pp. 105–139). New York: Wiley.

Shimanoff, S. B. (1987). Types of emotional disclosures and request compliance between spouses. *Communication Monographs, 54,* 85–100.

Sillars, A. L. (1980). Attribution and communication in roommate conflict. *Communication Monographs, 47,* 180–200.

Sillars, A. L. (1982). Attribution and communication: Are people "naive scientists" or just naive? In M. E. Roloff & C. R. Berger (Eds.), *Social cognition and communication* (pp. 73–106). Newbury Park, CA: Sage.

Sillars, A. L., Pike, G. R., Jones, T. S., & Murphy, M. A. (1984). Communication and understanding in marriage. *Human Communication Research, 10,* 317–350.

Sillars, A. L., & Weisberg, J. (1987). Conflict as a social skill. In M. E. Roloff & G. R. Miller (Eds.), *Interpersonal processes: New directions in communication research* (pp. 140–171). Newbury Park, CA: Sage.

Sillars, A. L., & Weisberg, J. Burggraf, C. S., & Wilson, E. A. (1987). Content themes in marital conversations. *Human Communication Research, 13,* 495–528.

Smeltzer, L. R., & Kedia, B. L. (1985). Knowing the ropes: Organizational requirements for quality circles. *Business Horizons, 28*(4), 30–34.

Smircich, L., & Calas, M. R. (1987). Organizational culture: A critical assessment. In F. M. Jablin, L. L. Putnam, K. H. Roberts, & L. W. Porter (Eds.), *Handbook of organizational communication* (pp. 228–263). Newbury Park, CA: Sage.

Smith, D. H. (1972). Communication research as the idea of process. *Speech Monographs, 39,* 174–182.

Smith, D. R. (1970). The fallacy of the "communication breakdown." *Quarterly Journal of Speech, 56,* 343–346.

Smith, M. J. (1984). Contingency rules theory, context, and compliance behaviors. *Human Communication Research, 10,* 489–512.

Snider, J. & Osgood, C. (1969). *The semantic differential technique.* Chicago: Aldine.

Sorrentino, R. M., Bobocel, D. R., Gitta, M. Z., Olson, J. M., & Hewitt, E. C. (1988). Uncertainty orientation and persuasion: Individual differences in the effects of personal relevance on social judgments. *Journal of Personality and Social Psychology, 55,* 357–371.

Spitzberg, B. H., & Hecht, M. L. (1984). A component model of relational competence. *Human Communication Research, 10,* 575–599.

Stafford, L., & Daly, J. A. (1984). Conversational memory: The effects of recall mode and memory expectancies on remembrances of natural conversations. *Human Communication Research, 10,* 379–402.

Steeves, H. L. (1984). Developing coorientation measures for small groups. *Communication Monographs, 51,* 185–192.

Stephenson, W. (1967). *Play theory of mass communication.* Chicago: University of Chicago Press.

Stewart, J. (1972). Concepts of language and meaning: A comparative study. *Quarterly Journal of Speech, 58,* 123–133.

Stiff, J. B. (1986). Cognitive processing of persuasive message cues: A meta-analytic review of the efforts of supporting information on attitudes. *Communication Monographs, 53,* 75–89.

Stohl, C. (1986). Quality circles and changing patterns of communication. In M. L. McLaughlin (Ed.), *Communication yearbook 9* (pp. 511–531). Newbury Park, CA: Sage.

Stohl, C. (1987). Bridging the parallel organization: A study of quality circle effectiveness. In M. L. McLaughlin (Ed.), *Communication yearbook 10* (pp. 416–430). Newbury Park, CA: Sage.

Street, R. L., Jr. (1984). Speech convergence and speech evaluation in fact-finding interviews. *Human Communication Research, 11,* 139–169.

Street, R. L., Jr., & Buller, D. B. (1988). Patients' characteristics affecting physician-patient nonverbal communication. *Human Communication Research, 15,* 60–90.

Street, R. L., Jr., & Giles, H. (1982). Speech accommodation theory: A social cognitive approach to language and speech behavior. In M. E. Roloff & C. R. Berger (Eds.), *Social cognition and communication* (pp. 193–226). Newbury Park, CA: Sage.

Sunnafrank, M. (1990). Predicted outcome value and uncertainty reduction theories: A test of competing perspectives. *Human Communication Research, 17,* 76–103.

Sypher, B. D., & Zorn, T. E., Jr. (1986). Communication-related abilities and upward mobility: A longitudinal investigation. *Human Communication Research, 12,* 420–431.

Sypher, H. E., & Applegate, J. L. (1984). Organizing communication behavior: The role of schemas and constructs. In R. N. Bostrom & B. H. Westley (Eds.), *Communication yearbook 8* (pp. 310–329). Newbury Park, CA: Sage.

Tagiuri, R. (1968). The concepts of organizational climate. In R. Tagiuri & G. H. Litwin (Eds.), *Organizational climate: Exploration of a concept* (pp. 11–32). Boston: Harvard University Press.

Tan, A. S. (1985). *Mass communication theories and research* (2nd ed.). New York: Wiley.

Tan, A. S. (1986). Social learning of aggression from television. In J. Bryant & D. Zillmann (Eds.). *Perspectives on media effects* (pp. 41–55). Hillsdale, NJ: Lawrence Erlbaum Associates.

Taylor, D. A., & Altman, I. (1987). Communication in interpersonal relationships: Social penetration processes. In M. E. Roloff & G. R. Miller (Eds.), *Interpersonal processes: New directions in communication research* (pp. 257–277). Newbury Park, CA: Sage.

Thorson, E. (1989). Processing television commercials. In B. Dervin, L. Grossberg, B. J. O'Keefe, & E. Wartella (Eds.), *Rethinking communication: Paradigm exemplars* (Vol. 2, pp. 397–410). Newbury Park, CA: Sage.

Tompkins, P. K. (1987). Translating organizational theory: Symbolism over substance. In F. M. Jablin, L. L. Putnam, K. H. Roberts, & L. W. Porter (Eds.), *Handbook of organizational communication* (pp. 70–96). Newbury Park, CA: Sage.

Tompkins, P. K., & Cheney, G. (1985). Communication and unobtrusive control in contemporary organizations. In R. D. McPhee & P. K. Tompkins (Eds.), *Organizational communication: Traditional themes and new directions* (pp. 179–210). Newbury Park, CA: Sage.

Tracy, K. (1984). The effect of multiple goals on conversational relevance and topic shift. *Communication Monographs, 51,* 274–287.

Van Evra, J. (1990). *Television and child development.* Hillsdale, NJ: Lawrence Erlbaum Associates.

VanLear, C. A. Jr. (1987). The formation of social relationships: A longitudinal study of social penetration. *Human Communication Research, 13,* 299–322.

Van Rheenen, D. D., & Sherblom, J. (1984). Spoken language indices of uncertainty. *Human Communication Research, 11,* 221–230.

Villaume, W. A., & Cegala, D. J. (1988). Interaction involvement and discourse strategies: The patterned use of cohesive devices in conversation. *Communication Monographs, 55,* 22–40.

Vinokur, A., & Burnstein, E. (1974). Effects of partially shared persuasive arguments on group-induced shifts: A group-problem-solving approach. *Journal of Personality and Social Psychology, 29,* 305–315.

Vinokur, A., Trope, Y., & Burnstein, E. (1975). Decision-making analysis of persuasive argumentation and the choice shift effect. *Journal of Experimental Social Psychology, 11,* 127–148.

Walton, R. E. (1982). Social choice in the development of advanced information technology. *Human Relations, 35,* 1073–1084.

Ward, S., Wackman, D., & Wartella, E. (1977). *How children learn to buy: The development of consumer information processing skills.* Newbury Park, CA: Sage Publications.

Warfel, K. A. (1984). Gender schemas and perceptions of speech style. *Communication Monographs, 51,* 253–267.

Watzlawick, P., Beavin, J. H., & Jackson, D. D. (1967). *The pragmatics of human communication.* New York: Norton.

Weick, K. E. (1979a). *The social psychology of organizing* (2nd ed.). Reading, MA: Addison-Wesley.

Weick, K. E. (1979b). Cognitive processes in organization. In B. M. Staw (Ed.), *Research in organizational behavior* (Vol. 1, pp. 41–74). Greenwich, CT: JAI Press.

Weick, K. E. (1987). Theorizing about organizational communication. In F. M. Jablin, L. L. Putnam, K. H. Roberts, & L. W. Porter (Eds.), *Handbook of organizational communication* (pp. 97–122). Newbury Park, CA: Sage.

Weiner, M., & Mehrabian, A. (1968). *Language within language: Immediacy, a channel in verbal communication.* New York: Appleton-Century-Crofts.

Weiner, N. (1948). *Cybernetics or control and communication in the animal and the machine.* Cambridge, MA.: MIT Press.

Weiner, N. (1950). *The human use of human beings: Cybernetics and society* (Rev. ed.). Garden City, NY: Doubleday Anchor.

Werner, C. M., & Haggard, L. M. (1985). Temporal qualities of interpersonal relationships. In M. L. Knapp & G. R. Miller (Eds.), *Handbook of interpersonal communication* (pp. 59–99). Newbury Park, CA: Sage.

Westley, B. H., & MacLean, M. S., Jr. (1957). A conceptual model for communication research. *Journalism Quarterly, 34,* 31–38.

Wheeless, L. R., & Cook, J. A. (1985). Information exposure, attention, and reception. In B. D. Ruben (Ed.), *Information and behavior* (Vol. 1, pp. 251–286). New Brunswick, NJ: Transaction Books.

Whorf, B. L. (1956). *Language, thought, and reality.* Cambridge, MA: MIT Press.

Whyte, G. (1989). Groupthink reconsidered. *Academy of Management Review, 14,* 40–56.

Wiio, O. A., Goldhaber, G. M., & Yates, M. P. (1980). Organizational communication research: Time for reflection? In D. Nimmo (Ed.), *Communication yearbook 4* (pp. 83–97). New Brunswick, NJ: Transaction Books.

Wilmot, W. W., Carbaugh, D. A., & Baxter, L. A. (1985). Communicative strategies used to terminate romantic relationships. *Western Journal of Speech Communication, 49,* 204–216.

Winett, R. A. (1986). *Information and behavior: Systems of influence.* Hillsdale, NJ: Larwence Erlbaum Associates.

Witteman, H., & Fitzpatrick, M. A. (1986). Compliance-gaining in marital interaction: Power bases, processes, and outcomes. *Communication Monographs, 53,* 130–143.

Woelfel, J. C. (1977). Changes in interpersonal communication patterns as a consequence of need for information. *Communication Research, 4,* 235–256.

Wood, W., Kalgren, C., & Priesler, R. (1985). Access to attitude relevant information in memory as a determinant of persuasion: The role of message attributes. *Journal of Experimental Social Psychology, 21,* 73–85.

Wright, C. R. (1986). *Mass communication: A sociological perspective* (3rd ed.). New York: Random House.

Wright, P. L. (1973). The cognitive processes mediating acceptance of advertising. *Journal of Marketing Research, 10,* 53–62.

Wright, P. L. (1974). Analyzing media effects on advertising responses. *Public opinion Quarterly, 38,* 192–205.

Wright, P. L. (1981). Cognitive responses to mass media advocacy. In R. E. Petty, T. M. Ostrom, & T. C. Brock (Eds.), *Cognitive responses in persuasion* (pp. 263–282). Hillsdale, NJ: Lawrence Erlbaum Associates.

Yinon, Y., Jaffe, Y., & Feshback, S. (1975). Risky aggression in individuals and groups. *Journal of Personality and Social Psychology, 31,* 808–815.

Zillmann, D., & Bryant, J. (1986). Exploring the entertainment experience. In J. Bryant & D. Zillmann (Eds.), *Perspectives on media effects* (pp. 303–324). Hillsdale, NJ: Lawrence Erlbaum Associates.

Zuckerman, M., DePaulo, B. M., & Rosenthal, R. (1981). Verbal and nonverbal communication of deception. In L. Berkowitz (Ed.), *Advances in experimental social psychology* (Vol. 14, pp. 1–59). New York: Academic Press.

Author Index

Subject Index